Visual Editing

A Graphic Guide for Journalists

Howard I. Finberg
The Arizona Republic

Bruce D. Itule
Arizona State University

Wadsworth Publishing Company
A Division of Wadsworth, Inc.
Belmont, California

Mass Communications Editor: Kris Clerkin
Editorial Assistant: Tamiko Verkler
Production Editor: Deborah Cogan
Managing Designer: Carolyn Deacy
Print Buyer: Barbara Britton, Martha Branch
Art Editor: Edie Williams
Copy Editor: Thomas Briggs
Compositor: Graphic Typesetting Service, Inc.
Cover Designer: Rob Hugel

Printed in the United States of America   85

1 2 3 4 5 6 7 8 9 10———94 93 92 91 90

Library of Congress Cataloging-in-Publication Data

Finberg, Howard I., 1949–
    Visual editing / by Howard I. Finberg and Bruce D. Itule.
       p.   cm.
    Includes index.
    ISBN 0-534-11736-8
    1. Newspaper layout and typography.   2. Newspapers—Illustrations—
Editing.   I. Itule, Bruce D., 1947– .   II. Title.
PN4778.F55   1989
    070.4'1—dc20   89-14816
                                                        CIP

Preface

We wrote *Visual Editing* to guide students and professionals in the effective use of informational graphics, photographs and illustrations in newspaper design and layout.

The book presents a realistic picture of how the various visual elements can be used at newspapers of any size, from the smallest weekly to the largest daily. It can be used by students in college journalism classes, by staffers at college newspapers and by professional journalists looking for guidance *without* preaching.

We describe the entire newspaper graphic process so reporters, editors, photographers and designers can understand how all the visual elements of the paper interact and how they need to be handled with the same care and understanding as an important story.

In each chapter we offer background, advice and extensive examples, as well as "Suggested Exercises" at the end of each chapter. Many chapters include an "Inside Look," an interview with a working visual journalist. The journalists interviewed are real people in real situations who make the lessons of the book come alive and who serve as instructional models.

We have learned while writing this book that visual editing is changing rapidly. The growth of graphic elements in newspapers in the last decade has been remarkable, and art, photography and informational graphics are playing a greater role in newspaper publishing than ever before. More than ever, publishers and editors are realizing that words alone do not sell newspapers; even words with pictures are not enough.

Journalists are no longer isolated workers in a newsroom. Reporters are expected to understand the importance of informational graphics and to gather the numbers needed to make a chart. Copy editors are expected to look at an illustration and write headlines that reflect the tone of the story and the accompanying artwork. Section editors are expected to combine all of these elements on the page to achieve good-looking, easy-to-read pages. Designers are expected to understand the news value of stories so they can put the proper emphasis on each story and photo.

Because universities and colleges only now are beginning to realize the great need to train students in newspaper visuals, virtually every school has a unique approach to teaching visual editing. Some schools, for example, touch on it in basic editing, others offer discussions on visual editing in photojournalism courses, still others offer a separate class. Because the approaches are so diverse, we have written a book that is flexible enough to meet the needs of most schools and instructors.

FEATURES OF THE BOOK

Our book features the following:

- Practical advice from visual journalists. We have interviewed scores of professionals in actual newspaper situations to show the readers of our book how visual editing works. First-person accounts from the journalists bring to life the day-to-day trials and triumphs of visual journalists.
- Numerous current examples from a wide range of newspapers. We use examples from large, medium and small newspapers from throughout the United States. These examples, including a collection of 30 newspaper front pages from the same day, make it easier for readers of our book to understand the fundamentals we discuss.
- Thorough instruction in areas that receive only cursory treatment in other textbooks. We have written detailed, comprehensive chapters on design, reproduction and color, legal and ethical issues, informational graphics, picture editing and art and illustration.

- Exercises at the ends of chapters. We believe that these exercises can aid the retention of material and enhance the skills of readers of our book.

ORGANIZATION OF THE BOOK

Visual Editing can be used in several college journalism courses: basic news editing, advanced editing, design and layout, photojournalism and visual editing. It also can be used by professional journalists who want to learn more about the visual side of a newspaper.

Part I, "Introduction," provides an overview of visual editing and the role it plays in newspapers.

Chapter 1 examines how the visual revolution has changed forever the look of newspapers. Today, publishers and editors are concerned not only about which stories will run in their newspapers but about how those stories will be presented visually.

Chapter 2 explores how computers, from giant mainframes to PCs, have brought a technological explosion to newspapers of all sizes. The chapter traces the steps a story takes from the time it leaves an Associated Press computer in Washington, D.C., until it appears on a printed newspaper page.

Chapter 3 reviews the role that design plays in daily newspapers by examining the three main components of design: organization, pattern and structure.

Chapter 4 emphasizes the basic guidelines that visual journalists follow to prepare readable pages.

Chapter 5 is unique in its examination of 30 front pages from the same day to show how design elements are put in practice on an average news day.

Chapter 6 examines inside pages and the special challenges they create for visual journalists. Included in the chapter is a discussion of the layout of advertisements, editorial pages and section front pages.

Chapter 7 discusses the rudiments of reproduction and color. It looks at the various processes performed in the production of newspaper visuals, from "pre-press work" (the work needed to prepare material to be printed) to the "press run" (the printing of the paper).

Chapter 8 explores the legal and ethical framework within which all journalists work, whether they handle visuals or words.

Part II, "Informational Graphics," outlines informational graphics, which include diagrams, maps, charts and tabular lists. It begins with a look at the history of informational graphics and ends with a discussion of pitfalls that visual journalists should avoid.

Chapter 9 gives readers a history of informational graphics, tracing its roots to a diagram of a murder scene that appeared on Page One of *The Times* of London on April 7, 1806.

Chapter 10 studies the innovative and exciting job of the graphics editor, who must move between words and visuals.

Chapter 11 discusses tables and charts and how they can be used effectively in a newspaper.

Chapter 12 examines diagrams, which explain how something works or why or how an event occurred, and facts boxes, which distill important points of a story or event.

Chapter 13 explores maps, the oldest form of graphic communication. Even though maps have been used by newspapers for a long time, they are one of the most underappreciated and underutilized forms of visual communication.

Chapter 14 looks at the pitfalls of informational graphics and offers advice on how they can be avoided.

Part III, "Picture Editing," looks at the history of newspaper photography, how picture editors work, wire service photos, cropping, sizing, captions and photo manipulation and illustration.

Chapter 15 provides a brief look at the history of photography in newspapers.

Chapter 16 looks at the newspaper picture editor as he or she tries to direct and manage the paper's picture report.

Chapter 17 examines how visual journalists crop and size pictures and how they write captions.

Chapter 18 examines wire service photographs and how they are used in newspapers.

Chapter 19 discusses photo manipulation and illustration. Despite protests from many photographers who insist newspaper photographs are supposed to portray reality, some visual journalists and editors manipulate photographs to meet the needs of a page's appearance.

Part IV, "Art and Illustration," surveys the history of newspaper illustrations and how art directors work.

Chapter 20 examines illustrations in newspapers, from simple drawings carved by hand on small wooden blocks to the complicated color illustrations of today.

Chapter 21 discusses the art director, who performs a specialized function in the newsroom. Although many newspapers do not have art directors, those that do rely on them to supervise the artists working for the editorial side of the paper.

ACKNOWLEDGMENTS

Many people contributed to the research and preparation of our text. Individuals who were helpful through their insights, counsel and willingness to share during our careers include the following:

From San Francisco State University, B. H. Liebes, Dr. Leo Young and Lynn Ludlow; from the *Chicago Tribune,* Clayton Kirkpatrick, Maxwell McCrohon, Joseph Leonard, the late William Jones, the late John Wagner, James Squires, Jack Fuller, Peter Negronida, Dick Ciccone, Carl Sotir, Tony Majeri, Barbara Newcombe, Mary Wilson, the late Leanita McClain, Paul Dix, Susan Popson, Marty Fischer, Pat Bergner, the late William Sajovic, the late William O'Brien, Anne Cusack, Karen Engstrom, Scott Fincher, Dan Pribilski, Mitch Dydo, Nancy Reese, Tom Heinz, Judie Anderson, Jane Hunt, Jackie Combs, Colleen Dishon, Mary Knoblauch, Kathy Naureckas, Owen Youngman, Max Saxinger, Carl Caruso, Ovie Carter, Larry Townsend, Michael Argirion, William Aldrich, Randy Weissman, Jack Corn, Steve Stroud, Marcia Peters, Bill Parker and Mary Ellen Hendricks; from *The New York Times,* Al Siegel, David Dunlap, John Lee and Fred Andrews; from the *San Francisco Chronicle,* Bryan Moss, Gary Fong, Iris Frost, Matt Wilson, John Sullivan, Pam Reisner, Chris Stewart, Tom Levy, Eric Luse, Brant Ward, Steve Ringman, Fred Larson, John O'Hara, Deanne Fitzmaurice, Liz Halfalia, Jerry Telfer, Vince Maggiora, Dennis Gallagher, Eric Jungerman, Elizabeth Lada, Hulda Nelson, John Boring and Loudes Livingston; from the *San Francisco Examiner,* Topy Fiske and Tim Innes; from *The Orange County Register,* William Dunn and Tom Porter; from Knight-Ridder Tribune News graphics network, Wendy Govier and George Rorick; from the Society of Newspaper Design, Ray Chattman; from *The Milwaukee Journal,* John Mollwitz; from the *San Jose Mercury News,* Jerry Ceppos, JoAnne Izumi, Wes Killingbeck, Mark Wigginton, Jonathan Krim and Bob Ryan; from *The* (Myrtle Beach) *Sun News,* Bryan Monroe; from Whittle Communications, Brad Zuckroff and Bambi Nicklen; from the Poynter Institute for Media Studies, Mario Garcia, Robert Haiman, Don Fry, Roy Peter Clark and Billie Keirstead; from the American Press Institute, William L. Winter, John Finemann, Laurence Hale, Elwood Wardlow, Donald Lippincott, Carol Ann Riordan and Mike Hughes; from *The* (Providence) *Journal-Bulletin,* David Gray, who graciously gave us permission to use his bibliography; from *The Washington*

Post, Jeanne Fox Alston, Michael Keegan and Mark Potts; from National Press Photographers Association, John Faber, John Cognell and William Hodge; from the *Los Angeles Herald Examiner*, Mike Gordon; from *U.S. News & World Report*, Nanette Bisher and Rob Covey; from *USA Today*, Richard Curtis and John Walston; from the *Indianapolis Star*, Myrta Pulliam; from Chicago, Ken Love.

In addition, we would like to thank the visual journalists who took the time to be interviewed for an "Inside Look." They are Tony Majeri, John Walston, Pat Murphy, Edmund Arnold, Robert Lockwood, Warren Skipper, George Wedding, Frank Peters, Bill Dunn, Pegie Stark, Rich Clarkson, Carolyn Lee, Pete Leabo and Lynn Staley. Although some of the journalists interviewed for this book have moved to other jobs, references to them remain within the context of their jobs at the time they were interviewed.

Several of our colleagues at *The Arizona Republic* and at Arizona State University also helped. At *The Republic*, they include Pat Murphy, Alan Moyer, Mary Lou Bessette, Bob Franken, Steve Anderson, Joe Cole-man, Patti Valdez, Don Foley, Gus Walker, Kee Rash, Joe Willie Smith, Eric Baker, Maggie Delbon, Janice Kowalski, Anita Mabante, P. J. Erickson, Bill Hayes, Dave Haakenson, Bob Ogle, Anne Spitza, Chuck Henrickson, Jenny Sjoberg, Gary Ulik, Judy Tell, Francine Ruley, Keira Cox, Karen Outland, Nancy Fasano, Jeff Dozhaba, Terry Cornelius, Audrey Pelliocciotti, Amy Carlile, Bill Carlile, Terry Duke, Tracey Phalen, Mike McKay, Linda Vachata, Tom Bauer, Benjamin Hegre, Phil Hennessy, Pete Watters, Mike Ging, Suzanne Starr, David Petkiewicz, Tom Story, Tim Rogers, Charles Krejcsi, Mike Spector, Mike Meister and Peter Schwepker. At ASU, they include Doug Anderson, Jackie Eldridge, Betty Asher, Frank Hoy, Salima Keegan and Fran McClung.

We also would like to acknowledge those professors who reviewed all or parts of the manuscript: Warren Burkett, University of Texas at Austin; Samuel V. Kennedy III, Syracuse University; Charles Pearson, Wichita State University; Sheila Reaves, University of Wisconsin–Madison; Ruth Walden, University of North Carolina at Chapel Hill; and Laura Widmer, Northwest Missouri State University.

We would like to thank Kristine Clerkin, our primary editor at Wadsworth, who believed in our idea and helped make it happen.

Special thanks go to our families for their patience, understanding and willingness to handle extra responsibilities while we wrote this book: Priscilla, Dena and Justin Itule and Kathy Finberg. This book is dedicated to them and to the memory of Martin and Flora Finberg, who would have put this book on their coffee table.

In many respects, this book would not have been possible without the encouragement, guidance and editing skills of Kathlyn Oakley Finberg. She brought her professionalism and care for the reader to this project in the same manner as when she was our trusted colleague at the *Chicago Tribune*. She is the "invisible" third member of this project. Kathy: We will never be able to thank you enough.

Howard I. Finberg
Bruce D. Itule

Contents in Brief

Contents

CHAPTER 6 / INSIDE PAGES   77

CHAPTER 7 / REPRODUCTION AND COLOR   91

PART FOUR / ART AND ILLUSTRATION

PART ONE

Introduction

CHAPTER ONE

The Visual Revolution

Never before in American journalism has so much attention been paid to the way newspapers look. Twenty-five years ago, editors packed their newspapers' gray-looking pages with column after column of hard-to-read type and a jumble of one- and two-column headlines. Today, however, editors are concerned not only about which stories they will run in their papers' columns but also how those stories will be presented visually.

This increasing interest in the visual side of news editing has been driven in part by the growing dominance of visual messages in today's society, where each day potential newspaper readers are bombarded by bright graphics and color images wherever they look: in television entertainment shows and commercials, on billboards, in magazines, in commercial and cable TV news programs, through direct-mail advertising, and even on cereal boxes.

Although some editors may debate the overall value of design and graphics in newspapers, one thing is certain: Newspapers have had to embrace the visual revolution to protect their dwindling audience of readers and to attract new readers.

It is through the use of visuals—photographs, illustrations, graphics,

color and page design—that newspapers have found an effective tool for helping to hold on to their subscribers and to attract the increasingly important and growing segment of casual readers through single-copy sales. A readership survey sponsored by the American Newspaper Publishers Association estimates that about 20 percent of daily newspaper circulation comes from single-copy sales. And, according to the survey, for some major metropolitan newspapers that market percentage can jump as high as 75 to 80 percent of total circulation. An interesting visual presentation of the news, while not the only factor, helps the reader decide which newspaper he or she will buy at the newsstand.

Even after a newspaper has captured the reader's attention with a bold headline or a dramatic color photo, it still has to compete for the reader's time, less and less of which is spent reading. Consumers no longer get most of their news from their community's daily newspaper. They are informed through radio and television broadcasts, magazines, books and national and regional newspapers. Because they are bombarded with so much information each day, people can pick and choose their news sources. According to a 1987 market study for the American Society

Figure 1.1 *USA Today* front page

of Newspaper Editors of nine daily newspapers, 40 percent of the readers who canceled their subscriptions said they no longer could find the time to read the news. In other words, given today's active and fast-paced lifestyles, an uninviting, gray-looking newspaper may end up in the wastebasket, unopened and unread.

One newspaper that has recognized and adapted to the changing needs and tastes of today's readers is *USA Today* (Figure 1.1). Since its creation in 1982, the paper has helped foster enthusiasm for the use of newspaper visuals such as graphics and color. Even while critics call it television news on paper or "McPaper" and decry its sometimes indiscriminate use of color and graphics for their own sake, *USA Today* has proven that a newspaper can be a visual medium. *USA Today* is now the country's largest general interest newspaper, with a circulation of 1,800,000.

"VISUALLY ENERGETIC" NEWSPAPERS

The emergence of visuals has changed forever the way newspapers present the news. "We're discovering how static print can be, especially to a younger generation, so we're actively seeking ways to make newspapers visually energetic, as animated as possible," said William Dunn, managing editor of *The Orlando (Fla.) Sentinel.*

A visually energetic page contains elements such as photographs, informational graphics, facts boxes and special treatment of type to attract readers. Note, however, that too many of these elements can confuse readers and create a "visually frenetic" page that lacks a clear focus or visual direction.

Dunn considers television to be a major force affecting newspaper visuals today. "Newspapers are one-dimensional," he said. "They are competing with television, which moves. We need to find ways to make our product as engaging in a visual sense as television.

"We can create the illusion of movement in the pictures we select and the graphics we put on our pages, anything that will build on the time a reader spends with a newspaper. The computer people call it 'user-friendly.' Television is user-friendly; newspapers really haven't been user-friendly."

Dunn used the roller-coaster action of the world stock markets on Oct. 20, 1987, to illustrate how a newspaper can create an illusion of movement. There were plenty of charts available that traced the crash and recovery of the markets, but the charts didn't tell the entire story. In addition to the charts, Dunn's paper used photographs showing the frustrated looks on stock-brokers' faces (Figure 1.2). The photographs created excitement in the story and did a better job of portraying the news than just the charts, Dunn said. "Anything that a newspaper can do to add to the relatively short time a reader spends with a newspaper is well worth the effort," he added.

CHANGES IN NEWSROOM GOALS

The increasing use of visuals in news-papers has put new demands on nearly everyone in the newsroom. Added to the daily routine of compiling a news report that is accurate, balanced, well written and well researched is the task of planning and producing a good-look-ing end product. And everyone in the

Figure 1.2 *The Orlando Sentinel* front page, attempting to create the illusion of movement

newsroom—reporter, photographer, artist and editor—is getting involved in the visual editing process.

Reporters, while out on assignment, are gathering statistics for informational graphics. They also are discovering that editors may cut five or 10 inches from their prose if the same facts can be better presented to readers as a graphic or other type of visual.

Photographers, used to thinking in terms of bold action photos captured at crucial moments, are enjoying the luxury of taking the time to create attractive photo illustrations for feature sections. They also are being called upon to capture scenes on film that will be used merely as visual backgrounds for informational graphics.

Copy editors, the wordsmiths of the newsroom, are checking graphics for spelling and style errors and making sure that the graphic information agrees with the data in the story. They also are writing headlines for graphics. They sometimes are asked to distill a wire service story into a facts box. They might write the headlines for Page One **promotions,** which highlight inside stories or packages, or **refers,** several words or a sentence displayed inside a story that guide readers to a related story on another page.

Artists are learning about the elements of news in order to draw detailed graphics to accompany news stories. Like photographers, they also are becoming visual reporters who often go on assignment to create an informational graphic or illustration for a major news event.

News editors are giving top consideration to a strong visual presentation as they choose the final selection of stories, photographs and other visuals that will make up the day's news report.

Page designers, the newest journalists at some newspapers, are blending all the visual elements and stories on the pages to create exciting and attractive page designs, or *layouts*. At a growing number of newspapers, the news editors and/or page designers are using complex *pagination* machines that assemble all the stories and visuals electronically to produce the finished pages. (Pagination is discussed in detail in Chapter 2.)

Graphics editors, a new breed of manager in the newsroom, are becoming the liaison between the word journalists (reporters and editors) and the **visual journalists** (photographers, artists and designers). To do this job effectively, graphics editors must fully understand newspaper production. They also need to be good communicators.

VARIETIES OF VISUALS

The decision to use a visual to help tell the news is just the first step in this new editing process. The word **visual,** or **graphic,** is an umbrella term for a piece of newspaper artwork, of which there are eight types:

- **News** or **feature photograph.** An image "captured" on film or digitally by an electronic camera by a newspaper photographer either on the scene of a news event or during a prearranged meeting.
- **Photo illustration.** A type of photograph that, through its subject or visual trickery, makes an editorial point or comment.
- **Illustration** or **sketch.** A piece of artwork created by a newspaper artist. Often in color.
- **Map.** A device that shows where an event has occurred.

- **Table.** A list of information, displayed in tabular form. A quick and concise method of comparing a large body of data. The most common display of tabular information is the daily stock market report or sports box scores and standings.
- **Chart.** A visual display of quantitative information, such as the tracking of data over a period of time. A **line chart** shows an up or down trend with a continuous line. A **column chart** displays comparable statistics with vertical or horizontal bars.
- **Facts box.** A summary or outline that highlights certain points of a story or gives background information.
- **Diagram** or **schematic.** A drawing that shows how things work or how events occurred.

The last five visuals sometimes are referred to as *informational graphics,* and they also may be combined into one complex visual, sometimes called a *megagraphic.*

The demand for accuracy and quality journalism carries over to these visual devices. Stylish graphics must provide complete and accurate information. Good-looking pages always should help inform the reader about the day's news.

BIG CHANGES IN A SHORT TIME

In recent years many metropolitan newspapers have committed themselves to more and better visuals or graphics through major design changes. Some of the changes have been made in response to competition from other newspapers; some have been made because the publisher and/or editor wanted the newspaper to project another image to keep and cultivate readers; many have been made because of advances in computer technology.

Newspaper design (the overall appearance of the paper) always has been limited by the current technology. In the days of letterpress printing and manually set lead type, papers found their "look" and stayed that way because of the physical limitations of the machines and the time and labor involved in operating them. However, since the 1970s, computers and the equipment they drive, along with the switch to offset printing, have brought profound changes to newspapers. Now there is a much wider variety of ways to display stories and visuals, and they all can be produced quickly. (A complete discussion of newsroom technology is in Chapter 2.) Computer technology, which still is evolving rapidly, is indeed the driving force behind today's explosion of visuals in newspapers.

Along with the technological changes have come new jobs and responsibilities. When the *Chicago Tribune* named its first graphics editor in 1974, it became the first large metropolitan newspaper to do so. Now, almost all major newspapers employ someone in such a position.

Ten years ago, newspaper pages were *dummied* (laid out) by news editors who may or may not have had training in page design. Today, many newspapers have designers who have been schooled in the creative presentation of pages. Although news editors still decide what goes on which page, designers are increasingly responsible for laying out those pages in good-looking and readable visual units.

Not everything has changed so rapidly. The first use of a photographic halftone in a newspaper is credited to the *New York Daily Graphic* on March 4, 1880. The newspaper published a photograph (black and white, of course) by Stephen H. Horgan called "Shantytown." That photograph led to a reproduction method in which a continuous image was reduced to a series of dots of various sizes; the larger the dot, the darker the image. Although today's photos look sharper and cleaner because of technological advances, this method of reproduction, called a **halftone,** is still used by newspapers today and is discussed in Chapter 7.

LOSERS AND WINNERS

Although creative newspaper design has helped modernize newspapers and draw new readers, it has yet to rescue a failing newspaper. Some well-designed newspapers—the *New York Herald Tribune,* the *Philadelphia Bulletin,* the *Washington Star,* the *Chicago Daily News*—have failed. Their downfalls were blamed on changing economies and lifestyles of readers, which led to circulation and advertising declines. Visuals could not save them.

Chicago Daily News

In the case of the *Chicago Daily News,* some observers attributed the paper's rapid decline in circulation to a redesign that shocked and dismayed readers. In fact, the *Chicago Daily News* most likely failed because of a lack of advertising revenues and the high cost of producing an afternoon newspaper. But its final design was daring and modern, with extensive use of column rules and other typographical techniques that gave the newspaper a bold, almost magazine-like look (Figures 1.3 and 1.4). In some ways, the redesigned paper looked like

Figure 1.3 *Chicago Daily News* front page before final redesign (1974)

Figure 1.4 *Chicago Daily News* front page after design revisions (1977)

its own obituary—heavy black borders surrounding news and feature stories. Of course now, more than a decade after the paper folded, the *Daily News* design would not be considered shocking.

Chicago Tribune

More often than not, a newspaper benefits from design changes. A good example is another Chicago paper, the *Tribune*. In the early 1970s, the *Chicago Tribune* faced circulation and advertising competition, not only from other Chicago and suburban newspapers but also from other media outlets. Young, affluent readers, the ones advertisers wanted to reach, saw the *Tribune* as old-fashioned, stuffy and hard to read.

Until the early 1970s, the *Tribune* had done little to change its appearance,

looking much as it did in the 1930s. A front page from 1964 (Figure 1.5) had many of the same design elements as a front page from 1936 (Figure 1.6). For example, both papers contained **vertical layout** in which stories are run in long, often single, columns rather than spread across several shorter columns. One- and two-column headlines dominate the pages. When a story covers more than one column, the columns are not necessarily squared off.

In addition, in 1936, an editorial cartoon was the main illustration on Page One. It still was in 1964, although by the 1960s the cartoon was smaller and in color and there also was a news photo on the page. The presence of an editorial cartoon gave some readers the impression that news stories were slanted to match the paper's editorial stand.

Figure 1.5 *Chicago Tribune* front page in 1964

Figure 1.6 *Chicago Daily Tribune* front page in 1936

On both pages, columns of type were separated by thin **column rules.** The *banner headlines* (those that stretch across the top of the page), as well as most of the other headlines on the pages, were printed in all-capital letters. Because of the vertical layout and small headlines, the pages looked like gray masses, particularly *below the fold* (the bottom half of a page).

One significant change from 1936 was in the *Tribune*'s *nameplate* on Page One: By 1964, the word *Daily* had been dropped from the title and an American flag had been added. The slogan "The World's Greatest Newspaper" remained, however.

From the 1930s to the 1960s, while the *Tribune*'s design changed only slightly, its readers changed greatly. As surveys conducted by the *Tribune* showed, its readership no longer was

made up of persons whose primary source of news was a daily newspaper. Those readers had been replaced by an audience that was used to livelier news presentations from television and other sources, an audience with less time to read. Readers in the 1970s wanted a more lively newspaper, a newspaper that better reflected the times.

In 1972, the winds of change started blowing through the *Tribune,* and at the suggestion of editors and a design consultant, the paper made a number of visual changes (Figure 1.7). For one thing, its all-capitalized headlines were eliminated—the first step in making the paper easier to read. Also, although the nameplate was the same in 1972 as in 1964, the editorial cartoon was off Page One. And there were more photographs.

The display of the stories changed,

too, with the use of more modular layout and less dogleg layout. In **modular layout,** stories are run in short, squared-off columns or blocks, giving the stories a more packaged effect, and three- and four-column headlines are common. In **dogleg layout,** irregular shapes, such as inverted L's, are used. Today, most newspapers use modular layout because it is considered easier to read and design than dogleg layout.

Throughout the 1970s and 1980s, the *Tribune* continued to make design changes until it became one of the nation's best-looking newspapers. By 1987, the paper's layout was completely modular (Figure 1.8). Color and numerous visuals were used on Page One every day, as were promotions to guide readers to stories inside the newspaper. The background of the nameplate also was in color (blue), and

Figure 1.7 *Chicago Tribune* front page after 1972 design revisions

Figure 1.8 *Chicago Tribune* front page 1987

"The World's Greatest Newspaper" slogan was history. The American flag remained.

ELEMENTS OF REDESIGN

The design evolution at the *Chicago Tribune* illustrates the major elements of many newspapers' redesigns in the past decade:

- *Better typography,* including an easier-to-read body type and easier-to-read headlines.
- *Modular elements,* making it easier for readers to follow stories or groups of stories.

- *Stronger photo play,* enlivening the page and inviting the reader to stop and read the stories or captions.
- *More and better graphics,* including maps, charts and other devices to give the reader a better understanding of events.
- **Sectionalization,** or presentation of information in separate sections that specialize in one or two areas: news, entertainment, sports, business and food, for example. Within each section, daily or weekly features are **anchored** (assigned to specific places within the section) so that readers can locate them more easily.

INSIDE LOOK

Tony Majeri

Creative Director   *Chicago Tribune*

For Tony Majeri, creative director of the *Chicago Tribune* and 1988 president of the Society of Newspaper Design, a good-looking newspaper is one that is a "useful creature."

Majeri, who is currently in charge of the visual presentation of the *Tribune,* said: "I am a sincere advocate of useful things. Newspaper design should serve the function of the newspaper. The newspaper should know its role and what it is trying to accomplish. The person doing the designing needs to have an understanding of the function. For example, if you understand that you are putting out a sports page, then you understand that there are certain things that need to go along with a sports page. The page needs to be informative, but it has to present details such as results and statistics. There also has to be enthusiasm and excitement in the writing and photographs."

Majeri said a newspaper runs into design problems when it quits trying to be what *it* is and begins trying to be what other papers are. "Look how many newspapers have taken components of *USA Today* and put them on their pages. There has been an entire generation of decorators who have been born at newspapers, and there has been sensational pressure on them to decorate rather than communicate. People feel pressure to leave their mark on things. They introduce little triangles, stars, particular rules and whiteouts for the simple feeling that they need to assert their ability to play with things."

The Wall Street Journal is a terrific example of a paper with a direct focus, said Majeri, who has held various jobs at the *Tribune,* including art director, senior designer, associate sports editor and assistant editor of special projects. *The Journal's* pages "mirror its focus, which makes its design successful," Majeri noted. *The Journal's* aim is to present a digest of daily news and sound analytical coverage of financial trends to a national audience. "Its design creates a focus and direction. It has a formal feeling to it. It doesn't shout. There is a certain intensity that the page projects.

"*USA Today* has a different visual intensity. It has a whole different role and function than *The Wall Street Journal* does," he explained. "It is successful because it has defined its market and its role in that market."

Majeri has helped the *Tribune* fine-tune its design focus for two decades. He said: "In 1970 the Tribune was a grand, old, 1950s-looking creature that was losing circulation in a very competitive market. At that same time, we were doing a lot of product research. The research showed the *Tribune* was not responsive to needs of readers. One thing the research found was that people didn't like the scattering of standing features. They wanted them in the same place every day.

"An outline was produced showing what the *Tribune* wanted to do visually. Several things grew from the outline. The paper divided itself into a series of sections aimed at satisfying the demands of its audience. It added a food section, a new sports section, a section on fashion and a special business section on Monday. Typography studies also showed that the use of italic and condensed heads was hampering the communication process. We eliminated them to make the newspaper more accessible and easier to read."

By the 1980s, the *Tribune* had changed more. It was using more color. It also had adopted Standard Advertising Units (SAUs), a system of standardized ad sizes for newspapers, and had abandoned its old letterpress printing process for modern offset printing. "We again had to look at all the things we do with the newspaper," Majeri said. "For example, with offset, ink lays down differently, and color availability is impacted. We had to study how presses work and what implications the presses have on a newspaper. We changed our headdress (headline style) to take advantage of a cleaner medium that laid down ink differently."

Majeri said the design of the *Tribune* has been evolutionary rather than revolutionary. "This paper is very sensitive to try to appear that it is always evolving. We are still in the midst of redesigning this newspaper. We want to be closer to the term *visual journalism.* We're constantly re-establishing priorities as the technology changes. We're re-examining the way art directors and artists are working on the newspaper every day. We're hiring more graphic journalists who can make the kind of judgments a reporter or editor would make. That takes a more sophisticated approach than before."

SUGGESTED EXERCISES

1. Compare the Page One layout of a major U.S. newspaper such as *The New York Times, USA Today* or *The Wall Street Journal* to your local daily. How are they similar? How do they differ?

2. Describe some of the visual messages you see each day in places other than newspapers. Do they provide you with more or less information than newspapers do?

3. What does "visually energetic newspaper" mean? Can you find examples in your local newspaper?

4. What are the five types of informational graphics? Clip two examples of each from a daily newspaper and discuss what you like and don't like about them.

5. Clip examples from a daily newspaper of the following:
   a. Nameplate
   b. Banner headline
   c. Vertical layout
   d. Modular layout
   e. Dogleg layout

6. Discuss the Page One layout of the daily newspaper that serves your community. Is it modular? Are visuals used effectively? How would you improve it?

CHAPTER TWO

The Technological Explosion

Computers have done more to change newspapers than have any other development since movable type was developed by **Johannes Gutenberg** in the 1450s in Mainz, Germany. They have allowed newspapers to do things never before possible, and the technological explosion is far from over.

Today, newspapers of all sizes depend heavily on computers, not only in the newsroom but in the advertising and business areas as well. From word processing to billing, from creating detailed informational graphics to electronically outputting a finished page, computers play vital roles. For a visual journalist, a computer is a necessity.

THE ELECTRONIC STORY

By using an important yearly event—the release of the U.S. president's proposed federal budget—as an example, it is easy to see the impact computers have had. The president is required to present his budget plan to Congress each January, and traditionally, it is a big story for newspapers. The wire services will move many news stories, sidebars, highlight boxes and other information about the budget. Many local newspapers will take that information and develop their own stories about the proposed budget's impact on their communities.

Let's start from the beginning, when, for example, an Associated Press reporter in Washington, D.C., receives a copy of the budget from the White House. First, she will read and analyze the proposal and interview government officials for comments, analyses and reactions. Then, when she is ready to write, she will sit at an AP computer and compose her story. Fewer than 20 years ago, she would have used a typewriter. When the story was written, edited and ready to be sent to member newspapers, a telegrapher would have retyped the finished story onto a piece of paper punch tape for eventual transmission over the telephone lines. In each AP member's newsroom, Teletype machines would capture the story from the wire and type it onto paper for editing by the newspaper's staff.

Today's computers, a **video display terminal** (VDT) or a personal computer (PC), look much like a television set with a typewriter-style keyboard. While the reporter sees the letters that make up the words in a story, the computer "reads" only electrical impulses that tell it what to display on the screen. A personal computer at home converts these same types of impulses into a display of words, graphics or games on its screen.

Figure 2.1   Reporter using computer keyboard and video display terminal (VDT)

The reporter's VDT, as well as other VDTs in the wire service bureau and at newspapers, is linked to a powerful central computer, which often is referred to as the **mainframe.** The mainframe allows each VDT to perform a variety of functions simultaneously. To comprehend the storage power of a mainframe, consider that the standard Macintosh II computer is equipped with a hard disk that usually provides 20 to 80 megabytes of memory. (A **byte** is a unit of electronic storage that can hold 8 digital bits of information. It usually takes 8 bytes for each letter or character. A **megabyte** contains 1,000,000 bytes.) A newspaper mainframe computer might store as much as 1 gigabyte, or 1,000,000 megabytes, of information. The mainframe keeps track of what each reporter has written and allows him or her to save or store the data at any time. This type of computer system also allows editors to see what reporters have written and to edit that copy.

The reporter **inputs** (types) her story, using a keyboard that has more functions than a typewriter (Figure 2.1). These additional functions make it pos-

sible for the reporter to edit her story as she composes it. The computer uses a symbol called a **cursor**—either a flashing line or square—to indicate the point in the text of the story where the reporter is working. By using the arrow keys, the reporter or editor can move the cursor to various points in the story to change a word or delete or add information.

Some VDTs move the cursor with the aid of a **mouse,** a small device attached by a wire to the terminal. As the reporter "drags," or moves, the mouse across a flat surface next to the keyboard, the cursor changes position correspondingly on the VDT screen.

Before reporters worked on computers, they had to retype part of a story to make major changes, or they had to cut their stories into pieces and paste them back together. With a computer, they can edit and cut and paste electronically, which allows them to turn in neat, easy-to-read copy.

When she is through writing, the reporter saves, or closes, her story, committing it to the mainframe's memory bank. Now the story can be

Figure 2.2   A directory of stories in national news basket

"moved" to her editor, who will check and edit the story on another VDT before transmitting it to one of the regional bureaus in the AP's system for distribution to newspapers and radio and television stations. This system allows the AP to move its copy via satellite and telephone lines at thousands of words a minute to hundreds of newspapers and broadcasters nationwide.

THE ELECTRONIC NEWSROOM

When the reporter's federal budget story arrives at a member newspaper, it is captured, or received, by the newspaper's own mainframe computer. This computer "reads" the AP's transmissions and sorts the files or stores them in an appropriate **basket.** (Note that there is little standardization in computer terminology—different systems use different terms. For example, a basket also may be called a *queue* or a *desk.*)

The newspaper's computer captures not only the AP's federal budget story but also all the other AP stories being sent. If the newspaper subscribes to another wire service, the stories by that service are captured by the mainframe computer as well. At some newspapers, hundreds of stories arrive in the mainframe every hour. The mainframe thus is set to automatically purge, or erase, stories every day or two to keep its memory banks from clogging with too much copy.

At the local newspaper, a reporter can read the AP's budget story for background information to help him write his article on how the federal budget will affect his community. The local story likely will run as a **sidebar,** or supplemental story, to the national article.

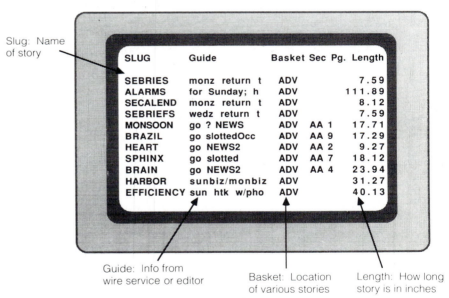

Figure 2.3   What an editor sees when looking at a directory

By typing a series of commands on a newsroom VDT, the local reporter "signs on" to the computer system (generally using a password to prevent unauthorized access). He "calls up" (asks the computer to show him) the national news basket (Figure 2.2), where AP's version of the federal budget story is being stored. When the reporter calls up the national stories, he sees a **menu,** or list of wire stories available for publication (Figure 2.3). Stories on the menu include all those sent into the national basket by the AP and other wire services.

By giving another set of commands, the reporter calls up all the stories with the word *budget* in the slug, or guideline—a one- or two-word description of a story (Figure 2.4). With the exception of information that the newspaper's computer has put at the top of

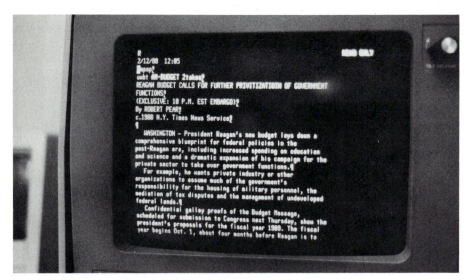

Figure 2.4   Display of a news story on a VDT

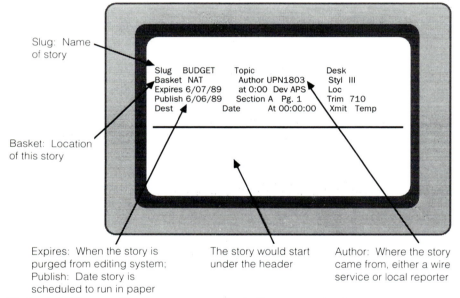

Slug: Name of story

Basket: Location of this story

Expires: When the story is purged from editing system; Publish: Date story is scheduled to run in paper

The story would start under the header

Author: Where the story came from, either a wire service or local reporter

Figure 2.5   What an editor or reporter sees when looking at a story header

the story in a field called a **header** (Figure 2.5), the AP story called up by the local reporter would be the same as the one sent from Washington.

After the local reporter has read the wire story for background information, he can make a paper printout—also called a **hard copy**—of it on a high-speed printer, or he can file an electronic copy of it in his personal basket or work area.

When he is ready to write his story, the reporter will call up a "take," which is an electronic version of a blank piece of paper in a typewriter. Only after the reporter gives the computer a slug and issues a "save" command does the computer add his story to its memory and store it in a basket.

The mainframe can store the local story in a different basket than the national story to avoid the confusion of too many stories in one place. A medium-sized newspaper might have hundreds of baskets, including one for each reporter, editing baskets for each department, baskets for production needs and baskets for the library to use when saving stories for its reference files.

THE ELECTRONIC COPY EDITOR

When the reporter is finished with his story, he sends it to a basket used by the newspaper's **city editor** or assistant city editors. While conferring with the reporter, the city editor reads and edits the story and then sends it to the copy desk basket. The **copy chief** or slot will assign a **copy editor** to call up the story, edit it for accuracy and style, prepare it for typesetting and write a headline.

The copy desk also will be sent the AP budget story. Using a computer with more powerful word processing and typesetting powers, a copy editor reads the wire story and the local sidebar. Through a series of editing commands, the copy editor can change words, move paragraphs, check spelling and style, adjust hyphenation and even combine elements from the two stories. The copy editor, who once used pencils, scissors and a glue pot to perform all of these functions, also prepares the story for its final stop, the electronic typesetter.

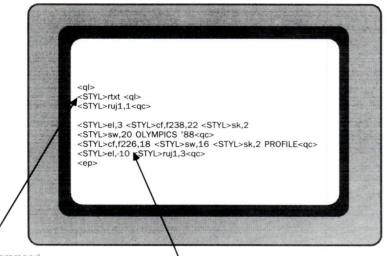

```
<ql>
<STYL>rtxt <ql>
<STYL>ruj1,1<qc>

<STYL>el,3 <STYL>cf,f238,22 <STYL>sk,2
<STYL>sw,20 OLYMPICS '88<qc>
<STYL>cf,f226,18 <STYL>sw,16 <STYL>sk,2 PROFILE<qc>
<STYL>el,-10 <STYL>ruj1,3<qc>
<ep>
```

STYL is the command that tells the computer the next piece of information is typesetting code

For example, cf means change font, f226 means use Franklin Gothic Bold, 18 indicates 18 point type

a

Figure 2.6 (a) Sample typesetting codes; (b) output resulting from sample codes

OLYMPICS '88
PROFILE

b

Figure 2.7 Galley of type being set by a typesetter

Figure 2.8 Production worker pasting up type on a makeup sheet

Photo by Gary Fong

At many papers, a **news editor** heads the copy desk. This key editor also may be responsible for story placement, headline size and design. News editors and their assistants generally monitor and edit the daily news wire report.

ELECTRONIC TYPESETTING

Before newspapers switched to electronic editing and typesetting systems, the hard copy was edited and marked with information that a member of the composing room staff, a printer, would use to set the story and its headline in lead type. With today's computer technology, the function of setting type resides with the copy desk.

The copy editor uses codes or typesetting symbols to tell the computer how to set the story in its final, printed form (Figure 2.6). The computer can set the story **justified** (by adding space between words or letters so that each line of the story sets flush right and flush left) or **ragged** (by letting the lines of the story end without adding space between words or letters to align the block of type vertically). Stories,

or any parts of them, also can be set in *italics* (slanted type) or **bold face** (heavier, darker type) for emphasis, as well as **medium face** (lighter than bold face but heavier than regular type).

At most newspapers, the copy editor is responsible for supplying the electronic version of the story with a headline, jumpline, byline, subheads, caption or any other special type treatment. That means that, along with improving the writing of a story and checking facts and spelling, the copy editor must understand computerized typesetting codes. This task of coding an electronic story has sparked debates in a number of newsrooms over the changing role of the copy editor, with some editors worried that the added production responsibilities take away from the time a copy editor needs to edit a story thoroughly.

Once the budget story is edited and coded, the copy editor releases the story to a computer for the complex process called **filming.** The computer reads the story, following the codes and special information on it, and instructs the typesetter, another sophisticated piece of equipment, to

output, or produce, the story on photosensitive paper called "film." The film is the actual "type" that will be used in the production of the finished news page.

The typesetting equipment is called the **front-end system.** The typesetter translates the computer information into the black-type images of letters and characters that make up a sheet of type, which also is referred to as a **galley** (Figure 2.7). A typesetter can be a basic model that outputs only galleys or a complex model that can set blocks of type, including story, headline, artwork and photographs.

Once the budget story is filmed (comes out of the typesetter), it is taken to a layout board where it is pasted to a full-scale page board according to the design instructions written on a paper dummy sheet (Figure 2.8).

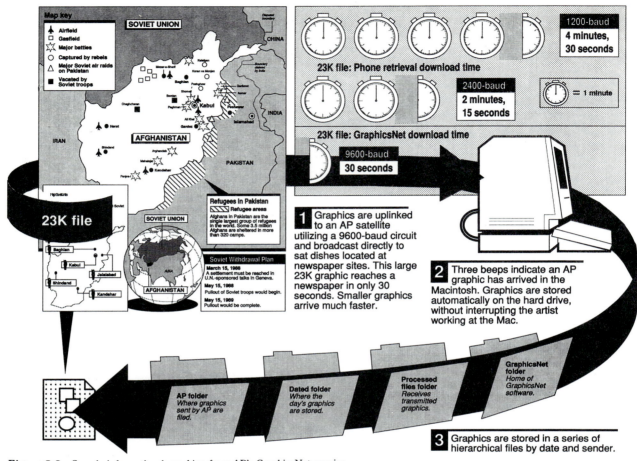

Figure 2.9 Sample informational graphics from AP's GraphicsNet service

PCs: NEW NEWSROOM TOOL

The technological explosion in American newspapers is in its infancy. Much of what has been described so far will be obsolete in coming years as advances in computers continue to change the way newspapers are produced.

Personal computers, such as those produced by IBM and Apple, are leading many of the advances in newspaper technology. In a 1988 survey of Society of Newspaper Design members, 92 percent said they use an Apple Macintosh computer at work. Some PCs are now as powerful as some of the computer systems currently used by newspapers, and a PC costs significantly less than a VDT connected to a mainframe.

The *Chicago Tribune,* which once had hundreds of VDTs connected to a mainframe computer, now is using a combination of VDTs and PCs. The

VDTs are used mostly for copy editing, while the PCs are used for writing.

The PC can be linked to a mainframe system for the transfer of stories, but reporters keep their copies on **floppy disks** (data storage devices), thus avoiding the need for and the expense of maintaining a great amount of computer memory space.

Personal computers also are being used by many newspapers to produce and edit visuals. Here are some of the uses:

• *Creating informational graphics and illustrations.* Newsroom artists use such software tools as MacDraw and Adobe's Illustrator to create maps, charts, diagrams and other visuals. Once the visual is finished, it can be stored on floppy disk or hard disk for later use or adaptation. The most popular program used for creating informational graphics

is MacDraw. It was the first drawing program released and it remained the standard drawing software until its mid-1988 upgrade to MacDraw II. Although Adobe's Illustrator and Aldus' FreeHand are more sophisticated, and more difficult to use, than MacDraw, some artists believe that both produce higher-quality graphics.

• *Receiving informational graphics on a newsroom personal computer via satellite or telephone.* A Macintosh can be used to access informational graphics from The Associated Press, the Knight-Ridder Tribune News graphics network or other, similar services. Such services, which store their graphics on large mainframe computers, make their visuals available to personal computers, equipped with a **modem,** a device that allows a computer to

Figure 2.10   Macintosh II

transfer information to and from another computer via telephone lines. A newsroom artist or editor uses a Macintosh to edit the informational graphic for publication. Both the AP and KRTN produce dozens of informational graphics daily, covering breaking news and feature stories, but the newsroom computer must be equipped with the same software as the graphics services for the artwork to be edited. In 1988, the AP started installing equipment that allows a newsroom Macintosh to receive AP informational graphics automatically via satellite. This service, called GraphicsNet (Figure 2.9), uses the same satellite that sends stories to the newspaper's mainframe computer.

• *Designing pages.* A visual journalist can use a personal computer—either a Macintosh or an IBM PC—with desktop publishing software to design news and feature pages. The personal computer allows the visual journalist to position visual elements, headlines and stories on an "electronic page." The elements can be moved quickly and easily to create the most pleasing design by using such software as Quark 'Xpress, PageMaker and AmperPage.

Many newspapers use either the Macintosh Plus or Macintosh SE as standard equipment. Some also use the Mac II, which was developed in the late 1980s and is faster and more powerful than its forerunners (Figure 2.10).

Almost all newspapers output—print—their Macintosh work on Apple's laser printers. The printer uses the same basic technology of copying machines and produces an image that has 300 dots per inch (dpi). A higher-resolution printer, the VT-600 (a 600-dpi machine made by Varityper), is being used at some newspapers, but its higher price has limited its acceptance.

As the personal computer becomes more powerful and is introduced into more newsrooms, it will serve even more functions. In the 1990s, look for personal computers—especially the Macintosh—to receive and manipulate digital photographs, capture and sort wire service stories, produce color separations, receive or produce and place advertisements and output a finished newspaper page. Even today, some small newspapers are being produced entirely on personal computers.

PAGINATION: THE FUTURE GETS CLOSER

Great changes are being made in the process that occurs after a story is edited and becomes part of a finished page. The manual pasteup process involving paper galleys of type and pasting wax is being replaced by an electronic layout process called **pagination**. In pagination, all the elements that make up a newspaper page—stories, photographs, cutlines, headlines—are assembled electronically by a highly sophisticated computer program. When the electronic page is complete, a complex typesetter films the page (Figure 2.11), much the same way as the first typesetter filmed the budget story. In the future, a typesetter will be capable of producing a negative that will be used to create a plate for the printing press or the printing plate itself.

Some newspapers use the term *pagination* to describe something less than full-page makeup. For example, it may be used to describe a computer-generated page that contains "holes," or space for the placement of photographs, advertisements and other graphic elements. Such output is more aptly named **area composition**.

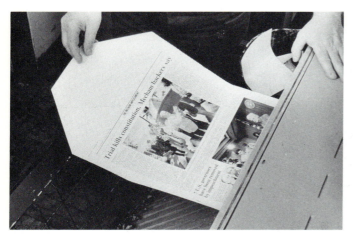

Figure 2.11   Sample filmed page

Figure 2.12   Pagination terminal and display of a page

A complete pagination system, which can store and display every element on a page, is expensive, and this factor has kept many newspapers from using pagination in its developmental stages. Those papers now using pagination have invested in sophisticated computers to store massive amounts of information. (Even a single photograph can take several hundred thousand bytes of information.) The pagination computers must keep track of each story planned for the newspaper, all of the photographs, the other visuals, the advertisements and even the page folios (publication date and page numbers at the top of each page).

There are two ways to paginate a newspaper—an interactive system and a passive system.

Interactive Pagination

The **interactive pagination system** allows for both the copy editor and the person using the pagination computer terminal (an editor, designer or printer) to edit or change a story. If a story is too long, the designer at the pagination terminal or the copy editor at a VDT can access the story and edit it to fit the page design.

Many newspapers believe this system allows for the most flexibility; however, it also means a page could be changed without editors being informed. Although safeguards can be established to prevent a pagination terminal operator

from changing copy, the temptation is still there, particularly when time is short as a deadline nears. Communication between the terminal operator and copy editor is extremely important when an interactive system is used.

Passive Pagination

Less flexible is the **passive pagination system,** which really is two separate computer systems. The passive system is based on the idea that the newspaper's front-end system, which sets the type, can be used to transfer that same "type" to the pagination computer. Using the system from Information International Inc. (Triple I) as an example, this is how passive pagination works:

The newspaper's front-end system transfers or films the story into type, but instead of going to a film processor, the story is sent to the pagination system by way of a computer "translator." The pagination system gives the story an identifying number or file "name."

When displayed by the pagination system, the story looks like a galley of type, exactly how it would have looked if it had been processed by the typesetter. The pagination operator takes the "galley of type" and places it on an electronic version of a full-size page board (Figure 2.12). The operator can have the type flow or go around photographs and advertisements. If the operator needs a change or trim in the story to fit the layout, the story is sent

back to the copy desk, where an editor makes the change on the front-end system and films the revised story to the pagination system. Once all of the elements are placed on the electronic version of the page, the pagination operator can output the page to a typesetter, which will produce the complete newspaper page.

The Arizona Republic in Phoenix uses a Triple I "passive" pagination system. The paper was fully paginated in 1988 and is producing more than 1,000 complete pages a week. The change has meant a re-examination of many traditional duties at the paper as editorial employees take on jobs that once were reserved for composing room employees and as lines of job responsibilities within the newsroom shift and blur.

ELECTRONIC PHOTOGRAPHY: THE NEXT REVOLUTION

There's still more change coming to newspaper technology beyond PCs and pagination. Filmless **electronic cameras** are being developed that record pictures on a video floppy disk, much like a computer floppy disk (Figure 2.13). The electronic camera resembles a 35mm camera, but it carries no film. The photographer points the camera at a subject, and a sensor inside the camera records the image by electronic signal. The images then can be viewed

Figure 2.13 Filmless electronic camera

Figure 2.14 AP's transmission print from an electronic camera

on a television monitor and printed out in color or transmitted via telephone lines to receiving stations, thus eliminating darkrooms, chemicals and the time it takes to process and print film.

Even though the resolution of images produced by an electronic camera still does not compare to the resolution of images on film, more and more newspapers are experimenting with these devices. One successful experiment was conducted by AP during the 1989 inauguration of President Bush (Figure 2.14). Using a Nikon electronic camera system, an AP photographer was able to take and transmit a picture within 40 seconds to member newspapers worldwide; normally, the procedure would have taken 30 to 45 minutes.

The Nikon electronic camera system cost about $20,000 in 1989. Another manufacturer of electronic cameras is Canon. As the costs of these systems drop in upcoming years, this type of photography will play an increasingly important role in newspapers.

ELECTRONIC PICTURES AND PICTURE DESKS

Beyond the electronic camera, and close to reality for many newspapers, are two pieces of electronic equipment that involve photographs: the electronic or digital photo transmitter and the electronic picture desk or darkroom.

The Electronic Photo Transmitter

The **electronic photo transmitter** requires only a negative to send photographic images from a remote site to the newspaper's office. Previously, a photographer needed to make a print and transmit that "positive" image with a print transmitter, which took eight to 10 minutes. By contrast, the electronic transmitter can send an image in less than one minute. It can send images from black and white film, color negative film (either in black and white or color) or color transparency film (either in black and white or color). In addition, the photographer who is transmitting the image can correct the photographic tones and color balances using a built-in computer system and software.

Currently, most newspapers receive photographic prints much like the transmissions from the Associated Press or United Press International. Eventually, however, images from the electronic photo transmitter will go directly into an electronic newspaper picture desk or darkroom.

John Walston

Deputy Managing Editor/Graphics and Photography   *USA Today*

John N. Walston, deputy managing editor/graphics and photography at *USA Today,* enjoys looking into the future, thinking about where the technological explosion will lead newspapers in the 1990s.

"We're getting ready to enter a new world," he said. "It will be a world where there will be a personal computer on every newspaper desk. The reporter can be writing a story on the screen, and if he needs background information, he can hit a key and up pops onto a section of the screen the information he needs. The writer, staying in the writing mode, can get the information right away. He can have available on the PC personal data bases, such as the World Almanac or biographies of everyone he's ever interviewed.

"I'm sitting here looking at a $10 million mainframe system that can't do any of that. The Apple Macintosh showed people in the newsroom that powerful PCs can do things that the big, expensive machines cannot do. The PCs can access data bases and sort data. They can be used to draw graphics. You can produce camera-ready graphics and put them in the newspaper. PCs showed us for the first time the potential of computers in the newsroom. We have been working with computers for 15 to 20 years, but none of them has showed us the potential that PCs show us."

Walston said as current newsroom computers wear out, newspapers will replace them with lower-cost, higher-power PCs. "Gannett has basically made the decision that for the future we will purchase no editorial system

that does not have a PC-based solution in its future," he added. "That means that even though a Gannett paper may not be purchasing a PC-based system at this moment, it will have the capability to do it in the future. We don't believe you should be out buying a new system every seven to 10 years because it is outdated. We say buy a system that can keep the mainframe computer and link computers that can be changed and modified as new innovations reach the market.

"What's been going on in the last five to eight years is we've had these little nerds sitting with personal computers in garages across the country inventing incredibly wonderful things. These things are not being invented in the laboratories. To keep up with these advancements, we want a computer system that can use a better wheel when someone invents it."

Walston predicted that by the late 1990s, nearly all newspapers will be PC-based. "The small newspapers will get them first because it's an investment that offers cheaper solutions. That's the way we're all going. It should be interesting to see how far people will take what the PC will do for them."

Walston has worked at newspapers throughout the country as a reporter and as a visual journalist. He started at his college paper. He joined *USA Today* in 1983.

He said: "By the time I got to *USA Today,* graphics were very much a part of what I did for a living. When I came here, the paper was looking for someone in the graphics department who also knew news. The graphics we do

are chock full of information. A lot of it is news or has news value of some sort."

Newspaper technology is not the only thing that is changing rapidly, Walston pointed out. He said that newspapers will have to continue to change editorially to meet the needs of their readers. "Until the 1970s, newspapers were cocky. They gave readers what they thought they [the readers] should have. I think we still should do that, but we have to look at how people have changed and give them something that can help them in their everyday life. I think the people here care more about their readers. That is a trend that has come into newspapers, partly because of us."

That does not mean every newspaper should try to be *USA Today,* Walston added. "Too many newspapers are doing things because *USA Today* does them. They are not looking at their audience and market and trying to figure out how to serve the people in that market area. Carrying short stories and a lot of color does not necessarily serve every readership.

"Too many newspapers look like us now. I think they have made a mistake. We created our look to serve our readership. I don't think it is an approach that works in every community. We were looking for a part of everybody's market, not their whole market. I think there are things about us that everyone can adopt, but I don't think community newspapers can serve *USA Today*'s readers. They need to concentrate on what makes them unique and different."

The Electronic Picture Desk or Darkroom

The **electronic picture desk** or electronic darkroom is designed to replace the conventional method of receiving wire service photographs. The wire services currently send positive images to a receiver, which produces a photographic print in the newsroom. This method uses an **analog** (continuous) signal, much like the signal a radio station transmits.

The electronic picture desk will allow for the **digital** (non-continuous) transmission of photographs via satellite or telephone lines at extremely high speeds directly into a computer. After the image has been received, an editor will be able to call up a picture on a monitor (a televisionlike screen) and consider it for publication. Before "outputting," or printing, the photo, the editor will be able to crop, size and improve the quality of the image.

Depending on the amount of computer storage, an electronic picture desk will be able to hold 100 to 500 local and wire photos. The picture editor will be able to look at the day's photo report listed on a menu (a visual preview of eight to 16 reduced-size pictures). After looking at the images in the system, the picture editor can save pictures, purge them or edit them. Once a picture has been edited, it can be sent to a wire photo receiver, which allows for a hard copy (or photographic print), to be made. Ultimately, the picture editor will be able to send the photograph directly to the newspaper's pagination system, where it will be joined with type and other elements in the finished page.

SUGGESTED EXERCISES

1. Discuss the computer system being used at a local newspaper. What type of video display terminals or personal computers does the paper use? How old is the system? What are the paper's plans for updating or changing the system?

2. Define and discuss the following terms:
   a. Mainframe
   b. Cursor
   c. Basket
   d. Purge
   e. Sign-on
   f. Password
   g. Menu
   h. Slug
   i. Header
   j. Hard copy
   k. Take
   l. Front-end system
   m. Galley

3. What is justified type? Ragged type? Clip examples from newspapers. Which style do you find more visually pleasing?

4. Is your local newspaper paginated? If not, does it plan to be in the future? If so, what type of system is being used?

5. Compare your college newspaper's computer system to your community daily's system. Is either using personal computers? If so, how are they being used in the production of the newspaper? If not, does either newspaper plan to introduce them?

CHAPTER THREE

Design and Newspapers

One of the greatest benefits of the technological revolution for newspapers has been the increased ability to visually present the news—and to do it attractively in ways that would have been unimaginable only a few decades ago.

The new electronic tools and machines of today's newspapers have removed all but a few production limitations—other than the physical size of the newspaper. With such wide-ranging production options available to even the smallest computerized daily paper, what's to keep the paper from looking chaotic and visually out of control from day to day?

Design. Each newspaper has an overall design that serves as the framework on which the ever-changing menu of news, sports, business and features is presented to readers each day. It is this design that gives a continuity and visual unity to the seemingly endless combination of words, photographs, graphics and advertisements that make up a newspaper.

HOLDING IT ALL TOGETHER

There are literally hundreds of elements that make up a newspaper's design, but the design itself has only three main

components: organization, pattern and structure. The design reflects the **organization** of the content of the newspaper—which sections go where, what features are anchored on which pages and so on. The design is the **pattern** of visual presentation—the rhythm or consistency of how the pages look day in and day out. The design is **structure**—what kind of type is used for body copy, which type for headlines, how many columns of type on a page and so on.

Choosing a newspaper design forces everyone involved to focus on what newspapers should be doing best—communicating ideas and information to their readers. The newspaper's design should encompass the complete and total awareness of every element that is published. A visual journalist who merely designs a page, without understanding the elements of the paper's organization, pattern and structure, fails as a designer.

DESIGN'S ORGANIZATION

The organization of a newspaper involves how it is physically put together and presented day after day. One of the major complaints from readers is that newspapers, for whatever reason—mechanical or lack of interest—aren't consistent

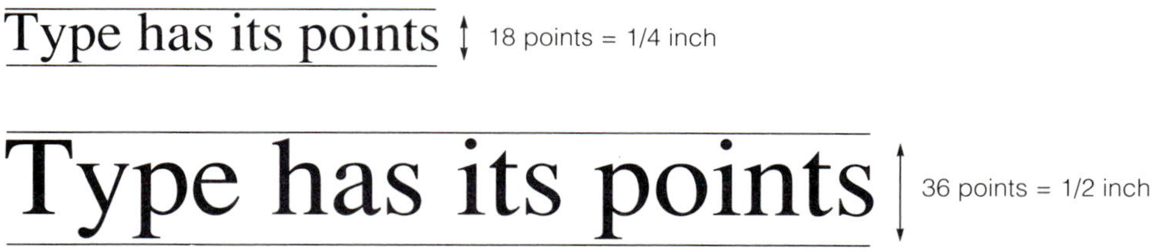

Type has its points ↕ 18 points = 1/4 inch

Type has its points ⏐ 36 points = 1/2 inch

Figure 3.1   Measuring type

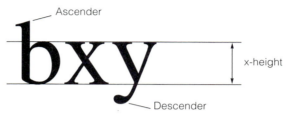

Ascender

bxy

x-height

Descender

Figure 3.2   Measuring x-height

in their presentation of the various parts of the paper. If sports has its own section five days a week, why can't it have it seven days a week? readers ask. This kind of organization of sections is not just a design function; it involves the limitations of a newspaper's production process. Some newspapers have pressroom limitations that don't always allow for the consistent presentation of sections. A successful design, however, will attempt to solve many of the organizational problems of a newspaper. And failing that, it will help guide the reader—with promotion boxes, indexes, refers—to news of high readership interest on the days when the newspaper's organization is different or confusing.

Organization also includes "anchoring" of popular columns and features within the various sections or pages of the paper: The editorial pages are always located on the last two pages of the first section; "Dear Abby" is always placed on the page following the comics; the team standings are always listed on the fourth page of the sports section.

DESIGN'S PATTERN

Part of design is the pattern of consistent presentation. It is visual style used in presenting the news and feature stories day in and day out; it is not the news per se, but the manner in which stories and visual elements are given to the reader from headline sizes to the style of photography. The reader needs to feel that today's newspaper will present the news in much the same approach as the edition he or she read six months ago. For example, Page One will contain the most important news of the day and an index to other news inside the

paper. And the biggest news of the day will have the biggest headline on Page One.

One newspaper's pattern of visual presentation might be to use large color photographs on each section front. Another paper might have a pattern of using mostly news photographs and very few "soft," or feature, pictures. Each newspaper sets the pattern of presentation for its readers. The task of the visual journalist is to understand that pattern and follow it fairly consistently. That doesn't mean that a page or a paper cannot contain a few surprises, but such deviations from the standard presentation should delight readers, not shock or confuse them.

One of the reasons many readers become upset when a newspaper radically changes its design is the loss of the familiar pattern of presentation. The readers feel, almost subconsciously, they can no longer understand how to get through the paper and find the day's news.

DESIGN'S STRUCTURE

Structure is the most important part of the design framework, and the most important part of structure is **typography,** the style and arrangement of type on a page. Typography entails more than the readability of the type on the

page; it identifies a newspaper's character, it creates an unspoken link between the paper and its readers. The typographic dress of a newspaper helps give readers a familiar, comfortable feeling each day.

Typographic Language

Although only a very small percentage of newspapers today are printed with the old-fashioned process of lead type, electronic typesetting still employs many of the universal terms and measurements used by the printing crafts.

Typography includes the size and character of the **body type,** the *face* or style of type used in everything from the story text to headlines. Type is measured two ways. The face of each letter or character is measured vertically in **points**—there are 72 points in an inch. The width of a line of type (the horizontal measurement of the column of type) is generally measured in **picas**—12 points equal 1 pica, and 6 picas equal 1 inch (Figure 3.1). Therefore, a headline set in 36-point type across an 18-pica column would be $\frac{1}{2}$ inch high and 3 inches wide.

There is another measurement of type that is important to a designer: *x-height.* This term refers to the height measurement of type without descenders or ascenders. *Ascenders* and *descenders* are the vertical parts of certain

Font No.	Face	Available Pt. Sizes
206	News Gothic Condensed	10 thru 96
209	**Techno Book Bold**	6 thru 48
212	Techno Light	6 thru 96
214	Techno Medium	6 thru 96
215	Techno Medium Condensed	6 thru 96
216	**Techno Bold**	6 thru 96
218	**Techno Extra Bold**	10 thru 96
220	**Techno Extra Bold Condensed**	10 thru 96
226	**Franklin Gothic Extra Condensed**	6 thru 96
228	**Gothic 13**	10 thru 96
234	**Cheltenham Bold**	10 thru 96
238	Century Schoolbook	6 thru 48
240	**Century Schoolbook Bold**	6 thru 48
244	Chelmsford	10 thru 96
248	**Bodoni Bold**	10 thru 96
249	*Bodoni Bold Italic*	10 thru 96
250	Bodoni Campanile	10 thru 96
263	Helvetica Light	6 thru 96
264	Helvetica Regular	6 thru 96
265	**Helvetica Medium**	6 thru 96
266	**Helvetica Bold**	6 thru 96
268	Franklin Gothic Light	6 thru 24
269	**Franklin Gothic Bold**	6 thru 24
270	Times Roman Light	6 thru 96
271	**Times Roman Bold**	6 thru 96

Figure 3.3   Sample typefaces from a newspaper

This is Times Roman Bold, a serif face

a

This is Franklin Gothic Bold, a sans serif face

b

Figure 3.4   Typeface (a) with serif; (b) sans serif

This is Century School Book

This is Century School Book Italic

This is Century School Book Bold

This is Century School Book Bold Italic

Figure 3.5   Type family; roman, italic, bold and bold italic

lowercase letters such as *p* or *b*. The x-height of type is measured using the lowercase letter *x*, hence the name (Figure 3.2).

Style of Type

There are hundreds of typefaces newspapers can use. Some of the more common faces include Spartan, Times, Chelmsford, Bodoni, Century, Caslon, Bookman, Helvetica, Franklin Gothic and Garamond (Figure 3.3). Some of these styles are **serif** faces, in which there is a fine cross stroke at the top and bottom of lowercase letters such as *b, d, h, i, j, k, l, m, n, p, s* and *z*. This stroke follows the lettering of medieval authors who lettered with a broad pen; others are **sans serif,** without the cross strokes (Figure 3.4).

A typeface can have different densities or visual weights: *light, medium, bold* and *extra bold* or *ultra.* The bolder the type, the thicker each letter. Type may be **condensed,** where the letters are thinner and spaced closer together, or **extended,** where the letters are

fatter and there is more white space between each one. Most type is set *roman,* or unslanted, but it also may be set *italic,* with a slight slant (Figure 3.5).

All of the type of any one design is called a *family.* For example, 12-point Century Bold, 72-point Century Italic and 30-point Century Light all are members of the Century family. A complete set of type characters and spacing in *one* size and style is known as a **font.**

Point Size

The sizes of type used in newspapers range from 5.5 points (used in some paper's stock market tables) to 96 points or larger (used in banner headlines on section pages). Most newspaper stories are set in 9-point type on a base of 10 points. That extra space, or "leading" as it is called, gives a little white space between each line of type and is more pleasing in appearance than lines of type set too close together. Leading also prevents the ascenders of one line

from running into the descenders of the line above it. Many newspapers are constantly evaluating the size of their body type in an effort to ensure that, as the U.S. population gets older, the paper is as readable as possible. One newspaper, the *St. Petersburg Times,* which serves a community with many retired residents, recently increased its body type size to 10 points from 8.5 points, believing that it could better serve its marketplace with larger body type. (You are reading Century Old Style, set 9.5 point.)

In addition to the size of the body type, the visual journalist must also be aware of two other readability factors: the optimum column width and the use of color type.

Readability studies have shown that the **optimum column width,** the length of a line of type that is most readable, is about 14 picas. (This paragraph has been set 13 picas wide; the columns in most books, because of their smaller page size, can be wider.) And although other widths in the range of

Mountain View editor wins contest

Trujillo

Guy

Seniors from three Valley high schools have won the top four local honors in the 1988 National Association of Hispanic Journalists writing contest.

First-place winner for the best published news story in English was Mario Mercado, 17, from Mountain View High School in Mesa.

Mercado,editor of the school's *Viewpoint* newspaper, won for his article, "Sophomore Dies in Plane Crash," reporting the impact of a schoolmate's death on her family.

Judges praised Mercado's story, saying he "tackled the toughest topic that can face a reporter" and produced a "sensitive, dignified" article.

ism major at Columbia University.

The second-place winner was Laura Trujillo, 17, of Alhambra High School in Phoenix.

Her story, "Date Rape," was published in the Teen *Gazette* section of *The Phoenix Gazette.* She won a $25 award.

The judges found Trujillo's article "compelling" and "well-researched," calling it "a professional piece" filled with "a sense of drama" of her subject.

Trujillo wants to major in print journalism at Loyola or the University of Santa Clara.

Two students from Camelback High School in Phoenix received honorable mentions.

Donna La May Guy, 18, received recognition for "Lights! Camera! Action!" a Teen *Gazette* feature story on students auditioning as hosts for a locally produced cable television show.

Krista Boggs, 17, was recognized for her analysis piece, "The Season for Fur: A Status or Sadist Symbol?" which ran in the school's *Blade* newspaper.

"The judges said the overall quality of entries was so high they had trouble making their decisions," said Holly Remy, the contest's coordinator and a reporter for *The Arizona Republic.* "This was the first time the contest has been held in Phoe-

Figure 3.6 Column on left is set too narrow for easy reading

Figure 3.7 Wide measure type

Caucus pushes Jackson to try for No. 2 spot

By DOUGLAS JEHL
Los Angeles Times

WASHINGTON — Seeking to invigorate the Rev. Jesse Jackson's tentative vice presidential bid, members of the Congressional Black Caucus Wednesday formally urged Jackson to seek the second spot on the ticket and said they would ask Massachusetts Gov. Michael S. Dukakis to make his rival his running mate.

Jackson said that he had not sought the caucus' opinion, and reiterated that he had not made up his mind whether to seek the office but believes that he has earned "serious consideration" for the job. He contended also that there was "obviously growing concern within the country that that 'serious consideration' be translated into being a part of the ticket."

Jackson also said he met privately earlier Wednesday with Dukakis' campaign chairman Paul Brountas, who is leading that campaign's vice presidential hunt. Asked if that meeting represented the consideration he sought, Jackson said only, "It was a very meaningful preliminary discussion."

"We need to know what the rules are and what the standards will be," he said later on CNN television.

The meeting was the first in which Jackson discussed the vice presidency with Dukakis or one of his aides. Dukakis' press secretary, Dayton Duncan, described the session as "part of the consultative process."

The formal statement from the black caucus, representing the consensus of 18 caucus members, added an influential voice of affirmation to the advice of some key Jackson advisers that the candidate "go for broke" and seek the vice presidential slot.

Other aides, however, have counseled caution, and Jackson has remained undecided. He explained Wednesday that "there is a relationship between leader and people" and that he hoped to "build a consensus" among his supporters for whatever course he eventually chooses.

In statements at a Capitol Hill news conference, six of the panel's members sought to counter the views of those who have counseled caution, arguing that Jackson should be regarded as the front-runner for the vice presidential slot and could bring great political strength to a ticket headed by Dukakis.

"We go into the convention not to put pressure on Gov. Dukakis," said Rep. Charles Rangel, D-N.Y. "We come in with a candidate. It seems to me that Gov. Dukakis has to come up with a better candidate."

14 picas (12 picas to 16 picas) are acceptable, stories set less than 6 picas or more than 18 picas wide should be avoided because too-narrow or too-wide type is hard for the eye to read. With too-narrow columns, the eye must dart back and forth (Figure 3.6); with too-wide columns, the eye grows tired faster reading the long line (Figure 3.7).

Special uses of narrow or wide type—captions, quotes, headlines—are not a problem because those elements contain very brief messages and readability is not affected. Some special typographic treatments can, however, have a negative effect on readability. They include:

• **Reversed type,** generally white type on a dark or black background.
• **Overprinting,** in which a black-and-white or color screen or pattern is printed over body type or a headline. This process is sometimes called an *overlay.*

Both of these treatments hinder the readers' ability to see and understand what they are reading. Some studies

have shown that reversed type is at least 20 percent harder to read than normal type. And when using overprinting, the designer must be careful to select a light screen or color to minimize the impact on the type's readability.

THE IMPORTANCE OF TYPOGRAPHY

Choosing the typeface that a newspaper will use is an important decision. The typeface helps a newspaper express its character or tone; it can give readers certain impressions of the content being displayed. For instance, when *The Arizona Republic* in Phoenix was redesigned in 1988, publisher Pat Murphy wanted a headline face that expressed a conservative, classic image. The paper replaced its Helvetica headline type, a sans serif face that it had used for nine years (Figure 3.8), with Times Roman, a serif face (Figure 3.9).

Sans serif headline faces were adopted by many newspapers in the 1970s because designers considered them more modern, a break from the more traditional newspaper designs of the 1960s. (Note that the use of sans serif headline style was nothing new—

Figure 3.8 *The Arizona Republic* page with sans serif headline typeface

Figure 3.9 *The Arizona Republic* page with serif headline typeface

it was popular in the 1940s.) Designers also believed that serifs did not help the readers scan the words and therefore served little function. Most newspapers did continue to use serif body type, though, and by the late 1980s, some of the "modernized" newspapers had switched back to serif headline faces as well.

Familiarity has much to do with readability, and because most textbooks and newspapers use serif type for their text, readers are used to such a typeface and find it easier to read. Moreover, many editors and publishers such as Murphy believe that serif headlines project a more stable, traditional image. Many visual journalists believe that serifs

add more visual contrast and typographical excitement to a newspaper page.

When *The Republic* tested the Times Roman headline face, it found that the new headline was perceived as more professional and more modern, as well as crisper. Like any newspaper that is redesigned, *The Republic* was careful to test its typographic changes with focus groups, carefully selected cross sections of readers and non-readers, before they were made.

COLOR AND READABILITY

The use of color also can affect the readability of the paper. Color, a relatively new addition to the newspaper

design toolbox, shapes the way the newspaper presents news and the way it is perceived by the reader. The most readable combination of type and color is black type printed on white newsprint. And although most newspapers have neither truly white paper nor truly black ink, unlike magazines or books, this combination is still the best.

As mentioned previously, one of the hardest combinations to read is white type on black, or reversed background. Most readers prefer not to read this combination and, when presented with type set in this manner, might choose to skip that element.

In the use of color, the best combination for readability is black type on a yellow tint. This is a combination of a dark type printed on a light background. The visual journalist should avoid the use of a dark type printed on a dark background (black type on purple, for example) or a light type on a light background (yellow type on white).

REDESIGNING FOR A NEW LOOK

Now more than any other time in newspaper history, the novice entering the newspaper industry can expect to find his or her employer embarking on substantial changes in the content and visual presentation of the product. According to a 1987 study by the Newspaper Advertising Bureau, between 1983 and 1987, more than 82 percent of the papers surveyed had altered their design to some degree through different typefaces, new column widths and new uses of graphics, color and layout.

The decision to try a new look in the paper reflected more than just a desire to see what the new machinery could do. Changing demographics, economic factors and new sources of competition all contribute to the decision to find a new look. There is, however, a serious caveat to design alterations: Change the content or the look of the paper too drastically or too quickly or without any explanation and readers will become confused and alienated.

Redesign is a jolting experience for everyone involved—from the publisher to the reporters and editors to the readers—and one that is not accomplished successfully without a great deal of patience, planning, adjustment and understanding. Any newspaper can decide to make changes in its design framework, but few newspapers do it quickly and without thought. (Remem-

ber, readers like consistency.) Redesign involves a lot of people—those who work at the newspaper *and* those who read it. Both groups are important in planning and executing a redesign.

The first step in a redesign is to set the goals to be achieved by the changes. The top editors of the newspaper generally make those decisions, often with the help of readership surveys and outside consultants.

The editors ask themselves what their newspaper's philosophy is, what they want to achieve with their product: Will it concentrate on crime and other sensational stories? Will it be flashy with a lot of color and big headlines? Will it have a classic look with small headlines and black and white photography? Scores of such questions must be answered before the design goals can be set. Once the editors know what they want, it generally is up to visual journalists to make the redesign work within the boundaries of the newspaper's philosophy.

For example, when *The Arizona Republic* redesigned, it established specific goals to be met:

- *Hierarchy/proportion.* Keep the day's news in proportion with the significance of the event. Try to give the reader a sense that the newspaper will get excited only when events are truly important.
- *Character.* Be understated; be a quieter newspaper that gives an order or value to the day's events.
- *Classic/high-tech potential.* Return to the paper's serif typeface, adopt a quieter headline dress with a design style that takes advantage of the paper's pagination equipment, such as the use of a 12-column grid.

- *Heavy traffic.* Convey a sense of movement on the page, not necessarily with more stories, but with more elements that provide information to the reader. Include more highlight boxes, more graphics and more refers to other stories.
- *Vertical movement.* Move the reader down through the page, especially on the front pages of sections. Make the paper look easier to read—big horizontal pieces of type seem overwhelming to readers.
- *Reliability.* Keep the paper consistent from day to day; anchor more features; be consistent on headline sizes and art sizes; be consistent in design style.
- *Elegance/symmetry.* Bring order and balance to the newspaper. Try to create a newspaper that is new but familiar, modern but comfortable.

Some of the results of *The Republic's* new design, as compared with its old design, can be seen in the accompanying examples (Figures 3.10-3.13).

The Importance of Readership Studies

Readers play the critical role in the design process. To find out what the readers want, newspapers conduct readership studies, which can tell them everything from what typefaces are the most pleasing to which pages in the newspaper are the most popular. The studies are especially important to determine how to package the newspaper more effectively. Most readers have a personal relationship with their newspaper, and when it changes, they may not like what they see. Those involved

Figure 3.10 *The Arizona Republic* Travel section before its redesign

Figure 3.11 *The Arizona Republic* Travel section after its redesign

in redesign must be ready for roses and thorns, but they can reduce criticism by listening to what readers are saying *before* they revise the paper.

Readership surveys can answer such questions as: Do you want more or less local news? More photographs? More color? Longer stories? Shorter stories? Different typeface? Bigger headlines? Here is a sampling of what such surveys have found:

- *Readers want consistency.* Many people follow a set routine when reading a newspaper, and they want their favorite features in the same place each day. They also want a newspaper to follow a certain structure. They want the top stories of the day on Page One, with the biggest headlines on the most important stories. Consistency of placement of stories and features gives the paper an image of reliability.

- *Readers want organization.* They look for groupings and packages of news that provide order and structure to the presentation. Indexes and refers are very important reading aids.

- *Readers don't necessarily read Page One first.* The sports section is the first place some readers go. The comics page, editorial page and local news pages are read first by many other readers. This means attention must be paid to the design of every page and every element in the newspaper.

- *Advertisements are important to newspaper readers.* What is on sale is valuable news to readers, too. How editorial matter is positioned in relation to advertisements thus is an important design decision. Readers don't want to confuse advertising matter with news stories because of an ambiguous layout.

In short, such studies have shown that readers want a paper that is easy to read and easy to follow, a paper that meets their need to know.

Figure 3.12 *The Arizona Republic* Sun Living section before its redesign

Figure 3.13 *The Arizona Republic* Sun Living section after its redesign

The Importance of Circulation

How and when the reader will get the paper also has an impact on the design. Is most of the paper's circulation through home delivery or single-copy sales? Is it a morning newspaper or an afternoon newspaper? There are different design considerations for each. For example, papers sold mainly through vending machines usually have larger headlines and photographs to catch the eyes of readers.

A morning newspaper generally is a *paper of record*, offering straightforward news accounts of what happened in the world, nation, state and community overnight or since the last edition. Afternoon newspapers, on the other

hand, usually are reporting events that will have occurred after their deadlines. They do so with comprehensive stories that offer unique interpretative angles on the news. In addition, afternoon newspapers are fighting for a reader's attention against all of the evening activities, such as television.

The Importance of Staff Involvement

An effective redesign also needs plenty of enthusiastic staff members working on it from the beginning. The process usually begins when a newspaper sets up a committee to provide ideas, enthusiasm and support. The committee should make sure that the entire staff

knows of the proposed changes before they are made.

Changes also need to be shared with other departments, such as circulation, advertising and production. Many redesign efforts have difficulty because editorial didn't tell production there was going to be a new way of putting together the newspaper or because someone forgot the new computer coding for the new typeface.

The key is communicating every step of the redesign to the entire newspaper. Copy editors should be involved early and often because they will have to learn new computer typesetting coding. Even the people in the telephone room of the circulation department need to know about the

Pat Murphy

Publisher   *The Arizona Republic* and *The Phoenix Gazette*

"Every publisher, editor or newspaper owner has to say, 'What kind of newspaper do I want? What is my market? What is the mission I am trying to achieve?' " said Pat Murphy, publisher of *The Arizona Republic* and *The Phoenix Gazette*. Murphy's answer to those questions is simple. He wants newspapers of distinction and excellence; he wants newspapers that look good.

"Afternoon newspapers such as *The Gazette* are different from morning newspapers," he explained. "An afternoon paper is an impulse buy rather than a habit. A morning newspaper has built-in assets because people have to start their morning with a newspaper. *The Republic* is a morning newspaper. It should have a dispassionate tone that says to a reader, 'You look at it and make a decision on whether or not to read it.' It should be global in reach, informing readers what is going on in the world, nation and their community.

It should be reserved and consistent. Its layout should be orderly. There must be a reason for everything on the page.

"A newspaper with a serious commitment to providing important information to sophisticated readers can't be packaged like a fast-food place. Look at *The New York Times* and *The Wall Street Journal*. They receive peer approval because they are classic. They are packaged in a serious way."

Murphy noted that when he became publisher in 1986, *The Republic* was a newspaper that did not aspire to excellence. "It sought mediocrity. There was no design order. It didn't look clean or comfortable. It was not user-friendly.

"I went to the staff and everyone mentioned design as the first thing that needed to be done. Some people wanted to go to more color, but I don't think color should be used for color's sake. The less color a newspaper uses, the more distinguished it looks. Everywhere you look there is color, on tele-

vision, in magazines, on billboards. Newspapers can't always do it well. A newspaper should not use color unless it can be done well and with reason."

One thing Murphy did was approve the change of the headline face of *The Republic* from Helvetica, a sans serif face, to Times Roman, a serif face. He said headlines send signals about a newspaper and can add to its character and integrity. "I picked Times Roman because it has taste, dignity, classiness and a sophistication about it that imparts the message that *The Republic* is trying to get across," Murphy added. "I think that newspapers that get away from sans serif and go to serif will achieve more if they are trying to send a message of classiness. Look at graphics in television, billboards and automobile designs. Classic lines are returning because they are solid, reassuring and comfortable."

redesign. That way, when a reader calls to ask or complain about the new look, the circulation employee won't say, "Gee, I don't know."

Newspapers are full of people who want lots of change, but often they do not want to change themselves. A redesign means a change in *their* newspaper. It is impossible to please everyone on the staff when the paper is redesigned, but the changes will be more readily accepted if staff members understand what is going on. Review sessions with the staff are important.

In addition, a timetable should be set that provides a starting and finishing

point for the redesign. The dates should be used for planning purposes only, because often it is difficult to meet those "magic" dates. And the process should be given plenty of time, because it's never any fun getting boxed into finishing a project under a tight deadline.

Finally, a *prototype* of a page, section or entire paper tells much about the redesign and whether it is practical. Some papers print their prototypes; others have type and visuals pasted up and then make photocopies of the page. A prototype allows a newspaper to experiment and test. It allows visual journalists to try new ideas and new

designs. The prototype can be shown to staff members and readers for their suggestions and to test a new typeface for readability. Readers should be encouraged to write letters to comment on the changes as they are made. Some newspapers also hire someone to organize focus groups in which readers are shown prototypes of a redesigned page and asked to comment on it. Usually, these groups include 10 to 15 people who study and discuss the changes while the newspaper's executives watch them through a one-way mirror.

Figure 3.14   *The Sun News* front page before its redesign

Figure 3.15   *The Sun News* front page after its redesign

SOME SAMPLE REDESIGNS

The Sun News in Myrtle Beach, S.C., the *Colorado Springs Gazette Telegraph* in Colorado Springs, Colo., and the *Daily Herald* in Arlington Heights, Ill., wanted to be more lively and reader friendly. To do that, these three medium-sized newspapers went through the redesign process, as outlined here.

The Sun News

This Myrtle Beach, S.C., morning newspaper has a circulation of 37,000. Designer Rob Covey was hired as a consultant in the newspaper's 10-month redesign project, which was introduced to readers in March 1988. According

to graphics editor Bryan Monroe, "The paper was unorganized" before the redesign. "There was good material, but it wasn't presented in the right manner. The new editor, Gil Thelen, recognized the need to change the visuals of the paper." Monroe said the goal was to make the paper "lively, reader friendly, entertaining, colorful and informative."

Thirty-five percent of *The Sun News'* circulation is through street sales, and it faces competition from nine other newspapers that are sold alongside it each day from sidewalk racks. That means the paper must grab readers with color above the fold, overlines referring readers to inside pages and a high headline count.

"The key [to the redesign] was the repackaging," Monroe said. "We created a local section and a cleaner, more modular look. With the new local section, readers perceive more local news. Our new presses allow for more and better color use.

"There is now a concept behind the design of the paper. There are now reasons why we do things" (Figures 3.14 and 3.15).

Colorado Springs Gazette Telegraph

This Colorado Springs, Colo., morning newspaper, with a circulation of 107,000, hired designer Robert Lockwood as a consultant in its redesign. The 13-month

Figure 3.16   The *Gazette Telegraph* front page before its redesign

Figure 3.17   The *Gazette Telegraph* front page after its redesign

project was introduced to readers in July 1987.

John Hutchinson, deputy managing editor, said: "We wanted to make it a reader-friendly newspaper, exciting and well organized. We wanted to build *windows of information* [a design device to give pieces of information quickly]. We wanted our covers to reflect our inside coverage, so we went with more summary or capsule information. We wanted people to know there was a lot inside.

"We wanted consistency, but not to formulate our pages. We wanted to be consistently flexible. We wanted a design that would adapt to the news of the day. We also wanted the look of the paper to reflect our immediate area,

something that reflected our community, such as the photo of Pike's Peak [or other local areas] in the masthead and the wider column measures to reflect our wide-open area of the country." Ragged right type was introduced throughout the newspaper to add to this "open" feeling.

Hutchinson said the redesign made the paper more organized. "Readers can easily find the information they desire, whether it is hard news or sports news or soft news," he said. "We've got a livelier product than before and a much easier-to-read newspaper" (Figures 3.16 and 3.17).

Daily Herald

This Arlington Heights, Ill., morning paper has a circulation of more than 90,000. It hired designer Rolfe Rehe as a consultant in its six-month redesign project, which was introduced to readers in January 1987.

"The last time we redesigned the paper it was only a touch-up," said graphics editor Robert Finch. "We were pretty much out of date. The paper was switching from letterpress to offset. We were going to use a lot more color and we wanted to make the paper more interesting looking. We wanted to reorganize the paper's content so the reader could go through the paper easier."

Finch said a highlight of the redesign

Figure 3.18 *The Daily Herald* front page before its redesign

Figure 3.19 *The Daily Herald* front page after its redesign

was the new nameplate and headline type. "We spent more than three weeks looking at type fonts. Italic headlines are gone. In the old paper we had six headline faces. Now we have just two. We use one headline face for news stories and a lighter version for columns and drop headlines.

"We have everything labeled—everything from brief boxes to obits—with reversed bars out of gray. The organization of the paper is better. We don't use any odd measure of type in the news pages. Only in a graphic or a feature front can type wider than one column be used. Every section, every page, except the feature fronts, is formatted the same way. We use more packages. And any type in a box is

set ragged right" (Figures 3.18 and 3.19).

THE VARIED LOOK OF NEWSPAPERS

This growing emphasis on newspaper design has some industry critics complaining that all newspapers are starting to look alike. They charge that when one newspaper goes through a successful redesign, other papers copy it in the hopes of also copying the success. This monkey-see, monkey-do mentality is homogenizing the look of the industry.

Phil Nesbitt, a design consultant who has worked on the *Sun-Times* in Chicago and on the *Record* in Bergen County, N.J., disagrees with them. In

an article in The Bulletin of the American Society of Newspaper Editors, Nesbitt comments on the design possibilities computers offer as a dawning of a new age of individuality for newspapers:

All newspapers use type . . . almost all newspapers use a photograph or two, or graphics and infographics. Most use logos and signatures, many use color. . . . Yes, from this point of view, American newspapers bear a family resemblance. We are limited in the tools and devices we have in our magic boxes to attract and, more importantly, communicate with the reader.

We can make the same analogy that all cars look the same—they have hoods, trunks, fenders, wheels, tires, etc.—or

Figure 3.20 The *Anchorage Daily News*

Figure 3.21 The *Richmond Times-Dispatch*

Figure 3.22 *The Providence Journal*

Figure 3.23 The *Fort Worth Star-Telegram*

Figure 3.24 *The Cincinnati Enquirer*

Figure 3.25 *The Sun*

that all houses look the same—they have doors, windows, rooms, roofs, etc. But few people mistake a Rolls-Royce for a Chevy Nova, and when was the last time you mistook your neighbor's house for yours?

The *Anchorage Daily News* (Figure 3.20) is unique. So are the *Richmond* (Va.) *Times-Dispatch* (Figure 3.21), *The Providence Journal* (Figure 3.22), the *Fort Worth Star-Telegram* (Figure 3.23), *The Cincinnati Enquirer* (Figure 3.24)

and *The Sun* in Baltimore (Figure 3.25). All of these newspapers report the news, some better than others. They all have sports pages, comics, editorials and obituaries. But each is an individual because of its design.

INSIDE LOOK

Edmund C. Arnold
Design Consultant

Edmund C. Arnold, author, professor emeritus and a design consultant well known around the world, has been involved in the design of scores of newspapers, but he's still bothered about the way newspapers look.

"In the last 10 years newspaper design has swung around in a circle," he said. "In the 1950s and '60s the big thrust was simplification, making it easy for the reader to get information real fast without distractions. Now we're coming back to things that were bad, and they are still bad. We're coming back to column rules and overlines (headlines over photographs), rules over pictures. Those overlines are so bad. The eye goes immediately to a photo on a page. The eye either refuses to read the overline or is irritated by it in the process of going to the overline first and then back to the picture.

"One of the things we have to remember is that the reader has a fixed amount of time to devote to reading a newspaper. When the time is used up, bang, that's the end of reading the newspaper. If the eye is spent on wild-goose chases, it's a waste of time."

There are more things that trouble Arnold. He said: "One of the things that bugs me now is the huge amount of type set ragged right. That's another irritation to the eye. When we have to do a job over and over again, the only way we can do it is rhythmically. Justified type makes that process easier. The eye does not have to adjust to a different sweep on each line. Now we have people who think ragged right type is the greatest invention since the zipper."

Although Arnold has retired from the classroom, he continues to travel and consult. "Retirement is only a figure of speech," the outspoken and sometimes controversial designer said.

For more than 30 years, newspapers throughout the world have sought his advice. "I was involved in redesigning *The Christian Science Monitor* when it went to a five-column broadsheet in about 1963. In about the same year I designed the two Louisville papers. They were the first regular metropolitans to use a six-column format. Before that there were a couple of papers that used six columns on the front page, but they used eight columns inside. Louisville was the first to use six columns throughout."

Arnold noted the 1960s and 1970s were a "heyday for consultants." He added: "In those days you didn't have anything like a graphics editor. I worked in Toronto, Boston, Kansas City, St. Louis and Chicago. Little by little, however, the metropolitans brought in their own people, and they didn't need me as much."

Still, Arnold keeps plenty busy. "I just had an interesting assignment in San Juan, Puerto Rico," he said. He also has written more than two dozen books, including "Functional Newspaper Design," "Profitable Newspaper Advertising," "The Student Journalist," "Ink on Paper," "Modern Newspaper Design" and "Designing the Total Newspaper."

In his books Arnold wrote that the first step in designing a front page was to put a strong *attention compeller,* an attention-grabbing element, in the *primary optical area,* the upper left corner where people naturally begin reading the page. He stated that the attention compeller may be a picture, a strong or interesting headline or a box. He warned against putting a one-column headline in the primary optical area because the eye would jump across it.

Arnold said the path of the reading eye is from top left to lower right. He labeled the lower right corner the *terminal area,* the last area readers normally look at before moving to another page. The upper right corner and the lower left corner were called *fallow corners,* areas outside of the normal reading diagonal from upper left to lower right. Arnold said strong *optical magnets* were needed in the fallow corners to draw readers to them.

"That will be the way people read newspapers until God redesigns our optical system and we abandon the Latin alphabet," Arnold said. "We will always read from left to right and top to bottom. The top of the page is the most important. The left side of the page is where you start.

"It bothers me that people sometimes ask me when my research was done on reading habits. We don't need to have a research project every five years to know you can't feed kids sawdust and call it cereal. We can't feed our readers sawdust. The way the eye works with the Latin alphabet isn't going to change. We don't need research to make reading from left to right, top to bottom, valid. It's a given."

Arnold said his philosophy of design is basic: Every element on a page should convey information as pleasantly and conveniently as possible. He added: "To convey information we have to get people to read. When we use bait, such as headlines or pictures, they have to be functional. They have to fit together. I am disturbed by papers that mix typefaces for headlines. I am disturbed by *USA Today,* for instance, which mixes serifs and sans serif headlines."

Arnold also criticized newspapers that mix headline weights on a page. "They will use the same face, but mix the weights. They will use bold Univers as their basic headline. Then they will drop in one-line decks in Univers Light. The light heads fade into the woodwork when they get on the page.

"My formula has been to use the same weight of headlines on a page. That maintains graphic consistency. You get variety by using roman and italic type and different headline forms. You can get variety by varying the number of lines and using kickers, hammers, wickets and tripods." [A *wicket* is a headline with two short lines of small type on the left of a single, larger line. A *tripod* is a headline with a single line of large type on the left of two lines of smaller type. Kickers and hammers are discussed in Chapter 4.]

Arnold hopes that in the 1990s the newspaper design pendulum will swing back from color-splashed jazzy pages to more traditional pages. "Newspapers have become too superficial. They're either going to turn into *USA Today* or People magazine, or they're going to shape up and become newspapers again. Readers don't want daily magazines. They don't want dessert. They want the meat and potatoes. They want a newspaper, not a television news story, where if there is no live footage, we'll wait until tomorrow to report the start of World War III. Some newspapers won't do anything unless they have graphics first. If they don't have graphics, they play down the story. That will be suicidal."

Arnold said newspaper managers are interested in two things: new equipment and design. "We're engrossed with the mechanical concept. We're enthralled with new typesetting machines, scanners and other new equipment. Design also is a new plaything, which we will play with for a while. But design will get relegated to a lower position. Things will get jazzier and jazzier for a while until someone realizes they aren't working."

He added that the basic function of a newspaper still is to convey news. "We've got to have all this sugar coating now to make the newspaper more desirable to readers, but our basic function is to be a newspaper. For example, we run color because it is color. Some of it is excellent; a lot of it is bad. I've seen color that is so far off register that it looks like a surrealistic poster."

USA Today's color is nearly perfect, Arnold said, because its management has demanded it. "Equipment is not the deciding factor," he added. "Many presses turn out crap because the people running them don't give a hoot. It depends on how nit-picking the boss is. Generally, I see better color in small newspapers than in metropolitans."

He recommended that when color is used on a front page, it should not be used in more than three areas. "That includes process color and spot color of any type. They can be three huge areas, but the reader's eyes get jerked around if you use any more color.

"*USA Today* wastes color. The color graphics in the lower left corner of each front page are a huge waste of color and space. They are often interesting, but more often than not the statistics in them can be used in a few sentences.

And *USA Today* uses them in a three-inch box."

Despite his criticisms of *USA Today*, Arnold said the paper is fine for the casual reader. He explained: "I read it frequently when I'm traveling. I like it because there are at least two items in it each day about the three states I'm interested in, Michigan, Virginia and New York. I can pick up the *Chicago Tribune* every day, and in two weeks Virginia won't be in there once.

"Another big contribution *USA Today* has made is its fact boxes, which present tiny nuggets of information real fast. Still, I think the people who designed *USA Today* designed a camel when they were supposed to design a horse. I think that, typographically, it is an abortion, not in terms of esthetics but from the point of view of not serving the reader well.

"The only way to fix *USA Today's* design is to start all over again."

SUGGESTED EXERCISES

1. Look at the design of your local daily and try to determine the newspaper's mission. Is the paper flashy or conservative? Does it emphasize visuals? Does it emphasize local or international news? How much color is used? Are the headlines serif or sans serif?

2. Compare your local daily to *USA Today* and *The New York Times*. How is its design similar to and different from those two newspapers?

3. Critique Page One of your local daily. How do you feel about its design? If you could redesign it, what would you do?

4. Do the same for an inside section front page as you did in exercise 3.

5. Examine the typography of your local daily. Is it consistent in all sections?

CHAPTER FOUR

Making Design Work

Although all newspapers try to be unique in their design, visual journalists must follow some basic guidelines. The guidelines are not ironclad rules; they often are changed and stretched, but they help visual journalists prepare readable pages.

A newspaper's design framework is articulated in its **layout,** an editing process in which headlines, stories, photographs and graphics are placed on a page. Each day, visual journalists try to construct pages that:

✔ *Follow the design goals of the paper.* There is room for creativity in page layout, but it is important that visual journalists live within their paper's design framework. Those who make radical design changes without authorization probably won't keep their jobs for long.

✔ *Follow the basic rules of layout.* Readers are comfortable and likely to spend time with easy-to-read pages; they are uncomfortable with jumbled, confusing pages.

✔ *Make the paper unique.* All newspapers look the same in some ways. All like to be unique in some ways. It is good to surprise the reader— pleasantly—every day.

In Chapter 3 we discussed the role of design in daily newspapers and how newspapers set their design framework. In this chapter we will discuss the basic rules of layout and how they are used to make a newspaper page consistent yet unique. Our goal is to show how visual journalists can make their pages road maps, moving readers from point A to point B without detours or road-blocks.

THE LANGUAGE OF LAYOUT

Page One is the main news page, the lead page, the window to the rest of the newspaper. Behind Page One, and the section it introduces, are other sections—local news, features, sports, business, entertainment. Every section begins with a main page, or **section front,** which contains the top stories of that section and guides readers to its *inside pages.* Although each of the sections may look distinct from the others, each has to fit into the overall design framework of the newspaper.

At a growing number of newspapers, pages are laid out electronically on a computer screen. Recall that this process is called *pagination,* which allows a page designer or another editor to view and produce an entire page as a

single unit. At other newspapers, the
pages are laid out on a piece of paper
known as a **dummy,** a miniversion of
the page that acts as a layout guide or
instruction sheet for a composing room
worker (Figure 4.1).

With a dummy, the visual journalist
has to conceptualize how the page will
look when it is produced and then draw
a detailed and precise plan of that page.
The production of a dummied page takes
place in a *composing room,* where a
composing room employee pastes up
sheets of type and visuals on a full-size
board according to the layout drawn on
the dummy.

THE PAGE AS A UNIT

Visualize a newspaper page as a single
unit of space about 13 inches wide by
21 inches deep (for full-sized newspapers), flowing from top to bottom. It
has a top half, a bottom half, four corners
and a middle, all of which have to fit
together in a neat, simple, clean package
of type and visuals. Sometimes the page
is open, which means it contains no
advertisements; sometimes it contains
advertisements.

Unity is an important concept in
layout because it brings harmony to a
newspaper page. Each story and visual
on the page is a subunit in itself, but
the stories and visuals should fit into
the design of the entire page. Such
unity should draw readers to the page
and keep them there longer than would
a helter-skelter layout where holes
simply are filled with anything that fits.

THE TOP HALF AND ITS CORNERS

The top half of a newspaper front page
is called *above the fold.* Newspapers

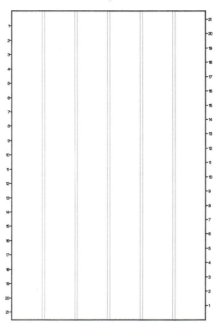

Figure 4.1   Six-column page dummy form;
numbers indicate depth in inches

Figure 4.2   Front page with top story in
upper right corner and top visual in upper left
corner

traditionally are folded in half when the
reader first sees them. If they are
hawked on a street corner, sold from a
vending machine or delivered to a
doorstep, they are folded to reveal the
paper's top, where the best stories and
photographs are placed. The above-
the-fold area of every other page in the
newspaper also is important because
readers tend to look at pages from top
to bottom.

One element that *has* to be above
the fold of a front page each day is the
nameplate, the name of the newspaper
or section, which usually runs across
the top of the page. The top story and
visual, having the greatest importance,
also should be above the fold. On a
front page, the top story traditionally
has been put in the upper right corner
and the top visual in the left (Figure
4.2). However, there is no rule against
putting the top visual in the right corner
and the top story in the left (Figure
4.3) or even putting the top visual in
the center (Figure 4.4). The visual
journalist needs to follow the design
style of the newspaper.

Other constant items that may be
used on a page each day are an *index* to
material on other pages, a weather
forecast or a *standing feature* such as a
syndicated column. Once the constant
items are placed on the page, the
remaining space can be filled. The layout
should not look the same every day,
nor should it be so different that the
newspaper lacks consistency.

Inside Pages

The same guidelines can be applied to
inside pages. The largest **headline**
(type that indicates story or informational
graphic subject matter) on the page
should be over the top story. It might
be a **banner headline,** which stretches
across the page (Figure 4.5), or it might
cover less space. Banner heads usually
fill one line, but sometimes they fill
two; other headlines might even run to
three lines. Headlines generally are
set in roman type and in regular weight,
although they can be set italic, bold or
extra bold depending on the newspaper's
design style.

Figure 4.3 Front page with top visual in upper right corner and top story in upper left corner

Figure 4.5 Banner headline on inside page

Figure 4.4 Front page with top visual in center

Advertisements, which are laid out on the page from the bottom up, will spill over to the top half of some inside pages. Each inside page has a *folio line,* a line of type at the top that provides the page number and date. The name of the newspaper and volume and number also may be in the folio line.

Progression of Headline Sizes

Readers expect to look at the top of the page and find the top stories, including the largest headlines. Traditionally, there is a progression of headline sizes on a newspaper page, starting at the top. That does not mean that a 72-point **head** (short for headline) should be on the top, over a 60-point head, which is over a 48-point head and so on down to an 18-point head. It does mean that headlines grade the news for readers. If the mayor dies in a car accident, the story should carry a 96-point or larger head and be placed on Page One. If the mayor speaks at a high school graduation, the story may

deserve a 30-point headline on an inside page.

The largest, heaviest head should be on the most important story, normally at the top or near the top of the page. The second most important story should be topped with the second largest and second heaviest head and so on. Two stories of equal importance may be placed in different spots on the page and carry the same size headlines.

Special Headlines

Special headlines, including decks, hammers and kickers, also can be used above the fold or elsewhere on the page. A **deck** is a supplemental headline that runs under a main headline (Figure 4.6). The days of a main head followed by two or three decks are gone because editors do not consider decks modern and recognize that such headline treatment delays readers from reading the story. Some editors also argue that decks occupy space that is better filled with body type and that it takes too much copy desk time to write additional

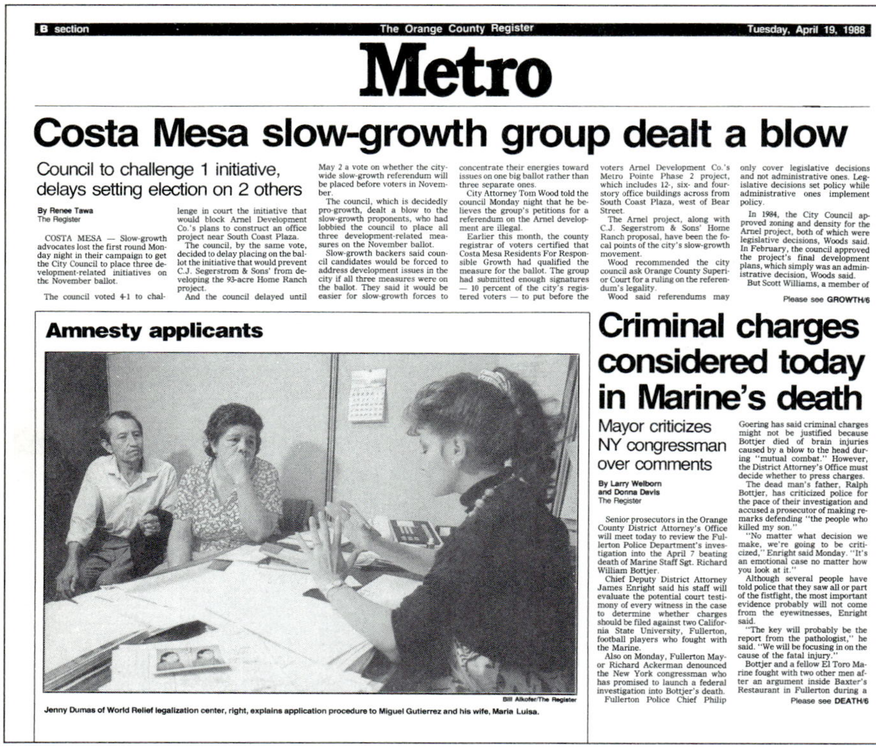

B section — The Orange County Register — Tuesday, April 19, 1988

Metro

Costa Mesa slow-growth group dealt a blow

Council to challenge 1 initiative, delays setting election on 2 others

By Renee Tawa
The Register

COSTA MESA — Slow-growth advocates lost the first round Monday night in their campaign to get the City Council to place three development-related initiatives on the November ballot.

The council voted 4-1 to challenge in court the initiative that would block Arnel Development Co.'s plans to construct an office project near South Coast Plaza.

The council, by the same vote, decided to delay placing on the ballot the initiative that would prevent C.J. Segerstrom & Sons' from developing the 93-acre Home Ranch project.

And the council delayed until May 2 a vote on whether the citywide slow-growth referendum will be placed before voters in November.

The council, which is decidedly pro-growth, dealt a blow to the slow-growth proponents, who had lobbied the council to place all three development-related measures on the November ballot.

Slow-growth backers said council candidates would be forced to address development issues in the city if all three measures were on the ballot. They said it would be easier for slow-growth forces to concentrate their energies toward issues on one big ballot rather than three separate ones.

City Attorney Tom Wood told the council Monday night that he believes the group's petitions for a referendum on the Arnel development are illegal.

Earlier this month, the county registrar of voters certified that Costa Mesa Residents For Responsible Growth had qualified the measure for the ballot. The group had submitted enough signatures — 10 percent of the city's registered voters — to put before the voters Arnel Development Co.'s Metro Pointe Phase 2 project, which includes 12-, six- and four-story office buildings across from South Coast Plaza, west of Bear Street.

The Arnel project, along with C.J. Segerstrom & Sons' Home Ranch proposal, have been the focal points of the city's slow-growth movement.

Wood recommended the city council ask Orange County Superior Court for a ruling on the referendum's legality.

Wood said referendums may only cover legislative decisions and not administrative ones. Legislative decisions set policy while administrative ones implement policy.

In 1984, the City Council approved zoning and density for the Arnel project, both of which were legislative decisions, Woods said. In February, the council approved the project's final development plans, which simply was an administrative decision, Woods said.

But Scott Williams, a member of

Please see GROWTH/6

Amnesty applicants

Bill Alkofer/The Register

Jenny Dumas of World Relief legalization center, right, explains application procedure to Miguel Gutierrez and his wife, Maria Luisa.

Criminal charges considered today in Marine's death

Mayor criticizes NY congressman over comments

By Larry Welborn and Donna Davis
The Register

Senior prosecutors in the Orange County District Attorney's Office will meet today to review the Fullerton Police Department's investigation into the April 7 beating death of Marine Staff Sgt. Richard William Bottjer.

Chief Deputy District Attorney James Enright said his staff will evaluate the potential court testimony of every witness in the case to determine whether charges should be filed against two California State University, Fullerton, football players who fought with the Marine.

Also on Monday, Fullerton Mayor Richard Ackerman denounced the New York congressman who has promised to launch a federal investigation into Bottjer's death.

Fullerton Police Chief Philip Goering has said criminal charges might not be justified because Bottjer died of brain injuries caused by a blow to the head during "mutual combat." However, the District Attorney's Office must decide whether to press charges.

The dead man's father, Ralph Bottjer, has criticized police for the pace of their investigation and accused a prosecutor of making remarks defending "the people who killed my son."

"No matter what decision we make, we're going to be criticized," Enright said Monday. "It's an emotional case no matter how you look at it."

Although several people have told police that they saw all or part of the fistfight, the most important evidence probably will not come from the eyewitnesses, Enright said.

"The key will probably be the report from the pathologist," he said. "We will be focusing in on the cause of the fatal injury."

Bottjer and a fellow El Toro Marine fought with two other men after an argument inside Baxter's Restaurant in Fullerton during a

Please see DEATH/6

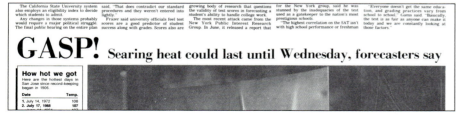

Figure 4.6 Section front page with decks running below main headlines

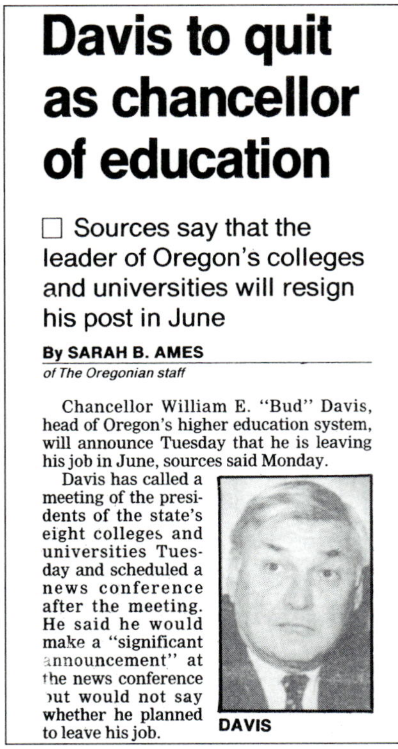

Davis to quit as chancellor of education

☐ Sources say that the leader of Oregon's colleges and universities will resign his post in June

By SARAH B. AMES
of The Oregonian staff

Chancellor William E. "Bud" Davis, head of Oregon's higher education system, will announce Tuesday that he is leaving his job in June, sources said Monday.

Davis has called a meeting of the presidents of the state's eight colleges and universities Tuesday and scheduled a news conference after the meeting. He said he would make a "significant announcement" at the news conference but would not say whether he planned to leave his job.

DAVIS

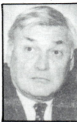

Figure 4.7 Decks used to "summarize" story

The California State University system also employs an eligibility index to decide which students to admit.

Any changes in those systems probably would require a major political struggle. The final public hearing on the entire plan said, "That does contradict our standard procedures and they weren't entered into lightly."

Frazer said university officials feel test scores are a good predictor of student success along with grades. Scores also are growing body of research that questions the validity of test scores in forecasting a student's ability to handle college work.

The most recent attack came from the New York Public Interest Research Group. In June, it released a report that for the New York group, said he was stunned by the inadequacies of the test used as a gatekeeper to the nation's most prestigious schools.

"The highest correlation on the SAT isn't with high school performance or freshman

"Everyone doesn't get the same education, and grading practices vary from school to school," Gams said. "Basically, the test is as fair as anyone can make it today and we are constantly looking at those factors."

GASP! Searing heat could last until Wednesday, forecasters say

How hot we got
Here are the hottest days in San Jose since record-keeping began in 1906.

Date	Temp.
1. July 14, 1972	108
2. July 17, 1988	107

Figure 4.8 Hammer headline, set larger than main headline and used for emphasis

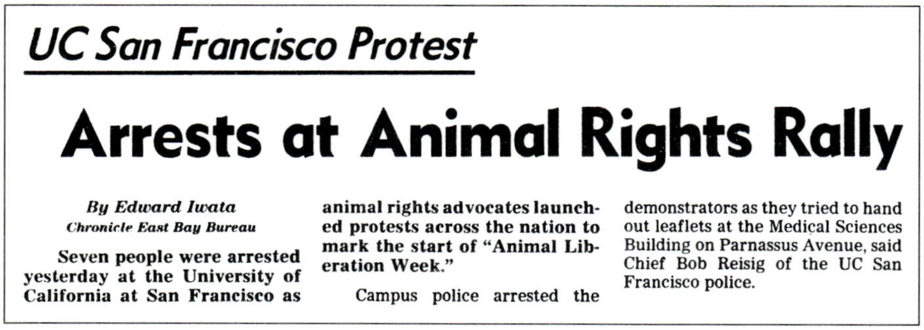

UC San Francisco Protest

Arrests at Animal Rights Rally

By Edward Iwata
Chronicle East Bay Bureau

Seven people were arrested yesterday at the University of California at San Francisco as animal rights advocates launched protests across the nation to mark the start of "Animal Liberation Week."

Campus police arrested the demonstrators as they tried to hand out leaflets at the Medical Sciences Building on Parnassus Avenue, said Chief Bob Reisig of the UC San Francisco police.

Figure 4.9 Kicker, set above main headline

headlines. There are exceptions to the no-deck rule, however. Some newspapers, notably *The New York Times* and *The Wall Street Journal,* have always used decks as part of their layout style. Other newspapers are using decks to provide additional information or a quicker "read" of a story. An unusual deck style is found in the recently redesigned *Oregonian* of Portland, Ore., which uses decks to provide a "summary" of a story. The decks are written not in a headline style, but more in a story style (Figure 4.7).

A **hammer** is a one- or two-word reference to a story that runs above or next to a main head and is set in larger and often heavier type (Figure 4.8). Hammers are strong descriptions of the story, such as "Victory," "Riot" or "Home Again."

A **kicker** is a two- or three-word summary of the story that also runs above the main head, but it usually is set half the size of the main head (Figure 4.9). Kickers, once very popular, seldom are used in newspapers nowadays. As with decks, some designers don't

Figure 4.10 Dominant visual, a news photo, placed above the fold on Page One

Figure 4.11 Dominant visual, a feature photo, placed above the fold on Page One

Figure 4.12 Front page with more than one visual

consider them modern, and editors are reluctant to have the copy desk spend time writing additional headlines that sometimes confuse readers.

THE DOMINANT VISUAL ELEMENT

Photographs, informational graphics and illustrations on a newspaper page are easily recognizable, and readers enjoy looking at them. Anytime a strong visual is used in a corner above the fold, it becomes the dominant element on the page. Readers naturally scan the top half of the page first; they will go to the visual first because it is human nature to look at visual elements before reading type. The visual becomes a *magnet,* pulling in readers. Visual journalists are well aware of the importance of the dominant visual, and they try to place the best one above the fold on Page One each day. Usually, the best visual is a news photograph, used large enough to dominate the page (Figure 4.10). Feature photographs or other visuals also can be used effectively as dominant elements (Figure 4.11).

Every page should contain a dominant visual element set above the fold and large enough so that readers can recognize its images. Once readers have looked at the dominant visual, their eyes tend to continue downward to other stories and other visuals on the page. Some researchers believe that readers' eyes follow an invisible S pattern on the page, with the top of the S being the upper right corner of the page. Other researchers suggest the eye follows a Z movement from the upper left to the upper right and then down to the lower corners. With this movement, the reader generally is following a banner headline across the top of the page before moving lower. If the dominant visual is put low on the page, it will draw readers, but they probably will not return to other elements above the fold.

More than one visual element should be used on a page, but only one should be dominant. If the dominant visual element is horizontal, a vertical visual should be used elsewhere on the page for balance and contrast. Visuals are

Figure 4.13 Inside page with more than one visual

like type; they should be used in various sizes and shapes (Figures 4.12 and 4.13).

Figure 4.14   Effective use of visual below the fold

A large headline or a special treatment of type also can be an effective magnet. **Spot color,** the use of one color on headlines or rules, or a **screen,** a gray tint used as a background, can also serve as magnets.

Color

A color photograph is a very strong magnet, although black-and-white photos and graphics also draw readers to a page. Many newspapers use a color photo on Page One each day. Surveys by the Poynter Institute for Media Studies in St. Petersburg, Fla., have shown that even a weak color photograph is a stronger magnet than a black-and-white photo and that color attracts readers. However, color does not appear to sell newspapers, because most single-copy buyers already have made the decision to purchase a paper before arriving at the news rack. Once there, color will aid the reader in the choice of *which* newspaper to purchase: Buyers choose color over a similar black-and-white product. It is hoped, however,

that visual journalists use color on the page because of its content and quality rather than its drawing power.

The Bottom Half

The layout of the bottom half of a newspaper page is critical. Readers naturally go to the top; they must be drawn to the bottom half. Visuals, headlines and other magnets must be placed in key spots to bring readers below the fold (Figure 4.14).

On inside pages, the area below the fold may be filled with advertisements, which means a visual journalist will have a more difficult job of layout. On those pages, the bottom corners might already be filled with advertisements, so the visual journalist must pay careful attention to the balance on the page and select strong elements for the top.

BALANCING A PAGE

Traditionally, visual journalists and designers have talked about the need to balance a page, but rarely is a newspaper page so formally balanced that everything on the left side is repeated on the right side. Instead, a page should contain an informal balance so that readers are attracted to the *entire* page and not pulled away from top or bottom by an unbalanced design.

Layouts

Scores of terms have been used through the years to define the patterns of layout on a page, though many of the terms and the styles they describe are now old-fashioned or out of date. In *balanced layout,* as the term suggests, elements on a page are carefully balanced, one

against another. In *brace layout,* one main story dominates and contains the strongest headline on the page, with other elements focusing attention on this element. In *quadrant layout,* the page is divided into quarters, with each quadrant containing a dominant element but none of the quadrants dominating the page. In *circus layout,* anything goes: different typefaces and fonts, bold, screaming headlines, big boxes, lots of color. In *modular layout,* a modern and popular style, rectangular rather than doglegged or ragged shapes are used. The drawback to both traditional and pure modular layout is that the page tends to have too many elements of the same shape and seems dull or boring.

Until the 1950s, stories usually were laid out in irregular shapes such as inverted L's, or doglegged type. Most newspapers' front pages also were laid out vertically, with long columns of type running from the top to the bottom of a page. One- and two-column headlines filled the page. Some newspapers, such as *The New York Times* and *The Wall Street Journal,* still use *vertical layout* on Page One to retain their traditional look. The *Times* and *Journal* do use easier-to-read modular and horizontal layouts on front pages of their major inside sections, however. Today's well-designed newspapers use a variation of modular layout, but with more vertical elements used on the page for variety.

Whatever style is used, layout should bring some order and balance to the page. The reader should not be confused. The page should flow from top to bottom so the reader can move easily from above the fold into the corners below the fold and into the middle.

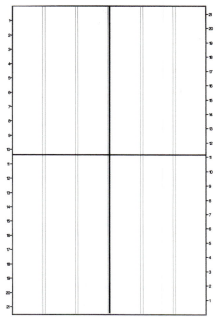

Figure 4.15 Symmetrical layout grid on page dummy form

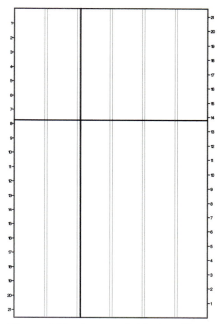

Figure 4.16 Asymmetrical layout grid on page dummy form

"Both symmetrical and asymmetrical layouts can work," said Tony Majeri, creative director of the *Chicago Tribune*. "Both are useful tools; it's just understanding when to use them."

Majeri, who is responsible for the visual presentation of the *Tribune*, explained that in a symmetrical layout, a newspaper page is divided into equal parts. "Take a piece of paper and draw a vertical line down the middle; draw a horizontal line down the middle. Now you have four equal quadrants. It is symmetrical. In symmetrical layout in a newspaper a page is divided the way you divided that paper. It can be divided into two parts, four parts or six parts. Nothing is highlighted. It's balanced and it's easy to access (Figure 4.15).

"It's also monochromatic; it's boring. Nothing dominates anything else. If a picture is used in the upper left quadrant, one is used in the lower right quadrant. The same size headlines are used in each quadrant. Some pages should be laid out like that, but others need to be asymmetrical."

An asymmetrical page is not divided into equal parts. "Take the same piece of paper," Majeri said. "Move the vertical center rule 3 inches to the left and the horizontal center line 3 inches up. Now you have created a different creature. Now there is a focal point where one element is more dominant than the other elements. You can promote hierarchy on the page" (Figure 4.16).

Majeri suggested most front pages should be asymmetrical because that is what readers expect. "Readers want the news prioritized. They want to know what is the most important element on the page, the second most important and so on. There should be some sense

of editing on the page that the reader feels."

Column Widths

Most newspaper front pages are five or six columns wide, with each column 12 to 15 picas wide. Between the columns is a gutter or white space or a column rule that serves to separate columns from each other. If white space is used for the gutter, the space is often 1 pica or slightly less.

Inside pages may contain more columns in narrower widths, and the news hole is determined by the amount of advertising on the page. Base column widths are only a starting point, however. Stories and art can and should be set in different widths to give variety to the page's design (Figure 4.17). Often, a rule will separate editorial matter and advertising.

The optimum reading width of a line of type is about 14 picas. Type set wider than 18 picas tires the reader's eyes because of the longer distance they must travel across the column. Type set narrower than 10 picas also will tire the reader's eyes because they have to keep flicking back and forth.

Figure 4.17 Front page with varying column widths

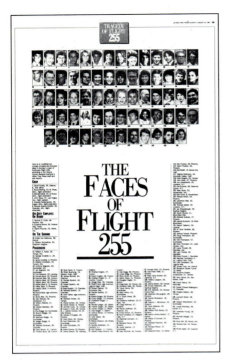

Figure 4.18 Creative use of white space on inside page

Figure 4.19 Section front page with "trapped" white space

Wide-measure type in itself helps to break the grayness of a page. For example, if a story is to be laid out in a four-column rectangular space, the type can be set in three equal legs of type. On a six-column page with 12.10 columns (that means each column is 12 picas, 10 points wide) a four-column space would be 51.4 picas wide. The type for the story would be set 16.4 picas wide, leaving slightly more than 1 pica of white space between the columns. It is best, however, to limit such usages.

White Space

White space (an area on the page where there is no type) can give a newspaper page an airy, uncluttered look. It is pleasing to readers because it gives them a break from gray type. White space should not be something that merely is left over on a page after all of the elements are laid out, however; visual journalists should plan so that the white space helps balance the page.

Typography that makes use of white space becomes a visual element in itself. For example, decks, hammers

and other special headlines can be used to create white space around stories to set them apart from other elements on a page (Figure 4.18). Photographs and other visuals can be used in odd shapes so that white space is created around them. Modular layout also adds white space, as does the elimination of rules between columns of type. In addition, white space separates stories and pictures, and advertisements and editorial matter, horizontally on the page.

White space is used most effectively on the outside edges of a page in unequal concentrations. It generally should be avoided in the center of the page, where it is "trapped," because it tends to push away the elements on the page and distract the readers' eyes from important news elements (Figure 4.19). Here are some tips for avoiding being "trapped" by white space:

✓ *Plan.* Treat white space like any other element on the page. Place it where it can be used most effectively. Sometimes that means placing white space in the corners or outside areas of a page.

✓ *Don't clutter a page with too many small elements.* The page should not look like a decorated Christmas tree with little pockets of white space spread throughout.

✓ *Don't use postage stamp-sized visuals.* Spread photographs, other pieces of art and headlines over two or more columns. Multicolumn visuals draw readers into a page. They also provide opportunities to use white space on their outside edges.

✓ *Vary shapes.* If a horizontal photograph is used above the fold, try to use a vertical one below the fold. Use various headline widths and depths. Set type in squares, horizontal rectangles and vertical rectangles. Think about how white space can be used with the modules in unequal concentrations on the page.

PACKAGING STORIES AND VISUALS

A major news event seldom is covered in a single story. Several stories will be written; photographs will be taken; graphics will be created. A visual journalist should try to lay out as many of these various items as possible on one page or neighboring pages. Such packaging makes newspaper reading more convenient. For instance, if record cold grips the city, the visual journalist might want to package a news story on the local weather, a feature on feeding the homeless who have sought relief from the cold at a local shelter and a wire story on the arctic blast in other cities. There also might be a photograph of a frustrated tow truck driver looking at a string of stranded cars, a facts box on staying warm and avoiding the dangers

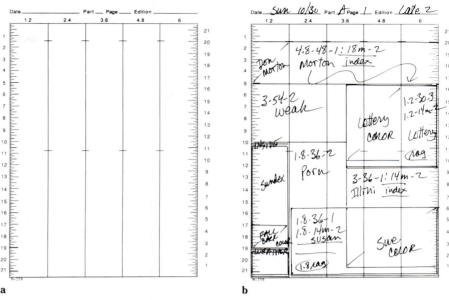

Figure 4.20 *The Milwaukee Journal* (a) blank and (b) marked-up front page dummy

a   b

of cold weather and an informational graphic on the cold temperatures compared with other cities or on how a low pressure area is creating the abnormal weather. The visual journalist must think not only about designing or laying out a page but also about gathering all the appropriate elements needed to present the most informative and pleasing package to the readers.

How Many of Each?

There is no ironclad rule on how many stories and visual elements should be on a newspaper page. An open page might contain three photographs, a graphic and five stories. Another might have four stories and two photographs. An entertainment section front page might contain a single photograph and two stories, while a sports page might have a photograph, a graphic and three stories. An inside page might contain a single visual or story.

A general guideline is to use at least two multicolumn pieces of art on an open page, one above the fold and one below, and four stories, but that is only a guideline. Variety is important. There is no need to give readers the same thing each day. Experiment. Let the news of the day dictate.

How to Do It?

How does a visual journalist actually put together a newspaper page?

Every visual journalist does it slightly differently. Even at the same paper, no two editors will work the same way in selecting and laying out elements for a page. However, there are some universal "hints" for doing a page layout. Remember, many of these steps happen simultaneously.

Layout begins with a close look at the space available on the page; usually, a page dummy (a miniversion of the page) will show if there are ads on the page and where such ads will run. The editor briefly visualizes the actual size of the page and amount of space available. The accompanying figures illustrate how the visual journalist plans the layout of a page (Figure 4.20) and show the final result of that process (Figure 4.21).

Because the amount of space available is fixed, depending on whether it is an open page or a page with advertising, the editor counts the number of stories planned for the page. How many inches are there for words? Which stories will lead the page?

The visual elements are placed on the page first. The photos are cropped and sized for optimum effectiveness. Many pictures can be used slightly smaller or slightly larger; these "flex" pieces can help make the page work more easily. If informational graphics are planned for the page, the visual journalist must keep in mind that graphics have far less "flex" than photographs have. Next, the number of inches the visuals will need is totaled. For example, a two-column by 5-inch photograph will take 10 inches; a three-column by $6\frac{1}{2}$-inch graphic will take $19\frac{1}{2}$ inches.

Figure 4.21 Actual *Milwaukee Journal* front page

Figure 4.22 *Chicago Sun-Times* front page

Figure 4.23 Tabloid section of the broadsheet *Orange County Register*

Having established the space requirements for all the stories, photographs and graphics, the visual journalist now measures the amount of space on the page: How many inches are available on the page? Even an open page has a fixed amount of space, usually 126 inches. Next, the editor subtracts any "furniture" needed for the page, such as nameplate or page header or column logo. These elements are fixed and can't be dropped. How much space is left?

The remaining space is divided: a portion for words and a portion for visuals. Although there is no set formula, some visual journalists try to maintain a ratio of 40 percent to 60 percent. This might mean on some pages, about half the space would be used for photographs and graphics. If that sounds like a great deal, consider that a four-column by 5-inch photograph uses 16 percent of the page; so does a 20-inch story.

By knowing what stories and visuals are most important and which can be trimmed or dropped or moved to another page, the editor begins placing elements on the page. Some visual journalists like to start at the top and work down; others first place the most important photograph (the one they don't want to crop or trim) and then work around that element with the most important

story; others will do the reverse—first the most important story and then the visuals.

One other element can't be forgotten—headlines. Headlines can take anywhere from 10 to 15 percent of a page's space. Not only does the head have its own space needs (a 72-point headline takes 1 inch per column) but there also must be space above and below the headline, usually $\frac{1}{8}$ to $\frac{1}{4}$ inch. And then there are little elements like captions for photographs, which can take another inch of space. Although that might not seem like much, a four-column caption that is 1 inch deep will total 4 inches of space, plus a little more for the space above and below the type.

This complex judgment process is repeated hundreds of times a week, and the visual journalist soon learns to do some of these steps automatically and to be able to size photographs, roughly, in his or her head. Sometimes, it is difficult to get the visual journalist even to explain the process because it has become so "second nature." With practice and experience, it usually does.

TABLOIDS

Although only a handful of daily newspapers are printed in the **tabloid** size, many weekly and college newspapers

Figure 4.24   *Newsday* front page

Figure 4.25   *New York Daily News* front page

are. A tabloid page is approximately one-half the depth of a standard or **broadsheet** newspaper page, which typically measures 13 inches wide by $21\frac{1}{2}$ inches deep. Most tabloids measure 11 inches wide by 13 inches deep, the smaller size making the tabloid easier to hold, much like a magazine. The *Chicago Sun-Times* is an example of a newspaper in a tabloid format (Figure 4.22). Many broadsheet newspapers do, however, also print tabloid sections, ranging from television listings and entertainment guides to special news reports (Figure 4.23).

A Unique Design Opportunity

A tabloid page offers a unique design challenge and opportunity. Even though a tabloid page is designed using many of the same principles as a full-size page, the designer must think differently when working in this smaller format.

For example, it takes less material to fill a tabloid page. While that may seem obvious, many tabloid pages suffer because they look like a shrunken broadsheet. An example of this form of tabloid presentation is *The Christian Science Monitor.* Although its design is clean and orderly, it does not take advantage of its unique size.

Another problem in designing tabloid pages involves the use of visuals. For

instance, a four-column photograph, a three-column photograph and a one-column informational graphic can be used in harmony with the other elements on a broadsheet page. On a tabloid page, however, the use of a four-column photo, a three-column photo and a one-column graphic would leave little room for anything else, and the visuals would fight each other for the reader's attention. On the other hand, the tabloid designer cannot simply shrink those visuals by half and put them on the half-size tabloid page because they would be too small and the readers would not have a dominant visual element.

Tabloid Front Pages

The typical tabloid front page is a window to the inside of the paper. Like a magazine cover, the front page often features only a photograph and/or headlines referring to stories and features inside. Many tabloids developed this technique because much of their circulation was based on street sales, and they needed to push each day's paper as something new.

For example, *Newsday* on New York's Long Island makes excellent use of its size. Its front page looks much like a news magazine, with the combination of a color photograph, color background

screen and a strong one-word headline clearly providing a dominant visual element (Figure 4.24). And although some traditional newspaper designers might argue against overprinting the "Panic" headline into the photograph, it is a technique typical of magazine design. By contrast, another New York tabloid, the *Daily News,* uses a more traditional format, but it still uses its front page as a way to attract buyers and move readers inside the paper (Figure 4.25).

TRACKING WHAT READERS SEE

Despite time-honored rules and regulations on newspaper design, a new form of research shows readers' habits are difficult to predict. Eye-Trac Research studies by the Gallup Applied Science Partnership have been used to provide an objective record of a reader's actual eye movement over a newspaper page. The research allows scientists to analyze what the readers actually look at rather than preferences or recollections of what they did. Dominant entry points, direction of eye movement and duration of viewing can be determined.

In the 1988 issue of "The Chronicles," published by the Society of Newspaper Design, findings of Eye-Trac Research were summarized in an article by Wendy Govier of Knight-Ridder Tribune News graphics network. They included:

- In a broadsheet, readers scan the top half and bottom half of section fronts without unfolding the page.
- In papers they are familiar with, readers tend to process more headlines than photos; in unfamiliar papers, they tend to process equal amounts.

Robert Lockwood

Design Consultant

- Readers typically process a page from left to right.
- Inside facing pages are typically viewed as one unit.
- Readers make note of about half of all section-front photographs and one-fourth of inside-page photographs.
- Banner headlines continue to be the most likely entry point.
- Regular readers appear to ignore promotion boxes more than do readers who have never seen the paper before.

In the same issue of the Society of Newspaper Design's "Chronicles," Jim Smith, manager of research for the *Fort Lauderdale* (Fla.) *News/Sun-Sentinel* commented on Eye-Trac. "One of the conventions that has been upheld since I was in high school journalism is that people read in a clockwise pattern from the upper left," he said. "Eye-Trac Research is showing this might not be true."

Roger Black, one of the country's leading designers and former art director of *The New York Times,* was quoted as saying: "Market research is like astrology. It's fun, but don't take it too seriously. The good news is that there is no permanent damage to the reader."

For Robert Lockwood, a painter and sculptor turned newspaper designer, there are no set rules for page design. "I feel strongly that you can't straightjacket journalists. My idea is that I can do anything I want as long as I do it well and it is well crafted," he said. "There has to be a reason for doing it. If type set ragged right reinforces the notion of casualness, why not use it?

"There is nothing written in anyone's Bible that says the rules of page design can't be violated. Rules may have applied at one time, when newspapers needed to funnel people into one way of thinking. But now we have the technology to do anything we want. We don't need to be bound by rules. We must find out what we need to do, and then get the tools to do that. Our pages must be well crafted, but they must give us flexibility to change with the news."

Lockwood's design philosophy is linked to his background as an artist. Taught by artists from the Bauhaus school, which promoted the adaptation of science and technology to architecture, Lockwood is driven by art and its relationship to technology. "We never separated words and pictures," he said. "We always communicated something. I always have taken a structural approach to information and how to communicate it."

Lockwood was teaching design at the Philadelphia College of Art in the 1970s when Ed Miller, editor of *The Morning Call* in Allentown, Pa., hired him to redesign the paper for the 1980s. Lockwood commented: "Ed Miller was interested in a paper driven by editors who thought about the needs of the

readers and how to best give a daily report that was visual. He had a conviction that most newspapers were dull and boring and readers would not stay with them.

"We started with a long examination of the entire newspaper. We established editorial intentions, which then became our goals. The redesign required a reorganization of the paper and the newsroom. We wanted content to determine the design of the page, and we wanted to gather journalists who were capable of doing that, journalists who could change quickly and graphically. If a big story occurred, such as the attempt on the pope's life, we would clear everything and have that as the story of the day. On another day we might run all photos on the front page, with windows to the inside. Then we would have a second page. We truly let the mix of news determine what we did.

"The Allentown redesign got some attention because people weren't talking a lot then about letting the content determine the design of the page. It was fun. We did some interesting pages. Still, in a profession where rules are cherished it caused some consternation among journalists."

Since Allentown, Lockwood has helped redesign three dozen newspapers. He enjoyed talking about his project at the *Colorado Springs Gazette Telegraph,* a paper that he helped design for the 1990s.

"In Colorado Springs we used some things that were begun at *The Call,*" Lockwood said. "Tom Mullen, the editor, started with the long process of review and analyzation to determine what type of paper we envisioned for the future.

Then we clearly defined the editorial goals.

"The process involved everyone in the newsroom, in production and in other departments. We reviewed the beats and the way reporters covered them. We looked at the structure of the newsroom, how we could rearrange the chairs to help us produce the type of paper we wanted. We looked at the city in a different way to try to determine exactly what type of community it was."

Lockwood added that the *Gazette Telegraph* became a newspaper built around communities of interest. "Colorado Springs is an area that has grown so rapidly," he said. "It is vast tracts of suburbia ringing a little village with Pike's Peak behind it. But there are communities of interest in the city, such as the military, medical and education. We looked at the newspaper in terms of those larger communities of interest."

By introducing labels in the paper— military, education and medicine, for example—Lockwood said stories could be better targeted to specific readers. "The labels gave us an avenue to the reader."

To reflect the wide-open spaces of the West and Colorado, the *Gazette Telegraph* changed from a six-column format to a three-column format. "It can be broken into six or 12, but it begins with three," Lockwood noted. "Everything is larger from the start. We went to ragged right columns to reflect a more casual, Western feeling. We put a moving picture nameplate on the top of Page One. The picture of Pike's Peak changes as the weather changes."

Lockwood said that like the *Gazette Telegraph,* every newspaper has traits that make it different from any other.

He added: "There are different goals, different publishing strategies at each newspaper. I believe in *indigenous design,* where design springs from the special things about the community and its newspaper. The paper itself has a tradition that should be continued in a redesign.

"The nation is filled with original newspapers that are not like each other. Newspapers are like storytellers. Two people can tell the same story. One can tell it so that it is interesting and exciting. The other can tell it and it is boring.

"Newspapers tell stories well when they put them on the page and give them impact for the reader. One paper can present a story, with a wire photo, and make it interesting. Another paper can take the same story and make it boring. The one boring the reader is the one that has preconceived ideas of how the job should be done. While one will run the picture a certain size because it has to be that size, the other will break down the page and restructure it to fit the story and picture. The exciting page may turn up the volume even more by doing a graphic."

Lockwood said the design of a newspaper page is much more than mechanics, where everything has to be placed or sized according to rules.

"My approach is more organic," he said. "When I design, I discover the content of a newspaper. That's not just the news content. It's the nature of the place, the skills of the journalists, the internal configurations, all of that. I try to ask the right questions that will allow the newspaper to come up with a design that fits its needs.

"Too many designers take the

mechanical approach: Head sizes are always a certain size; the type always is justified; hairline rules are used only at certain times; headlines never bump.

"I don't know why people worry so much about simple things like bumping headlines. When I look at a page, if a head is next to another and it is confusing, I know not to do that. But if one head is next to another and it is not confusing, why not do it? If a one-line bold head is next to a three-line medium head, no one in the world is going to confuse them. The issue isn't bumping headlines, it's clarity.

"We have built our newspapers with preordained structure. It should be the other way around. As content changes, so should design. An editor should have a range of headlines faces, for example, so he can turn the volume up or down according to the news."

Lockwood predicts that newspaper design will continue to evolve in the 1990s. "I want to continue growing and striving for improvement," he added. "As I expand my vocabulary I will continue trying to discover the essentials of communicating information by examining journalists and how they do their jobs.

"We will continue bringing more into the design process. We don't want to bore or tire readers. We want to make a newspaper more interesting. We're still in a transitional stage because people have not fully understood the impact of the information age. We're still hunting and gathering. We haven't seen the renaissance yet."

SUGGESTED EXERCISES

1. Reproduce the front page of your daily newspaper to scale on a dummy sheet. Mark the sizes of all heads, photographs and graphics. Also mark column widths.

2. Draw a dummy of a front page. After you have completed it, clip stories and art from a newspaper and paste up a page that fits your dummy. Compare yours to others.

3. Evaluate the design of two front pages from a local daily newspaper. Do all of the elements on the page fit together in a neat package? Are the corners anchored? Is there any trapped white space? How would you improve pages?

4. Evaluate the white space on two front pages and two inside pages. How does it fit into the design of the pages? Is it used effectively? If there is trapped white space, how would you eliminate it?

5. Evaluate the progression of headline sizes on a front page and an inside page. Do the heads effectively grade the news?

6. Evaluate two front pages and two inside pages for dominant visual elements. Where are they on the pages? Why are they dominant? What changes would you suggest?

7. Evaluate the bottom halves of two front pages. Are readers effectively drawn below the fold of each page? How would you improve the pages?

8. Find an example of a newspaper page that is symmetrical in quadrants. Find one symmetrical in six or eight parts. What do you like and dislike about the pages? Find an example of an asymmetrical page and explain why it is asymmetrical. What do you like and dislike about the page?

CHAPTER FIVE

From Idea to Page One

One of the best ways to study newspaper design and its effects on page layout is to examine newspaper pages. This chapter offers 30 front pages from the same day to show how the design elements discussed in Chapter 4 are put to practice on an average news day. The examples, all from June 21, 1985, come from every geographic section of the country, from large metros to small community newspapers. It was a typical news day with a normal mix of international, national, state and local stories. Editors had to choose what stories to put on Page One and what photographs and graphics to accompany those stories.

The biggest international and national stories of the day dealt with worldwide terrorism. One came from Beirut, where five American hostages under guard at a press conference urged President Ronald Reagan not to attempt a rescue. The other was from Washington, where Reagan offered extra military aid to El Salvador to track down and punish the killers of six Americans and to battle leftist guerrillas.

THE PERSONALITY OF A NEWSPAPER

Newspapers have personalities. They don't all look alike. In fact, they are as different as the journalists who work for them and the people who read them. The collection of 30 front pages in this chapter shows both the diversity of design and the commonality of news judgments that editors across the country made on one news date. These pages illustrate the great differences in **story play** (which stories will have the lead headlines) and **art play** (the mix of photographs and informational graphics and maps) among various papers. Some of the pages have similar design elements; far more follow their own path.

Before we look at the differences in the front pages, however, it is necessary to discuss the most common elements a journalist must consider when laying out a front page, including the nameplate, promotional devices, color and design, column widths, number of stories, photographs and informational graphics (Figure 5.1).

The Nameplate

A newspaper rarely changes its nameplate, because many publishers and editors consider the nameplate essential to the paper's identity, a link to its past. While other elements may change on Page One, the nameplate usually remains constant and reflects the style of typography used in past decades. When

Overline or promo line
(sometimes called sky boxes)

Elements in this area
called "ear"

Nameplate or flag

Date or dateline

Main story or lead
story; sometimes
banner story

Reader or feature
story with feature
treatment

Refer or promo
box; refers to
inside stories

Dateline
for story
location

Second play

Logo or bug

Photo caption
and credit

Byline and
credit lines

Promo or
refer box

Index

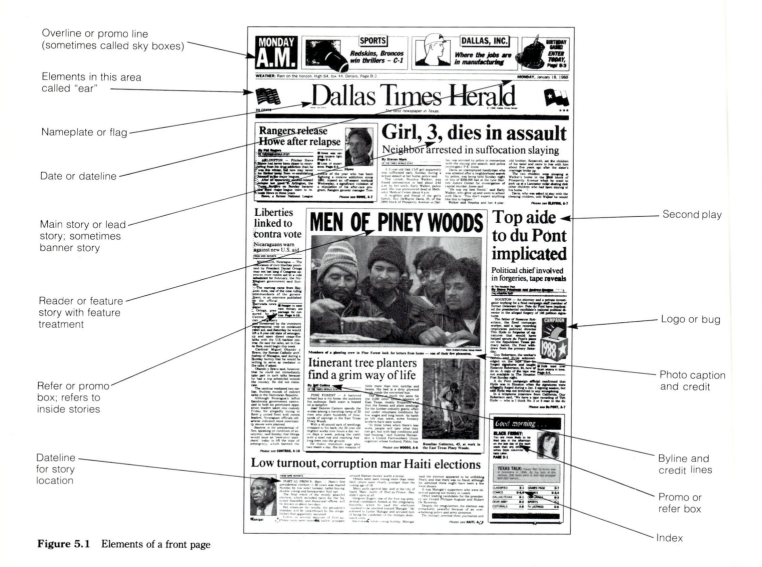

Figure 5.1   Elements of a front page

the nameplate is changed, or at least modernized, it is because the newspaper is going through a redesign to change its image.

As discussed in Chapter 1, one newspaper that has changed its nameplate several times since the 1930s is the *Chicago Tribune,* which wanted to become a more lively and colorful newspaper (Figure 5.2). In 1936, the nameplate of the *Chicago Daily Tribune* (as it was called then) was rather ornate (Figure 5.2a). **Ears** in the left and right corners note the price of the paper and the edition number; ears also can tell the weather or even sell advertising. (The most famous ear of all is found each day in *The New York Times.* It says, "All the News That's Fit to Print.")

Under the nameplate, separated by rules, is the *dateline,* which gives the volume number, day and date of publication and the daily cost of the paper.

By 1964, the *Tribune* nameplate had changed radically (Figure 5.2b). Not only had the name of the newspaper changed (the word *Daily* was removed) but the type also had been cleaned up by removing some of the serifs on many of the letters. The ear announcing the cost of the paper had been replaced by an American flag with the saying "An American Paper for Americans." The edition ear also had been reduced in size, and much of the dateline information had been eliminated, producing a cleaner look.

In 1972, the typeface used for the

Figure 5.2   Nameplates of the *Chicago Tribune* from 1936 to 1987
Reprinted by permission of the *Chicago Tribune*.

paper's name was made still cleaner and more modern by removing the strokes on the C and T (Figure 5.2c). The rest of the letters in the nameplate also were made bolder. The slogan under the American flag was removed, and the edition ear was given new treatment. One of the rules used to separate the dateline information was removed, giving the nameplate a more open, airy feeling.

By 1981, still more changes had occurred (Figure 5.2d). The slogan "The World's Greatest Newspaper" was removed, and the ears and the American flag were given a new treatment. The price of the paper and other dateline information were placed under the rule while the publication date remained

above it. The *Tribune* also began using **overlines** (or skyboxes or promo boxes), promotional devices that tell readers what is inside the paper or that summarize major news stories, in the top part of the nameplate.

The most radical change in the newspaper's nameplate came later in the 1980s (Figure 5.2e). In 1983, the type was *reversed*—made white on a blue background. The rule under the nameplate was colored red, and the dateline information was reversed out of a blue background. The flag was cut into the blue background and the overlines were given a more modern treatment. And in 1987, another design change removed the overlines as part of the nameplate design (Figure 5.2f).

Promotional Devices

Promotional devices such as overlines, indexes and summary boxes call attention to the unique stories and features inside the newspaper that day, especially in other sections such as sports or business. Generally, these devices run above the newspaper nameplate, although they can run at the bottom of a page or along the side.

Overline devices can be treated in various ways. *The Sun News* of Myrtle Beach, S.C., uses lines of type for its "live" news promotion (Figure 5.3). Such a device allows the editors to quickly change one of the lines to promote a different or more timely story. By contrast, the *Los Angeles Herald Examiner*'s overline is more rigid in its

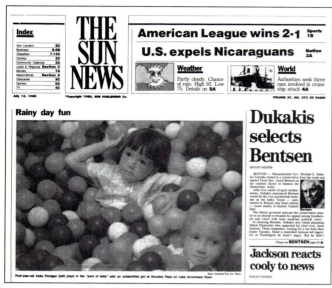

Figure 5.3   Flexible overline design

Figure 5.4   Rigid overline design

Figure 5.5   Example of standard use of summary box

Figure 5.6   Example of standard use of summary box

Figure 5.7   Untraditional placement of summary box on right side of page

uses of color throughout its format
(Figure 5.4). While the black type in
The Sun News is easily changed, the
Herald Examiner's color bar, which has
white type reversed out of a blue background, takes longer to change and set
up on the presses; therefore, it
promotes only features or nonbreaking
news stories and columns.

Page One almost always carries an
index that tells readers where they can
find daily features and columns inside
the paper. Some newspapers also
have a **summary box,** or **briefing
column,** which gives a brief description
of the content of stories in each section
of the paper.

The Today element on Page One
of *The Daily Report* in Ontario, Calif.
(Figure 5.5), and the Inside element of
the *Fort Lauderdale* (Fla.) *Sun-Sentinel*
(Figure 5.6) are two examples of the
standard use of summary boxes. These
elements are anchored or fixed on the
left side of the page, which reserves
the right side, the dominant focal point
of the page, for the major news stories
and art of the day. One newspaper that
breaks tradition and puts its summary
box on the right side is the *San Antonio*
(Texas) *Light,* which was redesigned
by Robert Lockwood in 1984 (Figure
5.7). Other papers run their summaries
across the bottom on Page One.

Wherever the index or summary
box is placed, it should guide readers
into the paper. It also can be used as a
visual element, but it should not take
up so much room and be filled with so
many rules, halftones and other graphic
ornamentation that it adds to page
clutter.

Color and Design

The use of color in newspapers, along
with the increased emphasis on graphics,
is one of the more significant changes
in newspaper design in the past decade.
Studies by the Poynter Institute for
Media Studies in St. Petersburg, Fla.,
show that more than half of the daily
newspapers in the United States use
color in some form; two-thirds of all
newspapers with circulation under 75,000
use color on a regular basis. Newspapers
use color in full-color photographs or
in full one- or two-color illustrations.
They also use it in **tint blocks,** a color
screen style. This use of one color is
called *spot color.*

Color affects the way visual journalists approach their jobs because its use
requires more planning time and preci-
sion in printing than does black-and-
white publication. It means earlier
deadlines because it takes longer to
position on the presses. Color also locks
in a page's design somewhat because
it is placed on the page first and the
other elements positioned around it.

Despite the extra effort color entails,
studies by Mario R. Garcia and Don
Fry for the Poynter Institute have shown
that readers like color and that they
prefer a full-color page to a black-and-
white page. Still, as Garcia and Fry
note, several of the top-rated newspapers in the country—*The New York
Times, The Wall Street Journal, The
Washington Post*—do not use color on
their news pages.

One important rule to remember
about color use is: If you can't take the
time to do it well, don't do it. Readers

Figure 5.8 Front page with both narrow-
and wide-measure columns

like color that looks good, that is
reproduced well, on the newspaper page.

Column Widths

Today's newspapers generally use about
the same column widths when setting
their stories—12 picas or 2 inches wide.
The 12-pica column comes close to the
desired or optimum visual width (14
picas) that the human eye can most easily
read. On some newspapers, 14 or 15
picas is the standard single-column
width. Although newspapers vary their
column widths, they try to keep them
near the optimum visual width.

For instance, the basic column width
in the six-column *Register-Guard*,
Eugene, Ore., is 12.3 picas (12 picas,
3 points) wide, but only one story on
the page is set in that measure (Figure
5.8). The top story on the page is set
about 15 picas wide, near the optimum.
However, the story in the lower right-
hand corner is set about 18 picas wide,
which is more difficult for the eye to
read.

Number of Stories

Editors always are concerned about placing the correct number of stories on Page One (or any page for that matter). They do not want too many stories and visuals, which makes the page look jumbled, or too few stories and visuals, which makes the page unattractive to readers. Generally, they strive for a balance of stories and visuals on Page One. Although sizes and numbers change each day depending on the news, usually there are four to six stories on the page and at least two visuals.

Page One philosophies also play an important role in the story-visual mix. Some newspapers require that Page One contain at least one local story, and perhaps one local photo, each day. Others reserve Page One for national and international stories and photos unless a major local story breaks. Still others require that one light-feature element appear on Page One every day.

Photographs

Almost all newspapers in the country, with the notable exception of *The Wall Street Journal,* use photographs on Page One. There are several reasons why: Readers like to look at photographs; photographs help illustrate or expand upon the day's news events; photographs prevent a newspaper page from looking massive and uninviting. Pictures also can help a newspaper change "pace." For example, a feature photograph can help brighten a page filled with news of disaster or destruction.

Newspapers have benefited from technological improvements that have brought more and better photographs from everywhere in the world. Cameras have become lighter and faster; film has become more flexible; offset printing has allowed for better reproduction. In addition to more photo wire services, newspapers in the past 20 years have increased the number of their own staff photographers. At the same time, photography and the photojournalist have become increasingly important.

Still, not everything is rosy. Photographs are finding increasing competition for space on the page from a desire for a higher story count and from graphics and illustrations. This competition often means fewer and/or smaller photographs on the page.

Informational Graphics

Informational graphics often are used on Page One. The growth in informational graphics comes mainly from a recognition that these devices help readers to better understand a complicated story. Technology also has allowed newspapers with limited artistic resources to generate their own graphics on computers or to receive graphics electronically from a news service or syndicate. Informational graphics should not, however, be used solely for their visual value, just a piece of art for a page. There should be a compelling reason to present information to readers in a graphic format that will help them understand the news quickly and easily.

FRONT PAGES OF JUNE 21, 1985

The following is a collection of front pages published on Friday, June 21, 1985. These pages indicate the variety in newspaper design and show the different approaches editors take to present the news and attract readers. The pages represent different geographic areas, circulation sizes and design approaches. It is important not to look at the pages as being right or wrong in their approaches, simply because designs are as individual as the newspapers themselves. Although there are certain design "rules" all newspapers follow, remember that the primary function of the design is to serve the reader.

Figure 5.9 *Albuquerque Journal*

Figure 5.10 *The Morning Call*

Albuquerque Journal

This morning newspaper (circulation 105,182) in New Mexico has a modular format (Figure 5.9). It uses spot color (blue) as an accent under its nameplate and at the top of the promotion box (Inside). The two stories at the top of the page are related and are packaged with an umbrella banner headline. Smaller and lighter headlines "read out" from the banner headline. The stand-alone photo at the bottom is boxed and refers to a story inside. Note that the *Journal* uses a different approach to **jump lines,** the lines that indicate a story is continued on another page: Its jump lines are ruled on the top and bottom.

The Morning Call

Page One of the Bethlehem edition of this morning newspaper (circulation 132,806) in Allentown, Pa., is exciting (Figure 5.10). It uses photos, rules and boxes to create graphic elements that enliven the news presentation. The design makes it seem that there are more than four stories on the page. The Inside promotion box on the left side of the page makes use of headlines and photographs to tell the reader about news inside the paper. In the lead story on U.S. hostages, a *refer box* alerts readers to related stories inside.

Figure 5.11   *Amarillo Globe-Times*

Figure 5.12   *The Asbury Park Press*

Amarillo Globe-Times

This afternoon daily (circulation 26,906) in Texas uses a vertical design approach (Figure 5.11). The Bug Zappers cartoon gives the pages a feature-page look. The only photograph on the page is a feature, stand-alone picture. A problem with vertical design can be seen on the bottom third of the page—six columns of gray type.

The Asbury Park Press

This evening paper (circulation 139,585) in New Jersey has a modern, colorful-looking presentation (Figure 5.12). It contains an unusual element: classified-style advertisements on the bottom of the page. Two stories at the top of the page are packaged in a modular format with the photo. The "shore summer fun" photograph is a stand-alone element, although at first glance it appears related to the story below; such devices are best boxed or ruled off to avoid any possible confusion.

Figure 5.13 *The Sun*

Figure 5.14 *Billings Gazette*

The Sun

Page One of this morning paper (circulation 221,941) in Baltimore has a high story count (eight) (Figure 5.13). Neither of the two photographs is dominant; they seem to fight each other for attention. Both are virtually square, a shape that is less appealing visually than a rectangle. The bottom photo is in color, however, which will draw readers quicker than will the black-and-white picture on top. The hijacking refer box in the upper right has a spot blue screen over it, which also draws the reader's attention.

Billings Gazette

This morning paper (circulation 57,620) in Montana has a feature-type design, with an "artistic" headline rather than a traditional headline over the hostage story (Figure 5.14). In addition to the bullet holes, the headline is printed in red ink, another feature-type design approach to a news story. A promotional box is in the upper right corner, and the lead story, about grasshoppers, is on the left. It also is unusual for a newspaper to put two different stories above the nameplate, which the *Gazette* did on this day.

Figure 5.15   *Butler Eagle*

Figure 5.16   *Sun-Times*

Butler Eagle

This afternoon paper (circulation 30,955) in Pennsylvania uses a design more typical of newspapers in the early 1900s (Figure 5.15). Its high story count, vertical makeup and unbalanced use of visuals produce a large gray area in the middle of the page. In addition, nine different typefaces and type styles are used on the page, which can cause visual confusion. The only visual above the fold is a small graphic from the Associated Press about a shuttle laser experiment.

Sun-Times

The *Sun-Times,* one of Chicago's two major morning newspapers (circulation 612,686), is a typical tabloid that uses large headlines and photographs to sell the paper (Figure 5.16). As part of that effort, a strong promotion box over the nameplate refers readers to a feature section of the paper.

Figure 5.17   *Chicago Tribune*

Figure 5.18   *The Christian Science Monitor*

Chicago Tribune

The *Tribune* (circulation 744,969) is the dominant newspaper in the Chicago-area market (Figure 5.17). The morning paper presents a high story count (six) and a long promotional box running down the left side of the page. The promotional box refers to sports stories, inside news stories and features. The page is a combination of modular and vertical elements; the main headline has two stories, one on each side, reading out of it. The layout on this page may cause some visual confusion because the story of the Marine deaths is placed under the hostage photo. Like the other two stories, it does deal with terrorism, but is not connected with the two Mideast stories.

The Christian Science Monitor

This nationally circulated morning newspaper (circulation 150,807) takes a different approach to covering the day's events, using a major news event as an opportunity to present the "why" and "how" of a story (Figure 5.18). This behind-the-scenes approach is illustrated on the paper's front page. The photos are more illustrative than news oriented. The paper's typography is quiet and subdued and lends a sense of authority.

Figure 5.19   *Concord Monitor*

Figure 5.20   *The Dallas Morning News*

Concord Monitor

This afternoon newspaper (circulation 21,479) in New Hampshire emphasizes local news—of the five stories on Page One, four deal with local or state issues (Figure 5.19). The main photograph is used to refer to a local column, which is not a typical newspaper design approach.

The Dallas Morning News

This morning paper (circulation 390,987) offers a solid, traditional Page One (Figure 5.20). The main story is at top right, with a related story, or *sidebar,* on the left. The main photograph on the page is in color. Color also is used as a background to the "Americans Slain in El Salvador" box in the middle of the page and in the map in the lower right.

Figure 5.21 *Erie Daily Times*

Figure 5.22 *The Fresno Bee*

Erie Daily Times

This afternoon paper (circulation 42,264) in Pennsylvania has a most unusual front page treatment (Figure 5.21). There are only two news stories on the page, although one has a sidebar. The four photographs have self-contained captions and are used as roundups for news and feature stories. Under the nameplate is a promotion box to inside stories, and at the bottom of the page is an index to features. Death notices also are placed at the bottom of the page, but they do not refer to obituaries inside the paper.

The Fresno Bee

This morning daily (circulation 139,689) in California offers a combination of horizontal and modular elements on its front page (Figure 5.22). All of the headlines on the page, except the banner head, are about the same visual weight, giving the page an unemphatic look.

Figure 5.23 *The Ledger*

Figure 5.24 *Lawrence Eagle-Tribune*

The Ledger

This morning paper (circulation 67,953) in Lakeland, Fla., offers a lively, active front page, with a strong combination of typographical elements, photographs and graphics (Figure 5.23). Although most of the type on the page is set in a wide measure, none of the blocks is overly long or visually imposing to the reader. Also of interest is the use of a facts box graphic on the left side of the page detailing the previous week's events.

Lawrence Eagle-Tribune

Every element on Page One of this Massachusetts afternoon paper (circulation 58,174), with the exception of the lead story, is in a box, a most unusual layout (Figure 5.24). The *Eagle-Tribune* also is unusual in that it does not have the usual promotional devices across the top of the page to enhance street sales. The *Eagle-Tribune*'s promotional devices look more like a morning paper's. Note the "This Weekend" feature, which promotes an upcoming community event and is not a news or feature story.

Figure 5.25 *Press-Telegram*

Figure 5.26 *Los Angeles Times*

Press-Telegram

Although this morning paper (circulation 124,488) in Long Beach, Calif., has a strong promotional device at the top of Page One, the most dominant visual image is the news photograph in the center (Figure 5.25). Using the photograph in this manner gives the page a design focus. Note the use of the refer box: Hijack ordeal: day 8.

Los Angeles Times

This morning paper (circulation 1,086,383) rarely uses visual elements at the bottom of the page, which often makes its makeup gray (Figure 5.26). The *Times* uses a style of design sometimes referred to as **brace** (layout that stresses just one story as the major news item and the unquestionably dominant visual element of the page). This typical *Times* front page also has a high story count (eight).

Figure 5.27   *The Miami Herald*

Figure 5.28   *The Miami News*

The Miami Herald

This front page in the morning *Herald* (circulation 433,027) is laid out modularly with a high story count (Figure 5.27). One interesting treatment is the placement of the refers before the lead of the main news story. Some editors may argue that this treatment delays the reader's entry into the story and is another design "roadblock." The coverage of the American hostages in Beirut and the coverage of terrorism in El Salvador are presented near each other but in their own visual packages.

The Miami News

Page One of this afternoon paper (circulation 57,035) is unlike almost any other in the country that day with its artistic magazine-like treatment of the terrorism headline (Figure 5.28). Note the informational graphic as part of the package. (Note: *The News* folded in 1988.)

Figure 5.29   *Newsday*

Figure 5.30   *The New York Times*

Newsday

This Long Island, N.Y., afternoon tabloid (circulation 603,172) also has a front page that looks much like a magazine, with a headline and photo that refer to the story package inside (Figure 5.29).

The New York Times

This Page One of *The Times* (circulation 1,001,694) is not typical for the paper because the main story headline is spread over four columns (Figure 5.30). On a more typical day, this national morning newspaper would run its lead story under a one- or two-column headline. The placement of the El Salvador photograph also is unusual for *The Times* and for newspapers in general because it runs under its related story. *The Times* generally has a high story count and uses multiple decks under its headlines.

Figure 5.31   *The Philadelphia Inquirer*

Figure 5.32   *The Providence Journal*

The Philadelphia Inquirer

Even though there are six stories on Page One of this morning newspaper (circulation 504,946), *The Inquirer*'s use of white space helps create an "open" look to the page (Figure 5.31). The hostage news story in a box, with a quote at the top of the photograph, is given almost a feature treatment. At the bottom of the page, the "Klan" story is given a hammer headline treatment, usually indicating that the story is different from the hard news on the page.

The Providence Journal

The striking balance between typography and photography makes the front page of this Rhode Island morning paper (circulation 94,220) interesting (Figure 5.32). Although the headline on the lead story seems too small in type size, its four lines and the four-line deck under it have enough weight to clearly announce the story as the main news of the day. Notice how rules and boxes separate unrelated items on the page. The promotion treatment at the bottom of the page also is unusual in its design approach.

Figure 5.33   *Roanoke Times & World-News*

Figure 5.34   *Times-Union*

Roanoke Times & World-News

This afternoon paper (circulation 44,779) in Virginia has a modular Page One with a typical left-side promotion device (Figure 5.33). Notice how the headlines go from large to small as stories are played from top to bottom. The informational graphic at the bottom of the page adds another strong visual element.

Times-Union

The front page of this Rochester, N.Y., afternoon paper (circulation 99,500) looks more like a morning newspaper with its understated layout (Figure 5.34). The lead is not on the traditional right side, but instead is a package of two stories boxed with a briefs column on the left side of the page. The index, a color promotion box and another news story are played at the top of the page. Every story or related package of stories is in a box.

Figure 5.35 *St. Petersburg Times*

Figure 5.36 *San Jose Mercury News*

St. Petersburg Times

This morning paper (circulation 291,202) in Florida was one of the pioneers in the use of newspaper graphics. The *Times* always has packaged stories effectively, as in this front page (Figure 5.35). Not only are the two stories on the hostages together but a box also ties in two other terrorism stories. The graphic element in the upper left ties all the elements together and also refers to other stories inside the paper.

San Jose Mercury News

Advance planning often produces a graphic element superior to the day's wire service photo report, as is shown on this front page from the *Mercury News,* a northern California morning paper (circulation 264,492) (Figure 5.36). It took days to plan and execute this graphic, and it could have run at any time while the hostage/terrorism stories were prominent.

Figure 5.37   *USA Today*

Figure 5.38   *The Washington Post*

USA Today

This front page is typical of this national morning paper (circulation 1.8 million); there are many elements and many stories (Figure 5.37). Given its excellent reproduction, *USA Today* is able to use multiple images on the hostages story. The news summary treatment along the left side of the page is constant, as is the color tint box on the lower right, which usually is where a soft news or feature story is placed.

The Washington Post

The Post, a morning paper (circulation 748,019), uses type widths and a rule at almost midpoint on the page to package five terrorism-related stories (Figure 5.38). The layout of the two stories at the top of the page gives readers the impression that they are of equal news value. Notice the rules between columns, which help reduce the effect of the bumped headlines at the bottom of the page.

SUGGESTED EXERCISES

1. What are the elements common to most front pages? Can you find examples of each in your local newspaper?

2. Clip from the front pages of daily newspapers two examples of the following elements:
   a. Ear
   b. Dateline
   c. Overline
   d. Index
   e. Summary box
   f. Tint block
   g. Spot color

3. What are the advantages and disadvantages of varying column widths? What is the optimum column width for newspapers?

4. Compare five to 10 newspaper front pages from the same date. Try to find newspapers from all geographic areas of the country. Discuss the similarities and differences in the following areas:
   a. Story selection and placement on the page
   b. The use of visual elements
   c. The use of color
   d. The use of promotional devices such as overlines and indexes
   Also discuss how regional and circulation differences affect the pages.

CHAPTER SIX

Inside Pages

Laying out a well-designed inside page is more difficult than it appears at first glance. Unlike the wide-open front page that provides an opportunity for lively and balanced display, inside pages often offer small *shelves* and *sleeves* of space for news. This means inside pages present their own special challenges to visual journalists. To begin with, there is always a much greater selection of stories, photos and graphics than there is space for them on the inside pages. And the visual journalist also must take into consideration the presence of advertisements on those pages. Two types of **ads** (short for advertisements) run in newspapers: **display ads,** which generally combine visuals and words and appear throughout the paper; and **classified ads,** which generally do not contain visuals, are run in a smaller type size and appear in a separate section.

THE MIX OF EDITORIAL MATTER AND ADS

Revenue from the advertisements in a newspaper pays the bills, which means that both the number and the positioning of advertisements in a paper are important. Many newspapers try to present a daily mix of 60 percent advertising and 40 percent editorial matter on their pages. Few newspapers, however, place advertising on front pages. The ads go on inside pages, some of which are filled with ads and others of which contain a mix of ads and editorial matter.

There is indeed competition for space between the advertising and editorial departments. Advertisers, who are paying precious dollars to the newspaper to place their advertisements in convenient spots for readers, want good play in the paper; some advertisers even pay a premium for special placement. At the same time, editors want to position their stories and visuals in spots where readers can find and read them easily.

This competition for space does not mean that the news and advertising departments must battle each day. It simply means that there should be a balance between the ads and editorial matter. Not every page can be open, but there should be a mix of inside open news pages and ad pages and partial ad and news pages. People read the paper for news; they also like to read advertisements. How the editorial matter and ads are positioned on inside pages can help make the paper user-friendly.

Figure 6.1 Modular layout of ads

ADVERTISING LAYOUT

Advertisements are placed on a page by the ad department before the page goes to the editorial department for the placement of news and features. Stories, headlines, photographs and graphics must be positioned in what space is left on the page in what is known as the **news hole**. Because the type and visuals used in the advertisements serve as magnets, visual journalists must use the remaining news holes to lay out inviting inside pages that draw readers to the editorial content.

The most common layout of advertisements in newspapers today is *modular*, in which the square and rectangular ads are squared off on each page. This enables the editorial matter to be laid out in a modular format as well (Figure 6.1). Two other ad layout styles are:

- **Pyramid.** The largest ads are placed at the bottom of the page, with smaller ads stacked on top to imitate a stair step.
- **Well.** Ads are stacked on each side of the page. A "well" is space reserved for news material on the

page. Very little design can be done with such space.

Most newspaper advertising is sold in *standard advertising units (SAUs),* which were created to standardize the sale and placement of newspaper ads. A broadsheet page is divided into 56 advertising units, and a tabloid page is divided into 33. SAUs eliminate the cost of extra production work by allowing advertisers to create a single-size ad that will fit the column specifications at almost any newspaper. For example, a two-column by 4-inch ad created by an advertising agency in New York City can be sent to newspapers throughout the country and placed on pages without modification. Before SAUs, advertisements had to be modified for almost every newspaper in which they ran.

Designing an Ad

As with anything in the newspaper, ads are created to draw the reader's attention. An advertisement should contain four basic elements:

- *Benefit headline.* The headline needs to talk to, to "benefit," readers in some way. For example, if the advertisement is targeting college students, the headline might say, "For College Students Only" or "Are You in College?" The headline must talk the prospective buyers' language. If it is trying to sell jeans to students, the headline might say, "Don't Just Be Smart . . . Look Smart, Too." If the ad is selling jeans to the students' parents, the headline might say, "These Jeans Will Wear Out Before They Go Out of Style."

- *Dominant art.* A photograph or some other visual element should show prospective customers what is being offered. For instance, if the ad is targeting women who buy cars, a photograph showing a woman driving a car can be used.
- *Informative body copy.* The body copy of an ad should get the readers involved by telling them what the product or service will do for them. Often, the selling points are highlighted by using typographical techniques such as bullets or bold face.
- *A clear display of advertiser's name.* If the potential customers don't know who is selling the product, then the advertisement has been wasted.

Dummying the Ad

The **ad dummies** showing the placement of ads on the page are prepared by the ad department from a **runsheet,** a daily list that contains the names of advertisers and the sizes of their ads but generally not the content or design. Most advertisers don't want to be on the same page or even facing pages with their competition, but ads generally are grouped. Male-oriented ads such as those for automotive goods or hunting and fishing supplies often are dummied in the sports section; restaurant and movie ads usually are placed in the entertainment section.

Because the runsheet does not show ad content or design, it is possible that very similar ads will be laid out next to each other. It also means that a visual journalist possibly could lay out editorial matter that clashes or blends with a neighboring ad. For instance, no one wants to lay out an airline crash story next to an ad for reduced summer air

Figure 6.2 News photo "blended in" with ad

Figure 6.3 Inside page devoted to specific topic—community affairs

Figure 6.4 Inside page devoted to specific topic—business

fares to Florida. No one wants to lay out a head shot of a speaker next to an ad for the speech that contains a head shot of the speaker. Luckily, these foul-ups can be caught and changed before the newspaper is printed. After the ad dummies are completed, a copy goes to the newsroom and a duplicate to the composing room, where the ads are created and placed on page boards in advance of the stories and visuals.

News and Advertising Photos

Strong pieces of art are as important in an advertisement as they are in a news layout. That means there always is a possibility of a news photo blending in with an advertising photo.

When the ad dummies are prepared, the layouts *should* show placement of photographs, but that seldom is done at most newspapers. The editorial department normally is given dummies with squares or rectangles drawn in to show where the ads are to run and how much space they will occupy on the page. Of course, the advertisements in a newspaper are generally ruled apart

or boxed, but if these two elements run side by side, one in a news space and the other in advertising space, readers are likely to be confused at first glance (Figure 6.2).

There are two ways to avoid this problem. The first is to not lay out a photograph next to an ad, which is not always possible but which can be done most of the time. The second is for the editorial department to establish a good working relationship with the advertising department and to persuade it to mark the placement of photographs in the advertising layouts.

The Benefit of Open Pages

It is important for the ad department to mix open and tight space inside the newspaper. Open pages allow visual journalists to best display the available editorial matter.

Today's news report is very different from that of 20 or even 10 years ago. Technology has allowed the wire services to use high-speed transmissions to send hundreds of stories and visuals daily. An increasing amount of sidebar

and graphic material is available with every major news story. Editors want—and readers deserve—related stories **packaged** along with photographs and informational graphics about the main news story of the day. This packaging of the news means a greater need for open pages.

PACKAGING INSIDE PAGES

Inside stories and visuals should be packaged in categories. For example, the inside pages in the first section of the newspaper may be reserved for stories about international and national news; inside pages in the second section may contain only local stories and art.

In a single-section paper, Pages 2 and 3 may contain international and national stories; Page 4 might be reserved for local news; Page 5, the editorial page; Pages 6 and 7, sports; and so on. Such packaging helps readers find categories of news stories each day; they don't have to search through the paper to find out what is happening in their area of interest (Figure 6.3 and 6.4).

Figure 6.5   Example of Page 3 treatment

Figure 6.6   Example of Page 3 treatment

Figure 6.7   Lively inside page with good photo use

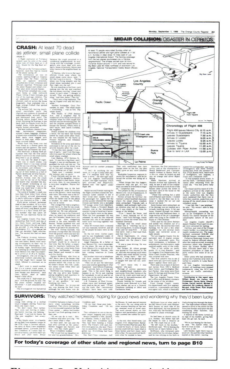

Figure 6.8   Uninviting, gray inside page

Page 3, The "Second Front Page"

Page 3, the page that readers see first when they open a section, is the second most important page in any section. Some newspapers use Page 3 as a "second front page," filled with editorial matter and devoid of advertisements (Figures 6.5 and 6.6). Most papers, however, must mix news, features and visuals with advertisements on Page 3 because the advertisers know the high readership of the page.

Again, a balance of editorial matter and advertising is important—whatever is on the page will affect a reader's reaction to the entire newspaper. Visual journalists usually put strong visuals and stories on Page 3, particularly in the upper half. At some newspapers, advertisers also are charged a premium to be positioned on Page 3.

Some newspaper redesigns have put an extra emphasis on Page 3, recognizing its unique position. For example, a newspaper may use it for the top national and foreign stories and pictures that did not make Page One; a summary of all the stories and features in the paper; or a "people" column of light, short items about show business and other celebrities.

Avoiding Gray Pages

When packaging major and often lengthy stories—wire or local—care must be taken to make the display as lively and interesting as possible (Figure 6.7). The visual journalist should avoid using large, unbroken blocks of type that add to the grayness of a page and make it less appealing visually (Figure 6.8). A gray page can be enlivened by using

ning elderly Americans

Figure 6.9   The use of subheads in a story

a combination of horizontal and vertical modules of type, boxes, photographs and graphics.

Sometimes, the visual journalist can suggest that parts of a long story be trimmed out and used as sidebars. The more visual elements in a major package, the more interesting the page will appear to the reader. Instead of publishing a 60-inch story, the visual journalist will work with the reporter and develop perhaps a 30-inch main story and three sidebars, each 10 inches long. In this way, readers can select only those elements of the presentation they are interested in reading.

In addition to photographs and graphics, other devices can be used to break up large stories:

- **Subheads** in long stories can serve as additional "miniheadlines" and provide a new point of entry (Figure 6.9).
- **Highlights** or **key points boxes** can summarize the major points in the story (Figure 6.10).
- **Quotes** from key people in the story can emphasize key points (Figure 6.11).
- **Series highlights** can be placed in a box if the story is part of a series.
- **Background boxes** can outline what is being discussed in the story or who the key people in the story are (Figure 6.12).

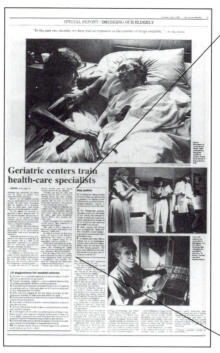

Key points

1. To combat the widespread lack of formal education and training in geriatrics, the federal government in recent years has funded 31 geriatric-education centers at medical schools across the country.

2. The Albuquerque geriatric-education center at the University of New Mexico has reduced the number of medications used on its elderly patients on an average of 30 to 50 percent and improved their health in the process.

3. Many patients and doctors have developed the "backward" view that their medical relationship must be consummated with a prescription drug.

4. An elderly, bed-ridden Illinois woman was on 13 medications, including three different antipsychotics, when she was taken into the New Mexico program. The drugs were reduced to only two, and several months later, she returned to a normal life.

Figure 6.10   Inside page enlivened by highlights box

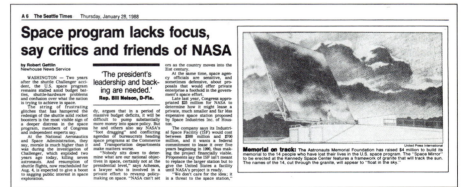

Figure 6.11   Inside page enlivened by quote

Figure 6.12   Inside page enlivened by background box
Reprinted by permission of the *Chicago Tribune*.

Such treatments are especially important with the group of readers who do not spend much time with the newspaper. These readers quickly "scan" through the paper looking for items that interest them. The more pieces of information—headlines, subheads, labels—the better the chance the newspaper can attract them into a story. Although newspapers may never give up the long story, they must realize that solid blocks of type do not invite the reader.

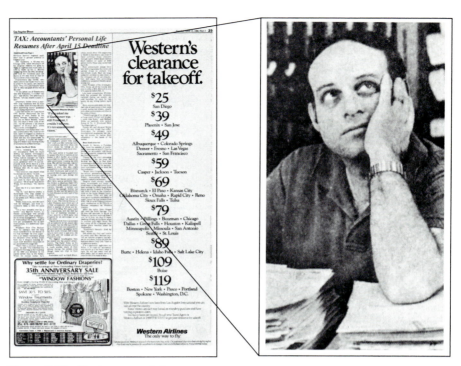

Figure 6.13   Head, or mug, shot

Head Shots and Portraits

Readers like looking at pictures of people in the news; therefore, photographs should be used liberally on inside pages. Often, the holes on inside pages are not big enough for multicolumn pieces of art, but a **head shot,** or **mug shot,** which shows a person's face, will work fine (Figure 6.13). A head shot draws readers visually to stories and also breaks columns of type or headlines. It normally is used in a one-column hole, 2 to 3 inches deep, but it can be used smaller or slightly larger.

A head shot should not be confused with a portrait. A head shot simply records a face. Readers look at the image and can decide if the person is old, young, white, Asian, whatever. A *portrait* is more than a face—it attempts to show the personality or character of a person. For example, face and hands or face and clothing tell much about personality, as does the environment in which a person is posed. A portrait can be used in a one-column hole, but it is used most effectively in two columns or more. A portrait is an excellent visual element and often tells a story as well as words can.

It always is best to use a head shot in which the person is animated. For example, a picture of a newsmaker smiling or frowning or not looking at the camera provides variety and avoids a posed look. Head shots also can be cropped out of a multicolumn picture, although such cropping probably will not make the photographer happy and may be a waste of a picture.

A head shot should not be played too big, especially if the image in the photograph is not animated. A multi-column hole should be a portrait opportunity rather than space for a large head shot. Sometimes, through careful picture editing, a visual journalist can use a portion of a photograph to produce a head shot for a tight inside news page. (A complete discussion of cropping is in Chapter 17.)

The Optimum Size of a Photograph

Although it is important to use photographs inside the newspaper both to present the day's news visually and to

break up long columns of type, a photograph should not be forced into the paper, especially when it means extreme cropping or sizing of the photo.

Photos have an optimum size, much like type. If they are too small, they are impossible to see or "read" (Figure 6.14). Small pictures need to be simple in form, showing something like a face or a close-up of one thing. Groups and complicated subjects should be avoided in small pictures. If pictures are too large, they are out of scale with the presentation of the news. The composition of large photographs can be more complex or complicated than that of small pictures. Even close-ups, however, can be powerful when they are played large, such as the portrait of the newly elected president.

Photographs on inside pages should be given their appropriate value, and pages that have room for photographs or graphics should have a dominant visual element. A visual journalist should play every photograph well so that the special ones, played even better, will have a greater value to the reader.

Figure 6.14   News photo that is too small

Graphics on the Inside

Because informational graphics do not have the same flexibility in sizing as photographs have—they cannot be enlarged or reduced more than 10 to 15 percent without greatly affecting their type size and artwork—the visual journalist must work closely with other editors to make certain there is room for graphics on inside pages. And although it is not always possible to quickly redraw a major graphic on deadline, the news editor or section editor and graphics editor can go through the dummies to reserve certain pages as potential places for inside informational graphics.

If there is not sufficient room to run the graphic at an appropriate size, the graphic probably should not run. By running a graphic too small, the visual journalist only teases the reader and gives the "hint of information" (Figure 6.15). Type that is too small is difficult, if not impossible, to read. One of the primary rules for informational graphics is to make them readable, with a pleasing type size, somewhere between 8 and 10 points.

Graphics also should not be placed next to an ad or be designed to look like an ad, because the reader might miss the graphic at first glance if he or she thinks it is an advertisement (Figure 6.16).

STORIES THAT CONTINUE

The Jump Page

If the most important stories are on Page One, then care must be taken in the handling and display of those stories

Figure 6.15   Informational graphic that is too small

when they continue inside the paper. Those continuations are often known as **jumps.** Although readers generally do not like to follow stories when they jump from one page to another, jumps are a necessity if a newspaper's front page is to offer in-depth news coverage in a lively page design with a number of stories and visuals.

Newspapers handle jumps in several

TEEN-AGERS GUNNED DOWN

2 youths wounded in Everglades

20%-50% OFF THE SEASON'S KEY LOOKS FOR WOMEN AND JUNIORS.

STARTS TOMORROW SPRING FASHION SALE

Burdines THE FLORIDA STORE

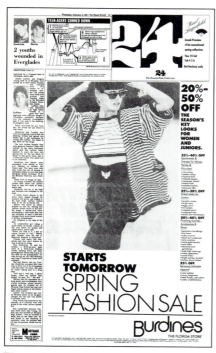

Figure 6.16 Informational graphic poorly placed, next to ad

6 A The Dallas Morning News Wednesday, July 20, 1988 H

Acquisition of 2 Texas bank holders expected

Continued from Page 1A.

H. Meyerson, and another bid submitted by the Ford Bank Group of Dallas.

Texas American and National had announced in April that they sought to merge with the help of the FDIC. Because both holding companies still report a positive net worth, sources said the deal would appear to be unique among recent bank rescues — and would preserve some investment for current shareholders of the two companies. Other details of the agreement were not known Tuesday.

A spokeswoman for Texas American on Tuesday said the company had no comment on its negotiations with the FDIC.

Pohlad became well-known nationally last fall with the World Series victory of the Minnesota Twins, the professional baseball team that he had bought just three years earlier.

But Pohlad had long impressed banking regulators and his Minnesota competitors by acquiring control of about 40 banks across the upper Midwest. Those banks now hold more than $4 billion in assets. The Minneapolis banker's purchases included several failed banks in previous deals with the FDIC.

"He's probably the best banker in Minnesota," said James H. Hearon III, chairman of National City Bank of Minneapolis. National City sits on

Carl R. Pohlad . . . financier reportedly will acquire Texas American Bancshares Inc. of Fort Worth and National Bancshares Corp. of San Antonio.

IC Industries Inc., Walt Disney, Avco, ITT, and McGraw-Hill Inc. Jacobs

Braniff's D/FW cutbacks to mean millions for airlines

Continued from Page 1A.

company with principal owners based in New York and Philadelphia. As part of the transaction, American agreed to purchase up to $23 million in Braniff assets and to lend the airline up to $21 million.

The airline's new management will announce next week that it is expanding service at its primary hub in Kansas City, Mo. At the same time, the airline is expected to announce service cutbacks in Dallas.

William G. McGee, the former chief executive officer of Piedmont Airlines who was brought in to run Braniff by the new owners, said last month the carrier may discontinue

"It's going to have a favorable impact. But it's not going to be so huge that we'll be dancing in the aisles."
— Michael Durham, American official

"Dallas would be just another city feeding the Kansas City hub, no more or less important to Braniff in the future than Denver or St. Louis," said Edmund Greenslet, publisher of The Airline Monitor, an

control a commanding 84 percent of the traffic. While Braniff's local market share is only 3 percent, American and Delta generally match the upstart's low fares on routes where they compete.

"When Braniff drops those routes, the low fares will go with them," Greenslet said.

This has been true in the past. When Braniff flew from D/FW to Boston, it offered a one-way coach fare of $197. Braniff dropped the route last September, and the one-way coach fare on American or Delta is now $486.

Henry Conley, Delta's district di-

Figure 6.18 Complete jump headlines

ways. Some package them on a single page, sometimes the back page of the front section or an inside page. This regular placement is more convenient for the reader and is easy to do on slow news days when there is little need to package sidebars and related stories with the jumps. Jumps also can be placed on a number of different inside pages in any convenient news hole in the section. This approach makes layout more flexible for editors, but it is more scattered for the reader.

One caution: Almost all newspapers avoid jumping from one section of the newspaper to another because readers usually read one section of the newspaper at a time; jumping sections may confuse readers.

Jump Headlines

Headlines for jump stories are handled in one of two ways:

- A one- or key-word treatment
- A completely new head on the inside page

The one-word jump helps signal that a story is a jump and is especially useful in alerting the reader looking to finish that story. A major drawback to such an approach is the key word often does not explain the story to readers who may have read the story and head on Page One. For example, for a bank robbery story, a key jump word of "Bank" is not specific and might not draw a reader into the story. Such headlines also are weak design elements on a page filled with jumped stories (Figure 6.17).

From Page One

Alleged forgeries found in Dole and Haig petitions in Texas

Jobless

1987 unemployment

Debate

Stocks

Reforms

Mecham

Money

SETTING IT STRAIGHT

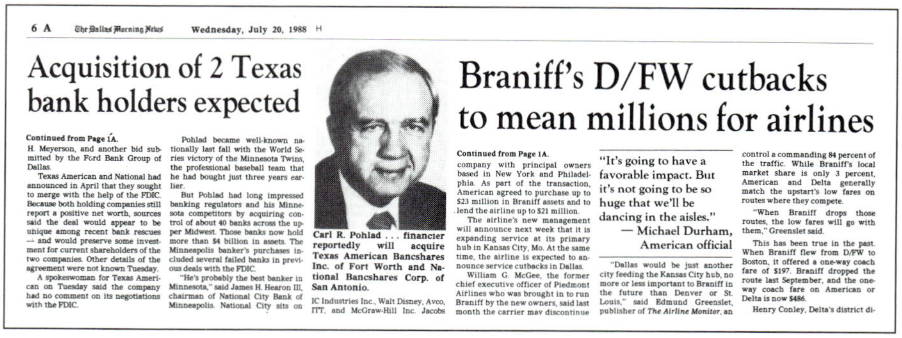

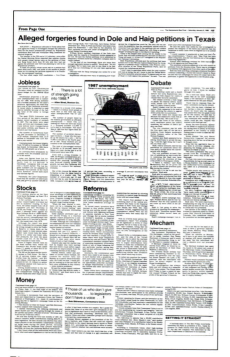

Figure 6.17 One-word jump headlines packaged on single page

One way to avoid this problem is to use complete headlines on jump stories (Figure 6.18). Although the use of complete headlines makes more work for the copy editor, who now has to write two headlines instead of one, a reader who is scanning through the paper has a greater chance of being drawn into a story.

HEADLINES ON INSIDE PAGES

Headlines grade the news on inside pages as they do on front pages. Because readers expect the top stories to carry the largest headlines, the biggest headline on an inside page should be at the top. Unlike an open front page, however, an inside page may have a news hole too small for large headlines. Some inside pages will have room for only a single headline and story. Thus, although the headlines on inside pages should be large enough to draw readers, they should not be so large or heavy that the page looks out of balance (Figure 6.19).

Normally, the largest headline used on an inside page with a limited news hole is 36 points; on a page that is open or nearly open, the headline sizes can be larger. Inside heads also should be used in a progression of sizes. Small heads, such as 18 points, can be used on inside pages, but they should be reserved for small one-column holes below the fold and should contain two or three lines.

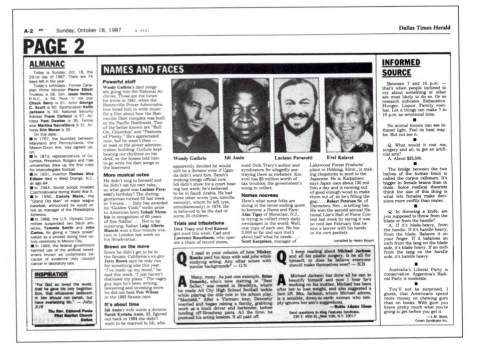

Figure 6.19   Too-large inside headlines

Standing Headlines

Standing headlines, which introduce columns or pages that appear in the newspaper each day, are useful in packaging the news but should be reserved for inside pages. There are scores of standing heads that may be used inside the newspaper, including world news, national briefs, editorials, comics, news summary and weather (Figure 6.20). Such heads may be placed on top of the page as an umbrella for the entire page, or they may be placed in a section of the page to introduce a package of related stories. Standing heads also top daily syndicated and local columns.

Standing heads and the stories or columns they introduce should be located in about the same place in the paper each day, so readers don't have to hunt for their favorite pages or columns.

Raw-wraps

A headline should stretch across the same number of columns as the related story under it. In other words, a four-column headline should have four columns of type under it or two columns of type and two columns of related art. Type should not, however, run next to it in column five or six. This **raw-wrapping** of type, also called **gray-wrapping** or **dutch-wrapping,** should be avoided because readers will tend to link the uncovered type with the story above it. Sometimes, raw-wraps are used on the tops of inside pages where there are no stories above the raw-wrapped type, but readers still may be confused (Figure 6.21).

Figure 6.20   Standing headlines

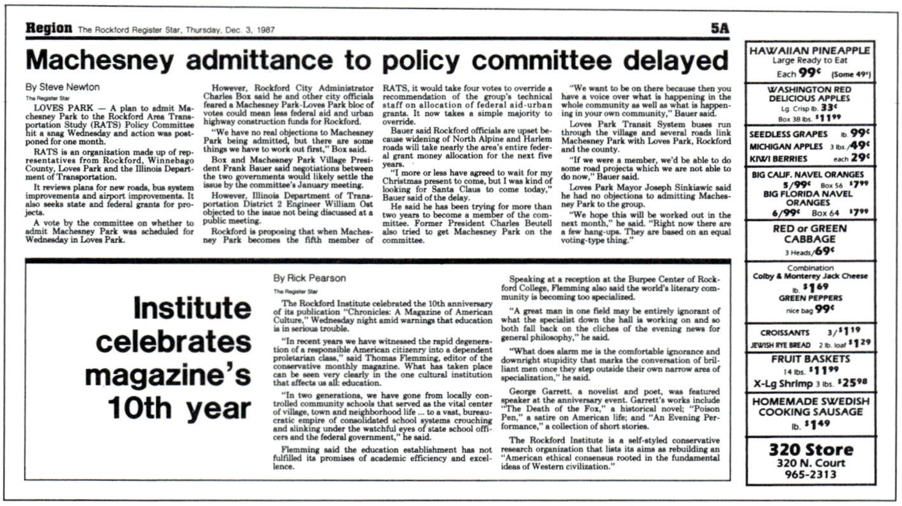

Region The Rockford Register Star, Thursday, Dec. 3, 1987 **5A**

Machesney admittance to policy committee delayed

By Steve Newton
The Register Star

LOVES PARK — A plan to admit Machesney Park to the Rockford Area Transportation Study (RATS) Policy Committee hit a snag Wednesday and action was postponed for one month.

RATS is an organization made up of representatives from Rockford, Winnebago County, Loves Park and the Illinois Department of Transportation.

It reviews plans for new roads, bus system improvements and airport improvements. It also seeks state and federal grants for projects.

A vote by the committee on whether to admit Machesney Park was scheduled for Wednesday in Loves Park.

However, Rockford City Administrator Charles Box said he and other city officials feared a Machesney Park-Loves Park bloc of votes could mean less federal aid and urban highway construction funds for Rockford.

"We have no real objections to Machesney Park being admitted, but there are some things we have to work out first," Box said.

Box and Machesney Park Village President Frank Bauer said negotiations between the two governments would likely settle the issue by the committee's January meeting.

However, Illinois Department of Transportation District 2 Engineer William Ost objected to the issue not being discussed at a public meeting.

Rockford is proposing that when Machesney Park becomes the fifth member of RATS, it would take four votes to override a recommendation of the group's technical staff on allocation of federal aid-urban grants. It now takes a simple majority to override.

Bauer said Rockford officials are upset because widening of North Alpine and Harlem roads will take nearly the area's entire federal grant money allocation for the next five years.

"I more or less have agreed to wait for my Christmas present to come, but I was kind of looking for Santa Claus to come today," Bauer said of the delay.

He said he has been trying for more than two years to become a member of the committee. Former President Charles Beutell also tried to get Machesney Park on the committee.

"We want to be on there because then you have a voice over what is happening in the whole community as well as what is happening in your own community," Bauer said.

Loves Park Transit System buses run through the village and several roads link Machesney Park with Loves Park, Rockford and the county.

"If we were a member, we'd be able to do some road projects which we are not able to do now," Bauer said.

Loves Park Mayor Joseph Sinkiawic said he had no objections to admitting Machesney Park to the group.

"We hope this will be worked out in the next month," he said. "Right now there are a few hang-ups. They are based on an equal voting-type thing."

Institute celebrates magazine's 10th year

By Rick Pearson
The Register Star

The Rockford Institute celebrated the 10th anniversary of its publication "Chronicles: A Magazine of American Culture," Wednesday night amid warnings that education is in serious trouble.

"In recent years we have witnessed the rapid degeneration of a responsible American citizenry into a dependent proletarian class," said Thomas Flemming, editor of the conservative monthly magazine. What has taken place can be seen very clearly in the one cultural institution that affects us all: education.

"In two generations, we have gone from locally controlled community schools that served as the vital center of village, town and neighborhood life ... to a vast, bureaucratic empire of consolidated school systems crouching and slinking under the watchful eyes of state school officers and the federal government," he said.

Flemming said the education establishment has not fulfilled its promises of academic efficiency and excellence.

Speaking at a reception at the Burpee Center of Rockford College, Flemming also said the world's literary community is becoming too specialized.

"A great man in one field may be entirely ignorant of what the specialist down the hall is working on and so both fall back on the cliches of the evening news for general philosophy," he said.

"What does alarm me is the comfortable ignorance and downright stupidity that marks the conversation of brilliant men once they step outside their own narrow area of specialization," he said.

George Garrett, a novelist and poet, was featured speaker at the anniversary event. Garrett's works include "The Death of the Fox," a historical novel; "Poison Pen," a satire on American life; and "An Evening Performance," a collection of short stories.

The Rockford Institute is a self-styled conservative research organization that lists its aims as rebuilding an "American ethical consensus rooted in the fundamental ideas of Western civilization."

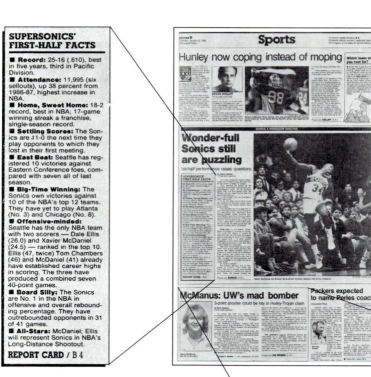

Figure 6.21 Raw-wrap on inside page

SUPERSONICS' FIRST-HALF FACTS

■ **Record:** 25-16 (.610), best in five years, third in Pacific Division.
■ **Attendance:** 11,995 (six sellouts), up 38 percent from 1986-87, highest increase in NBA.
■ **Home, Sweet Home:** 18-2 record, best in NBA; 17-game winning streak a franchise, single-season record.
■ **Settling Scores:** The Sonics are 11-0 the next time they play opponents to which they lost in their first meeting.
■ **East Beat:** Seattle has registered 10 victories against Eastern Conference foes, compared with seven all of last season.
■ **Big-Time Winning:** The Sonics own victories against 10 of the NBA's top 12 teams. They have yet to play Atlanta (No. 3) and Chicago (No. 8).
■ **Offensive-minded:** Seattle has the only NBA team with two scorers — Dale Ellis (26.0) and Xavier McDaniel (24.5) — ranked in the top 10. Ellis (47, twice) Tom Chambers (46) and McDaniel (41) already have established career highs in scoring. The three have produced a combined seven 40-point games.
■ **Board Silly:** The Sonics are No. 1 in the NBA in offensive and overall rebounding percentage. They have outrebounded opponents in 31 of 41 games.
■ **All-Stars:** McDaniel; Ellis will represent Sonics in NBA's Long-Distance Shootout.

REPORT CARD / B 4

Sports

Hunley now coping instead of moping

STEVE KELLEY
Times staff columnist

Which team will you root for?

SONICS' MIDSEASON ANALYSIS

Wonder-full Sonics still are puzzling

1st-half performance raises questions

McManus: UW's mad bomber

Packers expected to name Perles coach

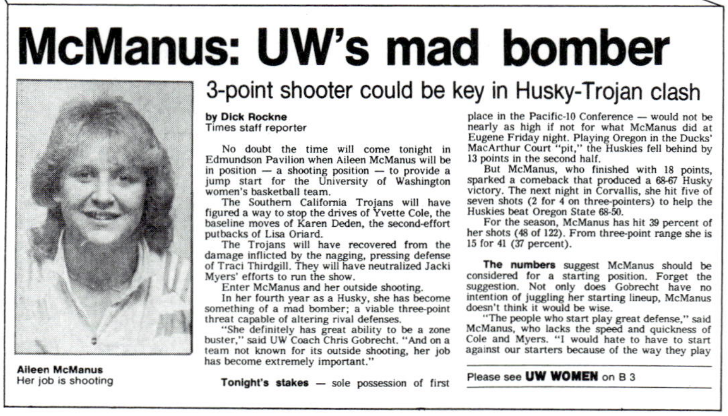

McManus: UW's mad bomber

3-point shooter could be key in Husky-Trojan clash

by Dick Rockne
Times staff reporter

No doubt the time will come tonight in Edmundson Pavilion when Aileen McManus will be in position — a shooting position — to provide a jump start for the University of Washington women's basketball team.

The Southern California Trojans will have figured a way to stop the drives of Yvette Cole, the baseline moves of Karen Deden, the second-effort putbacks of Lisa Oriard.

The Trojans will have recovered from the damage inflicted by the nagging, pressing defense of Traci Thirdgill. They will have neutralized Jacki Myers' efforts to run the show.

Enter McManus and her outside shooting.

In her fourth year as a Husky, she has become something of a mad bomber; a viable three-point threat capable of altering rival defenses.

"She definitely has great ability to be a zone buster," said UW Coach Chris Gobrecht. "And on a team not known for its outside shooting, her job has become extremely important."

Tonight's stakes — sole possession of first place in the Pacific-10 Conference — would not be nearly as high if not for what McManus did at Eugene Friday night. Playing Oregon in the Ducks' MacArthur Court "pit," the Huskies fell behind by 13 points in the second half.

But McManus, who finished with 18 points, sparked a comeback that produced a 68-67 Husky victory. The next night in Corvallis, she hit five of seven shots (2 for 4 on three-pointers) to help the Huskies beat Oregon State 68-50.

For the season, McManus has hit 39 percent of her shots (48 of 122). From three-point range she is 15 for 41 (37 percent).

The numbers suggest McManus should be considered for a starting position. Forget the suggestion. Not only does Gobrecht have no intention of juggling her starting lineup, McManus doesn't think it would be wise.

"The people who start play great defense," said McManus, who lacks the speed and quickness of Cole and Myers. "I would hate to have to start against our starters because of the way they play

Please see **UW WOMEN** on B 3

Aileen McManus
Her job is shooting

Figure 6.22 Boxes used to package related elements and separate stories

Bumping Headlines

When headlines are placed side by side on a page, they **bump.** If headlines in the same typeface and type size are placed side by side, they are called **tombstone headlines.** Tombstone headlines should be avoided because they confuse readers, who see the two headlines as one. The best way to separate headlines is with a visual element. If two stories must be laid out side by side, one should be boxed to lessen the impact of the bump, and the headlines should not be set in the same weight and size. Sometimes, a multicolumn headline can bump against a single-column headline so long as there is a great difference in their sizes or weights.

RULES AND GUTTERS

The most effective use of **rules** on a newspaper page is as a border for boxes. they often are used because they package related elements or help separate stories. Normally, boxes take 1- or 2-point rules and square corners (Figure 6.22). Traditionally, newspapers have used thicker rules around the obituary of a major news figure, but too many heavy rules on a newspaper page can make it look overly solemn.

The space between elements on a page is known as the **gutter.** Normally, rules are not used in the gutters that separate columns of type; therefore, gutters contribute to a more "open" feeling on a page. Gutters that run the length of an open page should be avoided because they pull the reader's eye away from the page's top elements. A full-length gutter also tends to divide a page into two symmetrical parts. A visual journalist can eliminate a full-length

gutter simply by rearranging the layout on a page and placing a mix of horizontal and vertical elements on the page.

THE EDITORIAL PAGE

The editorial page plays a unique role in a newspaper: Not only does it carry opinionated material, which is different from what's on other pages, but it also often differs in its design.

The design of an editorial page, which generally is an open inside page, is both a comfort and a challenge for a visual journalist. It is a comfort because it is filled with fixed elements each day, which convey a sense of consistency for the person laying it out and for the reader who by habit looks for certain things on the page. It is a challenge because the visual journalist probably does not want it to look like a dull gray mass of type that barely changes visually from day to day.

From a design standpoint, the editorial page should be distinguishable visually from the rest of the newspaper. A distinct design also clearly identifies the page and the unique role it plays in the newspaper (Figure 6.23).

Cutting the Editorial Page Gray

An editorial page does not have to be made up of five or six columns of gray type. All of the fixed elements on the page guarantee its layout will follow a pattern, but there are ways it can be made visually exciting:

- *Body type sizes can vary.* At some newspapers, editorials may be set in 10-point type, whereas the body type on the rest of the page may be 9 points, the same size as the type

Figure 6.23 Editorial page

on other pages in the newspaper. The larger type size sets the editorials apart from other items in the newspaper, as they should be, and also makes the editorial page more interesting visually.

- *Editorials can be set wider than other items on the page.* Setting the editorials in a measure wider than the rest of the items on the page gives them a distinctive look and also offers readers visual variety.

- *Editorial cartoons can run in different sizes.* An editorial cartoon should not run so small that it fails to give readers an immediate visual message, nor should it run so large that it overpowers the page.

- *Letters to the editor can be organized and easy to read.* Letters to the editor are widely read items and should not merely be stacked one on top of another. Small headlines over each letter, as well as extra white space above each headline, will make them more visually pleasing. They also can be set in a different measure than other items on the page.

Forum

"These are frantic and hectic days. Amid the crunch of unrealized legislation, the pressures of conflicting interests, the tensions of unrealistic demands, we pray for those who govern."

JUSTICE AT LONG LAST?

'She recalls bitterly the upbeat official attitude toward the explosions. "They told us to watch and be part of history. . . . It's just hideous what people went through." '

JACKSON AND THE BLACKS

PARADISE TO GO

'Barring aerial bombing by crazed environmentalists, development of the fast-food end of town is nearly complete.'

NANCY THE FIREFIGHTER

DOONESBURY

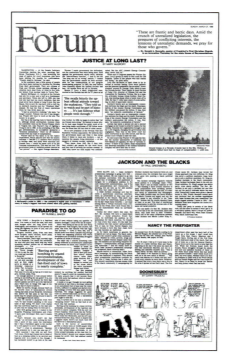

Figure 6.24 Op-ed page using boxes, rules and photos for visual interest

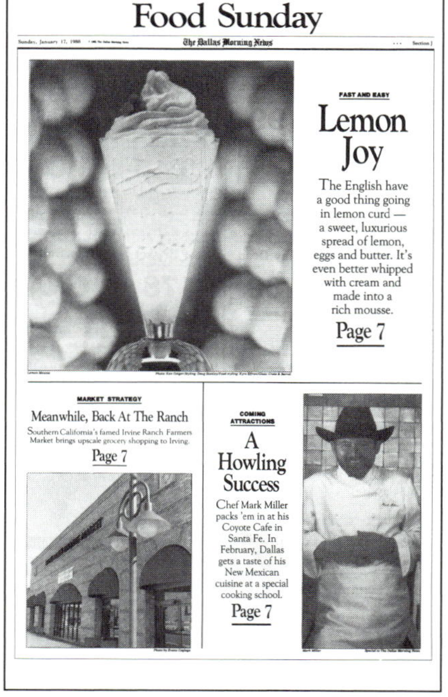

Food Sunday

The Dallas Morning News

FAST AND EASY

Lemon Joy

The English have a good thing going in lemon curd — a sweet, luxurious spread of lemon, eggs and butter. It's even better whipped with cream and made into a rich mousse.

Page 7

MARKET STRATEGY

Meanwhile, Back At The Ranch

Southern California's famed Irvine Ranch Farmers Market brings upscale grocery shopping to Irving.

Page 7

COMING ATTRACTIONS

A Howling Success

Chef Mark Miller packs 'em in at his Coyote Cafe in Santa Fe. In February, Dallas gets a taste of his New Mexican cuisine at a special cooking school.

Page 7

Figure 6.25 Example of strong feature section front with exciting, not excessive, design

The Op-Ed Page

At many newspapers, the page facing or following the editorial page is used for columns that offer readers additional or opposing viewpoints from those on the editorial page. That page is called the *opposite-editorial*, or *op-ed*, page (Figure 6.24).

Editorial cartoons, other visuals and letters to the editor, along with syndicated and local columns, may be used on the op-ed page. Like the editorial page, the op-ed page will have a standard format, but there should be some room for flexibility in how the type and visuals are displayed. The toughest task the visual journalist faces is laying out in a visually pleasing way a certain number of columns that generally are about the same length and that often aren't accompanied by illustrations or photographs. The same guidelines that apply to making an editorial page exciting can be followed on the op-ed page.

SECTION FRONTS

Section fronts are a special category. While they are neither inside pages nor the front page of the newspaper, they provide both special opportunities and obstacles for the visual journalist. Although not every newspaper has firmly entrenched sections for each department of the newspaper, most offer their readers many different sections during the course of a week. These sections, while offering opportunities for the designer to experiment and have "fun," still should maintain the overall design and typographic style of the newspaper.

Readers look for and appreciate consistency in their newspapers. This means body type and overall headline typography should be the same, or at least from the same family, throughout the paper. This does not mean, however, that the visual journalist must avoid experimentation, including the use of special headline faces, poster-size photographs or illustrations and other visual

Figure 6.26 Business section page with informational graphics

Figure 6.27 A sports page design

Figure 6.28 Sports page using table to present information

touches on section fronts to attract readers.

Here is a look at some of the considerations in and pitfalls of working on different section fronts.

Feature Sections

"Features" in a newspaper can be single pages or various sections, such as Home, Style, Food or Entertainment. Each presents different challenges to the visual journalist in both creative and journalistic ways. The biggest challenge is making the feature material look exciting and different each day without making the section or page appear out of place in the newspaper. There is a fine line between experimentation and design excess (Figure 6.25).

Business Sections

The skills of the informational graphics artist can be best used in a business or financial news section. Although many business stories have photographs, the visual presentation of the multitude of statistical information is best served by tables, charts and other informational graphics. The visual journalist should not, however, give up on getting good photographs. Photographers should be encouraged to study weekly business magazines to see how to make corporate photographs more exciting.

The section's informational graphics should be among the best in the paper, because the business section readers will be among the paper's most critical (Figure 6.26). Many of these readers work with statistics on their jobs and are aware of when a story runs with an incomplete chart. In addition, the visual journalist should avoid the temptation to make the informational graphic too cute or cartoonlike; the readers of business sections want information first, cuteness second if at all. An often overlooked technique is the use of "company at a glance" boxes that highlight the fiscal affairs of a corporation.

Sports Sections

Apart from satisfying sports fans' desire for photographs of sports action, the visual journalist should be aware of their hunger for statistical information (Figure 6.27). Many sports sections could be enhanced by the use of more tables and other graphic devices that present statistics and similar information (Figure 6.28). The visual journalist should, however, also watch for the opportunity to present a "how it happens" or "how it works" informational graphic in an effort to attract the less knowledgeable reader to the section; many sports sections tend to cater to the "expert" and forget the average or less than average sports reader.

SUGGESTED EXERCISES

1. What is the editorial news hole? How is it created? Clip five inside pages and explain how the editorial news hole on each page differs.

2. Find two examples of well-packaged inside pages. What makes them visually pleasing?

3. Clip Page 3 from two different newspapers. How are the two pages similar? How are they different? How would you improve them?

4. Are the jump heads in your local daily single words or full heads? Do they add to the total design of the paper? Which type of headline do you prefer and why?

5. Clip examples of the following elements from inside pages of newspapers:
   a. Highlights box
   b. Quote box
   c. Series highlights box
   d. Background box

6. Clip four informational graphics from inside pages of a daily newspaper. Are they used effectively? What do you like and dislike about them? How would you improve them?

7. Compare and contrast the use of head shots and portraits in newspaper stories. When should just the face be used? When should a portrait be used? When does a head shot become a portrait?

8. Find an open newspaper page with a full-length gutter. Redesign the page to eliminate the gutter.

9. Analyze the editorial page and op-ed page of a metropolitan daily serving your area. Are the pages visually exciting or are they drab and boring? How would you improve them?

CHAPTER SEVEN

Reproduction and Color

Newspaper production is complex and changing. Few newspapers are produced *exactly* alike; there are many types of equipment and production methods. Still, to do his or her job effectively, a visual journalist must understand the production processes that photographs and informational graphics go through before they are presented to readers on the printed page.

The purpose of this chapter is to provide a broad understanding of the various processes performed in the production of newspaper visuals, from *prepress* work (the work needed to prepare material to be printed) to the *press run* (the printing of the paper). Many of the processes discussed here have been touched on in previous chapters; here they are examined in some detail.

THE TYPE

Almost all daily newspapers use an electronic form of *typesetting* or **photocomposition** in which light-sensitive, specially coated paper is exposed with the images of the letters and symbols of the type being "set" by the newspaper's computer. Once the paper has been exposed, it is processed and dried in large, automatic equipment in much

the same manner as a photographic print. The machine that processes this type—stories, captions, classified advertisements and so on—is called a *typesetter.*

Depending on the model and complexity of the typesetter, a newspaper can set a single column of type, called a *galley,* or almost an entire page with all of the typeset elements in place, in a process known as *area composition.* Area composition is one step away from *pagination,* the computerized creation and output of a complete newspaper page with all of its elements, including photographs and advertisements.

Whether a newspaper typesetter produces a galley or partially complete pages, the next step is page *pasteup,* in which a printer assembles the typeset elements on a *page board,* which is the actual size of the finished page. The process is called "pasteup" because the elements are glued to the page with a waxy paste. (With a pagination system, page "pasteup" is done in the newsroom electronically.)

Printers have seen their craft evolve from a *hot metal* process, in which individual lines of type were composed in a metal form, to *cold type,* in which rolls of coated, photographic paper are pasted on a cardboard sheet, but they still are involved in producing the pages

Figure 7.1 Camera department employee checking page negative

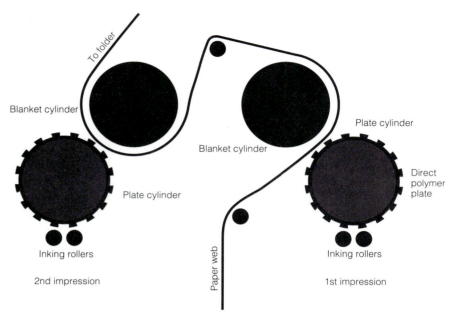

Figure 7.2 Diagram of rotary letterpress system; in this system, paper is given an impression directly from the plate cylinder

readers see in the newspaper. The printer, generally using a layout or dummy provided by the editorial department, needs to place all the necessary elements on the page, making sure stories, headlines, captions and visuals are cut and placed on the page straight and in the correct order. Even the advertising must be checked to ensure that the right ad is placed on the page.

When the printer is done, the page generally is taken to the plate-making department where a camera system will produce a full-page photographic negative of the completed page (Figure 7.1). From that photographic negative, a **printing plate**—either metal or plastic, depending on the type of printing process the newspaper uses—will be made and sent to the newspaper's pressroom.

THE PRINTING PROCESS

There are three major types of printing processes used by newspapers today: letterpress, offset and flexography.

Letterpress

Letterpress, a "relief" method of printing, is the oldest of the newspaper

printing systems. This process uses a printing plate with raised, reversed images of type and other page elements. The plate is coated with a thin layer of ink and rolled against paper, leaving an impression of the page in ink on the paper (Figure 7.2). The layer of ink is very fine, so only the top of the plate is covered before its image is transferred to paper, and areas on the plate—such as white space—do not collect ink. Where the letterpress method of printing once used heavy, rigid metal plates that were cast in molten lead, now it uses flexible plastic plates.

Offset

The popularity of offset printing of newspapers has grown tremendously in the past 20 years and currently is the standard for high-quality color printing. The **offset** printing process is based on the principle that oil and water do not mix. A thin metal plate is treated so as to be photosensitive, and the image of the newspaper page is exposed on the plate using the negative of the page. The plate's printing images—type, visuals and advertisements— are made "oil receptive," while its non-printing areas—the white space on the page—are made "water recep-

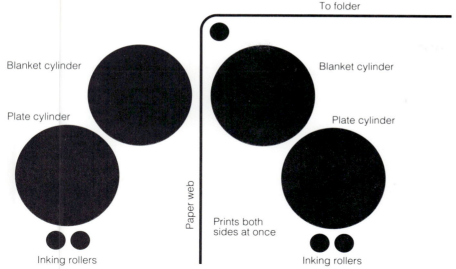

Figure 7.3 Diagram of offset printing system; in this system, the page's image is transferred via a blanket cylinder

Figure 7.4 Offset printing press

tive." On the press, the plate comes in contact with rollers of water and ink. The offset ink, which is made primarily of oil, will not mix with the water but rather adheres to the images of the plate that will be printed. The water prevents the ink from going into nonprinting areas.

Offset is so named because of the next step: The ink-covered plate is offset against (makes an impression on) a blanket, a rubber cylinder that picks up

the ink and then comes in contact with the paper (Figure 7.3).

Newspaper editors generally prefer offset over letterpress because it produces clearer images and its color reproduction is far superior (Figure 7.4).

Flexography

Flexography is the newest method of newspaper printing, although it is not a new method of printing. In flexography a raised, flexible printing surface using water-based inks delivered by an engraved cylinder known as an *anilox roller* picks up ink and applies it directly to the printing plate.

Flexography is used on everything from cereal boxes to toilet paper because of its simplicity—it uses only one printing plate and fast-drying, fluid inks. One reason that newspapers are considering flexography is that it is cheaper than offset printing. Because the ink is water based, it will not rub off on readers' hands as much as the oil-based inks of offset printing do. In addition, the flexo inks can be cleaned by water, which means newspapers can avoid the use of toxic solvents.

However, there are still questions about the suitability of flexography for printing newspapers. In some early uses of newspaper flexography, black-and-white photographs tended to be muddy

or splotchy, although color photography was brilliant or bright.

Among the newspapers printing pages by flexography are *The Providence (R.I.) Journal-Bulletin* and *The Miami Herald.*

REPRODUCING PHOTOGRAPHS

Familiarity with the major forms of printing is important in understanding the various methods of producing a photograph, a most important visual element on the printed page.

As we discussed earlier, the typesetter produces the type for a page electronically on photosensitive paper. The reproduction of this type is relatively easy—there is black (the shape of the letters) or white (the absence of any type). The reproduction of something in between—gray—is much more difficult. And because most photographs have blacks, whites *and* grays, something of a printing "trick" or "illusion" is needed to reproduce the grays.

Halftone Screens

The press process is "fooled" when printing a photograph's grays because of the use of a *halftone screen.* This method takes the original photograph or continuous tone print and rephotographs it with a **process camera,** a special camera that uses a transparent screen to alter the light reflected back from images during exposure to a high-intensity light beamed on the photograph. This light is transmitted through the transparent screen, which reproduces the photographic image in the form of thousands of tiny dots. In the final halftone print (some systems go through an intermediate step where a negative is made), the larger the dot, the darker the image; the smaller the dot, the lighter the image (Figure 7.5). Note that the actual dots throughout the halftone photograph are black—it is the absence of dots that produces the whites and a smaller number of dots that produce the grays. Thousands of dots are needed to create a pattern that will reproduce the photograph's tones and images (Figure 7.6).

The size of screen used for creating the halftone is rated by number of lines per inch. Most letterpress-printed newspapers use a 65-line screen. Offset newspapers generally use a finer 85-line screen. Some newspapers use an even finer screen, such as 100 lines.

Process camera work normally is done in a newspaper's engraving department, so named because at one time the engraving department took the screened negatives it produced and made metal plates from them by etching the dots on to the metal with an acid solution. (At many newspapers the name of the engraving department has been changed to the camera department.) Today, a photographic paper process is used to produce a halftone print. The halftone, which is developed either automatically or manually, is sometimes called a **velox** or *PMT,* a photo mechanical transfer. The velox is pasted on a page along with the stories, headlines and ads. When the printing plate is made, the varying sizes of black dots on the velox are recorded along with the blacks that make up the type.

In the future, paginated newspapers will use *scanners* that electronically scan photographs as halftones and process those screens along with the type when assembling the page for output to the typesetter.

Figure 7.5   Halftone print; the larger the dot, the darker the image

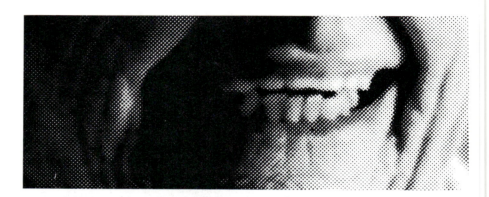

Figure 7.6   Photo progressively enlarged to show various-sized dots in halftone screen

How Various Newspapers Use Color

Color is playing an ever-increasing role in U.S. newspapers. It can be both a design and a content tool. As a design tool, color can help direct a reader's eye through a page. Or color can help sharpen or define the content of a story or a page. Newspaper readers like color that is reproduced well; they do not like color elements that cannot be reproduced and instead prefer a good-looking black-and-white page to a poorly printed color page.

Color Plate 1 *USA Today* prototype front page. The style of *USA Today* had a profound effect on newspapers across the United States.

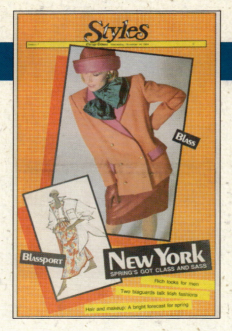

Color Plate 2 *Chicago Tribune* fashion section front, which makes a bold design statement, much like a poster.

Color Plate 4 *Dallas Times Herald,* another poster-like treatment with a striking color photograph.

Color Plate 3 *St. Petersburg Times,* an early pioneer in the use of color in daily newspapers.

Color Plate 5 *The Sun,* Baltimore, Maryland, uses two color news photographs on an otherwise traditional front page layout.

Color Plate 6 The color at the top of a *Dallas Times Herald* front page is "picked up" at the bottom of the page, helping to unify the page's design.

Color Plate 7 Color photography and informational graphics are used on the front page of the *St. Petersburg Times* to help tell the story of a powerful hurricane.

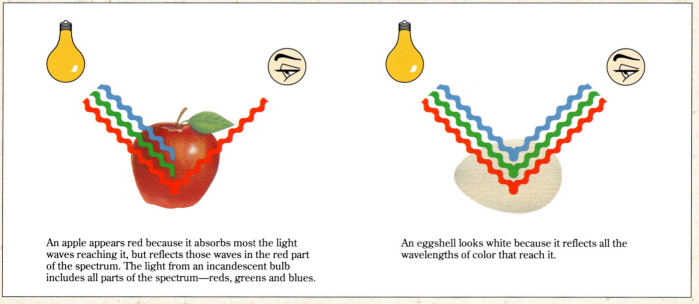

An apple appears red because it absorbs most the light waves reaching it, but reflects those waves in the red part of the spectrum. The light from an incandescent bulb includes all parts of the spectrum—reds, greens and blues.

An eggshell looks white because it reflects all the wavelengths of color that reach it.

Color Plate 8   Basic color theory

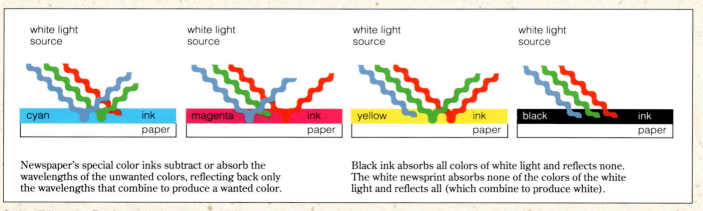

Newspaper's special color inks subtract or absorb the wavelengths of the unwanted colors, reflecting back only the wavelengths that combine to produce a wanted color.

Black ink absorbs all colors of white light and reflects none. The white newsprint absorbs none of the colors of the white light and reflects all (which combine to produce white).

Color Plate 9   Basic color theory for printing

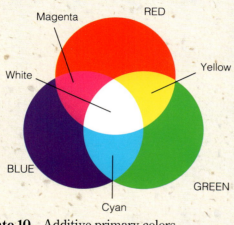

Color Plate 10   Additive primary colors

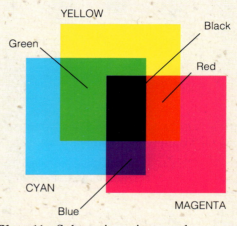

Color Plate 11   Subtractive primary colors

Color Plate 12   An example of spot (or single) color use as part of a graphic's design.

Color Plate 13   An example of spot color use as part of a front page's design.

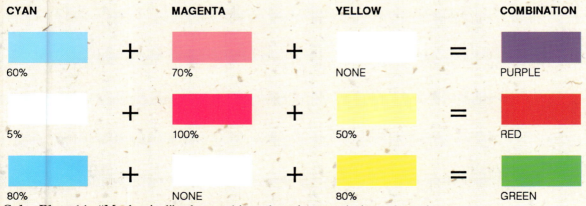

CYAN		MAGENTA		YELLOW		COMBINATION
60%	+	70%	+	NONE	=	PURPLE
5%	+	100%	+	50%	=	RED
80%	+	NONE	+	80%	=	GREEN

Color Plate 14   "Mechanical" color combines the primary printing colors of cyan, magenta and yellow to create different colors.

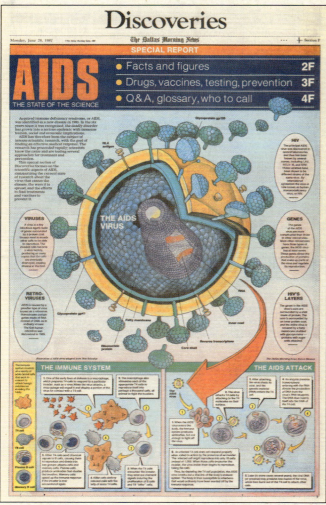

Color Plate 15 An informational graphic using "mechanical" color. This type of color is generally created by an artist or production worker cutting acetate (plastic) flaps that are used by the camera department to produce various screens or tones of color.

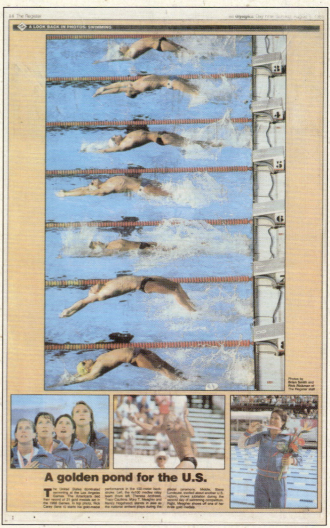

Color Plate 16 Reflective color refers to such material as a color photograph.

Color Plate 17 Sometimes color can overpower a page or an informational graphic.

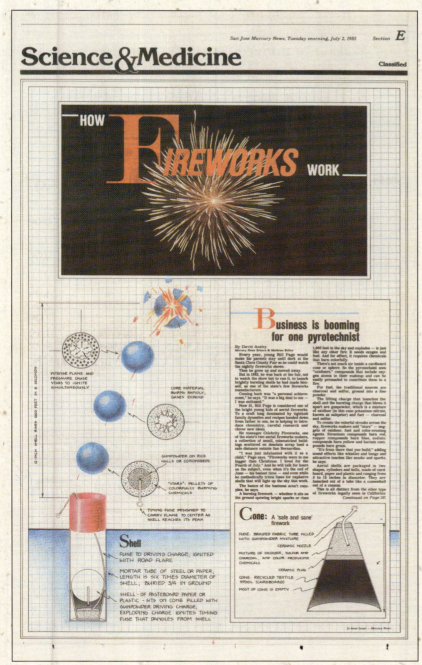

Color Plate 18 The proper selection of color in both a page's design and its graphics is always important, especially when dealing with "memory" colors.

Color Plate 19 Adding a color screen to a page can further intensify a design, sometimes creating a page that is too potent.

Color Plate 20 An exciting photograph, printed with excellent reproduction methods, energizes the front page of the *Sun-Sentinel* in Ft. Lauderdale.

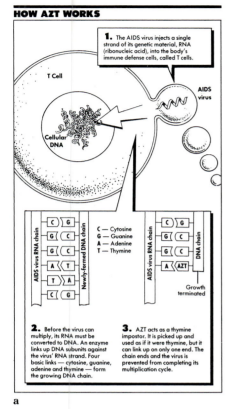

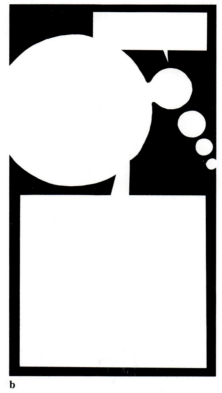

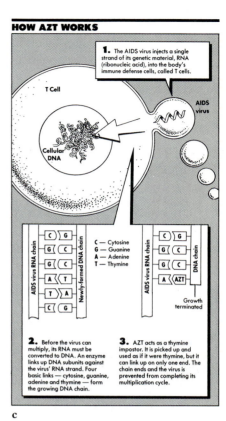

a   b   c

Figure 7.7 Graphic with acetate flap for screen: (a) original graphic, (b) flap, (c) graphic with screen

REPRODUCING GRAPHICS

When a map, chart or other informational graphic uses only black images or type, its reproduction is similar to the story type on a page. Those black images will be produced on the printing plate, and the reader will see a black box, line or image. Sometimes, however, an artist wishes to create a graphic that has gray in it. There are two main methods for the creation of gray tones in graphics:

- *A computer-generated image,* which creates its own grays through dot patterns
- *A screened image,* which is created in the engraving or camera department at the newspaper

To create those screens mechanically, an artist either indicates on a piece of

paper where the gray pattern should be placed or cuts an acetate or plastic film *overlay* (flap) in the exact position of the desired screen. When the artist cuts an overlay, the engraving department will make a separate negative of that pattern using a screen over the processing camera's lens. The graphic without the screen will be photographed as a solid black image. Then, the two negatives—the gray-tone screen and the black image—will be sandwiched together, and a velox will be made for placement on the page (Figure 7.7).

The *gray screens* can be used in a variety of intensities or tints and patterns (solid, crosshatch). Most newspapers use only a limited number of patterns, generally screens from a light 20 percent to a dark 80 percent (Figure 7.8).

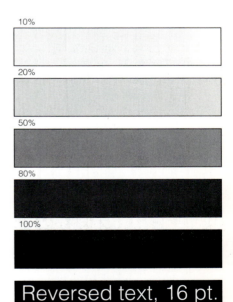

Figure 7.8 Sample gray screen patterns

THE BASICS OF COLOR

Color, partly as a result of the technological success of *USA Today,* has burst into the newspaper scene much like spring wildflowers. With the increased use of color has come additional pressures on the production and editorial departments.

Newspaper **color,** defined as a design tool that adds anything from a full-color photo to spot color to a newspaper page, is not new. The *Chicago Tribune* was making extensive use of color in the 1930s for both editorial and advertising purposes. As circulation grew, however, demands for faster letterpress output increased, making it more difficult to produce quality color. Not until the introduction of the high-speed, higher-quality offset printing method did the pendulum swing back to newspaper color.

With the introduction of *USA Today* in 1982, many publishers realized color could be produced daily on a high-quality basis (Color Plate 1). *USA Today,* because it prints at more than 30 sites across the country (and two sites in Europe and Asia), established rigid quality-control standards for printing color to ensure consistency no matter where the paper was printed. That high standard showed many publishers and visual journalists it was possible to achieve quality color on a regular basis.

Although *USA Today* has been a leader in the use of color, it certainly was not the first newspaper to establish consistently high-quality color. A number of newspapers were printing excellent color years before *USA Today* hit the newsstands, including the *St. Petersburg Times,* the *Chicago Tribune,* the *St. Louis Post-Dispatch* and *The Milwaukee Journal.* Many newspapers, however, looked at the success of color in those papers and, without understanding the need for higher production standards, began running color without regard to either editorial value or quality (Color Plates 2 through 7).

In the next 20 years, according to the National Advertising Bureau, almost all U.S. daily newspapers will be offering high-quality color. This infusion of color will come at the behest not only of editors but also of the advertising community. Advertisers see color as an effective way to attract shoppers to the hundreds of products displayed in a typical newspaper. And running more full-color advertisements will force publishers to establish strict quality standards that will benefit both the editor and the reader. How important is color to advertisers? A survey by the Newspaper Advertising Bureau found that the body copy of color ads is read 50 to 80 percent more than copy in black-and-white ads. The number of color advertisements in the weekly news magazines is evidence that advertisers and readers prefer color.

The Challenge of Color

Color presents more challenges than does black and white for the visual journalist. It simply takes longer to produce high-quality color graphics and photographs than it does to produce black and white, and there is more room for error. In addition, the pressroom has more trouble running color because the problems with *color registration* (the alignment of all the color plates), ink mix and press capacity. The more color a newspaper runs, the fewer pages it can produce and the more newsprint (paper) it wastes as it attempts to produce quality color.

A non-color newspaper need only concern itself with one plate per page and one color of ink—black—whereas a newspaper that runs color has four plates per page and four different inks. To run a color photograph, a newspaper press needs yellow, magenta (a red-like color), cyan (a blue-like color) and black plates and the ink for each one.

Printing Primary Colors

The human eye has three different types of *receptors,* each sensitive to a third of the *visible light spectrum*—red, blue and green. When a person views a color scene, the receptors are activated by the colors to which they are sensitive, and those impulses are relayed to the brain, which re-creates the scene. Light, such as that from the sun, illuminates these colors. When there is no light, the eye sees "black" (Color Plates 8 and 9). The "accuracy" of the colors in the scene depends on the condition of the receptors—a defective receptor can cause color blindness. The three colors—red, blue and green—are called **additive primaries** because, when added together, they produce white (Color Plate 10). (Note: The three *primary colors* of printing differ from an artist's primary colors of yellow, red and blue.)

What people see when they view a color object is not just the color of the object itself, but rather the object as it absorbs some colors and reflects others. A red apple reflects red light and absorbs the other colors, so the brain, using the eyes' receptors, perceives the apple as red.

Figure 7.9   Operator at color scanner

Color Separations

The process newspapers use for color on the printed page involves **subtractive primary colors,** which are created by the use of filters that subtract one color from the primary additive colors (Color Plate 11). The filters produce the printing plate images that will be used to create a faithful reproduction of the original. For example, placing a green filter over a photograph will subtract all of the green in the photograph, leaving only the red and blue of the original. The printing plate negative made from this filter is called the "magenta printer." A red filter is used to get a negative recording of all red and leave the blue and green. This process produces a printing plate negative called the "cyan printer." A blue filter removes the blue and leaves only red and green, which when combined produce the "yellow printer."

These three color negatives— each negative contains only those specific colors and is called a **color separation**—are used to create printing plates that, when used with their corresponding inks, produce the reproduction seen in a newspaper. The inks used to produce color are called process inks.

Sometimes, depending on the printing process, a fourth color plate is made—the black plate—which sharpens a photograph's grays and shadows. Many offset newspapers use the fourth, or black, printer; most letterpress newspapers do not.

The majority of newspapers use a camera to make the color separations. However, a newer technology—using an electronic light beam or laser light to scan the original —allows for greater flexibility and speed in producing color. The light beam that scans the original is split into three beams, each going to a filter that makes the proper separation for that color, generally in a negative form. The advantage of an electronic scanner for color is that it uses a computer to control variables such as inks, paper and tonal range. It also allows an operator to make adjustments based on the quality of the original photograph (Figure 7.9).

This scanned image—now in digital form that can be read by a computer —also can be manipulated by other equipment before the photograph is printed. Such prepress equipment, known as a **digital imaging system,** allows for anything from subtle adjustment of skin tone to the changing of a model's dress color from red to blue. Scitex is a well-known maker of digital imaging systems, which often are referred to as Scitex systems in the same way a cola drink is called a Coke.

The primary advantage of a digital imaging system is speed. More color photographs can be handled using a Scitex-type system than can be done manually at most newspapers, which saves labor and dollars.

MANIPULATION OF PHOTO-GRAPHIC IMAGES

The growing use of digital imaging systems also has sparked a debate over the manipulation of photographic images.

The highly sophisticated and expensive computer equipment of a digital imaging system uses a scanner to break a photograph into **pixels,** its tiniest components. A pixel—short for *picture element*—is the basic rectangular unit that, in combinations, forms the images on a screen. There are about four million pixels in a frame of 35mm film (the standard film for professional photographers). Because each pixel is a small unit of the picture, portions of the photograph can be manipulated or re-created without the reader being aware that the photograph has been altered. One example of such alteration occurred when the authors of a photography book, "A Day in the Life of America," manipulated the cover photograph of a cowboy, moving the cowboy closer to a tree and making the moon bigger in order to create what they said was a more pleasing and attractive cover. However, some visual journalists objected to this "unreal" photograph, claiming that, because it did not reflect the actual image captured by the photographer, it was not a true photograph.

Another example of such manipulation, although less noticeable, occurred when several newspapers changed the color of the sky in the photograph showing the U.S. space shuttle Challenger exploding shortly after takeoff. The editors who changed the color from its original purple hue to a truer blue argued that the photograph was "inac-curate" and they were merely adjusting its color balance.

As more newspapers buy equipment capable of such manipulation, the temptation to "edit" an average photographic image and make it "perfect" will increase. Many editors want to have such equipment in the newsroom, saying that they need total control. No matter who runs the machine, digital photographs can be both a blessing and a danger to the visual journalist. (Further discussion of the ethics of photo manipulation can be found in Chapter 8.)

TYPES OF NEWSPAPER COLOR

A complete understanding of newspaper color requires an understanding of the different types of color possible, including spot color, mechanical color and reflective or process color.

Spot Color

Spot color is the simplest form of newspaper color. Generally, it refers to the use of one (hence the word *spot*) of the three subtractive primary colors—cyan, magenta or yellow. The color can run in varying tints or screens from light—10 percent screen—to dark—90 percent screen. Research has shown that readers are attracted to any type of color, even a single color, which makes spot color popular in newspapers. It dresses up boxes, rules, screens and even headlines. And it requires only one additional plate (Color Plates 12 and 13).

Spot color has some disadvantages though. Because choices are limited to the three subtractive colors, there can be less creative use of color. In addition, the magenta used by American newspapers has a pink look and is not always attractive when displayed over large areas on a page. Also the yellow is too weak a color to run in the lighter screens (it will wash out or disappear) and is not a dominant color in the heavier screens. The cyan, probably the most attractive spot color, is able to hold almost all ranges of screens and look true blue.

If it is possible to mix one of the spot colors with black (type or other screen tones), the creative possibilities are increased. Black type will not reproduce over heavy tones of either cyan or magenta, however. That means the visual journalist must take care that percentage of color screen does not overpower the readability of the type.

Mechanical Color

Mechanical color is similar to spot color although the range of colors is far greater. This type of color is also called *flat* or *flapped color* because of the way it is created by an artist for use with informational graphics and other similar devices. An artist must cut individual acetate flaps for each color or color combination, hence the flapped color. Mechanical colors sometimes are called flat because they are used on one-dimensional objects.

Mechanical color is a full-color process that refers more to how the color is created than to the type of color. Mechanical color takes advantage of cyan, magenta, yellow and black to create other colors. By mixing 20 percent yellow with 10 percent magenta, for example, an artist can create a third color, in this case a sandy or flesh color (Color Plate 14).

Care must be taken when using mechanical color to create pleasing color combinations. Readers (and editors) have "memory colors"; they expect blue skies, green grass and red fire engines. (If you have ever been in a city where there are yellow or lime fire engines, you may remember how shocking it was the first time you saw them. That's because your memory color for fire engines is red.)

An artist tells the engraving or camera department what colors to create by noting them on a piece of paper or tissue or by cutting acetate flaps over the artwork. The engraving or camera department will photograph each flap or combination of flaps through a process camera with the proper screen or tint. Using the negative from that process, the engraving department will either make a paper print (velox) of each color or hold the color negatives until they can be combined with the finished page negative. The negatives are used to create the proper printing plates.

Mechanical colors are generally very bright or pure colors. They allow the visual journalist to add color easily to black and white graphics. By flapping an existing graphic, the newspaper can run color. If for some reason the color were unavailable, the flaps could be removed and the graphic could run in black and white, perhaps with some gray tone (Color Plate 15).

Reflective or Process Color

Reflective color refers to color photographs or color artwork, such as paintings (Color Plate 16). Although photographs and paintings are created differently, their reproduction in a newspaper is handled in much the same manner. The color artwork and the color photography are either photographed by the engraving department's process camera (with its screens) or placed on the drum of a color scanner, which offers increased speed and accuracy. The scanner's high-intensity, or laser, light source then "reads" the photograph or artwork. The image is digitized via color filters and converted into individual color separation negatives.

With either the process camera or a scanner, the color negatives (three colors and perhaps a black printer, depending on the type of printing process) are used to make the color printing plates in the same manner as mechanical color and spot color.

HOW MUCH COLOR IS TOO MUCH?

Color has brought great excitement to newspapers, but with its increased popularity comes a need for standards regarding its effective use. Few publishers, editors or readers want to see a paper that resembles a gaudy, excessive rainbow.

So how much color should a newspaper run? That is a question being debated in newsrooms across the country. Certainly, not every paper should, or can, look like *USA Today*, with its multiple use of color photographs, graphics, bars and screens (and that's just on the front page). At the other extreme, a single rule or a small piece of artwork in one color generally isn't effective. The use of color must be "designed" as part of the overall page design and not just as an afterthought. Striking the proper balance between too little color and too much color is a difficult task.

Few newspapers—*USA Today* is a successful exception—understand the proper relationship of color elements on a page. Too often, a visual journalist will add "just one more piece" of color to a page design, enough to make the page into a helter-skelter pattern of colors. Color can attract readers, but too much of it, like a plaid necktie with a Hawaiian shirt, also can turn observers off (Color Plate 17).

While some newspapers are rushing headlong into more color use, others are watching and waiting for improved technology to overcome one of the disadvantages of color —the time it takes to produce it. And because color takes longer to produce—sometimes five times longer than black and white—it is difficult to use it on breaking news stories, either photographically or in an informational graphic.

GUIDELINES FOR HANDLING COLOR

The use of color never should make it more difficult for a reader to see, read or understand printed material. Visual journalists need to understand color before it can be used effectively. For instance, some colors, such as red, have important psychological meanings. Red "says" hot or danger and is exciting. Blue, on the other hand, "says" ice or cold and is more calming than red. Examples of the effect color has on emotions can be seen on the walls of a dental clinic, where gradations of blue

INSIDE LOOK

Warren Skipper

Production Manager, Seminole Production Center   *The Orlando Sentinel*

are used to ease patients' fears, or on the walls of a fast food restaurant, which are painted orange to stimulate the appetite. Understanding the relationship of color to emotions can greatly improve the use of color in the newspaper.

An example of an improper choice of color would be the use of blue and green in a graphic about fireworks. More appropriate colors would be red and orange—"hot" and "exciting" colors (Color Plate 18).

Sometimes, a newspaper will use color to help project an image. By limiting the use of certain colors, the paper can "tell" readers that it is a "calm" or "exciting" publication.

Pleasing colors, such as a combination of light red and light yellow to produce sand or a combination of blue and red to produce purple, are preferable. Readers should not be repelled by odd or unusual combinations of color unless the story specifically calls for them (punk hairdos, for example).

When color elements such as photographs or illustrations are combined with color type, the visual journalist needs to be aware of what the primary colors are in each element. Sometimes, the most attractive pages are created by "picking up" a color from a photograph or illustration and using it in a color screen. A color in the primary piece of art or a complementary color may be used. If too many color elements are used, however, the result may be a page that is too intense (Color Plate 19).

Care also should be taken to ensure good quality in color photographs. A

Warren Skipper, production manager of the Seminole Production Center of *The Orlando Sentinel,* said it takes "total company commitment" to produce a consistently good newspaper.

He said *The Orlando Sentinel* became a leader in quality reproduction and the use of color because every department at the newspaper was committed to improving the product. "Top management said, 'Let's buy the equipment and let's train the people.'" Skipper added: "Once you have commitment from top management, you can begin to break down barriers that make it difficult for editorial people and production personnel to work together on problems.

"We purchased a lot of new equipment, such as a color scanner and high-speed offset presses. We wanted to know the potential and limitations of this new equipment. Through meetings and constant analysis we were able to improve the paper. We reached a level of sophistication that allowed us to produce a product, with daily color, that few other newspapers could produce."

Skipper, who has overall responsibility for the products, property and employees in one of *The Orlando Sentinel*'s two printing plants, did not start out in production. He was director of photography of *The Sentinel* until 1982 when he transferred to the production

side of the paper as one of the two people assigned to quality assurance.

The other person in quality assurance was Bob Crandall. He and Skipper were given the job of working with all divisions of the newspaper to produce standards that would allow *The Sentinel* to publish consistently good color.

"My strength at the beginning was photography and layout," Skipper said. "His was production. Between the two of us we could evaluate and correct the problems that prevented the newspaper from achieving a higher level of excellence.

"In the early 1980s, we set up a quality-control committee that started weekly meetings, which still continue, to bring together representatives of various divisions of the newspaper to discuss different quality problems. Departments like advertising, editorial and production talk about problem solving in a no-holds-barred meeting where no one gets wounded. It is an educational process. We have discovered how little we understand about the process various departments have to go through to produce a daily product."

Throughout the early 1980s, Skipper and Crandall worked hard to bring together the departments at *The Sentinel* and to gradually improve the quality of the paper. When the position of production manager of the Seminole Production Center opened in May 1987, Skipper said he "wanted the challenge and they threw me at it."

He said along with a commitment for excellence must come standardization of the production process. He noted: "To maximize the equipment, everyone has to do things to a standard. You have to standardize the process and make it predictable. You must establish a norm, and once you have mastered that on a consistent basis, you can rise to the next level. You raise your standard slowly from a given reference point, and you can begin to improve the process."

He added that a newspaper can produce a high-quality product without spending huge amounts of money on the latest equipment. "The best you can do in the production of a newspaper, from the photographer on the street to the kid on a bike delivering the paper, is maximize the process.

"You can take a standard automobile straight from the showroom floor, and if you neglect it by not paying attention to details, you'll only get so much mileage and it will only go so fast. But if you work with it every day, use the right oil and gas, keep it cleaned and lubed, the same car will run better and faster longer.

"Newspaper reproduction and color is the same. It will be better quality over a period of time because people paid attention to it. Our equipment is fairly standard. Our presses and scanner are several years old and are not state of the art anymore. We have a standard mix of photographers, some just getting in the industry, some who have been around for a long time. They use standard equipment. There is nothing extraordinary, nothing 'Star Wars' about the equipment we use. We don't have Scitex or pagination.

"But the commitment and the communication between departments are still there. All the shared information over the years has raised the level of awareness and quality in all areas of the newspaper. It has allowed us to find problems quickly and go in and correct them."

Throwing megabucks at the latest equipment will not solve any problems, Skipper added. "It will just give you mega-headaches," he said. "Instead of spending time looking at and talking about equipment, the newspaper industry needs to spend more time training the people who run the equipment. The world's greatest camera with all the bells and whistles will not make a good photojournalist. Good equipment coupled with the proper training and experience make a good photojournalist."

Skipper said he does not see any great technologic advances in the 1990s at The Sentinel. "We're doing real well now. I don't see us making any major breakthroughs or changes in the foreseeable future in terms of what the product looks like. I do see constant improvement. But there won't be major improvements like in the early 1980s when we went from letterpress to offset and changed our color separations. That's when we went from not too good to pretty darn good.

"What I see in the industry in the 1990s is more newspapers getting better. There seems to be a stronger commitment now to improve the product. That will make newspapers look, read and reproduce better than 10 years ago. In 1978 there were few good-looking newspapers. In 1988 there were a bunch. There will be more in the 1990s as the difference between newspapers' production methods becomes smaller and smaller. We are beginning to look more and more alike. Computers will continue to make reproduction and color more consistent in the 1990s. They will give better controls to those newspapers that look good one day but bad the next."

picture should not be used simply because it is in color—a bad color photograph will detract from the good ones on the page.

In a speech to the American Newspaper Publishers Association, Craig C. Standen, president of the Newspaper Advertising Bureau in New York, said three factors contribute to the effective use of color.

✔ Rigorous standards
✔ Proper training of editorial and production people
✔ A commitment from the publisher to produce quality color

More than anything else in a newspaper's production cycle, color requires attention to many details. By paying attention to even the smallest of those details, a visual journalist can create successful color pages (Color Plate 20).

SUGGESTED EXERCISES

1. Define the following terms:
    a. Typesetter
    b. Galley
    c. Area composition
    d. Pagination
    e. Hot metal
    f. Cold type
    g. Velox
    h. Overlay
    i. Pixel

2. Explain the following printing processes:
    a. Letterpress
    b. Offset
    c. Flexography

3. Explain the process in which a half-tone screen is made.

4. What are the primary colors? How are they processed for reproduction on a newspaper page?

5. What is spot color? Mechanical color? Process color? Clip examples of each from a daily newspaper.

6. Critique two front pages that contain color. Is it used effectively? Is there too much color on the pages? How would you improve the pages?

CHAPTER EIGHT

Legal and Ethical Issues

All journalists, whether they handle visuals or words, must be familiar with the legal and ethical framework within which they work. Neither the court of public opinion nor the U.S. legal system distinguishes between "visual" and "written" material in newspapers; that is, pictures and graphics, as well as words, that defame can be ruled libelous.

Even though the First Amendment to the U.S. Constitution says Congress shall make no law abridging freedom of speech or of the press, there are limitations placed on journalists. Quite simply, the courts decide, on a case-by-case basis, whether actions taken by journalists are legally permissible. That means journalists must be knowledgeable about significant decisions.

Although the ethical problems that journalists encounter might not mean an expensive lawsuit, an outcry of public opinion against a newspaper sometimes can be more damaging than a courtroom drama. Newspapers do not exist in a vacuum. Any publication that continually disregards community standards of good taste and obscenity is headed for problems caused by loss of trust, readership and advertising support.

The visual journalist is confronted with many of the same issues that affect reporters and editors in the newsroom: libel, privacy and copyright.

LIBEL

Three requirements must be met before a person can sue for **libel** and win:

- *The information must be communicated to a third party.* If a visual is published in a newspaper, it is communicated to a third party.
- *Identification.* The person being defamed must be clearly identified, though not necessarily by name.
- *Harmful effect.* The person being defamed has to be held up to public hatred, ridicule or scorn.

Most libel suits do not grow from aggressive news reporting, but rather result from carelessness. For example, an informational graphic on drug abuse among teenagers probably would present no problem. But what happens if, in an effort to use a photograph inside the graphic, a visual journalist goes to the photo file and pulls a picture of a teenager sitting on a street curb who turns out to be a member of a prominent family in town, never has used drugs and is easily identified in the graphic. The visual journalist and the newspaper could face a lawsuit.

Like the reporter or editor, the visual journalist always must be careful with the meaning of words. Every cutline and every informational graphic should be checked to make certain the words they contain do not damage a person's reputation.

Quotes

A newspaper is responsible for every statement that it prints, even if the statement is a quote from a source. Consider a photographer taking pictures at an accident scene. While getting cutline information, the photographer is told by a police officer, "I'm happy that no-good thief was in a wreck. Now he'll be off the street for a while and won't be able to burglarize homes in the neighborhood." Because in the United States a person is presumed innocent until proven guilty, it could be libelous to call a person a thief. The fact that a police officer made the statement does not reduce the newspaper's level of liability. Just because a source says something does not necessarily make it correct or libel-proof.

Other statements beside those that imply the commission of a criminal offense are potentially libelous as well. A statement that suggests infection with a communicable disease could have a harmful effect. So could statements that impute inability to perform the duties of office or employment or statements that prejudice a person in his or her profession or trade. In truth, every sentence is potentially libelous. So is every visual. That should not make journalists afraid to do their jobs, but it should help them realize how important it is to have a basic understanding of libel law.

Libel Defenses

A number of defenses can be used if a libel suit is filed. **Conditional defenses** are viable if certain conditions or qualifications are met; **absolute defenses** have no conditions or qualifications.

The conditional defense most often used by reporters is the **privilege of reporting.** This defense flows from fair and accurate reporting of official proceedings and fair and accurate reporting of information from official documents and court records. Privilege of reporting allows journalists to cover state legislative sessions, court trials, congressional hearings and other official proceedings. But it is limited to fair and accurate reporting; extraneous libelous matter cannot be used. If a school board member accuses the superintendent at a board meeting of embezzling district funds, a photographer can take the superintendent's picture and repeat the charge in the cutline. However, any interpretation of the board member's charge would not necessarily be protected.

Another conditional defense is known as **fair comment and criticism.** This defense covers journalists who write or illustrate opinions about matters of public concern. In these cases it must be clear that the allegedly libelous statement or illustration is an opinion, not an expression of fact. The defense does not protect erroneous factual reporting.

There are several absolute defenses, the most ironclad being the **statute of limitations.** A libel suit must be filed within a specified period set by state law; normally, the period is one, two or three years. In most states, truth is an absolute defense. (In a few states, truth is a conditional defense; the statements must have been published for justifiable ends and with good motives.) Another conditional defense, known as **consent** or *authorization,* can be used if a journalist obtains a source's permission before making a libelous statement about the source.

If conditional or absolute defenses cannot be used successfully, the defendant probably will be assessed damages. However, the defendant can cite **partial defenses,** which may help mitigate the damages. Partial defenses include publication of a **retraction,** which clearly admits erroneous reporting, or the introduction of facts showing that even though the defendant erred, there was no gross negligence or ill will.

The New York Times Rule

Common and state laws do provide journalists with defenses against libel suits. A federal rule, commonly called the **actual malice defense** is a constitutional defense first articulated by the U.S. Supreme Court in the 1964 *New York Times Co. v. Sullivan* case. In its ruling, the court nationalized the law of libel to provide a constitutional defense when public officials are the plaintiffs.

Suit was filed after *The Times* published an advertisement in 1960 that said, in essence, that certain Southern officials were meeting the civil rights movement in the South with a wave of aggression. L. B. Sullivan, a Montgomery, Ala., commissioner, filed the suit. The Alabama courts awarded Sullivan $500,000 in damages for the false portions of the advertisement. Subsequently, however, the U.S. Supreme Court reversed the decision, ruling that

to collect damages, a public official, such as Sullivan, would have to prove the defendant acted with *actual malice,* that is, with knowledge that the information was false or with reckless disregard of whether it was false or not.

The Sullivan ruling gave the media protection against suits brought by public officials, even when the statements in question were false, as long as the statements were not published with actual malice. Even though the Sullivan ruling has been modified over the years, journalists are still well-protected if the plaintiff is a public person. They need to be careful, however, when dealing with private people.

PRIVACY

Although the visual journalist deals with the issue of privacy mainly from an ethical point of view, he or she also must pay attention to the legal issues of privacy. According to the Reporters Committee for Freedom of the Press, the major areas of privacy affecting the visual journalist are unreasonable intrusion, placing a person in a false light and misappropriation of a name or likeness.

Unreasonable Intrusion

Photographers must acknowledge that not all events or people can be nor want to be photographed and that the press must avoid intrusion into a person's privacy. Generally, if the event or person is in a public place and there is not an **unreasonable intrusion** on privacy, the photographer has the right to take pictures. For example, a photograph of a drunken football fan is not an

intrusion, the courts have ruled. However, a photo of a woman with her dress unexpectedly blown up in an amusement park fun house was found to be intrusive.

In semipublic places such as restaurants, the photographer needs to secure permission of the owners to avoid trespassing charges. In places where a person has a reasonable right of privacy, such as a private hospital room, permission must be given by the person before pictures can be taken. Consent must be obtained from someone who can grant it validly. A child cannot give consent for a photographer to enter the family home and take pictures; likewise, renters can give a photographer consent to take pictures only of the portion of the building they are renting.

Placing a Person in a False Light

If a photographer knowingly places a subject's image in a **false light** or in an untrue setting or situation, the photographer may face a lawsuit. The courts have ruled, however, that such "false light" must cause injury and must be offensive to a "reasonable" person.

Most often, it is not a photograph that puts a false light on a subject, but the caption or accompanying story. For instance, running a photograph of an honest taxi driver in a story about dishonest ones is actionable. Likewise, using a photograph of a group of young men on a street corner in an informational graphic about the unemployed might be a dangerous practice —perhaps the men were on a lunch break.

Misappropriation of a Name or Likeness

A photographer does not need permission to photograph a crowd of people at a public event, so long as the material is used only for news stories. When an image is used for commercial purposes without permission, however, the photographer (and his or her newspaper) can be held accountable for **misappropriation of a name or likeness,** that is for the *appropriation* of that person's image. For example, a photographer takes a striking photograph of a child at a parade. The image is so beautiful that the photographer has a poster made of the picture. Sale of the poster without the consent of the child's parents would be considered an appropriation of a person's likeness.

COPYRIGHT

In simple terms, **copyright** represents a claim to ownership. Generally, a newspaper owns the material its employees produce. Most newspapers have a copyright notice on their front page, which means that another company or individual has no right to copy and distribute the material in the newspaper without permission.

When the visual journalist is seeking material to illustrate stories, he or she must pay careful attention to the proper use of copyrighted material. Someone else's work cannot be used without permission from the copyright holder. It would be a *copyright violation,* then, to reproduce photographs from a book to illustrate a news or feature story on the same topic. Without permission from the copyright owner—either the book publisher or the photographer—

the newspaper could be held responsible for the "theft" of the material. In addition, an informational graphic from another newspaper cannot be used without permission to duplicate it. Copying such a graphic would be similar to plagiarizing written material—both unethical and illegal.

Material from a wire service or syndicate is handled differently, however. That material is purchased by the subscribing newspaper, which may use the material as it sees fit. That allows a visual journalist to combine material from an Associated Press or syndicate graphic with a locally generated graphic, as long as the newspaper is a member of the Associated Press or subscribes to the syndicate. Subscribers to a syndicate cannot *sell* the material, however, because the resale could be a violation of copyright ownership.

When gathering statistics for informational graphics, the visual journalist should be aware of any copyright restrictions on the source material. Some surveys, for example, are done for a company, and permission must be obtained for their use. Generally, the surveys are available for use if proper credit is given the company that owns the copyright.

Information that is not, and cannot be, copyrighted includes material obtained from the U.S. government. All of the statistics and other information generated by the hundreds of government agencies are available without copyright restrictions.

CAMERAS IN THE COURTROOM

It is against the law to take pictures in courtrooms in some states and in federal courts. And although most of the states

do allow some form of photographic coverage in a courtroom, certain guidelines, usually set by the presiding judge, must be followed.

For example, a judge may allow one silent television camera and one still camera, as long as the shutter cannot be heard and flash is not used. The photographers must remain in one location. In this case, the cameras become **pool cameras,** and their pictures are shared with all of the media. By permitting a limited number of cameras, the judge can maintain the decorum of the courtroom.

Obviously, a photojournalist does not want to break the law. Therefore, he or she should check the rules in the courtrooms in his or her state regarding the use of cameras. Most courts have public information officers who can provide details on courtroom cameras.

ETHICAL CONCERNS

Society calls for journalistic accountability. Although there is no law mandating that journalists be responsible or ethical, journalists should feel bound to certain standards of behavior. With this in mind, many newspapers have established codes of behavior; others follow the Code of Ethics published by the Society of Professional Journalists. Visual and word journalists who violate these codes risk losing their readers and, perhaps, their jobs.

In his book on journalistic ethics, "The Imperative of Freedom," Professor John Merrill of Louisiana State University outlines some of the ethical concerns faced by journalists:

It has always been difficult to discuss this; law is much easier, for what is legal is a matter of law. What is ethical transcends law, for many actions are legal, but not ethical. And there are no "ethical codebooks" to consult in order to settle ethical disputes. Ethics is primarily personal; law is primarily social. . . . It is well to establish that ethics deals with voluntary actions. If a journalist has no control over his decisions or actions, then there is no need to talk of ethics. What are voluntary actions? Those which a journalist could have done differently had he wished. Sometimes journalists, like others, try to excuse their wrong actions by saying that these actions were not personally chosen but assigned to them— or otherwise forced on them—by editors or other superiors. Such coercion may indeed occur in some situations (such as a dictatorial press system) where the consequences to the journalist going against an order may be dire. But for an American journalist not to be able to "will" his journalistic actions—at least at the present time—is unthinkable; if he says that he is not able and that he "has to" do this-or-that, he is only exhibiting his ethical weaknesses and inauthenticity. The journalist who is concerned with ethics—with the quality of his actions—is, of course, one who wishes to be virtuous.

The visual journalist must be concerned about two major ethical issues:

✓ *Taste.* Is the material acceptable to the wide range of readers of the newspaper?
✓ *Privacy.* Does the public's right to know outweigh the news subject's right to privacy?

A MATTER OF TASTE

What constitutes good taste has been discussed, argued and shouted about in countless newsrooms. First, journalists, always anxious to grab readers with stories and visuals, may be more open or liberal in their treatment of sensitive material than their readers would be. Second, it is difficult to get a clear understanding of a community's standards because one group's vocal representation may not accurately reflect the majority's opinion. Third, tastes vary from community to community and country to country. What is acceptable in one community or country may not be in another; what is acceptable to one group of readers may not be to another.

Many of the mass-circulation papers in England, for example, are tabloids that run pictures of women naked from the waist up. The photos often run on Page 3 and are used solely as sales gimmicks; they have no news value. No daily newspaper publisher in the United States has yet dared to use the same gimmick to sell newspapers. Of course, tastes do change—what was unacceptable five years ago might be accepted five years from today. Nevertheless, it appears unlikely that American newspapers will follow the lead of some of the racy tabloids in England. Instead, the issue of taste will involve more subtle material, and it will continue to be decided on a case-by-case and newspaper-by-newspaper basis.

When dealing with material of questionable taste, the visual journalist must weigh both the public's right to know and the news or educational value of the material. The journalist's role is not to play censor with either words or pictures. However, a visual journalist is one of the ethical gatekeepers at a newspaper, and a picture of questionable taste and little value should not be allowed through the gates.

When visual journalists talk about taste and acceptability, they often are referring to photographs. Among the major types of images that stir readers are extremely violent photographs, those that depict the moment of death or that show bodies; photographs of grief or private moments in public places; and photographs of nudity or sexual behavior that go beyond some citizens' sense of good taste.

Extremely Violent Photographs

Although striking images of violence are becoming more commonplace, many editors debate the appropriateness of them, insisting that sensitivity take precedence over censorship. Even though newspaper readers—and television viewers—today see more graphic images of death than they did 10 or 20 years ago, graphically violent photographs are still shocking. The world is not necessarily any more violent now than it was 20 years ago, but the media's ability to bring back news and images is much greater than ever before.

Since the Vietnam War, newspapers have had to deal with the question of how to show death and violence. Vietnam was no more violent than any other war, but it was reported and photographed unlike any other. During World War II, because of censorship, primitive technology for transmitting photographs and a different sense of what was tasteful, the more graphic photographs never were published.

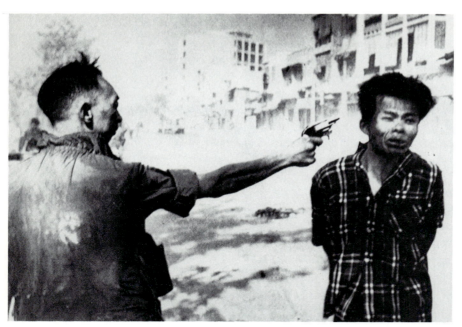

Figure 8.1   Eddie Adams's photo showing execution of Viet Cong prisoner in Saigon

The Vietnam War was different. Technology and changing tastes and standards enabled Americans to see the war on television nightly and in magazines and newspapers. One of the most graphic photographs from that bloody conflict was taken by Associated Press photographer Eddie Adams on Feb. 1, 1968. His photograph, which won a Pulitzer Prize, showed the execution of a Viet Cong prisoner by a South Vietnamese police chief in the middle of a Saigon street (Figure 8.1). The photo shocked and horrified readers around the world. And it presented a dilemma for newspapers: Was it too graphic?

Some editors argued that such a photograph accurately depicted a major news event and reflected the brutality of war. Others said it was too brutal and hence too shocking for readers to see. Many editors applied what is known as the **breakfast standard:** How shocking will the picture be to people as they read the newspaper over the breakfast table?

While Adams' photograph is still powerful and shocking today, and its news value is still clear, it has been followed over the years with other events and other shocking photographs.

When former Pennsylvania Treasurer R. Budd Dwyer called a press conference on Jan. 22, 1987, journalists expected him to resign because of his conviction in a kickback scandal. Instead, he pulled out a gun from an envelope and killed himself in front of reporters and photographers (Figure 8.2).

Dwyer's public suicide presented a news judgment dilemma: How important were the explicit photographs and how much play should they receive? Except in Pennsylvania and nearby communities, there was little notice of Dwyer's conviction. Most newspapers in the United States ignored the conviction of a relatively minor state official. However, when Dwyer killed himself in front of the cameras, he became a national story. The sequence of photographs recording the event included several gruesome images. Editors faced two challenges: Where and how to play the story and what picture or pictures to run or not run.

Few U.S. newspapers used the most violent and graphic photographs; most used only the photograph showing Dwyer holding the gun and waving off journalists (Figures 8.3-8.7). Editors said that their readers did not need to see the more graphic pictures to understand the brutal and shocking nature of the story.

Most editors and visual journalists, and many readers, would agree that it is appropriate to use a violent photograph accompanying a *major* news story. But what of a story that becomes major only because of the violent photographs taken at the event? In an unscientific survey done for a report presented to the Associated Press Managing Editors' convention in 1987, 21 percent of the editors questioned received strong

Figure 8.2   Sequence of photos showing R. Budd Dwyer committing suicide at press conference

Figure 8.3   Dwyer suicide photos in the Philadelphia *Daily News*

Figure 8.4   Dwyer photo in *The Raleigh (N.C.) Times*

Figure 8.5   Dwyer photos in *The Philadelphia Inquirer*

Figure 8.6 Dwyer photo in the *Gloucester* (Mass.) *Daily Times*

Figure 8.7 Dwyer photo in *The Bakersfield Californian*

objections from their readers after running photos of Dwyer's suicide. Twenty-three percent said they received modest objections, and 48 percent said they received no calls or letters.

Photographs of Grief or Private Moments

Sometimes, a national story can have a devastating impact on a family. When Mount St. Helens erupted in 1980 in Washington, a *San Jose Mercury News* photographer, George Wedding, photographed the body of an "unidentified" young boy lying in the back of a pickup, a testament to the volcano's violence (Figure 8.8). The photograph, shot from a helicopter, was one of the first visual reports showing the death and destruction caused by the volcano. It would be followed by scores of pictures and stories as the world's eyes focused on this northwest corner of the United States.

When the *Mercury News* published the photograph, the boy's family did not know if he was alive or dead; they learned of the tragedy from the photo. Speaking at a seminar on privacy and the press in 1986, Wedding said he believes the public's right to know outweighed the family's right to privacy.

The Mount St. Helens photograph was of significant national news importance, but what about photos with only local interest? They can stir up problems. In 1985, *The Bakersfield Californian* ran a photograph by John Harte on the bottom of Page One that showed a drowned boy and grieving members of the boy's family (Figure 8.9). Readers protested the publication of the photograph so vociferously that the paper

now has a strong policy against taking photographs of deceased persons. *The Californian* originally ran the photograph because it believed that it might help prevent further deaths in the community by alerting readers to a rise in drownings. But the storm of anger from the community that followed the publication of the picture highlighted a major ethical concern of editors: How close is too close when showing death?

When dealing with photographs that show violence or death, editors must consider proximity, the closeness of the event to the newspaper's readers. The closer to home an event occurs, the more likely readers will be upset over the use of graphic news photographs of the event. Photographs of dead Iranians are probably less shocking to American readers than are photographs of American solders killed in a rescue attempt of U.S. hostages (Figure 8.10). And those photos are less shocking than one in a community newspaper showing a drowning in town.

The standard of proximity to determine story and visual play always has been used by newspapers. They generally present news that relates to their readers; the number of deaths or injuries may not be as important. That's why a public suicide in India or a ferry boat sinking in Thailand would get little play in U.S. newspapers. A photograph and story of a local car accident would take precedence. Such devotion to local coverage can be a double-edged sword, however. Readers *are* interested in coverage of their community, but when local events such as accidents are covered, many readers will know the victims and may protest the use of photos showing grief and private moments.

Figure 8.8   Photo of young boy killed by Mount St. Helens eruption

Figure 8.10   Photo of American soldier killed in hostage rescue attempt

Figure 8.9   Photo of drowned boy and grieving family members

Sensitivity Toward Victims and Readers

Visual journalists must realize that running a particularly violent or graphic photograph may upset many members of the community. The decision to use or not use a picture must be made on a case-by-case basis. Factors in the decision include:

✓ *Proximity.* Is the event relevant locally?
✓ *Timeliness.* Is the development old or new?
✓ *Conflict.* Is the event unresolved? Does anyone care?
✓ *Prominence.* Are newsworthy people involved?
✓ *Consequence.* What impact will there be on readers?

Figure 8.11   Photo of grieving daughter holding picture of murdered mother

✓ *Human interest.* Are there unique, interesting elements?

A visual journalist should be aware that a visual has the potential to do more harm than good and can cause more pain than enlightenment. An increasing number of readers—and some editors— are expressing concern over the news media's occasional disregard of an individual's or a family's right to privacy, especially during a time of grief. Although television often is blamed for being more intrusive than newspapers, newspaper photographers also must be sensitive to the issue.

Newspapers are concerned about the rights of victims. Some are issuing guidelines to staff members on how to deal with family members during moments of grief. Often, those guidelines place strict limits on intrusion by staff members. Some editors, however, strongly believe that not publishing a photograph of a news event represents a form of self-censorship and a failure to live up to the responsibility of the media to accurately and fairly portray events in the town, city or area they cover. There must be a balance then between covering the news and self-censorship based on sensitivity toward members of the community.

Visually, one of the more difficult events to deal with is a funeral. Often, family and friends (and readers) view photographs taken at a funeral as an invasion of privacy. But what happens when the newspaper believes the deceased person was important enough to warrant coverage of his or her funeral?

There is no easy answer, as editors and photographers at the *San Francisco Chronicle* learned. While covering the

funeral of a local couple who were murdered, *Chronicle* photographer Eric Luse photographed the daughter holding a picture of her slain mother (Figure 8.11). The news editor on duty when Luse turned in his photograph saw the picture as an invasion of the family's privacy and did not run it. The photograph eventually ran with a follow-up story, but the impact of a breaking news story was lost. Who was right? Unfortunately, there is no ethical codebook that gives the answer.

Photographs of Nudity or Sexual Behavior

Each photo must be judged on its news and its photographic merits. And visual journalists must encourage the news-

paper's photographers to select the most appropriate image. For instance, when former Vice President Nelson Rockefeller gave the "finger" to a group of hecklers at a New York rally in 1976, editors had to weigh the newsworthiness of the photograph against the shock value of the gesture (Figure 8.12). Many newspapers ran the photograph, believing that the news value of the vice president getting that angry and expressing himself in a "normal" manner outweighed the bad taste shown in the gesture.

But where do the editor and visual journalist draw the line? When does news value become shock value? When Jessica Hahn, a former church secretary, brought down the television ministry of Jim Bakker in 1987, she became

Figure 8.12   Photo of Nelson Rockefeller giving the "finger" to hecklers

Figure 8.13   Photo of Jessica Hahn in *Playboy* magazine as sent by the Associated Press

Figure 8.14   Photo of protesters "mooning" the camera

Figure 8.15   Photo of revellers "mooning" the camera

genuinely newsworthy. However, when Hahn posed for *Playboy* magazine and the Associated Press moved a photograph (from *Playboy*) of her in a see-through outfit, the visual journalist had to apply standards of good taste along with standards of newsworthiness (Figure 8.13). Would the publication of such a photograph add anything to the story? Would it offend many readers?

And what about bare bottoms? Few newspapers would print a picture of them, no matter how newsworthy. Two examples, one from Agence France-Presse during an anti-nuclear demonstration (Figure 8.14) and the other from a celebration honoring the Golden Gate Bridge in San Francisco (Figure 8.15) probably would offend too many readers for the little news or information they contain. With these type of photos, the visual journalist must ask: How much is too much?

George Wedding

Director of Photography   *The Sacramento Bee*

In 1980, George M. Wedding, then a photographer at the *San Jose* (Calif.) *Mercury News,* made a photo that he, and the world, never will forget.

It was a picture of Andy. But no one knew the boy's name when his picture was taken. To the world, he was merely an "unidentified" boy lying dead in the back of a pickup after the May 18, 1980, eruption of Mount St. Helens in Washington. The dead child had his hands on his stomach, in a wrenchingly peaceful pose.

Wedding was in a helicopter when he took the picture of Andy, who along with his father and brother had gone camping and were asphyxiated by volcanic ash that blanketed their campsite $4\frac{1}{2}$ miles from the mountain. Wedding had no way of knowing who the boy was. His photo was distributed worldwide by the Associated Press even before Andy's mother had known her son's fate.

Why didn't Wedding's ethics prevent him from taking the photograph of Andy? Did the public's right to know overshadow a family's right to privacy at a tragic moment? Wedding said he has asked himself these questions in the years since Mount St. Helens and he's still convinced he did the right thing.

"There certainly was a collision of two principles of the public's right to know versus privacy," Wedding said. "As a journalist on the scene seeing all of the devastation, I felt overwhelmed. As I look back on it, the feeling of being awed by the mountain is still with me.

"I felt at the time that I had made an important picture. I knew that if I got back to the wire service office on time, and we got the picture transmitted, editors would have to make a difficult

decision whether to print the picture or not. As a photographer you try to make pictures as they happen, and then you make decisions after the fact on whether they should be used or not."

Wedding said he could not quit thinking about the picture after he made it. "I thought about it driving back to the AP office and while I was developing and printing the photo. I decided it was the most vivid scene that I had been exposed to. It communicated the type of feeling that I was experiencing. I made my decision when I decided to print it and show it to editors. Nearly 10 years later, I still feel I made the right decision."

After the photo was transmitted, newspapers throughout the world used it. A relative of Andy saw the picture and informed Andy's mother. According to Wedding: "The mother did not look at the picture for a long time. She didn't ask to see it."

Wedding said that months after the eruption, Andy's mother contacted him after tracing the source of the photograph. "We met on the campus of Stanford University and took a two- or three-hour walk. She expressed concern about how the media make decisions. She was articulate and sensitive. She was trying to work through what happened. She was a sweet, sweet person who didn't express anger or resentment.

"She asked a lot of questions that you would expect any reader to ask, like why it was necessary to publish a picture like that. We talked about the reasons, and I think she finally understood that there was a different point of view. In her last gesture to me, she opened an envelope and pulled out a family portrait of her husband and two children. She told me that she didn't

want me to carry that awful image of her son with me the rest of my life. The faces were sweet and lovely. It was a moving, touching gesture. It really affected me. I remember that moment to this day."

Wedding noted that a photographer's ethics are personal, and they play a role in every picture he or she takes. "When you are out in the field, you have to bring with you a sense of journalistic ethics and training and all of those things that make up who you are. You use all of that background when you decide what to make pictures of. It's not an easy task to go out into the world and make a picture that tells a story. You have to make subjective decisions.

"I think photographers should think about self-censorship. Editors will not like this, and I am an editor now, but as a photographer I never showed an editor a picture that I didn't want published. If I saw something that I questioned in my mind and arrived at the conclusion that it shouldn't be published, I simply never showed it to an editor. Photographers with a strong sense of purpose probably do a lot more editing in the camera than people realize. That probably would horrify many editors, who believe a photographer should shoot everything and decide later, or let the editors decide what to publish. My ethics drive me on whether or not to show a photograph to an editor."

He added that he does not shoot a photograph if "in my subjective opinion it does not communicate the ideas that I think are important to telling a story. At times that may be pictures that horrify people. It also may be images more

Continued

INSIDE LOOK

simple than that, such as pictures that don't tell the story that I think needs to be told. Reporters and photographers make these subjective decisions all the time.

"Part of the artistry involved and part of the challenge is to make a photograph that communicates what an event felt like. But it must be done so that people will be touched and will be aware of what happened. The goal is not to make readers turn their eyes away and forget about the picture. The goal is to communicate in an effective way. Many photos fail because they communicate only the horror or the sensational part of an event. They fail to give an insight into what we are seeing."

After a photographer has made a subjective decision on what pictures to shoot and print, an editor makes subjective decisions on how to use the pictures. Today's computer technology allows an editor to crop, size and even manipulate the image. Once again, ethics come into play.

"I'm a great believer in techno-logy," Wedding said. "Computers and digitized images are changing the technology of photography, but the technology can be used ethically. The very real danger is that this editing power of digitizing photos and altering them is coming to personal computers. When it gets into that realm and out of the realm of $350,000 machines, then a whole new level of people have power that only photographers previously had. Those people may not have training or exposure to traditional values of documentary photography. We're going to have all these people faced with the decision whether or not to manipulate pictures. Aunt Emma will be able to pixel out Uncle John after the divorce so that she can still have her wedding picture in the album.

"Photo manipulation has the potential to erode the power of a photograph as a document of fact. And with a digital image, we don't even have a negative to go back to. There's no more 'photo-graphic proof.' "

Wedding also criticized the use of *illustrative photojournalism* (posed photographs) in newspapers, if it is used to trick readers. Illustrative or conceptual photographs usually are perfectly executed in terms of lighting, detailing, propping and composition. They often are taken in a controlled studio environment, using models. They may or may not represent fact. Although such photographs have been used for years in advertising and are now being used in more and more newspapers, Wedding said they are dangerous if the reader doesn't know that they are not real moments in real life. Wedding added that although "there are a lot of exciting images created by studio photographers and advertising pho-tographers, there is not much good illustrative photography created by photojournalists. Many are trying to do with a shoestring budget what has been pioneered with big bucks, and they're trying to do it in too little time."

He said *The Sacramento Bee* is trying to work out a policy on docu-mentary and illustrative photo-graphs. "In 1988 we don't have a policy on what we will or won't do in terms of manipulating pictures. A news publication's credibility is its most important asset. We recognize the value and need for illustrations, but the readers need to know. Rather than pose the picture and pretend it's real, we need to be honest. All newspapers and magazines need to develop policies on how to handle manipulation in illus-trations and digital images to head off future problems. Digital capabilities necessitate this.

"The technology for digital picture editing also should remain in the hands of photographers and picture editors and not on news desks and in art departments. It is the best way to ensure consistency in approach.

"Photographers should inject whimsy and fantasy into their illustrations so readers do not confuse them with documentary photojournalism. Those who make illustrations too real are compromising the traditional values of photojournalism—truth, fairness, accurate reporting with a camera and objectivity whenever possible."

Figure 8.16   Graphic photo of S. Brian Willson after being run over by train

SUGGESTED EXERCISES

1. What three requirements must be met before a person has grounds to sue for libel?

2. What are conditional libel defenses? Explain each one.

3. What are absolute libel defenses? Explain each one.

4. Discuss the actual malice defense. When was it first articulated? What protections does it give to journalists?

5. What is unreasonable intrusion? Give an example of what you would consider unreasonable intrusion.

6. What is false light? Cite an example.

7. What is misappropriation of a name or likeness? Give an example.

8. You see an informational graphic in another newspaper that you want to use for a story in your newspaper. Describe the procedures you must follow so that you do not violate copyright laws.

9. What is the "breakfast standard"? Can you find at least two examples of photos that you think violate the standard?

10. What are the factors that should be used to weigh a visual for newsworthiness?

11. After S. Brian Willson was run over by a Navy train during a demonstration at the Naval Weapons Station in Concord, Calif., the Associated Press ran four photographs, three from *The (Oakland) Tribune* and one from *The (San Francisco) Examiner*. Willson, of San Rafael, Calif., had been leading a protest opposing alleged arms shipments from the Navy facility to Central America. He was injured critically when he was hit by the train while kneeling on the tracks after a press conference. The photos were graphic; the cutlines on them warned editors that they may be objectionable to some readers. In the photo showing the train, Willson's severed foot inside his shoe can be seen next to the track (Figure 8.16). Look at the photo carefully. Would you use or not use it and why?

12. A photographer takes a picture of a dramatic rescue of a 2-year-old boy submerged nearly 30 minutes in an icy lake. The picture shows a firefighter holding the boy and giving him mouth-to-mouth resuscitation. At the point the picture is taken the boy is still alive, although in critical condition. An hour later, an editor has the picture in hand, she's right on deadline and she still does not know if the boy is going to live. If you were this editor, would you use the photograph? What legal and ethical considerations would weigh on your decision?

PART TWO

Informational Graphics

CHAPTER NINE

The History of Informational Graphics

Newspaper informational graphics—diagrams, maps, charts, tabular lists—were not invented by the *Chicago Tribune* or *USA Today*. To find their beginnings, we can go back at least 180 years to April 7, 1806, when *The Times* of London ran a diagram of a murder scene on Page One (Figure 9.1).

The use of informational graphics can be traced even farther back than the early 1800s, when newspapers started using them. The earliest maps, created on clay tablets, were geography maps that showed only locations. The true informational graphic emerged in 1686 when Edmond Halley published "An Historical Account of the Trade Winds, and Monsoons, Observable in the Seas Between and Near the Tropicks: With an Attempt to Assign the Phisical Cause of Said Winds." This account included a map that used symbols and varying lines to give a statistical look at the trade winds (Figure 9.2).

Another example of an early graphic involved an 1854 map in which Dr. Robert Snow plotted deaths from cholera in a London neighborhood. Dr. Snow also marked the sites of water pumps, which led him to conclude that the cause of the epidemic was the water being drawn from one specific pump.

The earliest known chart is believed to be a 10th- or 11th-century work showing the orbits of planets as a function of time. The chart is thought to have been part of a text for monastery schools (Figure 9.3). It wasn't until the development of modern graphic designs, however, that charts became a means to communicate information.

WILLIAM PLAYFAIR, A "FATHER" OF INFORMATIONAL GRAPHICS

One of the "fathers" of informational graphics was William Playfair (1759–1823), an English political economist. The first known "business informational graphic"—a time series (or line) chart using economic information—was published by Playfair in 1786 in "The Commercial and Political Atlas," one of 43 such charts in his atlas (Figure 9.4). He also published the first bar chart, a style of presentation he invented because he did not have year-by-year statistics for Scotland's exports and imports. Using only the single year of data he did have, Playfair created the bar chart, complete with scale of values at the top and a legend on the right side (Figure 9.5).

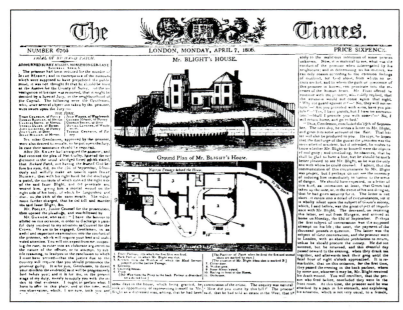

Figure 9.1   Early newspaper informational graphic (1806)

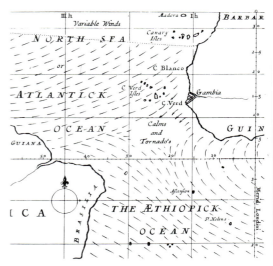

Figure 9.2   Informational graphic by Halley (1686)

Another of the pioneers of informational graphics was Charles Joseph Minard (1781–1870), a French engineer. Edward R. Tufte, a scholar of statistical presentation, said Minard created what "may well be the best statistical graphic ever drawn." Minard's graphic traced the losses incurred by Napoleon's army as it marched into Russia in 1812 (Figure 9.6). Minard, using five different series of information, showed how the army invaded Russia in June 1812 with almost a half million men and retreated in December with only 10,000 men. His graphic showed the size of the army, the location of the force at different dates, the direction of the army's movement and the temperature on various dates.

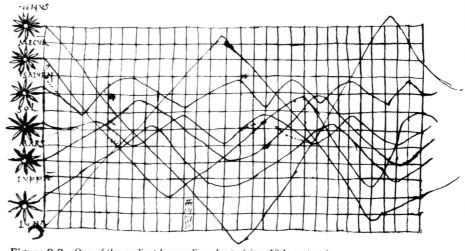

Figure 9.3   One of the earliest known line charts (circa 10th century)

It is from this type of work that modern informational graphics grew. With the development of methods to plot statistical data, information became easier to understand. Playfair, in describing the principles behind his presentations, said: "The advantage proposed by this method is not that of giving a more accurate statement than by figures, but it is to give a more simple and permanent idea of the gradual progress and comparative amounts, at different periods, by presenting to the eye a figure (chart), the proportions of which correspond with the amount

of the sums intended to be expressed."

Playfair understood the idea that vast tables of statistical information are difficult to understand and that the graphic presentation of such information would have a more lasting impression upon the reader. More than 100 years after Playfair's death, Otto Neurath, an Austrian statistician, put forth the same argument while discussing the discrete character of two languages—visual and verbal. Neurath said in 1925 that "words divide, pictures unite . . . to remember simplified pictures is better than to forget accurate figures."

THE EARLY USE OF INFORMATIONAL GRAPHICS

The use of informational graphics in newspapers was for many years limited by the time needed to create such devices and by the technology of printing them. Only maps and simple diagrams were used and only with major news stories. One such example is a 1909 *Chicago Daily News* map depicting the route taken by the discoverer of the North Pole (Figure 9.7). Another is the 1906 *New York Press* map showing the scenes of disaster from the San Francisco earthquake and fire (Figure 9.8).

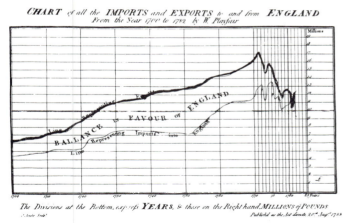

Figure 9.4   First known economics informational graphic (1786)

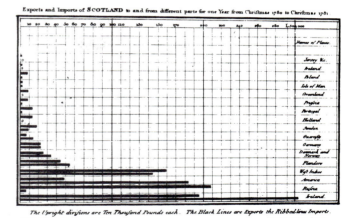

Figure 9.5   First known bar chart (circa 1780)

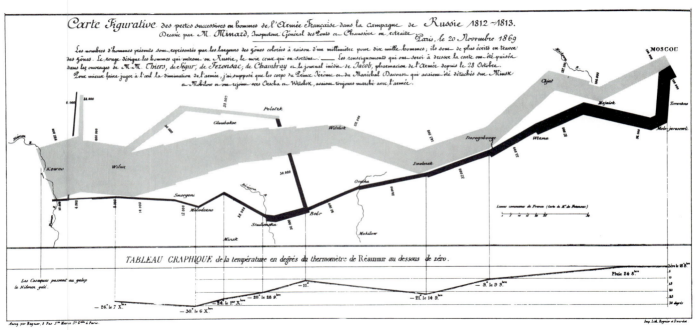

Figure 9.6   Minard graphic incorporating five series of information (circa 1812)

Early maps in newspapers often were used to help clarify and interpret information about a city. An example published by the *Los Angeles Times* in 1889 shows the arid areas of Los Angeles (Figure 9.9).

Not all newspaper informational graphics in the early part of the 20th century were maps; occasionally, there were diagrams or charts. They were crude according to the artistic standards of today, but they depicted information in much the same way as today's charts and diagrams do. *The Chicago Record-Herald* diagram showing the location of

Figure 9.7   Early newspaper map of North Pole expedition route (1909)

Figure 9.8   Early newspaper map showing San Francisco earthquake damage (1906)

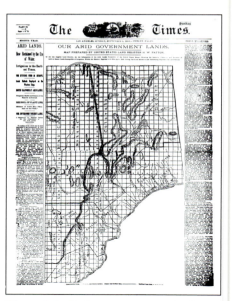

Figure 9.9   Early newspaper map showing arid areas in Los Angeles (1889)

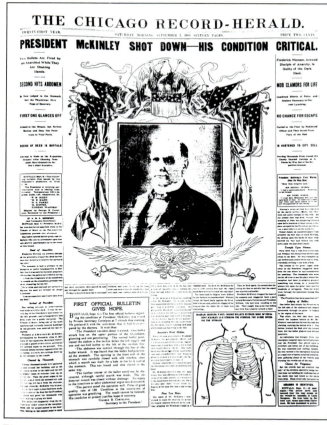

Figure 9.10   1904 diagram depicting location of assassination bullets

Figure 9.11   1981 diagram depicting location of assassination bullets

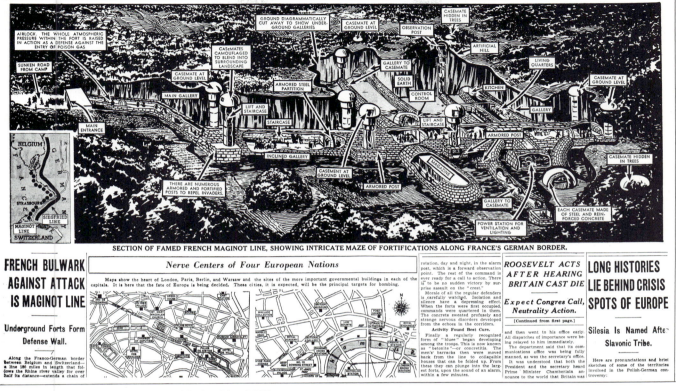

Figure 9.12   Complex graphic showing Maginot Line (1939)

the bullets that killed President William McKinley is an example of an early informational graphic (Figure 9.10). Although lacking the artistic touch of today's diagrams, this 1901 informational graphic serves the same purpose as did the informational graphics that depicted the bullet wounds of President Ronald Reagan in another assassination attempt 80 years later (Figure 9.11). Both show information visually that would be difficult to convey to readers with words.

THE ROLE OF WAR IN THE DEVELOPMENT OF INFORMATIONAL GRAPHICS

During World War I (1914–1918), informational graphics in the form of maps were used to communicate events occurring halfway around the globe. These maps were unpolished, with hand-lettering, but they must have seemed revolutionary to readers.

By the late 1930s, when war again was stretching across Europe, detailed and complex graphics were being published by some newspapers. Even by today's standards, some of these graphics are extremely sophisticated. One such example is a page-wide graphic published in 1939 by the *Chicago Daily Tribune* depicting the Maginot Line, a series of fortifications between France and Germany (Figure 9.12). The informational graphic showed the underground posts and living quarters of the troops defending France. Its style might not be modern, but the graphic provided as much detailed information as the most complicated and detailed graphic today would.

Another example of the *Tribune's* early commitment to informational graphics—and somewhat in the style of *USA Today*'s graphics that aid readers in understanding an event—was the full page of maps published the day after the Japanese bombed Pearl Harbor

(Figure 9.13). The maps, in the Monday, Dec. 8, 1941, newspaper, were headlined "Maps With Which to Follow Developments in the War Between Japan and the United States" and showed the Pacific theater of war and close-ups of the Hawaiian island of Oahu and the Philippines. Another informational graphic in that same issue used photographs and type boxes (balloons) to highlight details about the Japanese warships, including the location of their guns and the type of armor on the ships (Figure 9.14).

The next phase in the growth of informational graphics started with World War II. During this period, many editors introduced modern visual devices such as "at a glance" boxes that provided war news, detailed maps of battles and diagrams and other informational graphics that described ships, planes and other equipment. For instance, a page from the *Topeka Daily Capital* in 1945 gave readers a visual summary of

Figure 9.13   Map showing Pacific theater of war after Pearl Harbor bombing (1941)

Figure 9.14   Informational graphic highlighting features of Japanese warships (1941)

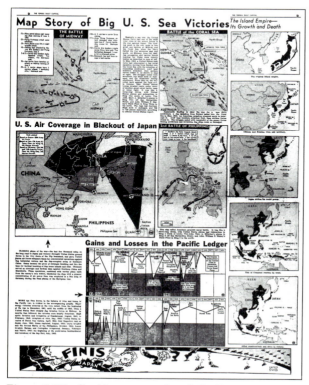

Figure 9.15   Graphic summary of war in Pacific (1945)

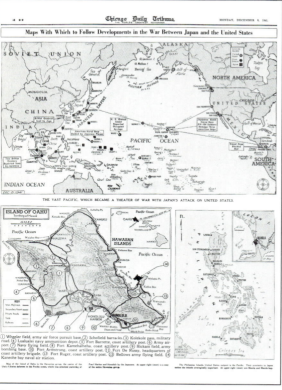

Figure 9.16   Newspaper graphics come of age (1970)

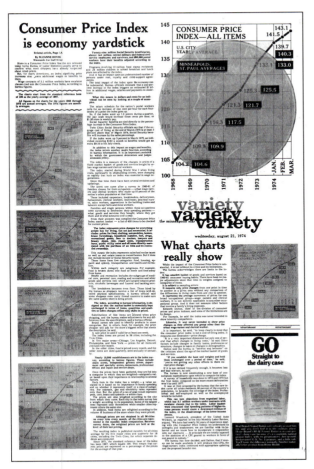

Figure 9.17 Effective graphic treatment in the *Minneapolis Star* on inflation (1974)

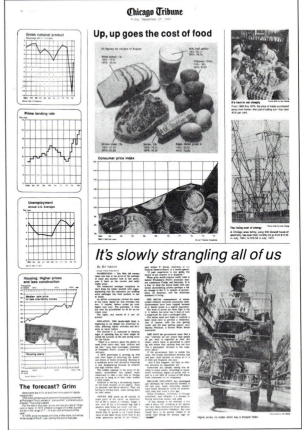

Figure 9.18 Effective graphic treatment in the *Chicago Tribune* on inflation (1974)

the war in maps and graphics. An unusual presentation of such information is found in the chart showing gains and losses in the Pacific Ocean by both sides (Figure 9.15).

MODERN NEWSPAPER INFORMATIONAL GRAPHICS

Newspapers continued to use informational graphics in the years after World War II, but it was not until the 1970s that they realized the full and exciting potential of presenting information in a visual form. American newspapers that were pioneers in the use of informational graphics included the *St. Petersburg Times,* *The Christian Science Monitor,* the *Chicago Tribune* and *The New York Times.* They showed other newspapers that informational graphics

could delight and inform readers (Figure 9.16). An excellent example of how two papers, the *Minneapolis Star* and the *Chicago Tribune,* used charts and text to try to explain the Consumer Price Index and the cost of living in 1974 can be seen in the accompanying illustrations (Figures 9.17 and 9.18).

In 1974, the *Chicago Tribune* created a new position in the newsroom—graphics editor. This editor, one of the country's first full-time visual journalists, worked with the reporters and editors in the newsroom and the artists in the art department. Maxwell McCrohon, then managing editor of the *Tribune,* said the role of the graphics editor was to bridge the gap between two different worlds. The readers, who would be presented more information in an easier-to-read form, would benefit. Prior to the creation of the graphics

editor job at the *Tribune,* informational graphics were handled by almost any type of editor—news editor, sports editor, features editor, picture editor, makeup editor. (By 1988, however, more than 17 percent of the 2,000 members of the Society of Newspaper Design listed their job as either graphics editor or graphics coordinator.)

By the late 1970s and early 1980s, more and more newspapers were using informational graphics effectively. A second wave of leaders emerged, including the *Allentown* (Pa.) *Call Chronicle, The Seattle Times, The Orange County* (Calif.) *Register,* the *San Jose* (Calif.) *Mercury News, Newsday* (on Long Island), *The Orlando* (Fla.) *Sentinel, The Louisville* (Ky.) *Courier-Journal,* and the now-defunct *Baltimore News American,* the *Philadelphia Bulletin* and the *Washington Star.*

GRAPHICS IN THE 1980s

The early 1980s provided newspaper editors with some unique stories that were helped greatly by informational graphics and that stimulated even more use of the devices. Some of these stories included the space shuttle, the eruption of Mount St. Helens in Washington, the failed attempt to rescue U.S. hostages in Iran and the attempted assassination of President Ronald Reagan. A look at two efforts to describe the bullet wounds Reagan suffered reveals the roots of today's graphic treatments. Even though these informational graphics—from *The Sun* (Baltimore, Md.) (Figure 9.19) and *The Washington Post* (Figure 9.20)—are less than a decade old, they're nothing like today's complex and detailed graphics being created on deadline.

On the heels of the big news events of the early 1980s came *USA Today,* which was born on Sept. 15, 1982, and which forever changed the newspaper industry and its use of informational graphics and color. Whether newspaper editors liked or disliked *USA Today's* treatment of the news and its visual impact, they could not dismiss the concept of a newspaper devoting so much attention to informational graphics. *USA Today* does not use informational graphics out of some design whim or fancy but rather in response to what it perceives as its readers' needs for more information presented in an easier-to-grasp manner. Although not all of the paper's graphics succeed—some are too trivial, some are too simple—they have helped change the way the rest of the industry looks at informational graphics. They have evolved from big-city luxury to journalistic necessity.

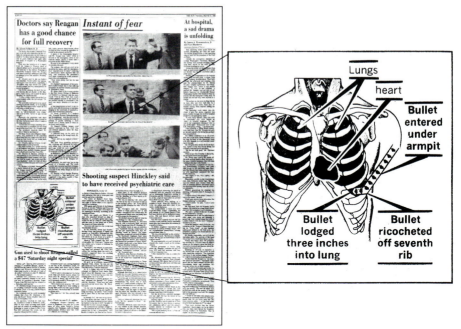

Figure 9.19   Informational graphic in *The Sun* (Baltimore Md.) on Reagan assassination attempt

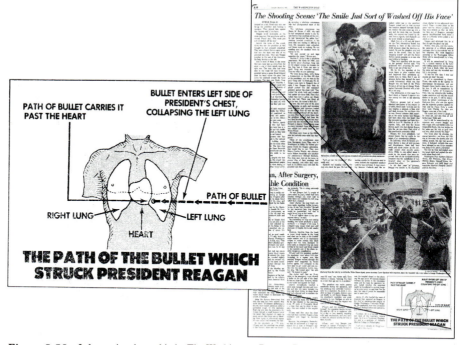

Figure 9.20   Informational graphic in *The Washington Post* on Reagan assassination attempt

Frank Peters

Artist   *St. Petersburg Times*

Today, graphics editors and coordinators are common in newspaper newsrooms. Working with computers and with other visual journalists, they are a far cry from the artists who not long ago hand-lettered maps and charts. Despite the massive changes, today's visual journalists should not lose sight of what William Playfair wrote more than 200 years ago about his new method of presentation: "On inspecting any one of these charts attentively, a sufficiently distinct impression will be made, to remain unimpaired for a considerable time, and the idea which does remain will be simple and complete."

The goal of complete understanding based on visual presentation of information is now more than ever in sight. Even the smallest daily can produce visual packages that inform and delight. Playfair would be amazed.

Frank Peters, a staff artist at the *St. Petersburg Times,* has witnessed the development of informational graphics from the "pioneer" days of the 1960s to the high-tech era of the 1990s. He started at the *Times* in 1958 as a copy boy but became a graphic artist shortly afterwards through a summer intern program in the paper's advertising department.

He said the *Times* began to change graphically in 1959 when Don Baldwin became editor. "One thing he did was fire the entire news art staff. They did only photo retouching and cartoons, and Baldwin was looking for something different. His approach to illustrating newspapers had more finesse. He was looking at the hard news side rather than the features side."

Peters was one of the advertising artists who moved into the newly formed news art department. He said Baldwin had informational graphics in mind for the newspaper.

"I had been doing some informational graphics as a part-time thing," Peters explained. "In those days, when an editor wanted a map, he would ask an advertising artist to do it. The only artists available were advertising artists."

Baldwin began to emphasize informational graphics in the news sections of the paper, Peters recalled. The paper was divided into four sections: A for national and international news, B for local and state news, C for sports and D for features. "We worked with editors, primarily doing graphics in the A and B sections," Peters said. "And Baldwin wanted them in color."

The artist said that even though the *Times* was printed letterpress, "We were doing a remarkably good job of

printing color. In late 1950s and all through the '60s, there was color on the section fronts every day. There was a responsibility on those of us, the editors and artists, who had to carry out Baldwin's wishes. It made us stop and think about the use of color and informational graphics.

"It was a time of experimentation. There was no format for it because no one really tried to use graphics and color like this before. It was a great deal of fun and a hell of a challenge. The way Baldwin pressed us to do it, we did a lot of innovation and pioneering."

Peters said newspaper graphics have changed greatly over the years, not only at the *St. Petersburg Times* but also throughout the country. "For so long newspapers didn't give informational graphics serious consideration. They were nothing more than one-column cartoons used to brighten up a page or fill a hole. Newspapers didn't see graphics as useful tools to help readers understand complex issues or subjects. I think that's entirely different now. Finally, newspapers have recognized how important graphics are. Newspaper artists no longer are thought of as people who do one-column cartoons and retouch pictures. We now think of ourselves as visual journalists. The professionalism that has come to newspaper art is very gratifying to see."

Peters credited *USA Today* with helping change newspaper graphics. He said: "The *St. Petersburg Times* has had some impact because it was one of the first to do them. But because the *Times* is a regional newspaper it has not had the wide-ranging effect

Continued

INSIDE LOOK

that *USA Today* has had on both graphics and color."

The way graphics are presented has changed in the past decade, Peters noted. "In general, newspapers want to make graphics more simple to read. If you look at *The New York Times* of 10 or 15 years ago, its maps were terribly cluttered. There was lots of detail. What we're trying to do with a news graphic now is give the reader a quick understanding of where something is. We don't need an oil company road map to do that. The simplest approach is often the best approach."

Peters suggested artists also should avoid trying to be too clever in how they present factual information to readers. He used as an example a line chart on dental care and hygiene in which the graphic was drawn into a set of teeth. "It was imaginative, but when a graphic lacks sophistication, it looks like it is out of a high school publication," he said. "I see too much of that. Sometimes, our focus becomes too much on the cleverness and not on the information itself and how best to present it to the reader."

One of the best tools that has come to newspaper art has been the computer, and Peters said it has helped him in his work. "The main thing a computer does is give us another tool that we can use in our creativity. It is not a replacement for the artist. Its biggest asset is the speed it gives us when we make our changes in art.

"On my desk now, I have an assignment to do a map on landslides in Turkey. Before, I had to call the library, which has an extensive file of maps we have done, and ask for the file on Turkey. When I got the file, I'd look through it for a map that would best fit this story. I'd try to find a map that already has been drawn."

If Peters could not find a map he could use, he would have to draw one. Then he would have to set new type, wait for it to be sent from the composing room, cut it out, wax it and paste it on the map. Finally, he would send the map to the desk that requested it.

Now if he wants to make changes, he can call a map up on the computer and simply make changes in the type. "There's no typesetting, no waxing, no pasting up on a board," he said. "I don't have to work with it by hand."

He added that the storage capability of computers is another big asset. "We can call things up instantly instead of going through the extensive library filing system, which requires a lot of space. The computer gives us an easy way to go through files and do changes easily. That really helps when you are fighting deadlines."

Peters said the evolution of newspaper graphics will continue into the 1990s. "Computers will open up a lot of creativity. We're also going to be using color in more sophisticated ways. There will be more sophistication in the use of art, both in ideas and in execution."

SUGGESTED EXERCISES

1. Look through microfilms to find a graphic in your local newspaper that is more than 50 years old. Compare and contrast it to a graphic you see in today's paper.

2. Look through microfilms of *The New York Times* to find a map that is at least 25 years old. Compare and contrast it to a map in a recent issue of *The Times*.

3. Find two newspaper graphics on the same subject, such as the weather or the economy. Which one does a better job of telling the story and why?

4. Study the graphics in a recent issue of *USA Today*. Do they do a good job of presenting information? Are they too clever? How would you improve them?

5. Discuss the use of graphics in your local daily newspaper. Does it use graphics? How about color? Are the visuals in the paper used effectively?

CHAPTER TEN

How Graphics Editors Work

Of all the jobs created in the newspaper industry in the past 100 years, the graphics editor is perhaps the most innovative and daring. Here is an editor who moves between words and visuals and has become a vital part of the newsroom of the 1990s.

Just as no two newspapers look exactly alike, no two graphics editors operate exactly the same. Each has a unique set of responsibilities, based on the needs of the newspaper and the editor's experience. The role of the graphics editor has expanded and changed along with the increased use of informational graphics. Only a few years ago, the graphics editor was responsible for a small portion of the newspaper's presentation; now, he or she may be responsible for the total presentation and packaging of news and features.

At many newspapers, the graphics editor oversees part or all of a newspaper's informational graphics. At some papers, the art director, picture editor or news editor performs this function. In this chapter, we discuss the role of informational graphics regardless of who is responsible for their creation.

HOW TO SUCCEED IN GRAPHICS

The graphics editor must be a journalist first—not a word journalist or a visual journalist, but a newspaper journalist who cares about the reader. Too often, the battle for space pits word and visual journalists against each other, with the graphics editor stuck in the middle. While in that "stuck" position, the graphics editor needs to think about the reader.

Thinking about the reader means understanding what is and isn't news. Graphics projects must have news value, and they must be of interest to readers. In some ways, the graphics editor applies the skills of a news editor, picking and choosing the most newsworthy items. Instead of selecting the stories to go on Page One, however, the graphics editor identifies the stories that will be served best by an informational graphic.

The graphics editor also must guard against the creation of informational graphics that are overly complex or busy—the more complicated the graphic, the more likely the reader will skip over the material or be confused. Because no rules dictate, for instance, that 12 arrows are too many or that a graphic that looks like Carmen Miranda's tropical

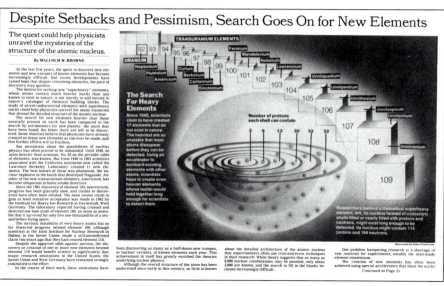

Figure 10.1   A very complicated graphic

fruit hat may be overdoing it, the visual journalist must use common sense. In addition, he or she must plan ahead and understand what the readers' needs are.

Preparing for the News

The graphics editor must anticipate the news. He or she needs to know what scheduled events are coming up and must prepare to cover them graphically. Some stories are indeed **spot news,** that is, breaking events such as earthquakes or traffic accidents that are reported on as they are occurring or shortly afterward. Few stories, however, are unexpected. The graphics editor can plan for the release of the federal budget or for an election or for the Super Bowl because these events are set months or years in advance. Even some "one-time" events, such as a major policy announcement or the release of monthly financial statistics, are scheduled in advance.

The graphics editor must know not only what *is* happening but also what *will* happen. It is not always possible to anticipate a major news story that will need accompanying informational graphics, but the graphics editor can at least plan for major events. Although specific news events do not repeat themselves, types of events do. An example of such repeating news might

be hurricanes in the South. If not this year, then sometime, there will be a major, destructive hurricane in the South. Planning for the event means paying attention to weather forecasts and collecting information (visual and written) about hurricanes that can be used in informational graphics. Note, however, that a major informational graphics package on hurricanes might be inappropriate at a newspaper in South Dakota, though it would certainly be important to a newspaper in Florida.

Knowing the Reader

The successful graphics editor needs to think of the reader, continually asking the same questions a reader might, such as how to protect a home from a hurricane. The graphics editor also must look at information much like a reader who is seeing it for the first time would. Too often, an informational graphic is overly complicated and assumes knowledge on the part of the reader (Figure 10.1). Conversely, some graphics give the reader too little information (Figure 10.2).

Anticipating and planning for the news, as well as asking questions that a reader might, are elements that a graphics editor can control. He or she cannot control the unexpected news happenings, which occur frequently, but

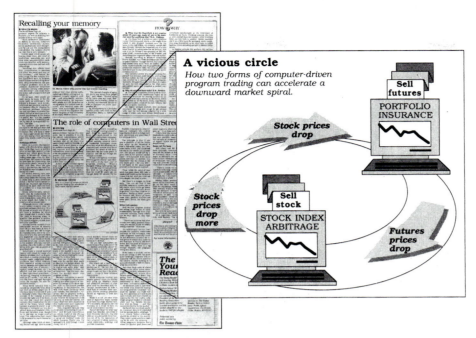

Figure 10.2   A very simplistic graphic

by developing skills in the areas he or she can control, the graphics editor will be much better prepared when big stories break.

CREATING INFORMATIONAL GRAPHICS

The process of creating an informational graphic begins with information. The graphics editor gets information for the graphic from a variety of sources, but the two most common are staff reporters and the wire services (either in story form or in an already created graphic).

Getting Help from Reporters

Ideally, a reporter who is developing a story will realize that the story could be helped by an informational graphic and will turn to the graphics editor for assistance. Many reporters understand how graphics can enhance stories and thus result in their stories getting better play in the newspaper.

Reporters who take the time to research graphic information—such as annual statistics—also gain a greater appreciation of the scope and depth of the stories they are reporting. Even stories about the latest developments will benefit from a "look back in history." A reporter working on a story about bank failures in the United States, for example, might have three or four years of information that show a trend. With more research, however, the reporter might find 20 or 30 years of information that point to a more significant trend and could be turned into a graphic. Ultimately, both the reporter and the reader will gain a better understanding of the story.

Gathering data for an informational graphic also can uncover additional facts for the story and help the reporter to avoid making statements based on too little knowledge.

Editing the Information

Once the information has been gathered and turned over to the graphics editor or coordinator, it should go through the same editing process that a news story goes through when it is given to a city editor. The graphics editor must ask:

✔ Is there enough information to make a graphic, or should the data be incorporated into the text of the story?

✔ Is this graphic needed only to add visual relief to the page?

✔ Is the information complete? Are there missing years or explanations?

✔ Is the information clear enough that an artist can create a graphic readers will understand?

If there are "holes" in the information, the graphics editor should work with the reporter or city editor to fill them. Incomplete information in a graphic can be much more obvious, and embarrassing, than incomplete information in a story.

The graphics editor must look at the information for a graphic in much the same way readers might see it when they open the paper. It is safe to assume that readers don't bring any background knowledge or inside understanding of a graphic before they look at it. Therefore, what is understood by or apparent to the reporter or even the graphics editor might not be so clear to the reader. Even graphics on simple topics like the three-point range on a basketball court need complete information so the reader doesn't have to guess at what is being shown (Figures 10.3-10.5).

Filling Out the Art Request Form

Once the decision has been made that there is enough information for an informational graphic, the graphics editor, working with either the art director or an artist, needs to decide on the type of graphic device that will best display the information. It might be a table, a chart, a diagram, a facts box or a map, or a combination of several.

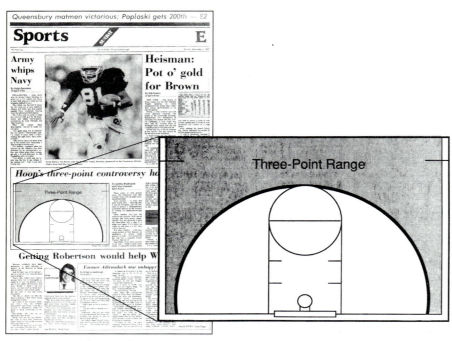

Figure 10.3   Three-pointer graphic in *The* (Glens Falls, N.Y.) *Post-Star*

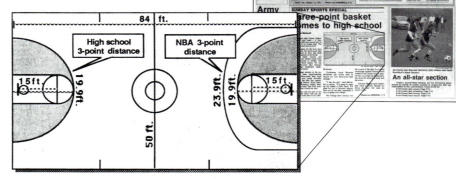

Figure 10.4   Three-pointer graphic in *The* (Nyack, N.Y.) *Journal-News*

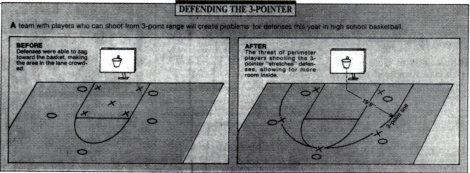

Figure 10.5   Three-pointer graphic in the Fort Lauderdale *Sun-Sentinel*

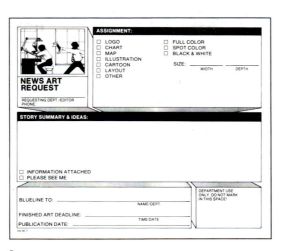

a   b

Figure 10.6 (a) Blank and (b) filled-in art request forms

(Each type will be discussed in detail in the next three chapters.)

At this point, either the reporter or the graphics editor requests that a graphic be made. The use of a *graphic request form* (or art request form) facilitates communication between all parties and helps avoid misunderstandings (Figure 10.6). The type of information that should be on the request form includes when the graphic is needed (what day or edition), what section is running the graphic and how big the graphic will be (this information should be filled out by the graphics editor or the art director and discussed with either the section editor or news editor). The headline and source line for the graphic also are noted on the form. The form may include information as to where the story that will run with the graphic can be found in the newspaper's computer system.

It is important for those who fill out request forms to understand that as much information as possible should be included. And although it is not necessary for the form to tell an artist *how* to draw the graphic, the artist needs to have all of the available data.

Working with an Artist

The next step involves the graphics editor and the artist. Together, they should decide on the possible direction, size and nature of the graphic. The artist should ask questions if any points are unclear. If the graphics editor can't answer those questions, the reporter should be brought into the discussion.

Sometimes, on more complex informational graphics, the artist and reporter will work as a team, discussing and tailoring the information for the

graphic until both are satisfied. The graphics editor would be part of this process as well, making sure the graphic meets standards set by the newspaper and also satisfies the needs of the reader.

While the graphic is being drawn, the graphics editor should be aware of its progress and be available to answer any questions from the artist. Such questions could range from a concern about the placement of information to confusion over data in the graphic. The graphics editor must be prepared to answer questions quickly by checking with the reporter or other sources of information.

During this process, the graphics editor also needs to communicate with either the news editor, if the graphic is planned for news pages, or the editor of the section where the graphic will run. Information that must be communicated includes what type of graphic, how big a graphic and whether or not it is in color.

Checking for Accuracy

When the artist is finished with the graphic, the graphics editor should check it for accuracy. He or she also should examine the graphic's overall visual approach. Although there shouldn't be

any change in the approach of the graphic if the artist and the graphics editor communicated earlier, it is still a good practice to double-check.

Here is another chance for the graphics editor to look at the material as an editor and also as a reader. The graphic must "make sense"—it must stand on its own merits. Few graphics should need a story as support; each one should tell its own story with its own headline. It should communicate information clearly.

In addition to checking the "concept," the graphics editor must do "fact" checking, asking the following questions:

✓ Are all the words spelled correctly?
✓ Are all of the months in a chart in the correct order?
✓ Are the oceans labeled properly in a map (the Pacific and Atlantic sometimes get flopped)?
✓ Do all of the figures add up? Sometimes, errors are caught when addition or subtraction is double-checked.
✓ Is the chronology correct?
✓ Does information in the graphic agree with information in the story? For example, if a graphic shows the number of people injured in accidents, the story should use the same numbers.

In other words, even minor details should not be overlooked. If any element is incorrect in an informational graphic, the credibility of the graphic in particular and the newspaper in general is called into question.

Even the reporter can help check the information. It is generally a good practice to give the reporter a copy of the graphic. The copy editor working on the story also should have a copy of the graphic as the story is being edited. Both the reporter and copy editor can provide additional sets of eyes to help prevent errors in the graphic.

"VISUAL REPORTING"

Often, the graphics editor will do his or her own research for a graphic. In these cases, the graphics editor becomes a graphics reporter, seeking specific information to create a visual report. At many newspapers, an in-house library—at one time known as a **morgue** and now more commonly called a **reference center**—offers materials and assistance in research projects. Like any good reporter, the graphics editor also maintains a personal file of sources, including:

- The person who keeps state unemployment statistics
- A good contact at the local office of the National Weather Service
- Librarians at public and university libraries who can research specific topics
- Public affairs officers and other officials of trade associations
- Contacts at other newspapers who might provide information (or even graphics) during a big story

In addition, the graphics editor can consult scores of reference books. There are far too many newsroom sources to try to list all of them here, but the major ones include:

- Clippings. Previous stories and graphics provide a wealth of information.
- Encyclopedias. They do indeed provide information from A to Z.
- World Almanac and Information Please Almanac. These reference books contain a little bit of everything.
- Jane's All the World's Aircraft. This reference book describes aircraft throughout the world.
- Jane's Fighting Ships. This volume is a major reference on military ships throughout the world.
- Lloyd's Register of Shipping. This reference book describes non-military ships.
- Military Balance. This annual, published by the International Institute for Strategic Studies in London, provides information about the military forces of various countries.
- State directories. These state "blue books" include information on the executive, legislative and judicial branches of state government. They give official rosters of elected and appointed officials, their salaries and other data, as well as maps of legislative and judicial districts.
- Biographies. The list of Who's Who books seems endless. It includes Who's Who in American Colleges and Universities, Who's Who in Communist China, Who's Who in American Politics, The International Who's Who, Who's Who in the United Nations and Who's Who in

the World. Current Biography is published monthly, except August, and is available in many newsrooms. The Dictionary of American Biography contains information on deceased distinguished Americans. There's also The New York Times Biographical Edition, Obituaries on File and Biography Index.
- Facts on File. This reference, published weekly, summarizes and indexes the news. There is information on national and foreign news events, deaths, science, medicine, sports, crime books, plays and much more.

Public or university libraries also contain scores of reference books that reporters can consult. Many provide computerized reference services that can access material almost instantly. Other sources include, but are not limited to:

- Newspaper indexes. *The New York Times,* the *Los Angeles Times, The Wall Street Journal, The Washington Post* and other newspapers index their stories and publish them in bound volumes.
- American Statistical Index (ASI) and Statistical Reference Index (SRI). ASI lists, by subject, areas in which there are federal government statistics. SRI lists statistics gathered by organizations, university research centers and state governments.
- Monthly Catalog of U.S. Government Publications. This catalog can help in the search for specific information.
- Statistical Abstract of the United States. Statistical data collected by the U.S. government and a variety of private agencies are listed.

- Gallup Opinion Index. This monthly index provides analytical and statistical data.
- The Address Book. This volume provides information on how to locate more than 3,000 celebrities, VIPs and corporate executives.
- Congressional Quarterly. This publication is a useful reference on national politics and legislation.

GRAPHICS SERVICES

The wire services and syndicated informational graphics services are major sources of graphics. They are commercial ventures, charging fees that run from $10 to several hundred dollars a week and offering completed informational graphics in different formats and delivery methods. The major graphics suppliers are The Associated Press, Knight-Ridder Tribune News graphics network, Infographics and the Chicago Tribune Graphic Service.

The Associated Press

The AP serves a broad base of newspaper members as part of its cooperative mission. It sends graphics to its member newspaper two ways—via its Laserphoto network and via satellite delivery direct to a newspaper's Macintosh computer.

The Laserphoto delivery method works much like the first transmissions of informational graphics in 1935 when an AP artist created a diagram of plays during the Rose Bowl game between Alabama and Stanford. A copy of the graphic is placed on a drum for transmission via phone lines or satellite. The finished graphic is produced at the member newspaper's office in a

Figure 10.7 AP Laserphoto graphics

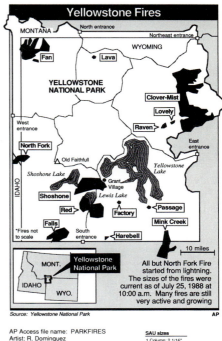

Figure 10.8 AP GraphicsNet graphics

processing machine. The newspaper can make a velox from the graphic and use it as is, or it can use information in the graphic as a reference for another piece of work (Figure 10.7).

In 1988, AP established *GraphicsNet,* a service that delivers graphics by satellite automatically to newspapers with Macintosh computers and satellite receiving dishes. With this high-speed delivery method, it takes AP about 15 to 30 seconds to send a graphic from

its headquarters in New York to newspapers receiving GraphicsNet service. The AP graphics can be modified, changed or even cut apart and combined with other graphics so long as the newspaper uses the same type of **software**—a program that tells the computer what to do—as the AP artist used to create the graphic (Figure 10.8). AP's Macintosh graphics are mostly created with a software drawing program called MacDraw II.

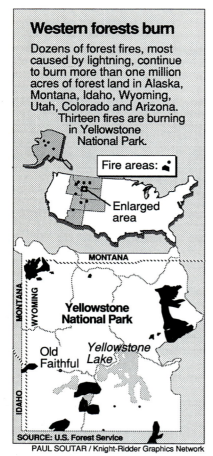

Western forests burn

Dozens of forest fires, most caused by lightning, continue to burn more than one million acres of forest land in Alaska, Montana, Idaho, Wyoming, Utah, Colorado and Arizona. Thirteen fires are burning in Yellowstone National Park.

Fire areas:

Enlarged area

MONTANA

MONTANA
WYOMING

Yellowstone National Park

Old Faithful   *Yellowstone Lake*

IDAHO

SOURCE: U.S. Forest Service

PAUL SOUTAR / Knight-Ridder Graphics Network

BULLETIN BOARD: Today's Graphics
SUBJECT: Yellowstone, forest fires in western states
ARTIST/ORIGIN: Paul Soutar, KRGN
RECOMMENDED WIDTH: 1 column (25% reduction)
ENTERED: 07/25/88

NOTE: This graphic was designed to be printed at 25%. To create a headline larger than the 25% printing allows, either use the program Font Sizer to specify a larger hed or print a headline separately (for example, a 36-point hed printed at 50%) and strip it onto the graphic.

Figure 10.9 Knight-Ridder Tribune News (KRTN) graphic on Yellowstone fires

Knight-Ridder Tribune News Graphics Network

Another Macintosh-based graphics service, the Knight-Ridder Tribune News graphics network, creates informational graphics from its Washington, D.C., offices for distribution through a central computer system. Newspapers call a local phone number and then are linked, through a computer service, to the KRTN service. In addition to the graphics created by staff artists at KRTN, informational graphics from Knight-Ridder newspapers, Tribune Co. newspapers such as the *Chicago Tribune* and others are submitted to the service for distribution over the network.

KRTN uses MacDraw II and another drawing program called Illustrator to create most of its graphics. Newspaper clients also might use different programs to draw graphics that are shared via the network (Figure 10.9).

Infographics

Graphics from this syndicated service are distributed by mail or express delivery service or satellite to a Macintosh. Subscribing newspapers receive several slick or glossy printed sheets that can be used as original graphics. Infographics is a service of North American Syndicate and King Features.

Chicago Tribune Graphics Service

The *Tribune* service, the first syndicated graphics service in the world, was launched in 1981. Graphics from this service, which are sent to clients twice a week, are based on work done for the *Chicago Tribune*. In addition, the *Tribune* distributes its Macintosh graphics via the KRTN graphics network.

Other Graphics Sources

Besides the major sources of syndicated graphics, there are several smaller sources. The Newspaper Enterprise Association sends a graphics package to its members, mainly small newspapers. The syndicated Gallup Poll also offers a graphics package, and several financial news syndicated services provide graphics as well.

Maintaining Quality in Wire Service Graphics

Wire services do make errors, and some of the graphics they send are outdated. That means the burden falls on newspapers to make certain the graphics they receive from wire services are checked and double-checked for factual accuracy before they are used. The use of computers has helped newspapers maintain quality. For instance, a graphic drawn by a Knight-Ridder artist in Washington, D.C., on a Macintosh can be handled, modified, adapted and updated as if its artist were working for the newspaper.

ONE GRAPHIC, SEVERAL TREATMENTS

After U.S. warships attacked Iranian ships in the Persian Gulf in 1988, the wire services sent graphics along with

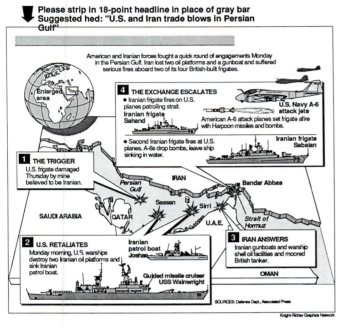

▼ Please strip in 18-point headline in place of gray bar
Suggested hed: "U.S. and Iran trade blows in Persian Gulf"

American and Iranian forces fought a quick round of engagements Monday in the Persian Gulf. Iran lost two oil platforms and a gunboat and suffered serious fires aboard two of its four British-built frigates.

Enlarged area

4 THE EXCHANGE ESCALATES
● Iranian frigate fires on U.S. planes patrolling strait.
Iranian frigate Sahand
American A-6 attack planes set frigate afire with Harpoon missiles and bombs.
U.S. Navy A-6 attack jets
● Second Iranian frigate fires at U.S. planes. A-6s drop bombs, leave ship sinking in water.
Iranian frigate Sabalan

1 THE TRIGGER
U.S. frigate damaged Thursday by mine believed to be Iranian.

Persian Gulf   **IRAN**

Bandar Abbas

SAUDI ARABIA   Sassan   Sirri
QATAR   **U.A.E.**   **Strait of Hormuz**

2 U.S. RETALIATES
Monday morning, U.S. warships destroy two Iranian oil platforms and sink Iranian patrol boat.

Iranian patrol boat Joshan

3 IRAN ANSWERS
Iranian gunboats and warship shell oil facilities and moored British tanker.

OMAN

Guided missile cruiser USS Wainwright

SOURCES: Defense Dept., Associated Press

Knight-Ridder Graphics Network

BULLETIN BOARD: Today's Graphics
SUBJECT: Persian Gulf: Map of U.S.-Iranian fighting
ARTIST/ORIGIN: George Rorick, Paul Soutar and Howard McComas, KRGN
RECOMMENDED WIDTH: 3 column (25% reduction)
ENTERED: 04/18/88

© Copyright 1988, Knight-Ridder Graphics Network Inc.
Reprint with permission only.

Figure 10.10 KRTN graphic on clash in Persian Gulf

Figure 10.11 KRTN graphic as adapted by one newspaper

scores of stories. One of the graphics sent by the KRTN graphics network showed the military action that took place between the United States and Iran and the types of weapons the United States used (Figure 10.10). How the graphic was modified by various newspapers illustrates the editing process performed on many wire service graphics. Some merely adjusted the graphic's type to their own style; others made major changes. The (Providence, R.I.) *Journal,* for example, electronically "clipped" part of another Macintosh graphic from the KRTN service and added it to the graphic it titled "Combat in the Gulf," a process that probably took no longer than five minutes (Figure 10.11). Other newspapers changed the headline of the graphic to match their own style (Figures 10.12 and 10.13).

Figure 10.12   KRTN graphic as used by the *Dayton Daily News*

Figure 10.13   KRTN graphic as used by the *San Antonio Light*

SUGGESTED EXERCISES

1. Critique four graphics from a community daily in your area. They don't all have to be from the same day. Are there any holes? Is the information clear? Complete? Is there news value?

2. Use the World Almanac to gather information for a sports graphic. For example, you could look up home-run leaders or teams with the best win records. You pick the subject, but it has to be about sports, and the information has to come from the World Almanac.

3. Look up an American battleship in Jane's Fighting Ships. Describe the battleship and explain how you would produce a graphic that informs readers about it. What would you say on your graphics request form?

4. List five graphics that you would plan for upcoming events in your community or school. Where would you obtain the information that would be contained in the graphics?

CHAPTER ELEVEN

Tables and Charts

Choosing the right informational graphic for a story is just as important as choosing the correct writing approach. A reporter picks a writing style based on the nature of an event and available information; a graphics editor picks a type of informational graphic based on the same two factors.

Each type of informational graphic—table, chart, map, facts box and diagram—has particular strengths and weaknesses. That means the visual journalist must have a good working knowledge of the various graphic forms in order to select the best way of presenting the information.

TABLES

The purpose of tables is to display data in an orderly and visually pleasing form. A newspaper runs many tables each day, including temperatures around the state, country and world; horse racing handicaps; baseball averages; basketball and football scores; and stock market prices (Figure 11.1). These tables provide specific pieces of information that are important to readers. For example, an investor may want to read a story about the general trend of his or her investments, but he or she also will want to look up opening and closing bids on particular stocks or bonds.

Information in a table must be organized so that it can be viewed quickly and easily. The type must be readable. The columns of type should run in equal lengths, with enough space between them to separate the information but without so much space that it is difficult to follow the rows. If the information is to be presented horizontally in wide columns, rules (lines) between each five or 10 lines may help a reader's eyes travel across the table (Figure 11.2). Gray or color bands can be overlaid to achieve the same result.

Each table should have a headline telling readers what information is being displayed. Any explanatory information should be at the top of the table. A source line can run at the top or the bottom to tell the reader where the paper obtained the information.

LINE CHARTS

Line charts, which also are called *fever charts,* are common in newspapers. They are technically referred to as *rectilinear coordinate charts,* which means that the information in them is plotted from two intersecting lines—a horizontal (X) axis

Figure 11.1   Tables in sports section

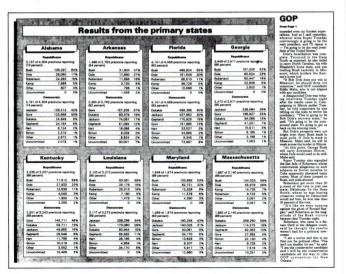

Figure 11.2   Tables broken up by horizontal rules to aid comprehension

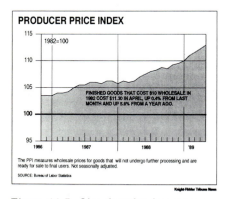

Figure 11.3   Simple line, or fever, chart

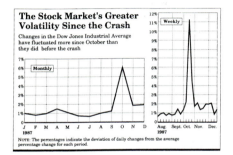

Figure 11.5   Line chart that does not use zero basing

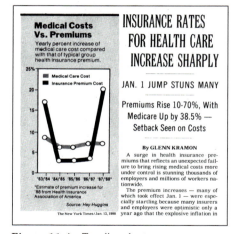

Figure 11.4   Two-line chart

and a vertical (Y) axis (Figure 11.3). An artist plots the graphic information from the points on the X and Y axes.

Line charts are most effective when they are used to display information that has changed markedly over a period of time, such as a two-line chart comparing medical costs and premiums from 1983 to 1987 (Figure 11.4). In such a chart, each of the five years is indicated on the X axis, with each year at an equal distance from the other years to make the time unit consistent. The Y axis, which indicates the yearly percent change, starts at zero to avoid a visual distortion of the information. The scale on the Y axis should be marked in con-

secutive numbers (0 to 10, for instance), in fives (0, 5, 10, 15, etc.), in 10s (0, 10, 20, 30, etc.) or in some other combination (3, 6, 9, etc.). The Y axis scale generally is on the left side of the graphic because the information is read from left to right.

There are some types of information that do not lend themselves to **zero basing** (starting the vertical scale at zero). For example, in a line chart showing the Producer Price Index, a year, 1982, equals 100. In this case, the vertical axis would show the index point, or 100, and the chart would not begin at zero (Figure 11.5).

There is more to a line chart, however, than the vertical and horizontal axes; line charts also may contain headlines, scale type and source line information. And like the axes, each of these elements must be consistent and accurate.

Headline

The headline should summarize the information in the chart. It can be written as a news headline, with subject and verb, as in "Plane crashes increase in U.S. since 1980," or it can be a *label head,* as in "U.S. plane crashes since 1980." Most charts carry label heads, particularly if they are displayed next to a story, to eliminate the possibility

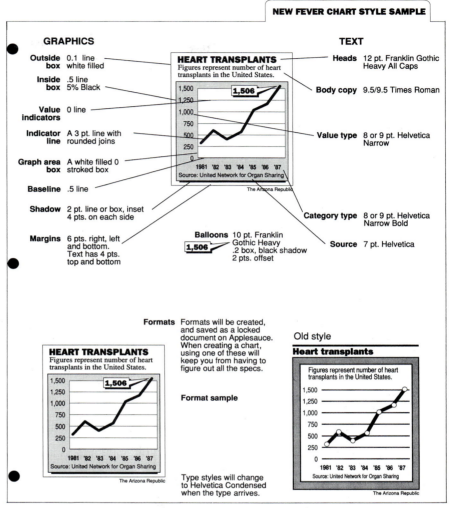

Figure 11.6   Sample type specifications for line chart

of the chart's headline repeating the wording of the story's headline.

The headline should be larger and/or bolder than other elements in the line chart. Normally, the headline is set in 14- to 18-point type while the rest of the chart's type is set in 9- to 10-point type.

Scale Type

It is not necessary to label each point on the X or Y scales; an excess of type will confuse readers. Instead, only the major points should be marked. For example, if the Y scale has 20 marks on it, from 0 to 20, it is best to mark only selected increments, such as 0, 5, 10, 15 and 20. The size of type used for scales should be the same on the horizontal and vertical axes.

Source Line Information

As in a news story, information in a graphic needs to be attributed to a source through the use of a **source line.** Telling readers the source of information adds to a graphic's credibility. Generally, the source line is in the bottom right corner of a graphic and is set in smaller type than the rest of the graphic's type. If the regular type is 9 point, for instance, the source line can be set in 6-point **agate.** Here are several examples of source lines:

Source: U.S. Census Bureau
Source: Commerce Department
Source: The Associated Press
Source: News reports

Graphics editors also need to know the source of information for the graphics

they receive over the wire or in the mail. That way, if they want to gather additional information, they'll know where to start.

The accompanying diagram of a line chart explains all of its potential elements (Figure 11.6). This diagram is used as a style sheet for artists at *The Arizona Republic.* It shows type sizes that would be used when a chart is made up on a Macintosh computer, before it is reduced to fit into a one-column space.

BAR AND COLUMN CHARTS

Like line charts, bar and column charts are used to display statistical informa-

tion. A **bar chart** is a horizontal display of information, with the vertical axis on the left side of the chart serving as the baseline (Figure 11.7). In a **column chart,** the bars are based on the horizontal axis at the bottom of the chart.

Bar and column charts are useful in comparing size or totals over a period of time. An example is the percentage change in wholesale prices. The U.S. government releases this information monthly detailing the amount the index has changed from the previous month. A column chart, unlike a line chart, could show the current month's specific growth rate while comparing it to the rates of the previous months (Figure 11.8).

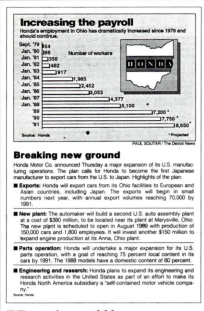

Figure 11.7 Bar chart on auto company employment

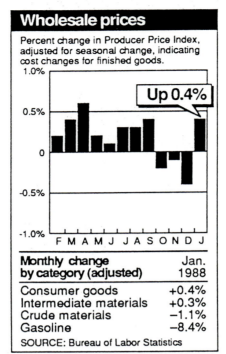

Figure 11.8 Wholesale prices column chart (with negative numbers)

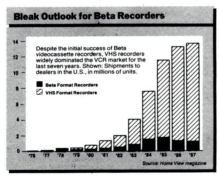

Figure 11.9 Grouped-column chart

Bar and column charts also are used to compare two or more items with each other against a time frame, such as the average income of farm workers versus the average income of urban workers during the past 10 years. A bar or column chart showing multiple items often is called a **grouped-column or grouped-bar chart** (Figure 11.9).

If only two items are being compared over a period of time, there is little research indicating which is easier to read—a grouped-bar chart or a grouped-column chart. If three or four items are being compared, however, a column chart with a legend explaining what each column represents probably is easier to read. The bars' lengths quickly tell readers how much larger one category is than others. Generally, the largest category is shown in the top bar and the smallest in the bottom bar.

More complex, and hence more difficult to read, is a bar chart with subdivided bars. This type of graphic shows each bar's total at 100 percent and various subdivided amounts (Figure 11.10). Because this type of bar chart is difficult to follow, it should be avoided.

Sometimes, items in a bar chart that shows comparisons are listed alphabetically, which enables readers to quickly identify those items of primary interest. For instance, in a bar chart ranking all 50 states in some category, an alphabetical listing would allow a reader to quickly see how his or her state ranked.

As in other graphics, the scale on a bar or column chart should be based on zero so that the chart will not give the wrong visual impression. If there is a big jump from the low figure to the high, the zero based scale may be broken, but some visual indication must alert readers that the chart is not to scale.

Bar and column charts do allow for the use of negative numbers, numbers below zero. This is particularly useful when depicting the profit and loss figures of companies or the percent change of a group or category. For example, if XYZ Corporation showed three periods of profit and two periods of loss, the column chart could show the wide swing of the numbers by using a scale that contains both the plus and the negative side of zero.

It is also possible to combine a line and columns on a single chart when showing items on different scales (Figure 11.11). One disadvantage of these charts is that they are difficult to comprehend quickly, which defeats a major goal of an informational graphic: showing readers useful information at a glance.

PIE CHARTS

A **pie chart** shows the relationship of various items to a total. An example of this relationship to a total can be seen when using a polling question that has three answers. In a pie chart, each answer, or sector of the pie, would be in relation to the other two pieces. By using two or more pies and keeping the visual relationship the same for all of the sectors (for instance, "yes is portrayed by black in all the pies"), attitudes can be portrayed visually (Figure 11.12). Pie charts also are used to depict changes or relationships between different groups, such as age or income groups (Figure 11.13).

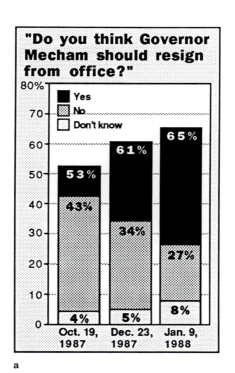

a

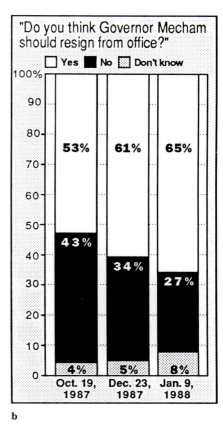

b

Figure 11.10   Charts with subdivided columns (a) incorrectly drawn and (b) correctly drawn

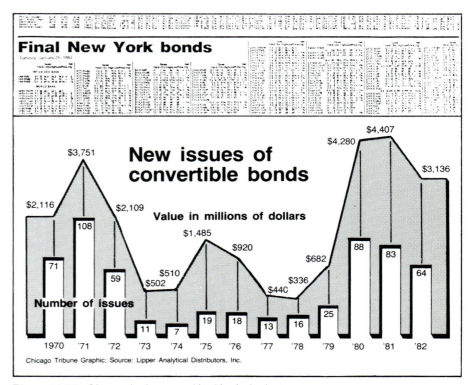

Figure 11.11   Lines and columns combined in single chart

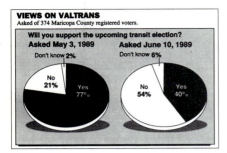

Figure 11.12   Sample of pie chart

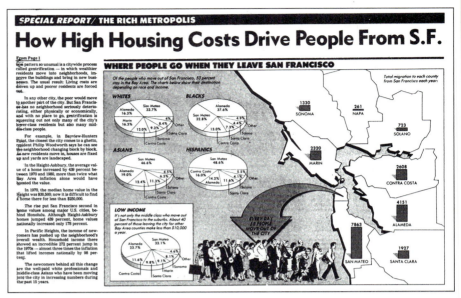

Figure 11.13   Pie charts depicting movement of various ethnic groups

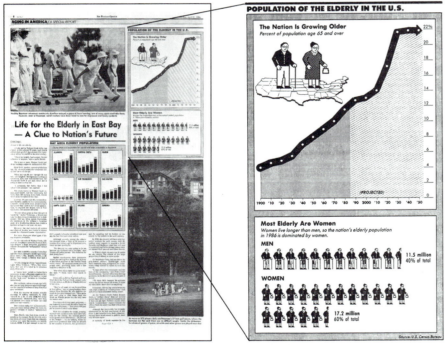

Figure 11.14   Pictograph using symbols instead of bars to display information

The pie chart, however, does have its limitations. It should not be used with information that has numerous categories because the pie would be divided into so many pieces that comprehension would be hindered. A pie chart also cannot be used to display information over a long period of time, such as with a polling question that was asked monthly for a year. Other types of graphics, such as line or bar charts, are better suited to display such information.

One warning about pie charts: Avoid letting an artist add too much visual depth or dimension to a pie chart, which can distort the information and deceive the reader.

PICTOGRAPHICS

The **pictograph,** or **pictographic,** only recently has made an impact on newspaper pages. Visual journalists are using pictographics to display information because these charts have unique artistic qualities.

There are three types of pictographics. In one, symbols are used instead of basic bars or lines to display information (Figure 11.14). This type of pictographic has been used for years, primarily in books and encyclopedias.

Figure 11.15   Pictograph using symbols as scale-based units of measurement

Another type of pictographic uses symbols as units of measurement (Figure 11.15). The symbols are based on a scale, with each unit having a specific value. The symbols then change size to represent an increase or decrease. For example, one house might be used to depict 100 houses sold; to show 200 houses sold, the artist would double the size of the house. Nigel Holmes, art director of Time magazine, is credited with making this form of pictographic popular among newspaper artists, and it sometimes is known as a "Nigel Holmes graphic."

This type of pictographic is the toughest to produce because the graphics editor and artist are using three-dimensional figures to illustrate one-dimensional numbers. When the one-dimensional data change, the three-dimensional size of the symbol used in the graphic must change correspondingly. It is not enough merely to adjust the height and width of the symbol. In fact, the new size of the symbol must be calculated mathematically as if it were a three-dimensional drawing.

For example, in the pictographic in Figure 11.15 showing the rise in building permits in Cecil County, the number of permits increased to 358 in 1987 from 184 in 1984. A mathematical formula based on volume is used to find the correct size of the symbols each time they change. Here is how it is done: First, divide the larger number being shown (358) by the smaller number (184). That equals 1.95, which can be rounded off to 2. Next, take the cube root of 2, which is 1.26. The height and width of the smaller figure then are multiplied by the cube root to find the correct dimensions of the larger figure. The smallest house is 8 picas deep and

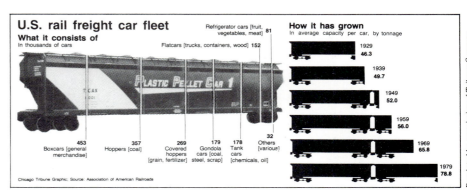

Figure 11.16   Pictograph using objects to convey information

11 picas wide. Eight multiplied by 1.26 is equal to 10.08 picas; 11 multiplied by 1.26 is 13.86. That means the largest house should be 10 picas by 14 picas, not 14 by 20 as it was in the graphic shown in Figure 11.15.

The third type of pictographic takes the most liberties with the information being presented. It uses objects, such as freight cars, to form sections of a pie chart (Figure 11.16), or it forces objects, such as exhaust from a jet, into the curve of a line chart (Figure 11.17). These types of charts tend to be the most misused. They often represent cartoons that serve to break up columns of type rather than graphic presentations of statistical information. For example, the use of the jet in Figure 11.17 is an inappropriate symbol for conveying information about Medicare spending.

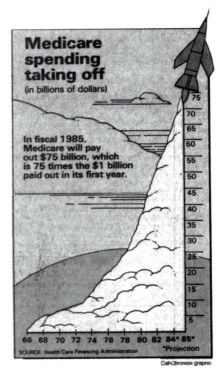

Figure 11.17   Inappropriate symbol in a pictograph

INSIDE LOOK

Bill Dunn

Graphics Editor   *The Orange County Register*

Bill Dunn, graphics editor of *The Orange County* (Calif.) *Register,* said that when he evaluates a story for an informational graphic, he looks to see "if there is a way to go beyond the common number presentation, if there is a way we can incorporate visuals or spice it up to make it more entertaining without distorting the numbers. I might introduce an element of art that signifies the story. Let's say we are doing a story on pro football salaries. I might introduce the NFL logo or a football helmet or dollar bills to go with the chart, just to make it stand apart from other information on the page and get readers into the information quicker.

"Sometimes we go overboard, where we try to get too cute for our own good. I think most newspapers are guilty of this. They try to be so slick that they forget the basic job, which is to present information."

Dunn said his decision on whether or not to do a graphic for a story is based on the article's importance. "We have to sort out the bigger stories from the smaller stories. We can't do graphics on the smaller stories. If we are talking about something that will affect people's pocketbooks—and in Orange County that's real important—I do a quick sketch, either in a fever or line chart or in a bar chart. I might brainstorm with the editor or I may just go right back to the artist to discuss the information."

He added that his biggest challenge each day is getting the information to do a graphic and then completing it on time. "On breaking news stories you scramble to do what you can do. Sometimes, you eliminate any visual enhancement and create a bare-bones chart or map. You just have to strip it to its basic information. If it is on a

deadline situation, you have to think about juggling other projects in the art department. If there are major components in a graphic, you might split the assignment among three artists, with one person responsible for a different element of the graphic.

"For example, on a plane crash, we might have one artist doing an overall locater map, a second artist doing a detailed locater map and a third artist doing a graphic on the airplane involved. These would all be packaged together."

When Dunn is given an assignment for a graphic, he passes the information to an artist, who is responsible for creating the graphic. The artist is able to call up information for the graphic from a computer terminal. Dunn said: "It is important that the artist checks the electronic copy to see if there are any notes from me or an editor. The artist then has a period of time to reflect on the information before he leaps into the assignment. I try to check the assignment during its progress. And then I'll see it at the end, when we start the proof process."

Two copies of each graphic are prepared, Dunn explained. One is given to the assigning editor and one is given to the copy desk of the department using the graphic. The graphics are corrected, initialed by the reading copy editor and returned to the artist, who makes the corrections and then makes another set of proofs.

"Then we go through the process again, where the proofs are reviewed, initialed and returned to the artist," Dunn said. "We continue this process until everyone signs off on the graphic. Sometimes it takes three or four passes; sometimes it only takes one."

SUGGESTED EXERCISES

1. Clip two examples of tables from a local newspaper and critique them. What do you like and dislike about them? How would you improve them?

2. Do the same for two line charts.

3. Do the same for two bar charts.

4. Do the same for two column charts.

5. Do the same for two grouped-bar charts.

6. Do the same for two pie charts.

7. Clip from newspapers two examples of each of the types of pictographs. What do you like and dislike about them? How would you improve them?

CHAPTER TWELVE

Diagrams and Facts Boxes

Tables and charts display statistical information, but there also are informational graphics used daily in newspapers that display non-statistical information. These non-statistical informational graphics can be classified into two categories: *Diagrams* or *schematics,* which explain how something works or why or how an event occurred; and *facts boxes,* which distill important points of a story or event. Facts boxes also can include visual representations to make it easier for readers to absorb the information.

DIAGRAMS/SCHEMATICS

Diagrams and schematics reduce complicated events or mechanical things to simplified, but not simple, one-dimensional drawings. They often provide the visual what, where, when, why and how of events and are among the most striking and powerful of graphics.

The explosion of the space shuttle Challenger on Jan. 29, 1986, is a good illustration of how diagrams can be used effectively. While a reporter might go into great detail to explain how the space shuttle's "O-rings" failed and caused the tragic explosion, the visual journalist could create a diagram graphic on the same subject and almost instantly give the reader specific visual information about the disaster.

When the shuttle exploded 73 seconds after liftoff, killing the seven crew members aboard, television recorded the event in graphic color and ran the video over and over. Television also offered graphics to explain the tragedy, but they were fleeting images on a screen. Only newspapers were able to give readers detailed information about the complex rocket systems that were operating aboard the Challenger. The diagrams that appeared in papers provided information that could be studied and restudied (Figures 12.1 and 12.2).

The Challenger disaster diagram should not have been difficult to create. The National Aeronautics and Space Administration published a number of lengthy briefing books for reporters about every part of the shuttle program. From one of these briefing books, the visual journalist could find background information about the rocket booster system, in addition to diagrams of the rockets and related systems (Figure 12.3). Working from such diagrams, an artist was able to diagram the rocket system and create a graphic that would show not only where the shuttle was when it exploded but also the degree of separation among the rocket elements.

Figure 12.1   Diagram tracing flight of Challenger

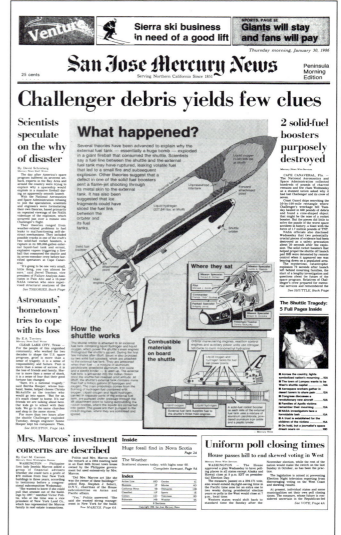

Figure 12.2   Diagrams showing details of Challenger disaster

A VISUAL FRAME OF REFERENCE

Many of the complex stories newspapers report involve things and places about which most readers have little understanding. Few newspaper readers have seen a space shuttle; even fewer have witnessed its launch. A diagram graphic can give them a "visual frame of reference."

Such a visual frame of reference is important in everyday life. For example, a computer manual may use dozens of words to describe a new piece of equipment, but until the consumer sees a diagram or a picture, he or she cannot accurately visualize what the new invention looks like. In much the same manner, a good diagram graphic can give readers a visual frame of reference on the faraway events of the world or even of their own town. Diagram graphics show *what* the story is reporting or *where, when, why* and *how* the event occurred.

The Chernobyl Disaster

When a fire erupted in a reactor at the Soviet Union's nuclear power plant at Chernobyl in April 1986, American journalists had to respond quickly with

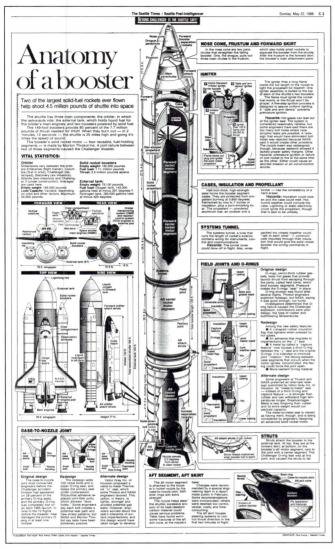

Figure 12.3   Diagrams showing complex rocket systems aboard space shuttle

Figure 12.4   Diagram of Chernobyl reactor

news reports based only on sketchy information. To make matters worse, the Soviet Union at first refused to release photographs of the nuclear accident site. Thus, diagram graphics of the event helped newspaper readers clarify the mental pictures they had made based on written reports; they gave readers a frame of reference on the plant, its size and its various elements.

A *San Francisco Chronicle* diagram provided both graphic and pictorial information (Figure 12.4). The *Chronicle* graphic, taken from an International

Atomic Energy Agency book, was combined with a 1982 Tass (the Soviet news and photo agency) photo to show readers the reactor's core and how such a reactor works. The *Chronicle* was able to produce the diagram because one of its science reporters remembered reading about Soviet nuclear power plants in a reference book.

Having such information is critical to creating accurate and complete diagram graphics. A reporter's copy can present a vague, general idea of a location or event, but a newspaper artist needs specific, detailed information to

create such diagrams. Source material can come from reporters, the wire services, the newspaper library or a university or public library. (A complete discussion of source materials and reference works can be found in Chapter 10.)

Figure 12.5   Early map in *The Detroit News* showing airplane crash location

Figure 12.6   Map in later edition of *The Detroit News* showing airplane crash location

Figure 12.8   Diagram of airplane that crashed in Detroit

Figure 12.7   Map in out-of-town paper showing airplane crash location

An Airliner Crash in Detroit

The Aug. 16, 1987, crash of an airliner taking off from Detroit Metropolitan Airport, in which 158 persons were killed, illustrates how diagram graphics can help explain the where and how of a major news story. The diagrams played an important role in giving newspaper readers information that may have been difficult to grasp in the initial print and broadcast reports.

When Northwest Airlines Flight 255 crashed, the first graphic information available concerned the location of the crash. By using reference materials showing Detroit's airport and its runway system, an artist could draw a detailed and accurate map, which also could be used in later diagrams (Figures 12.5 and 12.6).

Another piece of information readily available after the crash was a diagram of the plane, a MD-80 made by McDonnell Douglas Corp. This type of information is found in Jane's All the World's Aircraft. Again, an artist could take this information and create a diagram showing readers where passengers and crew were on the plane when they fell

FOOD: Now's the time to harvest herbs 1E

Storms

ROARIN': Tigers top Twins 11-2; Jays win, keep lead 1H

RACE TO THE TOP THE A.L. EAST

Toronto

Detroit ½

New York 3

METRO: Gang, lawyers indicted 1B

Wednesday August 19, 1987

The Detroit News

15¢

Winds probed in crash

Wind as a factor in takeoffs

Winds from the West

How a plane stalls

How a wind shear works

Inquiry: Temperature, tail winds, shear studied

Theories: Stall alarm is easily triggered

Survivor: Little girl brings joy amid grief

Frog turned prince

Biggest winner plays it cool

Lotto's $13-million man to buy a new pickup truck

Glass wrote notes for aid in his blood

INSIDE....

ON THURSDAY'S SCIENCE PAGE: Haute couture from a computer

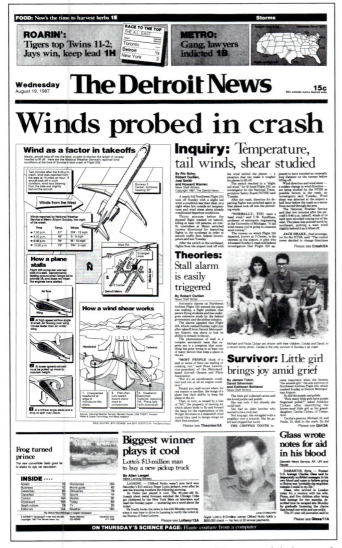

Figure 12.9 Early diagram illustrating possible causes of airplane crash

SCIENCE: Designing haute couture by computer 1D

Rain

RACE TO THE TOP THE A.L. EAST

Detroit

Toronto ½

New York 2½

TIGERS IN FIRST

Terrell records 7-1 win over Twins 1F

Thursday August 20, 1987

The Detroit News

15¢

Investigators say wing flaps weren't set for plane's takeoff

Cockpit: Interruptions cut into flight check

Wing flaps and other takeoff factors

Correct takeoff position

On takeoff of Flight 255

McDonnell Douglas model MD 80

Crew

Wind direction/load

Engine malfunction

THE CRASH OF FLIGHT 255

Miracle: Cecilia awakens, asks for mom, demands her doll

Toy guns cause real trouble on California freeways

INSIDE....

IN FRIDAY'S ENTERTAINMENT SECTION: Where to go to dance cheek to cheek

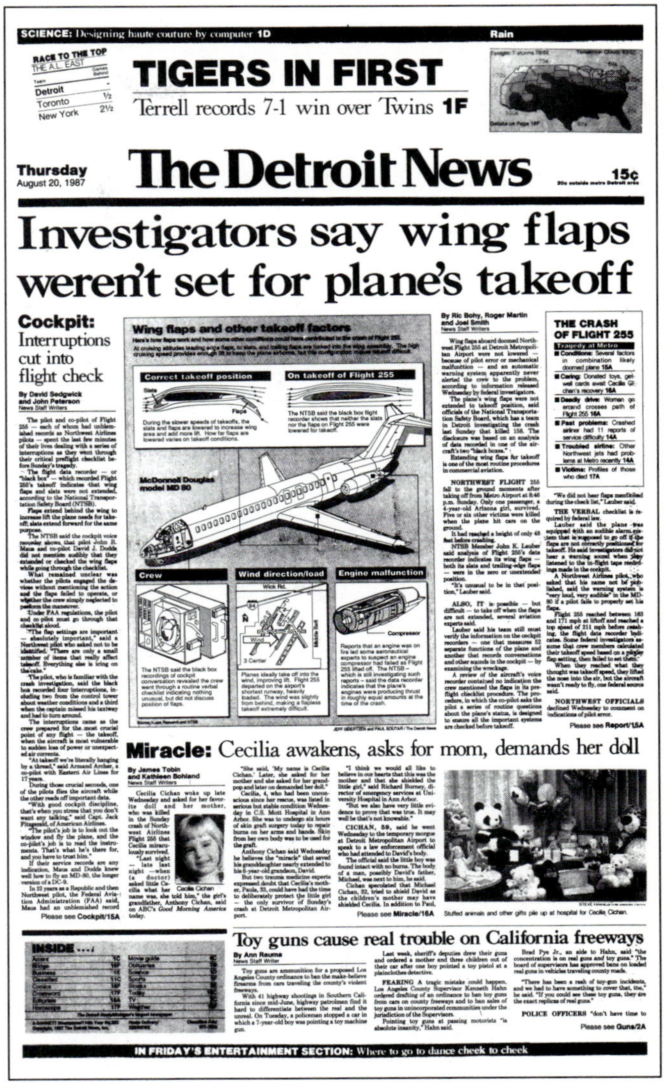

Figure 12.10 Subsequent diagram illustrating possible cause of airplane crash

to their deaths. The diagram also could show where the lone survivor of the crash, a 4-year-old girl, was seated.

For the newspapers in Detroit, diagram information as well as photographs were essential to illustrate the disaster. Out-of-town newspapers had to rely on wire service reports to show readers where the crash occurred. Some newspapers used only a location map of Detroit, without showing where the airport is situated in the city (Figure 12.7). Some editors would argue, however, that such a map is too simplistic and that Detroit's location relative to Michigan or the United States is unnecessary in understanding the plane crash story.

The Detroit News and the *Detroit Free Press* presented diagram graphics that showed not only the runway but also the plane's attempt to take off and its path of destruction (Figure 12.8). In the days after the disaster, speculation on the cause of the crash centered on the winds at the time of takeoff and the setting of the plane's wing flaps. Each time a new development occurred, the graphics staffs at the two Detroit papers responded with detailed and thorough informational graphics (Figures 12.9 and 12.10). The graphics provided specific information about what investigators were working on and background data that helped make the news stories more understandable.

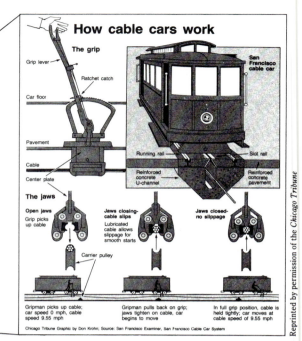

Figure 12.11   Diagram showing how cable car works

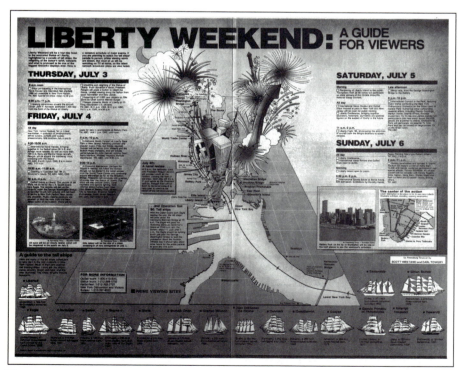

Figure 12.12   Diagram about Fourth of July celebrations

Non-Disaster Diagrams

Diagrams aren't used solely with disaster stories. They can explain common occurrences, such as how the San Francisco cable cars work (Figure

12.11), how to view Fourth of July celebrations (Figure 12.12), what's under a city street (Figure 12.13) or how a magician does his tricks (Figure 12.14).

The secret to creating these diagrams is finding the information for an artist to use. The information can come from reference books or through interviews with experts. When creating complicated diagrams, the artist must pay careful attention to taking technical jargon and putting it in language readers can understand. Visual journalists never should assume that readers are experts on the subject being diagrammed.

FACTS BOXES

A facts box is the simplest type of informational graphic from an artist's point of view; however, care must be taken when deciding on the information for the graphic.

By highlighting important aspects of a major story, facts boxes provide information to readers who have limited time to spend with the newspaper but who want to stay well-informed. Facts boxes allow a reader to skim the vital facts of a story, such as an income tax increase or a nuclear arms treaty,

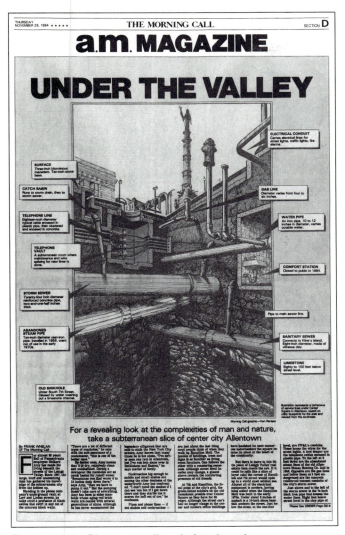

Figure 12.13 Diagram revealing what's under a city street

Figure 12.14 Diagram revealing how magician performs tricks

without having to read the entire report. Many editors believe a good facts box can help draw readers into the story because their curiosity may be aroused by something they read in the facts box.

There are several types of facts boxes from which the visual journalist or artist may choose.

Story Summary Facts Box

The *story summary facts box* highlights, as concisely as possible, key points in a story (Figure 12.15). Based on the information in the box, the reader can decide to read the accompanying story or move on to another. Such graphics are particularly helpful in lengthy investigative or in-depth articles or series.

Geriatric centers train health-care specialists

— GERIATRIC, from page 24

estimates that nationwide, the elderly may be taking 25 percent more medication than is necessary.

Stratton said the program actually may cut medications by as much as 50 percent. He said many medications that are assigned on an as-needed basis are never given, even though they are included in patients' records.

"In the elderly, the tendency to prescribe is there," Stratton said. "In the past two decades, we have had an explosion in the number of drugs available, and we in this country have adopted the erroneous philosophy that there is a drug for everything.

"Many patients and many doctors see the writing of a prescription as the consummation of the doctor-patient relationship. And we are backward in doing that.

"Improved awareness of drug utilization in the elderly is a major part of our program and is a part of the educational preparation of students and of practicing professionals through continuing education."

The center has taken its message to every corner of the state.

A conference in January drew 419 nurses, doctors, pharmacists and nursing and medical students from around

Illinois woman who was treated through the New Mexico program.

Dorothy, not her real name, was brought June 30, 1987, to Las Palmas Nursing Home, the other teaching nursing home served by the university program. Her son, who is in the Air Force and stationed in Albuquerque, literally brought her there to die.

"She was completely bedbound, she couldn't feed or dress herself, she had tongue-thrusting movements and she didn't know where she was most of the time," said nurse practitioner Jeanette Kelley, who managed Dorothy's case.

Nurse practitioners have completed courses beyond those required for a registered nurse's degree.

"She came in with a diagnosis of Parkinson's disease, hypertension and dementia," Kelley said.

As with all patients, the first thing Kelley did was to review Dorothy's medications. She found the patient was on 13 separate drugs for an unspecified "nervous condition."

Kelley knew something was drastically wrong when she noticed the woman was simultaneously taking three extremely powerful psychotropics, Thorazine, Mellaril and Haldol.

With the help of the center's team, Kelley diagnosed Dorothy as suffering from drug-induced tardive dyskinesia,

Key points

1. To combat the widespread lack of formal education and training in geriatrics, the federal government in recent years has funded 31 geriatric-education centers at medical schools across the country.

2. The Albuquerque geriatric-education center at the University of New Mexico has reduced the number of medications used on its elderly patients on an average of 30 to 50 percent and improved their health in the process.

3. Many patients and doctors have developed the "backward" view that their medical relationship must be consummated with a prescription drug.

4. An elderly, bed-ridden Illinois woman was on 13 medications, including three different antipsychotics, when she was taken into the New Mexico program. The drugs were reduced to only two, and several months later, she returned to a normal life.

Figure 12.15 Story summary facts box

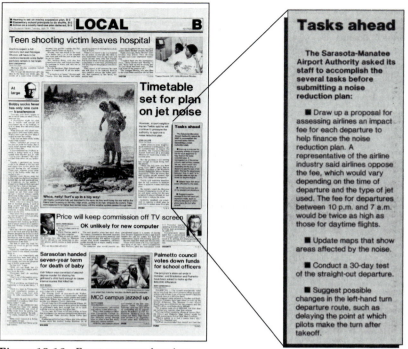

Figure 12.16   Event summary facts box

Figure 12.17   Event summary facts box with illustrations
Reprinted by permission of the *Chicago Tribune*.

Figure 12.18   Background facts box on person in news

Event Summary Facts Box

The *event summary facts box* shows major changes that occurred or will occur in the wake of a news event, such as a major decision by a government agency (Figure 12.16). It alerts readers quickly to changes that might affect them (Figure 12.17).

Background Facts Box

The *background facts box* provides the reader with necessary history about a story or person in the news (Figure 12.18). Because it details background information, the background graphic allows a reporter to focus on current events and helps keep the writing of the main story lively. This graphic

er case later

fit the description given by the witness.

Deputies were minutes from saving Patricia Greenfield's life.

"Everything went well" for Martin, Andersen said. "And everything went bad for Patti."

At the landfill, Martin took Greenfield out of the car and took her down an embankment. He tried to strangle her, but she did not become unconscious. He then took a five-inch filet knife and stabbed her once in the left side of the throat.

"I think I asked him if there was any other way to get around it. And he said that he had to kill her. There was no other way," Forbes said.

Two days later, George Greenfield said, he knew his daughter was dead. Sitting in a prayer meeting with Mary by his side, his daughter spoke to him, he said.

"In my spirit I heard Patti," George Greenfield said. "She said, 'Don't cry, I'm OK.' When I turned over that to [Mary] Monday night we knew she was in heaven with the Lord."

Greenfield's body was found four days later. Deep down, Andersen knew it would happen. But the glimmer of hope he had that Greenfield was still alive vanished when he saw her body that day.

"I hurt and I felt bad," Andersen said. "I was driving north on [Interstate] 95 and started to cry. And it was the only time I had really prayed."

Andersen said he felt as if he knew Greenfield as well as anyone. He went through her room, looked at letters, talked to friends and family.

"I usually try to find out as much as I can about the victim." Ander-

sen said. "When I went into her room I could really see the person. There was a lot of good there."

Martin and Forbes were arrested 10 days after the murder when a prostitute — tied, raped and threatened at knifepoint by Martin — escaped his apartment and called police.

Anderson said it didn't take him long to know who the killer was.

"After 20 minutes of talking to Nollie, I knew that he had killed her," Andersen said. "He was mean."

Forbes, on the other hand, was scared and sorry. He told detectives the whole story. And he begged them not to let Martin near him or his family.

Martin, he said, "told me one time he'd like to see how many people he could kill without being caught."

"It's been bothering me," Gary Forbes said on the day he was arrested. "He can do something like that and don't care. Just like a normal routine for him. Just like getting up in the morning. And I can't take that."

CHRONOLOGY

- **JUNE 25, 1977** — Convenience-store clerk Patricia Ann Greenfield is abducted during a robbery by Nollie Lee Martin and his cousin Gary Forbes. The woman is taken to Martin's house, where she is raped. Martin and Forbes then take her to a dump west of Lantana, and Martin stabs her.
- **JUNE 29, 1977** — Patricia Greenfield's body is discovered by a worker at the Lantana Landfill.
- **JULY 4, 1977** — Martin is arrested after he is identified by a prostitute he abducted and raped. Forbes confesses to abducting Greenfield and tells police Martin killed her.
- **NOV. 13, 1978** — Martin is sentenced to death by Palm Beach County Circuit Judge Marvin Mounts.
- **AUG. 8, 1984** — Gov. Bob Graham signs a death warrant scheduling Martin to die in the electric chair on Sept. 6.
- **SEPT. 6, 1984** — The 11th U.S. Circuit Court of Appeal in Atlanta grants Martin a stay of execution.
- **SEPT. 23, 1985** — Martin attempts to commit suicide by slashing his wrists in his death row jail cell.
- **OCT. 21, 1986** — Gov. Bob Graham signs Martin's second death warrant. He is scheduled to die in the electric chair on Nov. 18, the same day as serial killer Ted Bundy.
- **NOV. 14, 1986** — Martin's execution is once again stayed after his attorneys argue that Martin is insane. Common law and constitutional law prohibit the execution of insane inmates.
- **OCT 12, 1987** — Gov. Bob Martinez signs Martin's third death warrant. He is scheduled to be executed on Nov. 5.
- **OCT 28, 1987** — The Florida Supreme Court gives Martin a temporary stay of execution, ruling the state must first determine whether he is sane.
- **NOV. 5, 1987** — Martin wins a temporary stay until a circuit court judge and the state Supreme Court rule on his competency.
- **NOV. 11, 1987** — The Supreme Court declares Martin competent and the state schedules the execution for 7:01 a.m., Nov. 11. But U.S. District Judge James Lawrence King issues a permanent stay, saying there is not enough time for him to review the competency issue on appeal.

Figure 12.19   Chronology facts box

A DC-3, the rebels' lifeline, drops supplies of food, weapons and cash.

The Philadelphia Inquirer / ED HILLE

Nicaragua

POPULATION: 3 million

CAPITAL: Managua.

HISTORY: Since gaining independence from Spain in 1821, Nicaragua has been fought over by various factions. The U.S. Marines intervened several times early in this century to restore order on behalf of regimes friendly to the United States. U.S. occupation ended in 1932 after a five-year war against a guerrilla army led by Gen. Augusto C. Sandino. The Somoza family — father and two sons — ruled almost for 43 years. The Sandinista National Liberation Front, named for the martyred Sandino, overthrew dictator Anastasio Somoza Debayle in July 1979.

But Nicaragua's civil war did not end. Within two years, Nicaraguans disaffected by the Sandinistas' increasingly anti-democratic regime formed armed groups in Honduras. The Sandinistas called the armed bands "contras," a Spanish abbreviation for counterrevolutionaries.

At first the contras were trained by right-wing Argentine military officials. In December 1981, President Reagan ordered the CIA to aid the contras secretly.

With the aid, the contras' ranks grew from a few hundred fighters to several thousand. In 1983, an increasingly skeptical Congress capped the CIA's contra assistance at $24 million. And in 1984, after disclosures that the CIA had mined a Nicaraguan port, Congress cut off all aid and prohibited U.S. intelligence agencies from assisting the contras.

In June 1985, Congress approved $27 million in humanitarian aid to the contras. In September 1986, it increased the support to $100 million, including military aid. The CIA resumed supervising the contras.

A cascade of events in 1986 and 1987, culminating in disclosure of the Iran-contra arms deals, disclosed the extent to which Reagan administration officials had circumvented congressional restrictions on U.S. aid, including the diversion of at least $3.2 million in profits from U.S. arms sales to Iran.

LANGUAGES: Official language is Spanish.

GOVERNMENT: Republic. All state functions, military forces, police, key industries and much of the news media are controlled by the leftist Sandinistas.

HEAD OF STATE: Daniel Ortega Saavedra, one of the nine Sandinista commanders, was elected president in 1984.

INDUSTRY: Major exports are coffee, cotton, sugar, bananas, beef and gold.

RELIGION: Roman Catholic, 85 percent.

AREA: 57,000 sq. mi., about the size of Iowa.

SOURCE: U.S. State Department

Sandinistas by surprise, they failed to achieve what a State Department official called their major military objective — destroying a bridge near Muelle de los Bueyes that would have cut the highway.

A contra demolition team was killed trying to blow up the bridge. Two days later, the highway was reopened.

The Rama Road attack failed on another score as well — the contras managed to alienate some potential sympathizers.

The contras burned the municipal building at San Pedro de Lovago, which had contained a jail and offices for the local militia and the Sandinista party. But it had also housed the

He said a "psychosis of war" has paralyzed the town residents, who have witnessed five contra attacks in recent years.

"Nobody wants it to get dark now because the attacks have been in the night," he said. "So when night falls, everybody gets nervous."

U.S. officials said the Rama Road attack showed that the rebels could pull off a major coordinated military action, without killing or injuring many civilians.

But a subsequent attack on a small farm cooperative at El Juste, just off the Rama Road and about 10 miles west of San Pedro de Lovago, indicated that the contras' tactic of at-

Figure 12.20   Location facts box with map

sometimes is used as a sidebar to the main story and is given special treatment by an artist or graphics editor.

Chronology Facts Box

The *chronology facts box* provides key dates in the history of an event (Figure 12.19). Because it is not written in story form, the chronology graphic can allow for a more visual treatment of the information through photographs and drawings.

Location Facts Box

The *location facts box* explains basic facts about a country, state or city (Figure 12.20). It is useful with international news stories and often contains a map showing where the country is located. The information used in this facts box can be found in reference books from the U.S. State Department or Central Intelligence Agency.

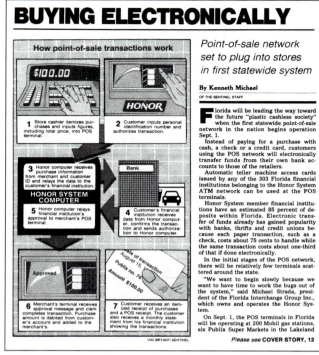

Figure 12.21   How-it-works facts box

Please see COVER STORY, 12

How-It-Works Facts Box

The *how-it-works fact box* uses visuals and words to explain a complex process. For example, this type of facts box might explain how purchases are made electronically (Figure 12.21) or how processors in a supercomputer "pipeline" function (Figure 12.22). Of course, that information could have been written in story form, but a facts box with plenty of visual elements does a better job of explaining the process.

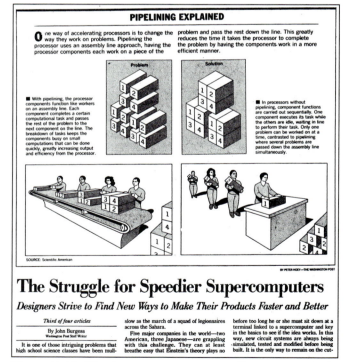

Figure 12.22   How-it-works facts box

Pegie Stark

Graphics Editor   *The Detroit News*

When Northwest Airlines Flight 255 crashed after takeoff from Detroit Metropolitan Airport on Aug. 16, 1987, *The Detroit News* graphics staff knew it had plenty of work to do. Pegie Stark, a graphics editor and researcher at the newspaper, was part of the team that covered the crash graphically. She works mostly on special projects, but when a story as big as the Northwest crash happens, she makes the late-breaking story her priority.

Stark said the first thing the graphics department did was construct a step-by-step 3-D map indicating the path of the plane on the airport runway. The map showed the way the plane hit a car rental building and ended up on the highway late on a Sunday night. The map files in the graphics department provided the artist with a base map from which to trace the path of the plane.

The first map/graphic was done as reporters worked on breaking stories on the tragedy. A graphics coordinator read the stories as they were being written, reconstructing the scene with the reporters. Stark explained: "During the night, an artist at *USA Today* was helping provide part of the graphic—the drawing of the plane—while our people provided the breaking news part of the graphic." (*USA Today*, like *The Detroit News*, is a Gannett newspaper, and they often share graphics or parts of graphics.) All of the crash graphics were created on a Macintosh computer and sent out on Gannett Graphics Network.

The next day, as officials worked to establish the second-by-second path of the plane, a more detailed map of the airport runways was needed. Although the airport people wouldn't cooperate by providing one, Stark said,

"Someone in the newsroom remembered that our advertising or PR department had done something on the airport and had a very good map. After some phone calls and persuading, the advertising department came through with a detailed map—the blueprints for the airport. It was exactly what we needed."

A day after the crash, the graphics staff of *The News* was working on visuals for the paper's second-day package. "At this point, the officials thought it was wind shear that caused the crash," Stark said. "We decided we could put together a very informative graphic on wind shear. We also ran a more detailed map/graphic, again with updated information, showing exact times of the events. We decided to show a detailed cutaway of the plane and to give its history, so we got a reporter to track the plane's day before it crashed."

At that time, the plane's black box was being discussed as well. "In that second-day package we included a cutaway of the black box and an explanation of what's in it," Stark noted. "It is really orange and becomes black when charred by fire. And it is really two boxes, a voice recorder and data recorder."

Stark said the staff's next step was to start calling people at McDonnell Douglas to establish contacts who could provide detailed information on the plane as the story developed over the following weeks.

"Every day some new theory developed as to the cause of the crash, so we tried to get on hand as much technical information as we could to anticipate describing graphically each theory," she said. "One of the reasons graphics worked so well was that photographs were only showing the total

devastation of the plane and the victims. There was absolutely nothing left at the crash site. So, when we wanted to explain the inside of the plane or the engine or to create the scene, graphics were the ideal visual explanation."

Stark said the graphics department kept digging for information. "We called the airline and manufacturer of the plane to get more and more details. Using Jane's All the World's Aircraft, we got a cutaway of the engine. Then McDonnell Douglas [the manufacturer] sent us [via facsimile machine] detailed diagrams of the flaps, slat, controls, cockpit and other equipment."

Stark wrote a sequence of events of what a pilot does right before and when he or she enters the cockpit of the plane and then had McDonnell Douglas check that information. She explained: "We couldn't find a photo of the cockpit, so we took a blueprint from McDonnell Douglas and a drawing of a general cockpit that we found in a magazine and drew a graphic from that information. Once we had it together, we faxed it to McDonnell Douglas to check it for accuracy. As the story developed, the cockpit graphic was used over and over to put the reader inside the cockpit. We provided an explanation of what is needed to get the plane up and flying."

Stark said much of her job involves asking reporters and sources "visual" questions. "I gather visual information and written descriptions that an artist can draw from. For example, someone might say, the pilot flips a switch and flaps go to the right position. My job is to dig for more, to ask: 'Where is the switch? How does it work? How do the flaps work? How are they different from the slats? How big are they?'"

SUGGESTED EXERCISES

1. Find two examples of diagrams in a newspaper and critique them. What do you like and dislike about them? How would you improve them?

2. Clip a diagram from a local newspaper and discuss how it explains what, where, when, why and how.

3. Discuss "visual frame of reference." Clip a diagram from a newspaper that can be used as an example.

4. Find an example of a story summary facts box in a newspaper and critique it. What do you like and dislike about it? How would you improve it?

5. Do the same for an event summary facts box.

6. Do the same for a background facts box.

7. Do the same for a chronology facts box.

8. Do the same for a location facts box.

9. Do the same for a how-it-works facts box.

CHAPTER THIRTEEN

Maps

Maps are the oldest form of graphic communication—even before there was paper, clay tablets were used to record information about the location of places and things within those places.

The oldest known map, drawn by Sumerians, has been dated to approximately 3800 B.C. and shows an estate in Mesopotamia. The Egyptians made maps in the 14th century B.C. that showed boundaries of property. The Greeks laid the foundation for modern mapmaking in about the 6th century B.C. when they developed the system of latitude and longitude, which is used today to map coordinates of locations in the world. For centuries, people have used geographic maps to tell others about places.

MAPS IN NEWSPAPERS

Maps were among the first types of graphics used by newspapers more than a century ago. In its coverage of the Civil War, for example, *The Philadelphia Inquirer* included a map to help tell the story of the 1862 battle of Antietam (Figure 13.1). Another example of early newspaper maps is a 1934 hand-drawn map that gave newspaper readers a better understanding of the violence that erupted between striking longshoremen and San Francisco police (Figure 13.2).

Even though maps have been used by newspapers for a long time, they are one of the most underappreciated and underutilized forms of visual communication. Few newspapers run as many maps as they could to provide readers with a geographic fix on news events. And the maps that are used often are not given the same play as larger, more glamorous informational graphics. Despite the lack of "excitement" in a one-column map, the visual journalist should look for stories that can be enhanced by the inclusion of maps.

Maps also are a much-needed graphic in today's newspapers because of the startling lack of geographic knowledge among readers. Surveys of U.S. high school and college students have revealed an appalling lack of knowledge of where various countries are in the world. Even journalists who are familiar with places in the news have a hard time correctly identifying countries on a map. For example, how many people could look at a map of the United States that showed the outline of states and correctly label each one (Figure 13.3)?

Figure 13.1   Early newspaper map (1862)

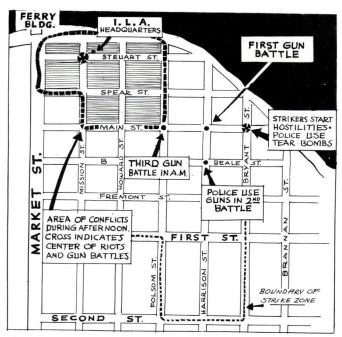

Figure 13.2   Hand-drawn newspaper map (1934)

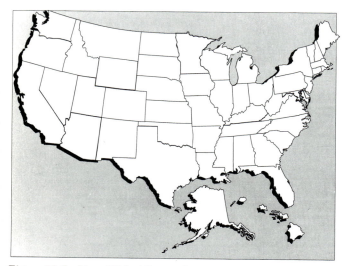

Figure 13.3   Map of United States—how many states can you identify?

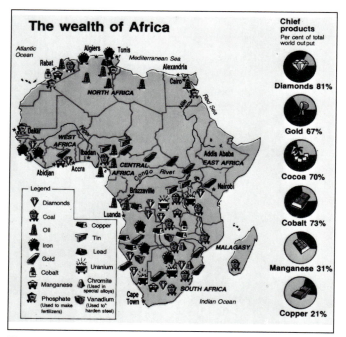

Figure 13.4   Distribution map

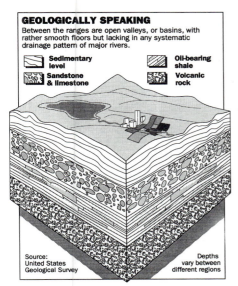

GEOLOGICALLY SPEAKING
Between the ranges are open valleys, or basins, with rather smooth floors but lacking in any systematic drainage pattern of major rivers.

Sedimentary level

Sandstone & limestone

Oil-bearing shale

Volcanic rock

Source: United States Geological Survey

Depths vary between different regions

Figure 13.5   Geologic map

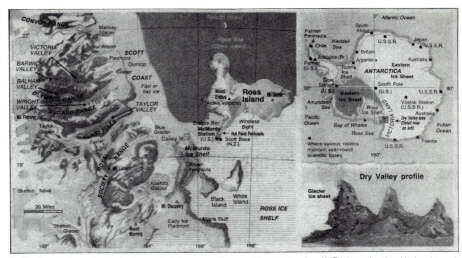

Looking like water from a dam that has burst, a glacier flows against the side of a Dry Valley mountain range. The valleys are free of ice and could contain great mineral wealth. The ice on the other side rises thousands of feet. Scientists are trying to determine why the valleys are free of ice.

Figure 13.6   Topographic map

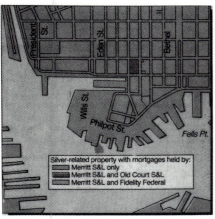

Silver-related property with mortgages held by:
Merritt S&L only
Merritt S&L and Old Court S&L
Merritt S&L and Fidelity Federal

Figure 13.7   Land use map

There are scores of map types available to the visual journalist. Here are the ones most commonly used by newspapers.

Distribution Map

Distribution maps show, for example, the location of endangered species or the occurrence of oil deposits (Figure 13.4). Another common distribution map appears on many weather pages to show the distribution of temperatures across the United States. Such maps use *isolines* or *contour lines* to show the gradual change in value.

Geologic Map

Geologic maps show formations of mineral or other surface deposits, as in a bedrock map, or the rock layers of the Earth, to help in understanding earthquake faults. These maps also are used to show land disputes, disasters and soil conditions (Figure 13.5). Sometimes these devices are called *cross-section maps.*

Topographic Map

Topographic maps show visible features of an area such as a mountain range or a valley (Figure 13.6). These maps also can use contour lines to show elevation relative to sea level. Topo-

graphic maps are useful to a visual journalist because of the vast amount of specific data found in them, such as roads, trails and power lines. Most topographic maps are produced by the U.S. Geological Survey department of the federal government.

Land Use Map

Land use maps show activity in a given area, such as residential and industrial areas within a city's boundaries (Figure 13.7).

Statistical or Data Map

Statistical or **data maps** show quantitative information across a geographic area, such as state-by-state unemployment rates in the United States (Figure 13.8).

Surface Map

The most commonly used maps in newspapers are **surface maps,** which show the location of places on a flat surface. They are sometimes called *transportation maps* because they generally show highways, roads, streets, airports, cities and major points of interest. A map showing the route Pope John Paul II took during his visit to

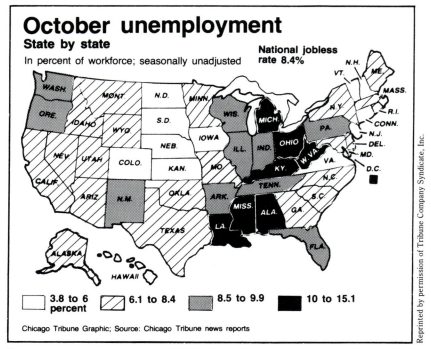

Figure 13.8   Statistical or data map

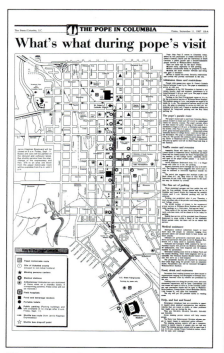

Figure 13.9   Surface map

Figure 13.10   Location map

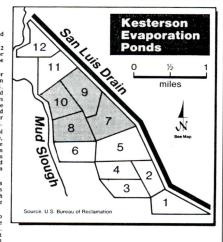

Figure 13.11   Location map that is too specific

Columbia, S.C., is an example of a surface map (Figure 13.9). Within the broad category of surface or transportation map, there are different types of maps newspapers can use to present geographic information.

Location Map

A **location map** shows an area being written about in an accompanying story (Figure 13.10). This common newspaper map is often the most poorly done because it fails to do the two things that successful location maps must do: first, show a location important to a story; second, relate the specific location to an overall area, as the "River" map did.

The map showing the Kesterson evaporation ponds is an example of a location map that is so specific, so

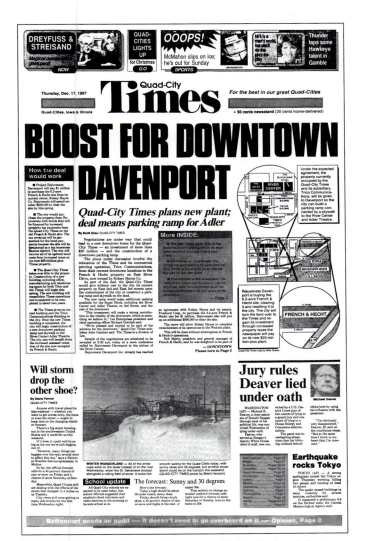

Figure 13.12 Location map showing specific location in relation to overall area

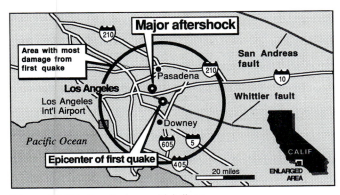

Figure 13.13 Location map with balloon

detailed, that it fails to give readers any sense of where the ponds are in relation to towns or cities they might live in or know (Figure 13.11). There are only two reference points, a mud slough and the San Luis Drain. If a reader doesn't have any knowledge of either site, the map serves virtually no purpose.

A better example of a location map is from the *Quad Cities Times* (Figure 13.12). This map shows not only the specific blocks being written about in the news story but also the location of the blocks in relation to the city and the Mississippi River, a reference point for most Quad Cities readers. By showing both a specific location and its relationship to an overall area, this map gives readers unfamiliar with the area a better chance of understanding the story.

Location Map with a Highlight Box or Balloon

This type of map, often used with breaking news stories, points to a location and, in a box or balloon, gives readers a three- or four-word explanation of the news (Figure 13.13). The balloon or box should tell readers, in as few words as possible, where an event occurred. The story should give the details. For example, instead of saying "12 West German miners die in accident," the balloon should say "Where miners died" or "Site of mine accident."

Event or Trip Map

The **event** or **trip map** traces specific events over a period of time, helping readers understand events that have occurred or upcoming events. As with location maps with balloons, the information in these maps needs to be con-

USA TODAY · THURSDAY, MAY 26, 1988 · 7A
REAGAN AND GORBACHEV: ROUND FOUR
Guide to Moscow summit
TV brings it home
Where Reagans are staying
Ambassador's host at Spaso House
THE SUMMIT
What leaders will discuss
What's in the stars
What Moscow's weather is like
Common Russian words to know
Kremlin: Center of attention
Palace of Congresses
Lenin Mausoleum
Red Square
Department store
St. Basil's Cathedral
Arsenal
Spassky Tower
Armory
Trinity Tower
Great Kremlin Palace
Patriarch's Palace
Cathedral Square
Council of Ministers

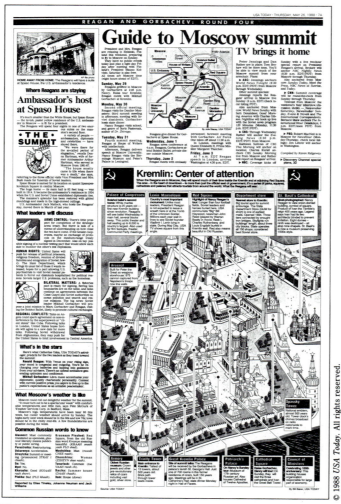

Figure 13.14 One type of trip map

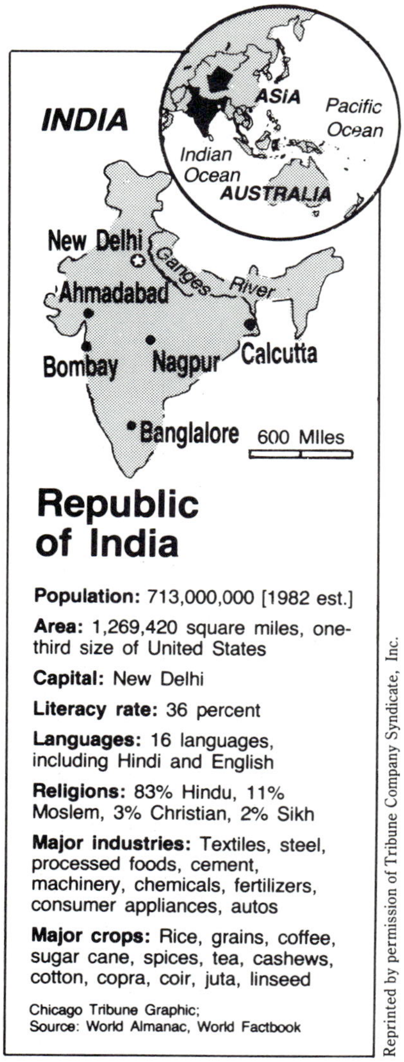

INDIA
ASIA
Pacific Ocean
Indian Ocean
AUSTRALIA
New Delhi
Ganges River
Ahmadabad
Bombay
Nagpur
Calcutta
Banglalore
600 Miles
Republic of India
Population: 713,000,000 [1982 est.]
Area: 1,269,420 square miles, one-third size of United States
Capital: New Delhi
Literacy rate: 36 percent
Languages: 16 languages, including Hindi and English
Religions: 83% Hindu, 11% Moslem, 3% Christian, 2% Sikh
Major industries: Textiles, steel, processed foods, cement, machinery, chemicals, fertilizers, consumer appliances, autos
Major crops: Rice, grains, coffee, sugar cane, spices, tea, cashews, cotton, copra, coir, juta, linseed
Chicago Tribune Graphic;
Source: World Almanac, World Factbook

Figure 13.15 Country facts map

cise. In addition, the information should be arranged so the reader can follow the sequence of events.

Another type of trip map shows the specifics of a city that a newsmaker is visiting. *USA Today*'s map of Moscow prior to President Ronald Reagan's 1988 visit does an excellent job of introducing a foreign city to American readers (Figure 13.14).

Country Facts Map

The **country facts map** presents both a map of a country and some specific information such as population and size, which makes it more like an informational graphic than a pure map (Figure 13.15).

Weather Map

Almost all daily newspapers run a **weather map** showing, at the least, temperatures for a featured area. Some papers run more than one. Readers demand such maps because weather is important to their lives and to the nation's economy. And everyone likes to talk about the weather. Although perhaps not as newsworthy as some informational graphics, the weather map is thus an important part of a newspaper's daily graphics presentation. The same amount of time, thought and attention to detail should be given to the weather map as to other devices. Fortunately, once the design of the weather map has been established, it remains constant from day to day. It is up to the visual journalist, however, to double-check all the figures and weather fronts in the map each day.

Weather maps can range from simple black-and-white forecast maps supplied by the Associated Press or another service (Figure 13.16) to more elaborate and colorful maps. *USA Today* has had

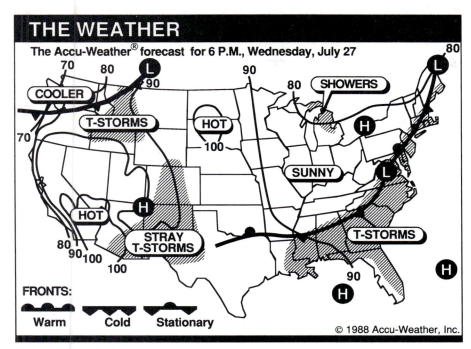

Figure 13.16 Weather map

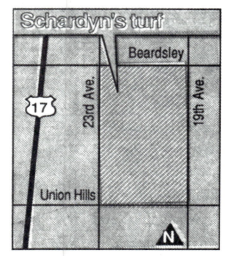

Figure 13.17 Map without a visual frame of reference

an impact on newspaper weather maps much as it has on all newspaper visuals. Shortly after the newspaper introduced its colorful weather map, many newspapers redesigned and improved their weather package to include more and better visuals.

An important element in the improvement of weather maps has been the arrival of forecasting services that are independent of the National Weather Service. These services, such as Weather Central and Accu-Weather, provide sophisticated weather information tailored to the needs of individual newspapers. In addition to supplying tabular information showing the highs and lows around the nation, these services will provide daily (or more than once daily) color weather maps produced on a Macintosh computer and transmitted to the newspaper via telephone lines. These transmitted maps can save valuable artistic time without a loss of quality.

THE ELEMENTS OF MAPMAKING

The simple, although hardly simplistic, location map should be created with the same care and attention to detail as any informational graphic. The visual journalist must pay attention to how readers will perceive the map; the use of type, symbols and tones; and the use of a scale.

How Readers Visualize a Map

Successful mapmaking for newspapers means understanding that the map is only a representation of a three-dimensional object, the Earth, on a one-dimensional plane, the newspaper's printed page. When taking points from a curved Earth and putting them on a flat map surface, it is impossible to show precisely the true size or relationship between points.

However, the purpose of newspaper maps is less to show true size relationships than to show a relative sense of distance between known objects. For example, newspaper readers in Dallas might have a good understanding of their state's geography—they know that Houston is south and east of Dallas and Fort Worth is west of their city. Such geographic relationships are easily understood when they involve areas that readers are familiar with.

But what about the relationship between Paris and Lyon in France? Unless a reader recently drove or took the train between the two French cities and knew that Lyon is south and east of Paris, he or she would have trouble visualizing the relationship between them. In this case, the success of the map depends on giving the reader a visual frame of reference, such as a well-known landmark, major highways or a country's shape or boundaries.

Some maps can show too much detail of a location and fail to give the reader a sense of the area being depicted. This problem is especially true in maps showing events in a large, spread-out city. If the map is "too close" in what it shows—that is, lacks a visual frame of reference—only the readers who live near the area being depicted will have a sense of location when they see the map (Figure 13.17).

State, focus locator for a city, area, event or incident within a state, 1 col. 100%

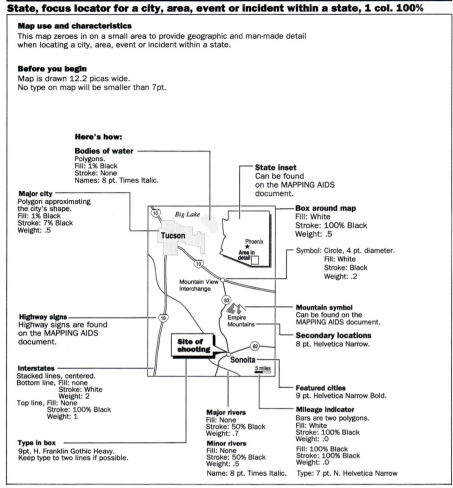

Map use and characteristics
This map zeroes in on a small area to provide geographic and man-made detail when locating a city, area, event or incident within a state.

Before you begin
Map is drawn 12.2 picas wide.
No type on map will be smaller than 7pt.

Here's how:

Bodies of water
Polygons.
Fill: 1% Black
Stroke: None
Names: 8 pt. Times Italic.

Major city
Polygon approximating the city's shape.
Fill: 1% Black
Stroke: 7% Black
Weight: .5

Highway signs
Highway signs are found on the MAPPING AIDS document.

Interstates
Stacked lines, centered.
Bottom line, Fill: none
Stroke: White
Weight: 2
Top line, Fill: None
Stroke: 100% Black
Weight: 1

Type in box
9pt. H. Franklin Gothic Heavy.
Keep type to two lines if possible.

State inset
Can be found on the MAPPING AIDS document.

Box around map
Fill: White
Stroke: 100% Black
Weight: .5

Symbol: Circle, 4 pt. diameter.
Fill: White
Stroke: Black
Weight: .2

Mountain symbol
Can be found on the MAPPING AIDS document.

Secondary locations
8 pt. Helvetica Narrow.

Featured cities
9 pt. Helvetica Narrow Bold.

Mileage indicator
Bars are two polygons.
Fill: White
Stroke: 100% Black
Weight: .0
Fill: 100% Black
Stroke: 100% Black
Weight: .0
Type: 7 pt. N. Helvetica Narrow

Major rivers
Fill: None
Stroke: 50% Black
Weight: .7

Minor rivers
Fill: None
Stroke: 50% Black
Weight: .5
Name: 8 pt. Times Italic.

Figure 13.18   Map style sheet

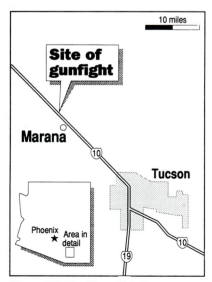

Figure 13.19   Map with balloon

Type, Symbols and Tones

Too much type can make a map unreadable; too little type may mean that the reader is not being given enough information to relate the map to the accompanying story. In addition to selecting the appropriate amount of type, the visual journalist must make certain that the type is readable. Type size is important not only for readability but also for readers' identification of key areas or information in a map.

The newspaper should have a style sheet that clearly details what size type should be used on locations such as cities, counties, roads and rivers (Figure 13.18). The style sheet can assign different type sizes for different locations. For example, a river might be set in 7-point type and a capital city in 9-point type. Although there might not be much of a difference in the two type sizes, when the map is printed, the city will be of greater importance visually than the river. And whatever the size of the type, it needs to be consistent from map to map. That's why a style sheet is important—it sets a standard for every person at the newspaper who will be working on a map.

Consistency also is important when selecting symbols to designate map features such as highways. Many newspapers simply use the same shape symbol for a U.S. highway that the federal government does. For state or county roads, most newspapers try to duplicate the standard symbols for such roads. Using standard symbols helps readers quickly "see" the type of road being shown on the map.

When information is presented in a balloon in the map, the wording should be terse. When pointing to a location within a city, for instance, the balloon might say, "Site of gunfight." Such information helps readers quickly understand the significance of the story as well as where the event occurred (Figure 13.19). Of course, not every map needs a balloon. Conversely, too many balloons can crowd the map and hinder comprehension. For example, the "Flooding in the Midwest" map has 13 balloons, which makes it difficult for readers to identify points on the map (Figure 13.20).

When selecting tones that are keyed to certain areas of a map, the visual journalist must be aware of the printing limitations at his or her newspaper—it does little good to present a map that has tones or gray screens that the newspaper can't print.

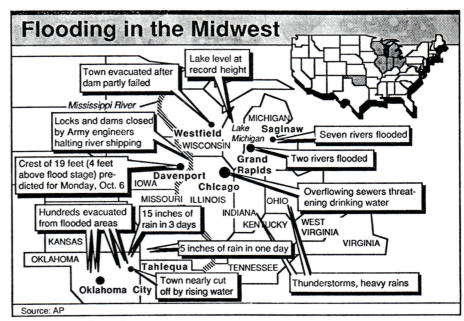

Figure 13.20   Map with too many balloons

The Scale

The *scale* of a map refers to the relationship between distance on the map and the corresponding distance on the Earth's surface. World maps show only a little amount of information because they are out of necessity made on a small scale. In contrast, a map showing a couple of blocks in a city can show a lot of detail because it uses a large scale. In newspaper maps, the scale tells readers how the space on the map relates to the actual space on the ground, either in feet, miles or kilometers. The scale thus must be clear and easy to understand.

Color and Contrast

A good map, whether in color or black and white, will use tones and shading to help focus the reader's attention on the most important part of the map. Often, a gray screen is used to shade the least important areas, thus allowing the key areas to be in white.

Color also can be used effectively to highlight key areas or designate certain information, such as blue for water. Care must be taken, however, to avoid using too much color, which can make the map confusing. And complementary colors should be used to prevent a gaudy look. A newspaper's color reproduction capabilities also must be taken into consideration, because information in the map can be obscured by poor reproduction of certain colors.

Color works well when it is used for individual keys in a statistical map. By using colors to portray distribution of information, as in state-by-state unemployment, the artist does not have to worry about the limited number of black-and-white tones that are available.

Figure 13.21   Map with the wrong visual impression

Avoiding Visual Trickery

While many artists strive to add visual excitement to maps and other informational graphics, the end result can be a graphic that "fools" the reader or wastes space in the newspaper. Such visual trickery should be avoided.

For example, in the map showing the West Bank of Israel below the rest of the country, the artist probably was trying to separate visually the two areas (Figure 13.21). However, he ended up giving the visual impression that Israel is "above" the rest of the countries on the map.

The artist who created the perspective map of the San Francisco Bay area to show the epicenters of two earthquakes also played a visual trick (Figure 13.22). The "mountains" on

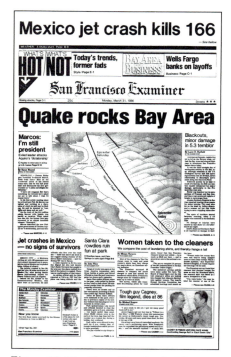

Figure 13.22   Map with a visual trick

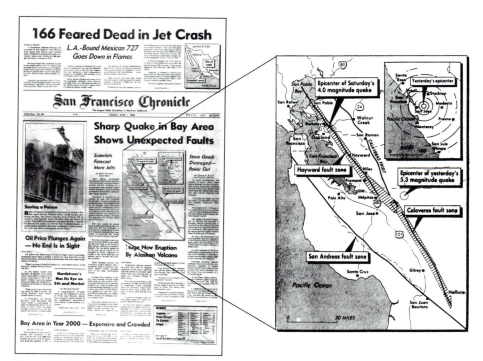

Figure 13.23   Straightforward quake map

the east side of the map bear no resemblance to fact or geography and give the map a cartoonlike appearance. For the amount of space used, little information was transmitted. In contrast, a quake map from another newspaper takes far less space and transmits far more information (Figure 13.23).

SUGGESTED EXERCISES

1. Look through several issues of the same newspaper, or different newspapers, and find examples of the following types of maps:

   a. Distribution map
   b. Geologic map
   c. Topographic map
   d. Land use map
   e. Statistical or data map
   f. Location map
   g. Location map with balloon
   h. Event or trip map
   i. Country facts map

2. After you have clipped examples of each of the maps, critique them. Do they contain too much or too little information? Are they easy to read? Do the symbols, scale and tones work? Can you suggest ways to improve them?

3. Clip the main weather map from *USA Today.* Also clip two weather maps from metropolitan newspapers that resemble the *USA Today* map and two maps from metros that do not. Which maps do you prefer?

4. Clip two examples of black-and-white maps that would work better in color and explain why you think they would.

5. Can you find an example of a map that tricks readers? What is wrong with it? How would you fix it?

6. On a blank piece of paper and without any reference tools, draw a map of your town and indicate where you go to school and where you live. Draw in the major streets. Now compare your map to a real map. Discuss how well your mental map illustrated the actual thing.

CHAPTER FOURTEEN

The Pitfalls of Informational Graphics

By the mid-1980s, newspapers realized that informational graphics could help their readers better understand complicated stories. Today, newspapers of all sizes are using maps, tables, charts, facts boxes and diagrams to provide information and/or highlight the essence of stories.

Most important, an informational graphic must be capable of standing alone without a story. Readers should be able to look at it as an independent element and draw meaning from it. That means editors and artists must avoid graphics that depend on stories for explanations. Graphics cannot be so complex that they confuse readers or so simplistic that they add nothing to the comprehension of a story. As with everything else in the newspaper, graphics must present meaningful information accurately, concisely and in easy-to-understand language. When they do not, the publication risks a loss of credibility with its readers.

Too often newspapers run faulty graphics, which fall into two categories: empty graphics, which contain too little information and serve only as window dressing to pretty up a page; and garbage graphics, which can mislead readers and distort information for the sake of artistic display. Some graphics editors and artists would argue that such faulty graphics are part of the creative process. Indeed, most readers will not even realize that there is a lack of data in an informational graphic if they are not interested in the story. But if they are, or if they have some knowledge of the subject, they will know they have been given an empty or garbage graphic. That is when the newspaper's credibility suffers.

The surge in the use of informational graphics and their increasing sophistication have created new problems and challenges for newspaper editors and artists. This chapter will examine those problems and challenges and offer some solutions.

THE EMPTY GRAPHIC

An empty graphic contains insufficient information to make a story clearer to readers. For example, the graphic "Room tax collections for Washoe County" takes up about 6 column-inches of space but offers little data (Figure 14.1). The information provided in the graphic could have been better expressed within the text of the story. For instance:

Figure 14.1   Empty graphic

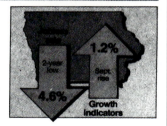

Figure 14.2   Empty and misleading graphic

Figure 14.3   Graphic containing too little information

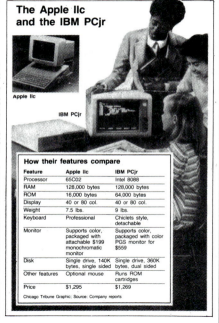

Figure 14.4   Effective graphic

Room tax collections in Washoe County totaled $1,016,235 in September 1983, 26 percent more than in the same month in 1982.

That one sentence of type takes up less than one inch of space; in this case, the editor could have saved valuable space by not running the graphic. Or the editor could have added more information to the graphic. For example, historical data could have been included to show trends in the room tax collections: Were they larger or smaller 10 years ago? Such information would help a reader understand the story.

Another example of an empty graphic ran on Page One with a story about Iowa's economy (Figure 14.2). Once again, the small amount of data does not warrant its placement in a graphic—the data showing the Iowa jobless rate

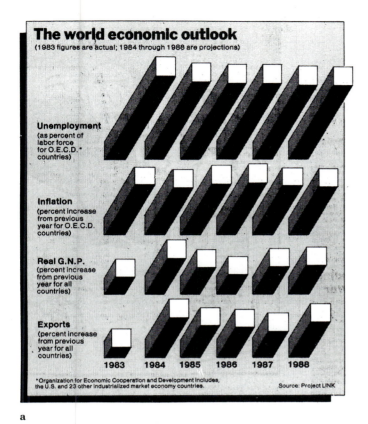

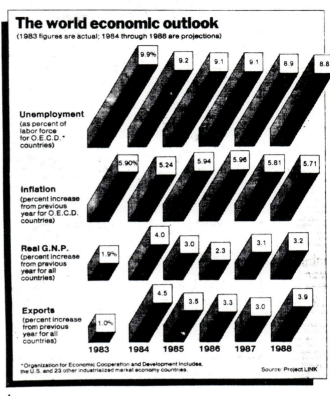

Figure 14.5 (a) Graphic with misleading bars as (b) percent increase figures indicate, as graphic was originally published

at a two-year low merely repeats the headline. The use of the directional arrows in the graphic also is misleading. The jobless rate did not drop 4.6 percent as the arrow indicates; it dropped 1.2 percent from the previous month to 4.6 percent. This graphic would have worked if it had included a more accurate summary of the information in the story, or if it had provided more background so readers could have seen historical trends.

Accompanying the graphic "Choosing a computer" is a story that reports on what the experts say about some of the most popular home computers (Figure 14.3). The graphic, however, contains little information. It shows only what the various computer systems look like. A better graphic would have included some information with the photographs, such as memory size, display screen size, keyboard type, disk drive data and price. All of this information is contained in the story and thus is available to the graphics editor or artist.

One graphic that does work, entitled "The Apple IIc and the IBM PCjr," appeared in the *Chicago Tribune* (Figure 14.4). The graphic provides basic information about the two computer systems in a clear display and in a minimal amount of space.

THE GARBAGE GRAPHIC

Lack of information is not the only reason for poor informational graphics. Sometimes, the editor and artist have solid information but the data are misused and distorted. Such misuse creates a "garbage graphic." The three major problem areas of garbage graphics are perspective, zero basing and time shifting.

Problems with Perspective

Because newspaper pages are one-dimensional, artists are tempted to add visual variety to graphics to give them perspective, or the illusion of depth.

A common technique involves creating bars that look three-dimensional. Unfortunately, such three-dimensional bars can be misleading; they may create a discrepancy between the reader's visual impression and the actual data in the graphic. Visual trickery should not replace accurate graphics.

An example of misleading bars is found in the chart entitled "The world economic outlook" (Figure 14.5a). When you look at the top row of bars, it appears that the highest bar is the first bar on the left and the lowest bar is the second bar from the right. Now look at the chart as it originally appeared with the percent increase that each bar supposedly indicates added (Figure 14.5b). The first bar indeed represents the highest percent increase, but it is the last bar that represents the lowest total.

The "Scandinavian popularity" chart is another example of a graphic that is difficult for the reader to follow and understand (Figure 14.6). This graphic creates a dimensional effect in the

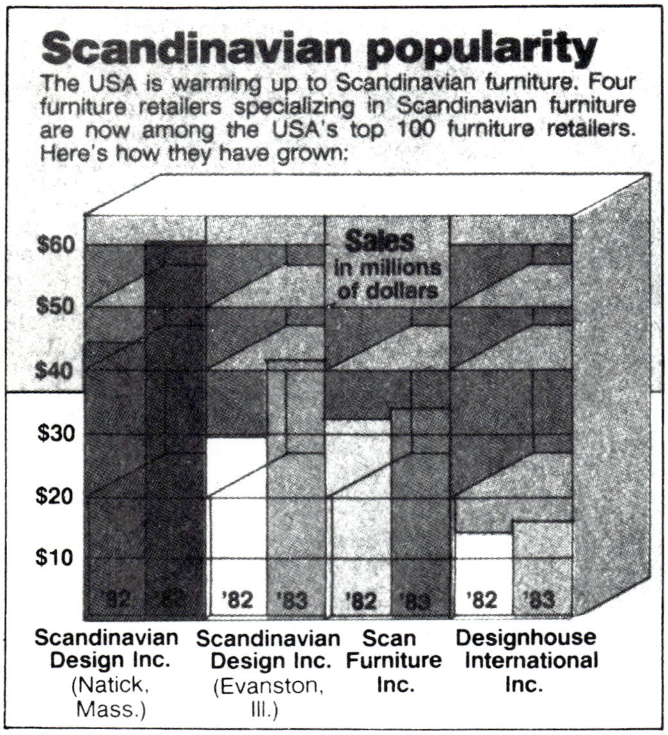

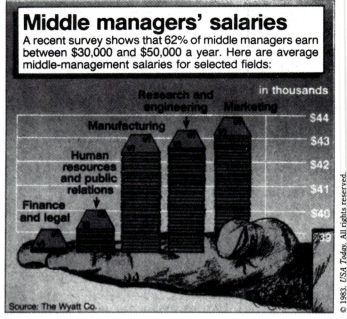

Figure 14.6   Graphic with confusing dimensional effect

Figure 14.7   Ambiguous graphic

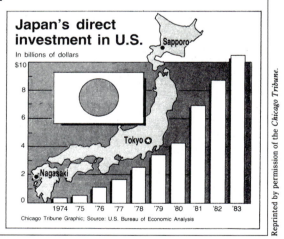

Japan forges presence in U.S. steel

By Robert Kearns

TO THE THOUSANDS of workers at National Steel Corp.'s three Midwest mills, the visit of 28 engineers of Nippon Kokan K.K., Japan's No. 2 steelmaker, to their plants late last year was nothing unusual.

For more that 15 years, National had had a relationship with Nippon Kokan whereby Japanese teams would visit their plants and people from National in turn would go to Japan in order to exchange technical information. So the National Steel employees had gotten used to Japanese visitors looking and asking all sorts of questions.

However, what they didn't know then is that as early as last summer Howard Love, chairman of National Intergroup Inc., National Steel's owner, had been talking with Nippon Kokan about making the relationship a good deal more serious.

Last week, National Steel's approximately 12,500 employees learned just how serious those talks had been: Love announced that Nippon Kokan would take a half-interest in National Steel, the United States' seventh-largest steel producer, in a $292 million deal that calls for payment of $273 million in cash and $19 million in notes by Nippon Kokan.

"WE'RE ALL VERY happy," Love said in an interview. "We're two very strong partners—godparents, you might say—and the deal ensures the long-term viability of National Steel. Steel is a worldwide commodity."

Figure 14.8   More effective use of dimension in column chart

background that causes the reader to lose track of the bars. This type of graphic is sometimes referred to as the "six-dimensional Salvador Dalí graphic," after the noted painter who worked with surreal images. In this graphic, the artist's attempt to create an appropriate background for the data overshadows the information itself.

Even in the best of cases, overdrawn dimensional charts confuse readers. In the graphic "Middle managers' salaries," the use of bars consisting of stacks of dollar bills is confusing (Figure 14.7). The reader does not know, for example, whether the marketing manager makes $44,000 (the back edge of the top dollar bill) or slightly more than $43,000 (the front edge). Such ambiguity diminishes the value of the graphic.

It is possible to use some dimensional effects in graphics, but such artistic considerations should not preclude the accurate display of information. For example, the bars in the *Chicago Tribune* graphic "Japan's direct investment in U.S." have shadows that give a sense of dimension, but do not affect the plots on the chart (Figure 14.8).

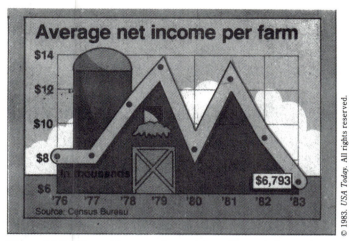

Figure 14.9   Chart without zero base, giving a distorted picture of farm income

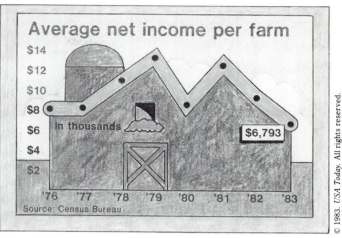

Figure 14.10   Farm income chart plotted on a base of zero to present a more accurate picture of information

Still, this graphic does not meet all the standards of good charting. The final bar "pops" out of the chart, which may be dramatic but which also creates confusion as to the actual point on the scale to which the bar is referring.

Zero Basing Charts

The use and misuse of the vertical scale, or Y axis, often creates problems for graphics editors and artists. The problem arises over whether to base, or start plotting, the graphic data at zero or break the scale and start plotting at another point. (Zero basing is discussed in Chapter 11.) By distorting the scale on which the information is plotted, the artist can create a visual impression that may be at odds with the information being presented.

For example, the graphic entitled "Average net income per farm" shows a dramatic drop in income between the high year of 1979 and the low of 1983 (Figure 14.9). Visually, this graphic, which starts the plotting of information at a base of $6,000, displays a bleak picture of farm income. The decline appears to be nearly 100 percent of the area shown in the chart. However, a closer look at the statistics suggests that the picture isn't that bleak. Farm income dropped 49.7 percent between 1979 and 1983, from $13,500 to $6,793. When the information is replotted on a base of zero, the visual impression of

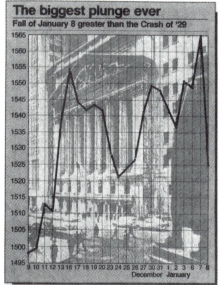

Figure 14.11   Misleading line chart

the change between 1979 and 1983 is quite different (Figure 14.10). It doesn't look like the bottom has fallen out of that income segment; readers can see the more than $6,000 the farmer still has.

The farm income chart points out the **lie factor** common to charts that are not zero based. The lie factor is the difference between the actual, or statistical, information and the visual presentation of that information. For example, if the change between two

years is 5 percent, a chart showing the change should give a visual impression of 5 percent. The lie factor is a formula put forth by Edward R. Tufte in his book "The Visual Display of Quantitative Information." Tufte blames the lie factor for graphics that are misleading.

"The biggest plunge ever" chart is a misleading graphic with a lie factor (Figure 14.11). It displays a scary picture of the largest one-day drop since 1929 (until 1987) in the Dow Jones Industrial

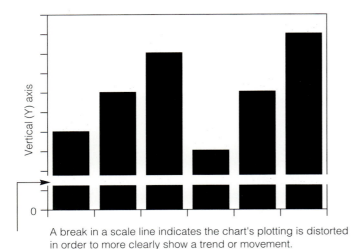

A break in a scale line indicates the chart's plotting is distorted in order to more clearly show a trend or movement.

Figure 14.12   Column chart with "broken" scale

Figure 14.13   Chart with distorted time axis

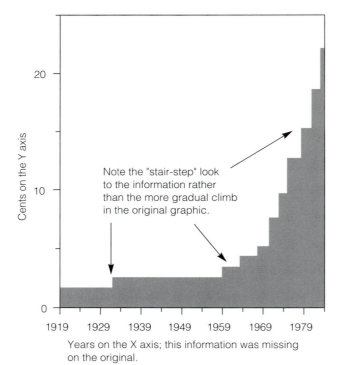

Note the "stair-step" look to the information rather than the more gradual climb in the original graphic.

Years on the X axis; this information was missing on the original.

Figure 14.14   Postal rates chart plotted with consistent time element

average. It is plotted with a starting point of 1,495. The drop was indeed the largest numerical change since 1929, but the change as a percentage of the entire index was only 2.5 percent. The graphic shows a drop in the Dow Jones not of 2.5 percent but of nearly 50 percent of the total area shown in the chart. In this case, the actual change is quite different from the visual presentation of the change.

The graphics editor and artist need to discuss when to plot graphics on a zero based scale. When dealing with charts based on percent change between statistical periods, the artist should always start the chart at zero. Decisions on when or when not to start the scale at zero should not be based solely on artistic considerations.

Ideally, the Y axis scale on charts should not be broken; however, that is not practical when subtle trends are being shown. When the scale is broken, extra care must be taken to ensure that the reader is being shown correct, undistorted information. In addition, there should be an indication on the chart that the scale has been broken. The most common way of breaking the scale is by leaving a gap in the bar (Figure 14.12).

BY THE NUMBERS
LIFE EXPECTANCY

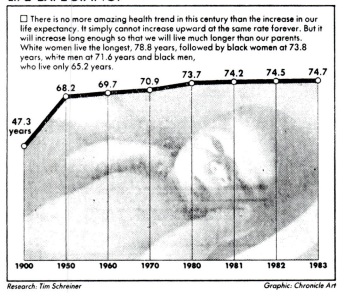

☐ There is no more amazing health trend in this century than the increase in our life expectancy. It simply cannot increase upward at the same rate forever. But it will increase long enough so that we will live much longer than our parents. White women live the longest, 78.8 years, followed by black women at 73.8 years, white men at 71.6 years and black men, who live only 65.2 years.

47.3 years   68.2   69.7   70.9   73.7   74.2   74.5   74.7

1900   1950   1960   1970   1980   1981   1982   1983

Research: Tim Schreiner   Graphic: Chronicle Art

Figure 14.15   Graphic with faulty time scale on X axis

BY THE NUMBERS
LIFE EXPECTANCY

☐ There is no more amazing health trend in this century than the increase in our life expectancy. It simply cannot increase upward at the same rate forever. But it will increase long enough so that we will live much longer than our parents. White women live the longest, 78.8 years, followed by black women at 73.8 years, white men at 71.6 years and black men, who live only 65.2 years.

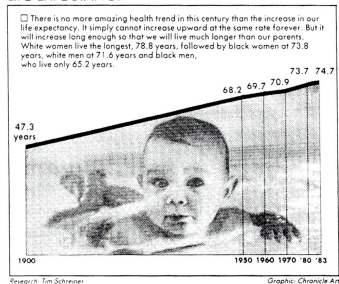

47.3 years   68.2   69.7   70.9   73.7   74.7

1900   1950 1960 1970 '80 '83

Research: Tim Schreiner   Graphic: Chronicle Art

Figure 14.16   Life expectancy graphic with corrected time scale

Time Shift Problems

Problems are created in graphics when the time element on the X axis is compressed or expanded, which in turn misrepresents the data. To be accurate, the distance between the points on the X axis should remain constant. For example, if the chart shows a passage of time between 1919 and 1981, the distance between any two points, say 1958 and 1968, must be the same as the distance between any other two points, such as 1968 and 1978.

In the chart "United States Postal Rates," the distance between years is compressed for the early years, 1932 to 1958, and expanded for the later years (Figure 14.13). Such distortion of the time axis means the graphic does not give a true indication of how long it was before postal rates changed. It leaves the reader with a visual impression of a rapid change in some time periods. Thus, to be accurate, the information needs to be plotted with a consistent time element (Figure 14.14).

Another example of faulty use of time on the X axis can be found in the graphic "By the Numbers/Life Expec-

ISU economists question effect of beef-industry concentration

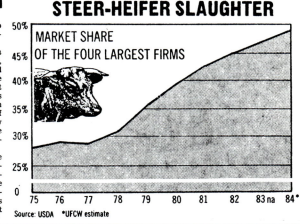

MEAT
Continued from Page One

firms extracting a market share so large as to create a position of economic dominance."

● Over 50 percent of the nation's hog slaughter occurs in Iowa, Illinois, Minnesota, Michigan and Ohio, and Iowa clearly dominates, with more hogs slaughtered than in the next three states combined. While Iowa's total reported slaughter declined from 1972 to 1982, the reported slaughter of the top four firms increased by 2,429,548 head, and their market share increased to 62 percent from 47 percent in 1972.

The top eight firms' market share increased to 93 percent from 83 percent during the same period, the congressional report says, adding, "These figures indicate that Iowa hog slaughter is dominated by the top four firms and that the top eight firms account for almost all of the state slaughter."

STEER-HEIFER SLAUGHTER

MARKET SHARE OF THE FOUR LARGEST FIRMS

50%   45%   40%   35%   30%   25%   0

75   76   77   78   79   80   81   82   83 na   84*

Source: USDA   *UFCW estimate

Figure 14.17   Inaccurate plotting of incomplete data

tancy" (Figure 14.15). The distance between 1900 and 1950, five decades, is a half inch, whereas the space between each decade from 1950 to 1980 is a half inch; after 1980, there is a half inch of space between each year. If the chart were plotted correctly, the spacing would

have to be consistent (Figure 14.16). There is one other problem with this graphic: The plotting over a photograph makes for difficult placement of type.

A more serious misuse of information is shown in the chart "Steer-Heifer Slaughter" (Figure 14.17). At first

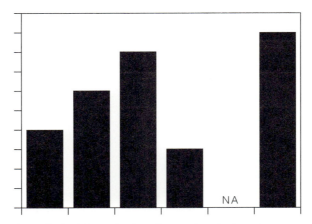

A gap in the information for a time-series chart can be handled this way. This method quickly tells the reader that some data is missing. NA means the information is not available.

Figure 14.18   Chart showing how to handle missing data

glance, the chart appears to show a steady climb from 1975 to 1984. Alongside the indication of 1983 is the notation of NA (graphic shorthand for *not available)*. If the figure for 1983 is not available, then connecting the plot points between 1982 and 1984 is inaccurate because it gives the visual appearance that the market share is 47 percent. This graphic would have worked as a bar chart, which, unlike a line chart, does not depend on a continuous flow of time. With a bar chart, the artist could have used a break in the X axis to indicate a break in the data (Figure 14.18).

One More Danger

Even if an informational graphic avoids the problems of lack of information, time shifting, perspective and zero basing, it can fail if it is so complex or convoluted that it intimidates readers. Research has shown that readers are faithful only up to a point. If they can not process the information in a graphic, they will skip it. For example, if a graphic contains an image with long and complicated explanatory copy blocks, most readers will be drawn to the visual image, but some will ignore the copy. The visual journalist must avoid the temptation to pile pieces of information upon pieces of information. Too many "bells and whistles" can embellish a graphic device to the point that it fails in its primary purpose—to convey information to the reader quickly and simply.

IMAGES THAT WORK

If an informational graphic contains a photograph or illustration along with the

type, all of the artistic elements should work together. For example, the use of cartoon characters on a graphic about suicide, murder or birth defects could be in bad taste. The use of dragons and knights in a Los Angeles Times–Washington Post News Service graphic concerning the AIDS virus should have been avoided (Figure 14.19). Even such "neutral" topics as construction spending can be made to seem less serious than they are when inappropriate graphics are used. The cartoonlike nature of the graphic entitled "Residential construction permits" belittles the seriousness of the information being presented and the story that accompanies it (Figure 14.20).

The key to successful graphics is teamwork among reporters, editors and artists. Careful planning, research and discussions should be part of the creative process of every graphic. Reporters gathering information for their stories play an important role. Usually, information for graphics and news stories comes from the same sources, which means reporters working on stories also can be working on graphics. Of course, not all reporters look at a story visually or statistically; it is possible for them to botch the assignment. Still, they can work with graphic editors and artists to make certain valuable information is being collected.

Once the information is gathered and the graphic completed, the graphics editor must work with other editors at the newspaper to make certain the visual element is used appropriately. An informational graphic is one of the elements on a news page that presents information to readers. It is not meant to be merely a decoration or a *type breaker,* a device used solely to divide columns of type.

CHECKLIST FOR GRAPHICS

Editors and artists can avoid the pitfalls of informational graphics. Here is a checklist that may help them:

✔ Make certain there is enough information for a graphic. Don't attempt to compose a graphic with missing figures or gaps in the information.
✔ Understand what the information is supposed to convey. Is the graphic trying to show the reader a subtle trend or a broader, more historical outlook?
✔ Make certain the artistic presentation does not overpower or interfere with the information.
✔ Make certain that if there is a break in the scale on a chart, the reader can see that the information has been compressed or expanded.

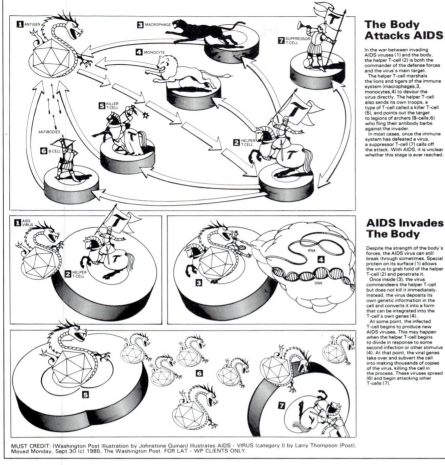

Figure 14.19 Inappropriate use of cartoon characters in graphic

SUGGESTED EXERCISES

1. Find an empty graphic in a daily newspaper and explain why it is empty. How can it be improved?

2. Find a graphic with perspective problems. How can it be improved?

3. Find a graphic with zero base problems. How can it be improved?

4. Find a graphic with time shift problems. How can it be improved?

5. Find three examples of effective graphics. Discuss why they work.

6. Define the following terms:
   a. Lie factor
   b. Y axis
   c. X axis
   d. Type breaker

Figure 14.20 Cartoonlike informational graphic

PART THREE

Picture Editing

CHAPTER FIFTEEN

The History of Newspaper Photography

Newspaper photographs give readers an opportunity to become part of the world, to see things that once were only written about. Photographs—especially news photographs—bring greater understanding and a sense of immediacy to world events.

The publication of **photographs,** which are continuous tone images reproduced on surfaces through the reaction of light and light-sensitive chemicals, became possible in newspapers once a method was found that would allow for suitable reproduction. When that method—halftone reproduction—was developed in the 1880s, the role of visuals in newspapers changed forever. (A complete discussion of the halftone reproduction method can be found in Chapter 7.)

Over the decades, however, photographs have had to fight their way into most newspapers. A century ago, many people at a newspaper, from publisher to reporters, looked upon photographs as money and space wasters. Reporters and editors argued that photographs took up space that should be reserved for words. And the artists who made drawings or linecuts from photographs viewed halftones with disdain, suggesting that readers preferred crisp, clear artistic interpretations of an event over the fuzzy, sometimes unclear halftones (Figure 15.1).

Times did change, however. In 1891, there were about 1,000 newspaper artists turning out 10,000 drawings a week. By the early 1900s, many of them were out of work.

THE "WORLD" OF NEWSPAPER PHOTOGRAPHS

When the *New York Tribune* published a picture on Jan. 21, 1897, of Thomas C. Platt, who had just been elected U.S. senator from New York, it was, according to some records, the first halftone reproduction to appear in a mass-circulation newspaper, although The Daily Graphic, a publication of a printing house, had printed a halftone in 1880 (Figure 15.2).

When Joseph Pulitzer tried to reduce the number of illustrations in his sensational *New York World,* readers didn't like it. Circulation dropped, and the illustrations, including photographs, were restored to the paper. Recognizing that pictures of ordinary people sold newspapers, Pulitzer began running photographs of teachers, actors and political figures. He even published a display of women entitled "Ladies Who Grace and Adorn the Social Circle." The photos were probably the first use

Figure 15.1 Newspaper linecuts showing an artist's depiction of an event

Figure 15.2 First known published halftone (1880)

of **cheesecake**—a suggestive picture of one or more women—used to sell a newspaper.

A HINT OF PHOTOJOURNALISM

Shortly after it published its first halftone, the *New York Tribune* printed a series of photographs depicting the slums that housed many of New York City's poor. It was an example of how photography could be used to capture reality and present it to readers.

By the early 1900s, other publishers realized that photographs helped boost circulation, and the rush was on to use more and larger pictures. Although newspapers still used artist's drawings of events, or an artist's drawing based on a photograph, the era of newspaper photojournalism was about to start. More and more photographers wanted to dig deeply into society's problems and present what they found through pictures. Most publishers, however, saw newspaper photographs as a tool to entice and hold readers.

Although some of the limitations of photo reproduction were solved with the invention of the halftone, the quality of newspaper presses in the early part of the 20th century made it difficult to reproduce photographs and type on the same page. To overcome the problem, photographic sections were printed in advance on rotogravure printing presses and inserted into the middle of the newspaper. *Rotogravure,* considered an excellent printing method for reproducing photographs, used a higher-quality printing plate than letterpress, but it was too expensive to use on a daily basis.

In 1914, *The New York Times* started a Sunday picture section that was

Figure 15.3 Sensational photo in a 1928 tabloid

printed by the rotogravure method. The section was so successful, and the war in Europe at the time offered so many photo opportunities, that *The Times* started a midweek pictorial section. Despite its current image as a newspaper "unfriendly" to the space needs of photography, *The Times* was a pioneer in newspaper picture usage.

THE ERA OF SENSATIONALISM

In 1919, the *New York Illustrated Daily News* was created. (It later dropped the word *Illustrated* from its title.) The paper quickly proved that photography could indeed sell newspapers. The paper was a *tabloid,* a newspaper that is about half the size of the typical broadsheet, and it showed readers that photography could be an equal partner with words. The *Daily News* was as aggressive with its photographs as other newspapers were in their reporting and writing. In 1928, when the *Daily News* ran a Page One photograph of the electric chair execution of Ruth Snyder, convicted of her husband's murder, its aggressiveness crossed over into sensationalism (Figure 15.3).

John Farber, in "Great News Photos and the Stories Behind Them," described how the paper got its picture. City editor Harvey Denell, picture assignment editor Ted Dalton and assistant picture assignment editor George Schmidt masterminded the project. They decided that a miniature camera, strapped to an ankle, probably would get past the guards and into the execution chamber. Guards would be frisking the length of the body but would probably miss the ankle, they figured.

The camera needed to be pre-focused, and so it was necessary to know the arrangement of the room. One staff member did the almost impossible: He obtained blueprints of the Sing Sing room where the execution would be carried out. It also was decided that all of the *Daily News* photographers would be recognized by police officers, so a photographer from the *Chicago Tribune,* Thomas Howard, was brought to town. He stayed in his hotel room, making test shots with the ankle camera, which was triggered by a long cable release running up his trouser leg into his pants pocket. To

get the picture, he had to lift his trouser clear of the lens. The camera used a glass plate about 35mm wide, and because there was only one glass plate, Howard had to get the picture in one shot.

Howard took his picture when the first shock was administered to Snyder. He then realized that a second shock would be given, so he quickly closed the shutter. When the second shock was administered, he exposed the glass plate again. After the members of the press were dismissed from the death

Figure 15.4   Composograph

chamber, Howard rushed back to the *Daily News*. The plate was developed, and the full-page picture ran on Page One of a Jan. 13, 1928, extra edition under the headline **DEAD!** In the cutline, the *Daily News* described the photo as "perhaps the most remarkable exclusive picture in the history of criminology."

In fact, the *Daily News'* picture of Ruth Snyder's execution was tame compared with what other newspapers were doing. By the late 1920s, sensationalism was in, as newspapers emphasized scandalous photos to lure readers. Some papers even resorted to faked photos and other trickery. For example, the *New York Evening Graphic* developed and exploited the **composograph,** a staged "news" photograph in which actors would pose for the newspaper's photographers. Later, the real faces of the parties involved were superimposed over the actors' faces (Figure 15.4). And while the newspaper admitted, in small type, that the picture was a composograph, such practice certainly raised ethical concerns over the manipulation of images.

THE DEVELOPMENT OF PHOTOJOURNALISM

Even though photographs helped sell newspapers, many newspapers in the 1920s were content to use photography as a feature item, much like a crossword puzzle. Little attention was paid to the value of photography as a means of journalism. Then, in the 1930s, two magazines were born that ushered in the era of photojournalism. Life magazine began production in 1936; Look started a year later. Both magazines—and several important magazines in Europe such as Berliner Illustrierte Zeitung and Münchner Illustrierte Presse—helped usher in the era of photojournalism.

At about the same time, new, smaller cameras such as the Ermanox and Leica were introduced, and once again technology gave photography a boost. While both the Ermanox and the Leica had fast lens, Leica's use of a strip of 35mm motion picture film allowed photographers to capture more than one image before having to change film. The Leica thus changed the way photographers

could work. It gave the journalist with a camera the ability to photograph subjects unobtrusively. Subjects no longer needed to pose for pictures; the photographer was able to capture them as they moved.

Photojournalism also was given a tremendous boost by the documentary work done in the 1930s by Dorothea Lange and Walker Evans for the federal Farm Securities Administration. Lange and Evans were part of a team of photographers that visually reported on the Dust Bowl conditions that plagued the American Plains during the Great Depression (Figure 15.5). Many newspaper photographers today are still influenced by the photographic poetry of Lange and Evans.

NEWSPAPER PHOTOGRAPHY CHANGES SLOWLY

While the picture magazines were making excellent progress in photojournalism, newspapers and their photographers lagged behind. In the 1950s and 1960s, many newspaper photographers were slow to use the Leica, preferring to stay with the bulkier, sheet-film camera called a Graflex (later models were called the Speed Graphic). These cameras used a large format for film, 4 by 5 inches, as opposed to the 1 by $1\frac{3}{8}$ inches of 35mm film, and carried their film in holders, two shots to a holder.

In a sense, the lack of interest by newspaper photographers in the more lightweight cameras that would allow them to capture candid scenes reflected the lack of interest editors and publishers had in photography in the middle of the 20th century. A look at newspapers from the 1930s through 1960s shows

Figure 15.5   Documentary photo by Dorothea Lange

Figure 15.6   An example of cutout photos used as decoration

a remarkable lack of photographic effort compared with the visually exciting and vibrant newspapers of today. Until the 1970s, few newspapers were advocates of strong visual elements. Even on the larger newspapers, a picture editor often merely coordinated photographers' assignments and had little voice in the discussion of how pictures were used. At many papers, news photographs were used as part of a layout device, cut into circles or triangles. Too often, less space was devoted to photographs than to words or the photographs were treated as decoration without regard to their visual integrity (Figure 15.6).

TECHNOLOGICAL CHANGES

Throughout the history of photojournalism, technological changes in the equipment a photographer carries and in the printing process have enabled newspapers to improve their visual presentation. Two developments in

particular—the Fairchild engraver and television—spurred newspapers to embrace photography as a vital part of their product.

The Fairchild Engraver

Until the mid-20th century, smaller newspapers generally were excluded from the daily use of photography because they were unwilling or unable to spend the money on equipment required to produce halftone engravings on metal. By the 1950s, however, technology had advanced to the point that engravings could be made on plastic. This photoelectric engraving process opened the door to widespread use of photographs throughout the newspaper in news and feature columns and in advertisements.

One system, the *Fairchild engraver,* used the same principle of the wire photo transmitter. The machine looked much like a lathe with two cylinders.

A photograph was attached to one of the cylinders and was scanned by a beam of light; a plastic sheet was placed on the second cylinder. As the two cylinders rotated, a cutting head on the second cylinder responded to impulses from the scanner, etching the halftone image into the plastic. This relatively inexpensive process allowed even the smallest newspapers to produce photographs more quickly and more cheaply.

The Influence of Television

By the late 1960s, photographs could be reproduced more effectively on offset presses, and better cameras and film had been developed. Added to these technological advances was the growing importance of television in society, which helped newspaper photography gain its prominence in newspaper publishing. Television made consumers more visually aware of the world, and editors realized that even the still newspaper

INSIDE LOOK

Rich Clarkson
Photojournalist

Rich Clarkson has helped mold photojournalism. In his more than three decades as a newspaper photographer, manager and free-lance photojournalist, Clarkson always has been a strong advocate for pictures.

"Photojournalism is a myriad of things," Clarkson said in an interview shortly before boarding a plane to cover a college football game for Sports Illustrated. "It has never been very well-defined because it isn't any one thing. The kind of photograph published on the fashion page or food page is different from the type of picture that appears on Page One. Each has a very different set of needs.

"Photojournalism is a term that probably encompasses everything from the special-interest magazine to the New York Daily News chasing a celebrity in Manhattan."

During his career, Clarkson has shot pictures for newspapers, magazines and books. He has contributed to Life, Time, The Saturday Evening Post and Sports Illustrated, where he continues under contract as a contributing photographer. Clarkson was the director of photography and senior assistant editor for the National Geographic Society from 1984 to 1987. He left the staff of the society in the spring of 1987 to become an independent book producer/editor and a consultant to newspapers and magazines.

Clarkson, one of the founding members of the National Press Photographers Association, said he has been a student of newspaper photojournalism since the 1950s. He added, "At that time I paid particular attention to The Milwaukee Journal, which was a real pioneer in lighting. It created

many of its pictures. They were quite marvelously done.

"At the same time a group of photographers at The Denver Post was doing a lot of pictures that had more to do with what was in the news. I watched those two papers a lot in those days because they had marvelous pictures and much different personalities."

Clarkson's first job out of college was in Lawrence, Kan. In 1957, he became director of photography at the Topeka Capital-Journal and helped make the paper a leader in the use of photography.

"I started rebuilding the paper along the lines of what I thought should be appearing on its pages," he said. "I had the support of the top editors and the publisher, but because what I was doing was new, some of the editors did not feel comfortable. I formulated a style that I didn't think was unique. I just thought it was what we needed to do."

Clarkson stayed at the paper for 23 years. During his tenure, Brian Lanker, one of the photographers at the Capital-Journal, won a Pulitzer Prize. The staff also swept regional competitions during those years, and seven staffers became NPPA newspaper or magazine photographers of the year—either while at the Capital-Journal or subsequently.

Quality photojournalism comes and goes at newspapers, Clarkson said. "The Milwaukee Journal and The Denver Post had an era. The Louisville Courier-Journal did too. The Eugene Register Guard certainly did some wonderful things when Brian Lanker was there. Today, I would say the Anchorage Daily News is doing some good things for

all the right reasons. The Charlotte Observer did a number of years ago. The Miami Herald has done some good things over the years."

He said photojournalism today has been influenced greatly by television and somewhat by USA Today.

"The world has become more visual," Clarkson added. "Lots of newspapers have upgraded with offset printing and now can publish pictures beautifully. Many publishers are concerned with using the capabilities that they have. And a growing group of kids, some of the brightest people in colleges, have looked at photojournalism as an interesting vocation and have taken it up.

"So what we have at this point is a lot of newspapers using pictures very elegantly and well. Hundreds of photographers are working on newspapers, more than ever, and there is a high level of local photojournalism taking place in a lot of places."

Still, there are problems, Clarkson noted. "USA Today has been wonderful in proving to publishers that they can print quality color quickly. But other than that USA Today has had a negative influence on photojournalism. It is a well-designed newspaper, looking only for certain types of pictures. It runs 'feel-good' pictures. It won't use a disaster picture on Page One if it can find a way out of it. There are smiling faces on every section front."

He added that there is a lack of leadership in the photojournalism community. "We need people who can tell editors how to use pictures. Photographers still are not full-fledged, participating members of the newsroom family. Somewhere in the ranks of those very bright college-trained photographers has got to be some leadership that will help photojournalism take off."

Clarkson also cautioned against the sameness in today's newspaper pictures. He said: "Through contests, particularly clip contests, photographers are emulating each other to the point that there is almost no originality at all. You see the same types of pictures appearing across the country. They may be good for the community, but they are not taking photojournalism into any new or interesting steps."

Clarkson said that throughout his career he has had problems with photo illustrations, pictures that are concocted and do not necessarily document reality. "Even though I didn't like it, some of the things I did when I first started out come close to illustrative pictures. I remember being assigned to take a picture during a beautiful spring day. The editor said go to a grade school and get a kid looking out the window and wishing that he was outside instead of inside. To do that, we called ahead to the school and made arrangements. We moved a chair close to the window. We moved other kids out of the background. We coaxed the kid to pose. We put the teacher in just the right spot. Everything was done in a way to make the readers think it really happened.

"I felt uncomfortable about doing such things and got out of it before anyone told me I shouldn't be doing it. Photography has at its core believability. I think when you start dabbling with photo illustrations, you start making people mistrust pictures. It's important to keep credibility in photography."

Figure 15.7   Dramatic photo use

photograph could have a great impact. Newspapers such as the *Chicago Daily News, The Milwaukee Journal,* the *Topeka* (Kan.) *Capital-Journal* and *The Louisville* (Ky.) *Courier-Journal & Times* began to use more and better-quality news pictures (Figure 15.7).

Along with the demand for better pictures came the demand for better photographers and managers, such as picture editors, to lead them. Programs such as the Missouri Workshop at the University of Missouri and the National Press Photographers Flying Short Course helped bring examples of excellent photojournalism to students and professionals around the country.

The ratio of words to photographs also began to change. Many newspapers have come to recognize that photographs are powerful communicative tools and that the photographer can be an equal partner in the journalistic process. Still, some papers have a ways to go. Too many newspapers are dominated by a strong word editor and lack an advocate for visuals. Unfortunately, until attitudes change at newspapers and more journalists are trained to think visually, the artificial separation will continue.

SUGGESTED EXERCISES

1. At your school's library or at a public library, search through microfilms of a newspaper from the 1920s. How big a part did photography play in the newspaper? Can you find examples of sensational pictures? Can you find any examples of photojournalism?

2. Do the same thing for a newspaper in the 1950s. What major changes can you find between the 1920s and the 1950s?

3. What is a composograph? Do you think it is ethical? Would you ever use one?

4. Critique the photographs on the front page of your community daily newspaper. Are they given good play, or do they take a backseat to the words? How would you improve the page photographically?

CHAPTER SIXTEEN

How Picture Editors Work

A newspaper picture (or photo) editor has a difficult job each day as he or she tries to direct and manage the paper's daily picture report. The editor must deal with the newspaper's limitations in terms of reproduction and available space and also be an advocate for quality photojournalism, which requires good reproduction capabilities and a certain amount of quality space.

Without a doubt, photographs represent an exciting, vibrant art form. A picture editor can help capture that excitement for the newsroom and readers. This chapter does not discuss picture-taking methods, such as lighting or camera angles; there are several excellent texts available that examine photographic methods. Instead, this chapter will look at the important role photography and the picture editor play within a newspaper. It will examine how a picture editor handles a finished picture that meets acceptable professional standards and what the editor's relationship is to the rest of the newsroom.

A PICTURE EDITOR'S RESPONSIBILITIES

A **picture editor** is one of the visual journalists at a newspaper, and although his or her role changes from newspaper to newspaper, there are some major responsibilities of a typical picture editor at a newspaper. The picture editor must:

✔ Understand the day's news report, and offer appropriate photographs within the limitations of space and reproduction.
✔ Have complete knowledge of all photographic assignments being covered by staff photographers; sometimes this includes selecting the right photographer for the right assignment.
✔ Manage the day's wire service photo report.
✔ Work with section editors and news editors to help crop and size photographs.

These responsibilities once belonged to other people in the newsroom. The city editor typically was responsible for assignments, the news editor sorted the wire photographs and the layout editor cropped and sized the day's photo report. And although to an extent this system may have worked, it failed to provide the same quality control and managerial authority over photos and photographers that city editors or section editors had over their reporters and stories.

Today, many newspapers recognize the value of entrusting a single individual with the responsibility of managing and editing the day's picture report. This manager of photography has different titles at different newspapers: director of photography, photo editor, photo coordinator, assistant managing editor/photography, chief photographer or picture editor. In this chapter, the term *picture editor* will be employed.

Understanding the Day's News Report

As part of the management staff of a newspaper, the picture editor must have a complete and thorough understanding of both the newspaper's philosophy of coverage and the day's events. Newspapers have different philosophies of news coverage, just as reporters have different styles of writing and photographers have different styles of picture taking. The picture editor thus must be familiar with the newspaper's philosophy and how it relates to photographs. Armed with that knowledge, certain decisions can be made in structuring (editing) the day's picture report. Just as reporting should reflect a newspaper's goals, so too should photographic coverage and display.

If a newspaper's goal is to put major hard news stories on Page One each day, it makes little sense for a city editor to offer any light feature stories. Likewise, it would make little sense for the picture editor to offer pictures of dogs chasing kites. On the other hand, if a newspaper wants to have a local color photograph on the front page every day, the picture editor must plan and develop a dependable selection of color pictures. He or she cannot rely solely on a breaking news event to provide excellent color possibilities.

To help plan the photo report, the picture editor should "read" the newspaper before it is published by looking at the amount of space that is available for words and visuals in the next day's edition. That space —the *editorial news hole*—is shown on the paper's dummies, which are sent to the editorial department after the advertising department has positioned the ads. By looking at the dummies, a picture editor can see which pages will accommodate photographs and which will not.

The picture editor can estimate the number and size of the pictures that will be required for the next day's paper. Although this task has little to do with editing pictures, it reminds the picture editor that he or she cannot work in a vacuum. It would do little good to offer 40 pictures when the paper only has room for 10 or 15. Even though all of the pictures might be good enough to run in the paper, they are much like the good stories that get left out for lack of space. There are many victims of hard editing choices at a daily newspaper.

Knowing the Day's Photo Assignments

If the newspaper does not have a director of photography or a chief photographer, the picture editor must decide which photographer gets which assignment. At many smaller newspapers, one person serves as both picture editor and chief photographer; it makes for a very busy and challenging job. To effectively make assignments, the picture editor must be part traffic cop, directing photographers around town so they can get to their assignments on time, and part cheerleader and motivator.

In matching assignment with photographer, the picture editor has an effect on the success or failure of the assignment. The picture editor must understand the strengths and weaknesses of each member of the photography staff, leading each photographer like a successful football coach leads his or her players—some players can perform well at many positions; others are best at only one. In that sense, the photographer who excels at sports coverage should be given assignments for the sports section; the photographer with a flair for photo illustration should get feature section work.

Handling Photo Requests

As any editor would, the picture editor must distinguish between the good and bad assignments. Some stories are worth covering; others are not. That is why it is important for reporters to work closely with the picture editor. Reporters may understand the value of having photographs with their stories, but they should not file a photo request form without consulting the picture editor (or a designated assistant). The editor can best decide how to get the most out of a photo assignment (Figure 16.1).

A good newspaper won't write about boring or trivial events, and it should not send photographers to such events. A picture editor must educate reporters and editors requesting photographs, reminding them that the "content" of an event will allow for good photographs. Wishful thinking or the need for a space filler will not make for good pictures.

San Jose Mercury News Photographic Request

PHOTOGRAPHER   DATE   TIME

ASSIGNMENT

LOCATION (INCLUDING ADDRESS, CROSS STREET, MAPS, ETC.)

REQUESTED BY   DESK   COLOR   BLACK &   NO. OF
                                                                            WHITE   ROLLS SHOT

FIELD CONTACT   TELEPHONE   PUBLICATION DATE

APPROVED BY_____
                        (PICTURE EDITOR)

STORY SUMMARY: (ATTACH ARTICLE IF AVAILABLE)

(BEFORE PLACING REQUEST, PLEASE USE TIME CLOCK STAMP AT PICTURE DESK)

Figure 16.1   Photo request form

Too often, the picture editor is not given the most important information on the photo request form—the nature of the story being written. Without knowing the who, what, where, when, why and how of the event, a photographer cannot capture the story visually. The picture editor must ensure that such information is available for every assignment before the photographer begins to shoot. The most important information, however, is a summary of the story itself.

When looking over the day's photo requests, the picture editor should watch for events that will make good pictures—real people doing real activities. To send a photographer off to an assignment that has no picture potential wastes the photographer's time, time that could be spent on another story.

Managing the Day's Wire Photo Report

At smaller newspapers, the wire or news editor, not the picture editor, edits or selects wire photographs for the paper. However, because many local stories are linked to international or national events, it is important for the picture editor to know what the wire services are offering in terms of photographs. That is why at most large papers the picture editor is responsible for both the local pictures and the wire service photographs. (Wire photos are discussed in detail in Chapter 18.)

In addition to understanding the day's wire service photo report and how it relates to overall photo use in the paper, the picture editor often gets story ideas from looking at photographs from other parts of the country. And many times it is possible to pair wire service and local photographs, thereby giving readers an understanding of the scope of the story being reported. For instance, a drought might be causing as much damage locally as it is in several neighboring states. By pairing a national photograph with a local one, the picture editor can offer a stronger visual package.

There's one additional chore in the handling of wire service photos. Many of them need to be distributed to section editors—sports, business, features— for use with specific stories. Usually, wire photos are marked for particular sections, but the picture editor still should check each wire photo for possible usage in a section other than news.

Working with Section and News Editors

Although many "word" editors would not like to admit it, editing newspaper photographs takes special skill. Unfortunately, many newspaper editors believe they have both the talent and right to edit pictures in any manner they please.

That puts the picture editor in a difficult position. Without antagonizing a section editor or news editor, the picture editor must ensure that photographs are being given the proper display and treatment. To do that, the picture editor must understand the goals and needs of each section and editor and also must be an articulate spokesperson for the proper use of photographs. That articulation should be firm but not confrontational; it should educate and lead without being dogmatic. Part of the process should involve teaching section editors (by example, if possible) about the effective cropping, sizing and display of photographs. (Cropping and sizing are examined in Chapter 17.)

At metropolitan newspapers, the display of photographs on a page often is determined by a group of people, including a designer or art director, a section or assistant section editor and a picture editor. Each person will bring his or her own perspective to a photograph or photographic project. Each will have a bias toward or against certain photographs. It is the job of the picture editor to recognize and overcome those predispositions. The picture editor needs to work with this group as a full partner,

Figure 16.2   Dramatic Page One photo use

Figure 16.3   Page One photo "reporting" major news event

aware that there will be not only a certain amount of text on the page but also perhaps other elements in addition to photographs.

THE POWER OF PHOTOGRAPHS

One of the real joys of working with photographs in a newspaper is when a big event occurs and the photos of it have an overwhelming impact on the readers (and even the newsroom staff). A picture editor needs to seize those special moments and urge other newsroom executives to let a photograph, rather than a headline or columns of type, tell the story first.

One example of the power of photographic images is from *The New York*

Times the day after Pope John Paul II visited New York in 1979 (Figure 16.2). *The Times,* not noted for its dramatic use of photographs, devoted the top half of its front page to a photograph of the pope greeting New Yorkers. Such treatment told readers instantly that a major news event had occurred.

The *San Francisco Chronicle* of May 25, 1987, also allowed photography to "report" on a major news event on Page One (Figure 16.3). With only a headline and a single photograph, the newspaper gave readers a sense of the biggest news story of the day—the 50th anniversary party of the Golden Gate Bridge.

Sometimes, a dramatic event, such as a high-rise fire in Chicago, can be conveyed to the reader through unusual cropping and sizing of a photo (Figure 16.4). Note how the photo became just one news element on the page, and the other, more important news did not get "lost."

Sometimes, an unusual photograph will surprise and delight readers. Most readers would not expect to see the strongly downward movement in the picture of roller coaster riders (Figure 16.5). Readers probably were startled at first and thought that something was wrong until they digested more information.

The picture editor should be aware, however, of unusual or surprising photographs of dubious taste. The photograph accompanying a story about a *National Geographic* magazine article on the human sense of smell raised questions of taste, even though it probably caught the attention of every person who saw it (Figure 16.6). The picture editor and other editors should discuss seriously whether or not to use such a picture; no one person should be responsible for deciding if a controversial image is suitable for viewing at the breakfast table.

MAKING PICTURES MORE READABLE

The picture editor, as the newspaper's arbiter of photographic standards, should keep the reader in mind when selecting and editing pictures. Sometimes, the picture editor forgets that the reader will see only a few of the numerous images that are offered to a newspaper each day. Those images thus need to be to the point and easily understood.

Figure 16.4 Page One photo "reporting" major news event but with other news on the page

Figure 16.5 Unusual photo that will grab readers' attention

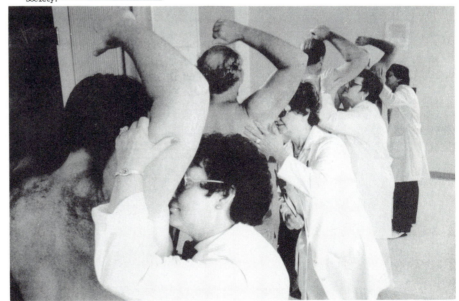

Figure 16.6 Unusual photo, but of questionable taste

Figure 16.7 *Chronicle* photo of tall plant that uses passerby to establish sense of scale

This rare plant, native to the Andes, surprised botanists by sprouting a 15-foot-tall flowering stalk after only 28 years

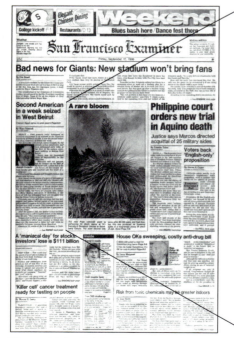

Figure 16.8 Original *Examiner* photo of tall plant that fails to establish sense of scale

The rare Puya raimondii plant is performing its death dance at UC-Berkeley's Botanical Garden in Strawberry Canyon. The plant blooms only once, after 80-100 years, and then dies, but this one produced its flowering spike at a surprisingly young 28 years of age. Story/Page A-9.

Horticulturist Peter Klement stands by the rare Puya raimondii plant, which is performing its death dance at UC-Berkeley's Botanical Garden. The plant blooms only once, after 80-100 years, and then dies, but this one produced its flowering spike at a young 28 years of age. Story/Page A-9.

Figure 16.9 Subsequent *Examiner* photo of tall plant that establishes sense of scale

Helping Readers Relate to Pictures

When editing photographs, the picture editor must select images that readers can "relate to." For example, if a photograph illustrates a story about a 15-foot-tall flowering stalk, it should be edited so that the reader sees the stalk and is given some visual sense of its size. When the *San Francisco Chronicle* and the *San Francisco Examiner* covered the story of the 15-foot-tall stalk, they presented readers with very different pictures. The picture from the morning *Chronicle* showed both the stalk and a woman walking by; she added scale or dimension to the size of the giant plant (Figure 16.7). By contrast, the afternoon *Examiner* in its first edition used a photograph of only the plant (Figure 16.8). The picture could have been of a plant 5 feet tall or 50 feet tall—the reader was given no sense of scale or dimension. By the final edition, however, the *Examiner* ran a picture with a sense of scale (Figure 16.9). Although the *Examiner*'s substitute picture lacked the visual clarity of the first one, it did a better job of telling the story.

Avoiding Misuse of Images

Even when dealing with relatively simple images, such as that of an attempted escape by a Tennessee prisoner, the picture editor must stay alert to possible misuse or mishandling of images. Honesty is extremely important in the photographic presentation each day. For example, in the *San Jose Mercury News*' presentation, the prisoner is heading head first through his cell's viewing window, with his body parallel to the door, yet it appears as if he has twisted his head 90 degrees (Figure

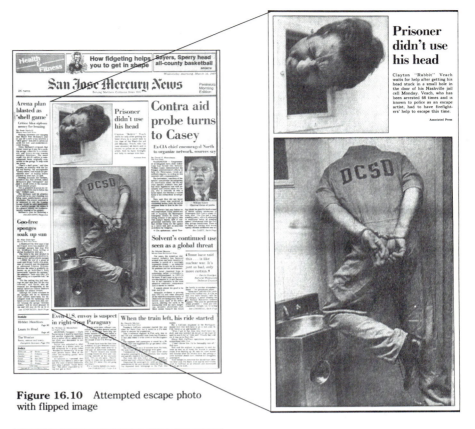

Figure 16.10 Attempted escape photo with flipped image

Figure 16.11 Attempted escape photo correctly laid out

16.10). In fact, an editor flipped or allowed the picture to be flipped to fit a layout. Readers who studied the *Mercury News* layout carefully probably shook their heads in amazement; readers of the *San Francisco Chronicle* were presented the "real picture" (Figure 16.11).

a   b

Figure 16.12   (a) Reversed and (b) correct photo of Joe Montana and Lily Tomlin (in the correct image, the lettering on the door reads backward through the glass)

Figure 16.13   Staged photo containing erroneous information

Avoiding Reversed or Improbable Images

One of the most common errors that a picture editor should guard against is the **flopped**, or **reversed, image,** when the photograph is printed backwards. Often, subtle points are the only clues to a reversed image—a wedding ring on the wrong hand or a man's coat buttons on the wrong side (the buttons for men's and women's clothing are on opposite sides). Reversed lettering is the best clue that a picture has been flopped. When the Associated Press transmitted "Ernestine Swept Off Her Feet," it had to send two pictures (Figure 16.12). Only one was correct.

Picture editors have to watch for the improbable. The photograph of a man walking away from a bank machine was "arranged" to illustrate a business story about the success of automatic tellers (Figure 16.13). However, a close look at the money in the photograph reveals an error. The man is carrying

$1, $5 and $10 bills in his hand. The machine in the background does not issue money in all of those denominations; it gives only $20 bills. In this case, the photographer failed to make sure all of the visual information was correct.

A PROPER MIX OF PICTURES

The picture editor must present an interesting visual report to readers, one that creates a proper mix. No reader wants to view page after page of political pictures or page after page of foreign disasters or car accidents. Readers deserve a well-edited picture report that has all types of pictures that illustrate the day's events, much like the day's story mixture does. To achieve such a balance, the picture editor must keep several things in mind: visual pacing, the size of photos, a picture package or page and the ratio of text to photos.

Visual Pacing

Visual pacing involves the editing of images so they are from different vantage points. If all the pictures in the newspaper one day were close-ups of people, the visual pacing would be too static or boring. By providing a report with both close-ups and pictures taken from a distance, a picture editor can positively influence the overall design of the newspaper.

Big and Small Pictures

There is no doubt that readers like large pictures. A research project on reader interest in newspaper pictures showed that larger pictures attract more interest. And although some professional pho-

Figure 16.14   Effective use of series of small photos

Reprinted by permission of the Chicago Tribune.

tographers believe that a picture always should run large, a better guideline is "Run the picture in the size most appropriate for its value." This guideline is based on the assumption that every picture has both a content and pictorial worth that, combined, determine the value of the photograph. A good picture played too small is of no value to the reader, much like a story with no information. Conversely, a bad picture played big becomes a big, bad picture.

A chronology of former Chicago Mayor Jane Byrne's years in office shows that a series of relatively small photographs can have more impact than two or three large pictures (Figure 16.14). The pictures of Byrne were selected carefully enough to clearly tell a story of her years in office. If only two or

three photographs had been used, more words would have been needed to fill in the gaps.

Another successful presentation of relatively small images can be found in *The Miami Herald* Viewpoint layout of the 1988 presidential candidates (Figure 16.15). Through careful use of lighting and image size, all the candidates receive equal treatment, yet the page still has vitality because of the different sizes of the men themselves. This type of project requires more effort in conception than in execution and once again points out the value of planning.

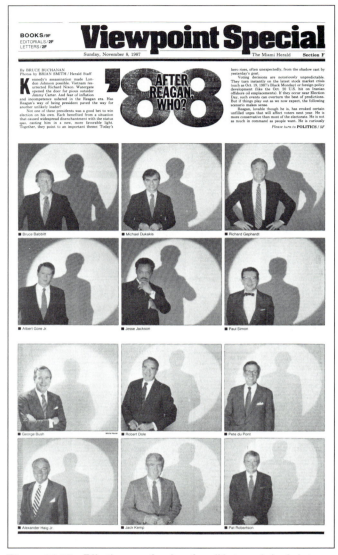

Figure 16.15   Effective use of series of small but equal-sized photos

The Picture Package and Picture Page

Although most newspapers no longer have a **picture page,** a page devoted exclusively to pictures, there are special occasions when the picture editor will edit and perhaps design a picture page or a **picture package** (layout). Even a picture package has elements of a good picture page, including a strong lead photograph that captures the reader's attention and sets a mood.

One of the chief concerns of a picture editor when confronted with such an opportunity is to determine whether there is a sufficient number of quality photographs to warrant such treatment. Weak pictures made into a picture page will result simply in a weak page.

Again, the picture editor must be concerned with the pacing of such packages. There must be a difference in the appearance of each picture and in the shape of each picture on the page. There should be a good mix of distance pictures and close-ups to help move the reader in and out of the visual package. For example, the picture layout of an elderly woman has a variety of pictures in a pleasing arrangement (Figure 16.16). Similarly, the picture

page on farm kids uses a variety of images that give the reader both a close-up view and a more distant sense of life on a Midwestern farm (Figure 16.17). The **double-truck layout,** in which two facing pages are laid out as a single unit, of Pope John Paul II's 1987 visit to the United States also illustrates picture page pacing. The *San Jose Mercury News'* double-truck layout has a dominate image, and the rest of the pictures are "satellites" to the main picture (Figure 16.18).

Sometimes, images in a picture package should be the same size, as in the example from the *Chicago Tribune* that displays police mugshots of gang members (Figure 16.19). The repetition of the images, and the careful placement of the type, gave readers a powerful impression of the vast numbers of gang members who had committed violent crimes.

The Ratio of Words and Visuals

At some newspapers, the ratio of words and visuals has been expressed in a simple formula. If an open page in the newspaper has 126 inches of space (six columns, each 21 inches deep), then 40 to 50 percent of that space (about 50 inches) should be reserved for visuals. Although this rule is not firm even at those newspapers that use a word-visual ratio, it does provide visual journalists with a measure of what space is available for photographs and informational graphics. It also helps maintain visually pleasing pages. Of course, some projects will have more or less space for visuals depending on the importance of the project and the availability of both photographs and graphics.

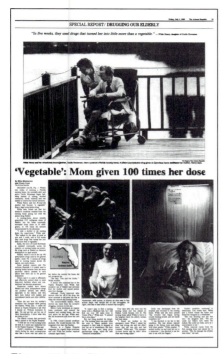

Figure 16.16 Picture package layout effectively combining distance and close-up photos

Figure 16.17 Picture page effectively combining distance and close-up photos

Figure 16.18 Effective double-truck layout

Figure 16.19 Effective use of single-size photos in picture package

INSIDE LOOK

Carolyn Lee
Picture Editor   *The New York Times*

Carolyn Lee, picture editor of *The New York Times,* manages a picture desk that handles photographs from around the world. She also directs staff photographers who cover not only one of the world's largest metropolitan areas but Washington, D.C., as well.

"First, we are not very bashful about asking [the wire services] for particular things," she said. "In particular, our foreign picture editor, who monitors broadcasts from abroad, will call the wire services early in the day and specify that we are looking for certain events. If the wire services aren't covering (a particular event) and don't see any need to for the network, then we'll ask them to cover it as a special for *The Times.*

"When we come in [to start the work day], one editor strips the machines of what has accumulated overnight and sorts out the material we saw the day before because there is some recycling for PMs. The editor then sorts by category for all the editors to look at. Foreign pictures are routed to the foreign picture editor, national are routed to the national picture editor and so on."

Besides wire service photos, *The Times* relies heavily on photos produced by its own staff. "I consider the direction of those photographers and the publication of their work to be the most important part of what the picture desk does," Lee said.

Editors on the picture desk evaluate the photos. "The [picture] editor, based on the merit of the picture itself and on the story list of his or her [word] desk, then makes further selection from what has come in and calls the wires for better or different pictures. Then late in the afternoon I'll skim the cream of the crop from their selections for the Page One board."

Lee said she looks for "floater pictures" that have no story as well as pictures that she may not like quite as much but, "because the story is being offered, the editors have to know there is a picture."

Lee prepares a board of pictures for editors to look at during their Page One meeting, a daily conference where the top editors at *The Times* discuss the pictures, graphics and stories that will go on the front page the next morning.

Lee said she and other editors at *The Times* look for a photo that offers not only a striking image but that also explains something to readers. "It tells them something that is going on in the world that they might not know about. There is more of a tendency, with current editors, to use pictures to get another story on Page One. We are sometimes using a picture of secondary merit as a photograph because it has merit in getting a story on the page. Naturally, we try to combine the two; we want the striking image that also has news merit. But if you don't have both, most times the news merit will win out over the beauty of the picture."

Lee said wire photos are "very important to our report because there is no way to begin to cover the ground that we want covered in the newspaper photographically without input from the four corners of the Earth from the wire services. No newspaper can afford photographers everywhere. You do depend on the wire services."

Lee said *The Times* depends on the wire services more for foreign pictures than domestic pictures. "We found the domestic offering, except on particular major stories, quite weak." That means Lee often sends staff photographers to national events rather than relying on the wires. "The staff views it [the event] in a different way," she explained. "They are not as concerned with the common denominator as the wires, which are trying to please all of their customers. The staffer knows the editors of *The Times;* he or she knows and can afford—because there is the backup of the wires if all fails—to take a chance on a different angle or a different view."

SUGGESTED EXERCISES

1. Look through two issues of a daily newspaper. Clip all of the photographs that are in the paper. How many were taken by staff photographers? How many were provided by the wire services? How well were the pictures edited? Was there a good mix of pictures?

2. Look through the same newspapers as you did in Exercise 1 and clip stories that should have been illustrated with photographs. Make out photo assignments for those stories, making certain that you tell the photographer the nature of the story and the type of picture you want taken.

3. Clip a picture page or a picture package from a newspaper. Discuss the visual pacing of the package.

4. What is the ratio of words and visuals on two open pages of the daily newspaper in your community? What percentage of the pages is visual? How would you improve the pages?

CHAPTER SEVENTEEN

Cropping, Sizing and Captions

Once the decision has been made as to which pictures will run in the newspaper, the picture editor or visual journalist must crop and size them and write captions for them. Because most newspaper photographs contribute to the overall design of the paper, how they are cropped and sized is important. Although cropping and sizing are distinct functions, they often are done together.

CROPPING

Cropping is one of the most powerful tools visual journalists have in shaping the day's photographic report. At many newspapers, especially small-circulation ones, the editor who lays out or designs the pages also crops the pictures. At medium- and large-circulation newspapers, cropping may be done by a variety of people, including the picture editor, graphics editor, page designer, news editor or copy editor.

Cropping a photograph means editing or removing the part of it that is unnecessary or that impairs the effective communication of the picture. Cropping can increase the impact and effectiveness of a photograph; however, overcropping can do the reverse and blunt a powerful image's visual punch.

The visual journalist cropping a picture should be aware of photographic composition and understand how his or her actions can improve or harm an image.

A visual journalist should crop in the way a city editor edits. If the story is well-reported and well-written, few changes will be made. If the story is poorly organized or poorly written, the city editor might make substantial changes to improve it. The same is true of photography. A well-composed, well-reported photograph will be difficult to crop; at best, it might be fine-tuned. However, a poorly composed photograph might benefit from cropping to help focus the reader's attention on the relevant material in the picture.

As with each story, each photograph is unique. Therefore, the rules on cropping are general at best. To tell someone there are only two or three methods of cropping would be misleading—there are as many ways to crop a photograph as there are photographs.

Identifying the Essence of a Photograph

Effective cropping entails getting to the essence of a photograph. For example, when Nancy Reagan visited the Tulsa area, both the *Tulsa World* and *The Daily Oklahoman* sent photographers to cover the event. Both

Figure 17.1   Photo with few visual distractions

Figure 17.2   Photo that could have been enhanced by cropping

brought back a good picture of the First Lady hugging a pupil before he boarded a school bus. Each newspaper ran about the same size photograph, but one was cropped tightly to focus on the subject (Figure 17.1), whereas the other used a wider shot that showed other students and even another photographer in the background (Figure 17.2). Clearly, the *Tulsa World* photograph is more dramatic and to the point—it shows the essence of the event more clearly. By contrast, the other picture is poorly cropped. The line of children behind the pupil being hugged distracts the reader's eye from the hug. Even the school bus door is a distraction because the opening pulls the eye away from the action.

Cropping can focus attention on the relevant point of a photograph. In the picture of firefighters climbing a fire escape, the ladder on the left side of the photograph is distracting; it leads the eye away from the action. A tighter crop directs the reader's attention where the photographer and picture editor want it (Figure 17.3).

A photographer capturing a train derailment might turn in an uncropped print showing the entire accident scene. However, the picture editor, realizing that the road leads the reader's eye away from the train's boxcars and up to the automobiles at the top of the picture, could crop the picture in such a way that all attention is focused on the accident (Figure 17.4).

It is important for the visual journalist to look for a better picture "inside" a good picture. For instance, the picture of a kindergarten's graduation ceremony is heart-warming—it captures the mood of the participants and shows a funny side of the event. Within the middle of the photograph, however, is a stronger

image of a girl kicking her fellow pupil. By cropping to the essence of the picture, the visual journalist eliminates the distraction of the other children and presents an even stronger image (Figure 17.5).

Sometimes, the good crop represents a subtle change. The image of an old man becomes stronger by cropping tightly on his head, which allows the reader to focus more on the man's eyes and mouth (Figure 17.6). The lines of the man's shirt also help direct the reader up to the face.

When cropping the human anatomy, the picture editor should avoid leaving parts of limbs "floating" in the picture. For example, it generally is better to crop an entire arm out of the picture rather than just a hand. If it is necessary to crop the bottom of a picture of a person standing, it might be preferable to crop at the waist rather than just above the ankles.

Overcropping

A good photograph can be damaged or ruined by a poor crop. And even though some editors feel a need to crop every picture they see, if a photograph does not need cropping, it shouldn't be cropped. Sometimes, it takes more editing skill to recognize the photograph that does not need cropping than to actually crop a picture. Other times, the trick is to know how much to crop. For instance, the photograph of a woman being helped from her home after a fire could have benefited from cropping (Figure 17.7). The full frame shows a man standing to the right of the action who pulls the reader's eye away from what is important. By cropping him out of the picture, along with

a   **b**

Figure 17.3   (a) Fire photo (b) cropped to focus attention on central action

a   **b**

Figure 17.4   (a) Train derailment photo (b) cropped to eliminate extraneous details

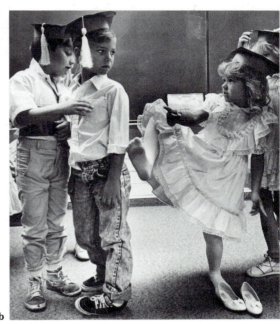

a

Figure 17.5   (a) Feature photo (b) cropped to focus on "inside" image in picture

b

a   **b**

Figure 17.6   (a) Portrait photo (b) subtly cropped to emphasize features

some of the house on the left side, the reader's attention is clearly focused on what is important. Cropping even tighter to focus just on the woman, however, would hurt the picture. With that tight a crop, the sense of a burned-out house is lost, and readers might wonder what was going on in the picture until they read the caption.

Cropping for Impact and Shape

Deep within a picture is often another, better photograph. Cropping can help bring out that picture, allowing the image to have greater impact upon readers, to dramatize an event for them. For example, an original frame taken at the scene of the ruins of a hospital after the 1985 Mexico City earthquake is powerful, but with a tighter crop, the picture can have even greater impact (Figure 17.8). Without the information on both sides of the frame, the picture's focus becomes the efforts of one doctor in the foreground. There also is a clearer view in the background of what is left of the hospital.

Not all dramatic images need to be news photographs. Full frame, the image of the Indian woman and child in the desert is a good photograph; when cropped into a more pronounced horizontal shape, the image becomes even

a

a

b

b

Figure 17.8   (a) Earthquake photo (b) given greater impact by cropping for tighter focus

c

Figure 17.7   (a) Fire rescue photo (b) enhanced by cropping and (c) hurt by overcropping

a

b

Figure 17.9 (a) Image (b) enhanced by cropping for shape and fixing horizon

Figure 17.10 Photo whose mood would be diminished by cropping

Cropping for Mood

The mood of a photograph can be either strengthened or hurt by cropping. That means the successful visual journalist must know when *not* to crop a picture. For example, the mood in the picture of a woman climbing a flight of stairs as sunlight hits her would be spoiled by cropping (Figure 17.10). The blackness surrounding the sunlight directs the eye to the woman and makes it seem as if she is going off into the darkness.

Too much cropping also could spoil the mood of the photograph of soldiers in a makeshift morgue during the 1985 Mexico City earthquake (Figure 17.11). By cropping off just a little of the left side, the visual journalist can heighten the mood of the photograph; any more cropping would destroy the effect.

The Dallas Morning News picture of a local boy near his apartment is stronger without cropping (Figure 17.12). The lines of the boards in the photograph lead the reader's eye toward the child. The boards also give the photograph a sense of mood.

Cropping must be used wisely and with great understanding of the purpose and value of a photograph. Cropping

more powerful (Figure 17.9). The crop on the picture of the woman and child illustrates how the visual journalist can edit for effect. By reducing the amount of information given the reader—that is, by taking out much of the foreground and some of the sky, the visual journalist has focused the reader's attention on what is important—the woman and child. The crop also helped fix the problem with the crooked horizon line by straightening the line and eliminating the visual distraction of the lopsided horizon.

Figure 17.11   Photo requiring only slight cropping

to make a picture "fit" a hole is equivalent to trimming a story without reading it or hacking off the bottom part. A city editor should not allow that to happen to stories; a visual journalist should not allow it to happen to photographs.

SIZING

The second step in preparing a photograph for publication is **sizing,** or scaling, it. Once the photo has been cropped, the visual editor needs to size the picture to fit its allotted space on the newspaper page or to let the news editor know how much space it will take.

Sizing is a mathematical function. The visual journalist first measures the original width and depth of the cropped photograph. At many newspapers, the width is measured in picas and the depth in inches, although some papers measure the depth in picas as well. Then, by using one of the dimensions of the finished size, usually the column width, the visual journalist can determine the printed size of the image. The mathematical formula works because both the original and finished work are proportional.

Usually, a **proportion wheel** is used to compute photo size (Figure 17.13). The proportion wheel works as follows: the original width, found on the inner scale, is lined up with the desired width. The original depth on the inner scale then will line up automatically with the proportional size on the outer scale. If the proportional size is not acceptable, the picture can be cropped and refigured. The crop can be done on the sides or the top or bottom of the original.

Figure 17.12   Photo requiring no cropping

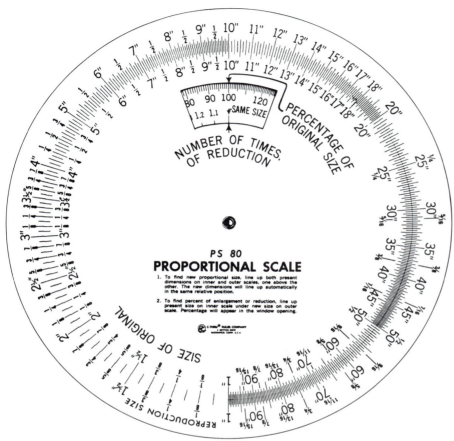

Figure 17.13   Proportion wheel

Figure 17.14   News photo at top of page overshadowed by portrait photo at bottom

For example, suppose an editor needs an 8-inch-wide by 10-inch-deep cropped photograph to run in a $5\frac{1}{2}$-inch or three-column space. On the proportion wheel, the original width (8 inches) is aligned with the desired width ($5\frac{1}{2}$ inches). The original depth (10 inches) will line up with the new depth ($6\frac{7}{8}$ inches).

The proportion wheel also will provide the percentage of reduction or enlargement, a number that is used by the production department to set its process camera to make a velox print. In the case of the 8 by 10 picture, the proportioned three-column photo will be 69 percent of the original.

Because most news, sports and business photographs run within normal or fixed column widths, figuring sizes of photographs is a relatively painless process. The visual journalist needs to know only the original width, the original depth and the desired width. The proportion wheel, or any other scaling device such as metal link rules, a slide rule, a calculator or scaling rules, will provide the new depth.

Image Size vs. Picture Size

Sometimes, it is not just the size of the picture that has the impact on the reader but also the size of the image within the picture. A multicolumn picture of a crowd at a sporting event has little image size, for example. However, a multi-column portrait of a newsmaker would have a huge image size.

The image size of a photograph should be considered when determining the published size, and it should be weighed against the image sizes of the other photographs on the page. The more dramatic photo on the *Minneapolis Star Tribune*'s front page of Dec. 13, 1987—a picture of a rescue helicopter landing on a burning oil tanker in the Persian Gulf—is greatly overshadowed by the portrait of a steroid user (Figure 17.14). Given the image size of the weight lifter, that photograph could have been made slightly smaller without losing impact. And a smaller picture would not have overpowered the news photograph quite as much.

In addition, the image size of a picture must be large enough to convey the message. For example, the two-column photo in *The Arizona Republic* of emergency workers taking a tornado victim out of a building is so small that it lacks visual impact (Figure 17.15). The picture does have impact, however, when it is used in a four-column display, as in the *Tempe* (Ariz.) *Daily News Tribune* (Figure 17.16).

As another example, when a New York bridge collapsed, both *The Washington Post* and *The Boston Globe* played

Figure 17.15   Photo sized too small

Figure 17.16   Photo sized large enough to maintain visual impact

Figure 17.17   News photo sized large enough

Figure 17.18   News photo sized too small

Figure 17.19   Portrait photo sized too large

the story on their respective front pages. However, the difference between *The Globe*'s $5\frac{7}{8}$-inch-wide photo (Figure 17.17) and *The Post*'s $4\frac{1}{4}$-inch-wide picture (Figure 17.18) makes it clear that sometimes photographs can be played too small for the amount of information in them. The bridge photo needed to be played large so the detail of the supports and the river could be seen clearly. (*The Globe* also ran a photograph of a

youngster riding his bike in the rain. By combining the youngster's picture with the bridge photograph, *The Globe* gave its readers a more complete and balanced visual package.)

Another example of image size involves a feature story about a Sarasota, Fla., minister (Figure 17.19). At first glance, the image—a large portrait overwhelming the page—is a powerful one. However, because the picture is

so large, the paper could not use additional photos on the page that would have better illustrated some of the points in the story about this energetic and active church leader. Conversely, powerful news photographs can be wasted when played too small.

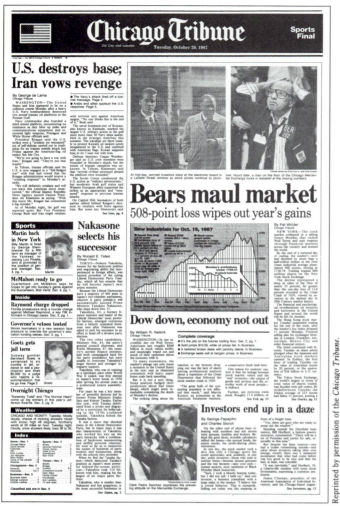

Figure 17.20 Photo used to accent other elements on page

Reprinted by permission of the *Chicago Tribune.*

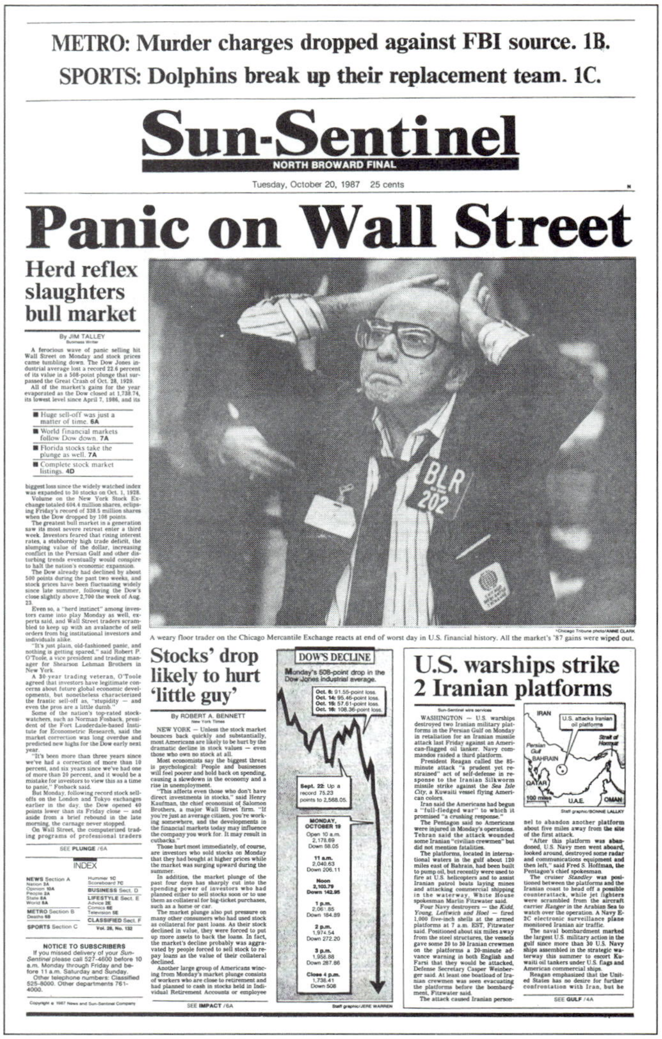

Figure 17.21 Photo used as "exclamation point"

How Big Is Big Enough?

Is a three-column picture too small? Is a six-column photo too large? Unfortunately, there are no ironclad answers. Every picture must be sized for maximum effect, which depends on the image it shows.

All newspapers have their own standards, their own design styles that indicate a direction the visual journalist can look to for guidance. Some newspapers use photographs as exclamation points; they want them to shout. Others prefer that pictures carry their own weight; only those photos with great news value are run large.

For example, the design style and use of photographs at the *Fort Lauderdale Sun-Sentinel* is different from the *Chicago Tribune,* even though they are owned by the same company. The *Tribune* photographed a weary floor trader on the Chicago Mercantile Exchange the day the stock market dropped 500 points, and both papers ran the photo. The *Tribune* used the picture as an accent to other visual elements on the page, including a hard-to-read photo of worried investors (Figure 17.20); the *Sun-Sentinel* used the photograph as an exclamation point (Figure 17.21). Similarly, when the United States and the Soviet Union

Figure 17.22 Photo sized large for dramatic effect

Figure 17.23 Photo sized smaller and lacking visual impact

signed a treaty to eliminate certain types of nuclear missiles, papers throughout the country ran a picture of the historic event. However, many could not or would not have played the photograph as large as the *Star Tribune* in Minneapolis did (Figure 17.22) even though the same photo played half as large lacks visual impact (Figure 17.23).

In most cases, the visual journalist must find, through error and experiment, the combination of sizes that works for both the design of the newspaper and the photographers. Often, the proper size of photographs is determined during the give-and-take that goes on between the picture editor and news editor as the pages of the newspaper are laid out.

CAPTIONS

A **caption,** or line(s) of type under or alongside a photograph, is of paramount importance because it is a prime entry point for readers of a newspaper page. Readership studies have shown that readers are attracted to a picture first,

then to the caption and finally to the story.

The information in a caption should explain or amplify what is visible in a picture. A good caption will give additional information without rehashing the obvious action going on in a photograph. In addition, the caption identifies the people shown in a photograph.

Most captions are written on the newspaper's copy desk. And although few picture editors write captions, they should be aware of the special skill that good caption writing requires. An effective caption can add understanding of or appreciation to the story the picture accompanies. It should be written after the story is read and the photograph is viewed. And, if the picture does not accompany a story, the caption must tell the story on its own.

Good captions begin with the newspaper's photographers, who must understand that part of their job as visual journalists is to bring back complete information to accompany the image. Some newspapers will refuse to run a photograph—no matter how striking

or important—if the photographer fails to do this. Complete information includes:

- First and last names of people in the picture, if possible
- A good description of the event being covered, without repeating what the image in the photograph shows
- An explanation of any part of the photograph that might be confusing

Because the photographer was at the scene of an event, he or she will have a greater understanding of the photograph than will an editor or reader who views the image for the first time. In fact, some newspapers also ask the photographer to act as reporter, bringing back quotes from the people being photographed or additional information.

Once the photographer turns in the caption material with the picture, it is up to the copy editor or picture editor to write the most complete caption possible in a limited amount of space. The Continuing Study Committee of The Associated Press Managing Editors (AMPE) put together a list entitled Ten Tests of a Good Caption:

✓ Is it complete?
✓ Does it identify, fully, clearly?
✓ Does it tell when?
✓ Does it tell where?
✓ Does it tell what's in the picture? (Captions writers, however, never should state the obvious in a photograph, such as "man sits" when it is clear the man is sitting.)
✓ Does it have the names spelled correctly, with the proper name on the right person?
✓ Is it specific?

✔ Is it easy to read?
✔ Have as many adjectives as possible been removed?
✔ Does it suggest another picture?

And the cardinal rule from APME: Never write a caption without seeing the picture.

In addition, the caption writer has to write all this according to size—an 8-inch-deep caption can't run under a 3-inch-deep photograph. Thus, the caption must be both concise and complete. Size requirements for captions will depend on the design style of the newspaper. Finally, caption writers must remember that a reader looks at the photograph *before* reading the caption. To assume otherwise can lead to the creation of weak, demeaning and repetitive captions.

SUGGESTED EXERCISES

1. Clip and discuss three examples of well-cropped pictures from a daily newspaper. Do the same for three badly cropped pictures.

2. Find two newspapers that run the same wire photo on the same day. Do they both use the picture effectively? Discuss the cropping, sizing and captions of each picture.

3. Use a proportion wheel to size the following pictures:
   a. An 8 by 10 into a 7-inch-wide hole
   b. A 5 by 7 into a $3\frac{1}{4}$-inch-wide hole
   c. A 4 by 5 into a 5-inch-wide hole
   d. A 5 by 7 into a 9-inch-deep hole
   e. An 8 by 10 into a 7-inch-deep hole

CHAPTER EIGHTEEN

Wire Service Photographs

Few newspapers have the staff or resources to cover every major national or international event. They depend on wire services such as the Associated Press and United Press International for the majority of their out-of-town coverage. By using the wire services, they are able to satisfy their readers' demand for a full range of local, state, national and international stories and visuals.

There are four major photographic wire services that offer newspapers a large number of photographs and other visuals each day from their networks of staff photographers, stringers and free-lancers: the AP, UPI, Reuters and Agence France-Presse. AP is a not-for-profit cooperative; it is owned by its member newspapers. UPI, Agence France-Presse and Reuters are commercial ventures, and their clients are called subscribers. AP and UPI are U.S. companies, Reuters is based in England and AFP is based in France. (UPI distributes Reuters' photos taken outside the United States in a cooperative venture, and Reuters has the rights to distribute UPI's domestic photo report to its clients outside the United States.)

Only the AP and UPI currently offer a full-coverage photo service, which means they cover major national and international events and also transmit feature, business, entertainment and sports photographs. They also honor member or subscriber requests for photographs of particular events. Reuters and AFP are referred to as "supplemental" services and limit their coverage to major news events. In addition, as members of the AP cooperative, newspapers are obligated to share their photographs with AP for possible widespread distribution. UPI, because it is a for-profit venture, has no such claim to subscribers' photographs, although it is a common practice for newspapers to share photographs with it.

AP's cooperative nature allows it to draw on the photographs of some of the best newspaper photographers in the country and to distribute the best of the photos to its members. Currently, more than 1,000 newspapers receive AP photos; more than 300 subscribe to UPI's photo service, although the service has suffered from financial difficulties in recent years.

A LOOK AT ONE DAY'S WIRE REPORT

In one 24-hour news cycle, hundreds of wire photos and graphics are available for scores of news, sports, business

a

b

Figure 18.1   Wire service photos of USS Stark from (a) Reuters/UPI and (b) AP

and feature stories. Even those editors whose newspapers subscribe to only one wire photo service are faced with many decisions. There usually are too many pictures and not enough space, which means careful editing is essential to ensure the best use of the wire photo report. There also may be too many visuals on subjects in which a newspaper is not interested, or there may not be enough visuals to go with a story the paper's executives consider important to readers. Again, creative editing is needed.

An example of the diversity and volume of the wire service report can be found in the 24-hour period, midnight to midnight, on May 19, 1987, when UPI in San Francisco moved the following 113 photos and graphics:

- 32 sports photos, which included more than 10 pictures involving the NBA playoffs, either Boston vs. Detroit or Los Angeles vs. Seattle
- 10 advance photos for stories planned for the weekend features or upcoming stories and columns

- 10 photos of specific regional interest to northern California, including six involving the disappearance of two Reno women and the disclosure by police of a suspect in the case
- four feature photos, two of which were from the Cannes Film Festival
- two informational graphics
- one satellite weather photo and one weather map
- 28 national photos, which included six involving the attack on the USS Stark in the Persian Gulf the previous weekend
- 25 foreign photos, including seven showing either the USS Stark as it was being towed to port in the gulf or headshots of U.S. sailors killed during the attack by an Iraqi jet and six concerning the recent military takeover of the island of Fiji

In the same period, the AP moved more than 100 photographs and graphics on its main wire photo network, including 19 pictures to go with national stories, 30 for international stories and seven for regional stories.

TYPES OF WIRE PHOTOGRAPHS
Page One Photos

On May 19, 1987, the most important news involved the investigations into the attack two days earlier by an Iraqi jet on the USS Stark, a warship stationed in the Persian Gulf. All the wire services offered pictures that showed the ship, with a large hole in its bow area, being towed to port. One picture from Reuters/UPI showed the bow of the ship; one from the AP showed the side (Figure 18.1). Such photos illustrated the top story of that day and provided readers with a greater understanding of the death and destruction caused by the missile attack. For many papers, it was the main or banner story on Page One.

Although the choice of which news subject is worth pictorial coverage usually is an easy one, the newspaper's picture editor must consider other factors in determining which photograph to use. If the editor is choosing between the AP and Reuters/UPI versions (assuming the paper receives both services), he or she must determine which

a   b

Figure 18.2   Secondary photos from UPI showing (a) parents of killed serviceman and (b) mother waiting for word about her son

picture does the best job of telling the story. The editor also must consider which version is likely to reproduce well in the newspaper. The size of the photograph on Page One must be considered. Will the AP horizontal or Reuters/UPI vertical picture fit better with all the other elements and stories scheduled for the page? The order in which photos move also must be considered when determining usage. A great picture that moves after deadline stands less of a chance of being used than an average photo that is sent earlier.

In the case of the USS Stark, although neither wire service could provide excellent transmissions from that remote site because of the distance involved, the Reuters/UPI photo probably was the best picture to use because it showed the bow of the ship. In addition, the speedboat in the foreground gave a sense of scale or size.

Secondary or Inside Photos

Often, with major news stories, there are secondary stories, or sidebars, that deal with other elements of the story, such as background or human interest angles. The wire services also will transmit secondary photos and visuals to accompany these stories.

Many of the secondary stories and photographs about the attack on the USS Stark involved the families of those servicemen who were killed or missing. These stories and pictures were important because they added a human or personal element to the event. Of the two secondary photos transmitted by UPI, one was from a newspaper, the *Roanoke Times & World News*. This photo, showing a mother waiting for word about her son, is more visually interesting than the other photo, which shows the parents of one of the men who was killed (Figure 18.2). However,

not every picture selection is based solely on photographic merit; if the family in the other picture were quoted in the story, then that may be the most appropriate photo to use. It is important to match, if possible, words and pictures in a story of this nature.

Of course, words and pictures don't always match. Often, because of staffing limitations or deadlines, a photographer cannot accompany a reporter on assignment. The photographer brings back pictures that are true to the nature and tone of the story but do not show specific people mentioned in the copy. In these cases, the visual journalist should pick the photograph that will best help readers understand the story. The photograph then would supplement the words rather than illustrate them precisely.

Figure 18.3   Photos of British prime minister candidates (a) Margaret Thatcher and (b) Neil Kinnock that would benefit from combo treatment

Combo Photo Treatment

Sometimes, the packaging of two photos can provide a more informative, pleasing presentation than could either photo alone. One example of such packaging, or *combo treatment* as it often is called, involves two photographs that were transmitted at the start of the British campaign for prime minister (Figure 18.3). The photo of Prime Minister Margaret Thatcher was acceptable in itself—in the United States, Thatcher is a recognizable newsmaker. However, her opponent, Neil Kinnock, was not well-known to most Americans. In addition, the photo of Kinnock is not as strong as the one of Thatcher. By using both photos, cropped and sized to about the same dimensions, editors could give readers a faster "read" or understanding. In a visual sense, the picture editor could pair off the two candidates—face to face—much as they were paired off in the race for prime minister.

Wire photos often are not cropped tightly, so editors can use them in a variety of shapes and sizes. Not only does effective cropping make packaging easier but it also increases image size and helps save space. (Cropping and sizing are discussed in depth in Chapter 17.)

Sports Photos

The sports section, depending on the season, can be overwhelmed by potential photographs to use in limited space. Newspaper editors always must keep in mind what teams are of interest to readers rather than to editors. By understanding that sports fans have certain loyalties even to losing teams, the picture editor can weigh various

Figure 18.4   Sports wire photo

Figure 18.5   Stand-alone feature photo

sports action photos and select those that are visually worthy and also important to the readership (Figure 18.4). The editor also should know enough about the contest to look for a good picture of the game-winning play.

Wild and Stand-Alone Photos

Newspapers often use photos without stories; such pictures are called **stand-alone photos** or **wild art**. The use of these photos can provide additional news to the reader and make for a more pleasing visual presentation on a news page. Sometimes, a stand-alone photo is used on Page One to give greater importance to a story that appears inside the newspaper. In this case, the photo's caption refers to the story inside.

For the sake of balance and tone, many newspapers run wild art features or "light" photos that give a visual counterpoint to the news photos that reflect the unhappier events of the world. Often, these photos involve the weather, children, animals or humorous subjects (Figure 18.5). These stand-alone photos seldom are used if they

are not important to the visual mix of the news.

When a stand-alone photo is used, care must be taken not to place it next to a story and headline that deal with a tragedy or other somber news event. There is nothing worse, for example, than a color stand-alone photo of a crowd laughing at a clown inadvertently placed next to a story of a tragic accident.

THE WIRE PHOTO NETWORK

When a photographer wants to send a print to a wire service's main office, he or she uses a photo transmitter (Figure 18.6). Although the process varies slightly from wire service to wire service, the principle is basically the same.

The photographer using the AP's system places a print on a drum that will rotate while a beam of high-intensity light scans the photo. The light is reflected off the print, and sensors measure the amount of reflection. The intensity of the reflected light is converted into electronic intensities of sound; the intensities are different vol-

umes on the same sound frequency. The lighter the area of the print, the more light is reflected and the louder the sound; the darker the print, the less light reflected and the quieter the sound.

These sound impulses are transmitted over leased phone lines to a newspaper's receiver or via satellites directly to a receiving dish. A photo receiver converts the impulses of sound into impulses of light, which are exposed on light-sensitive paper. The paper then is processed into a finished print. Under a microscope, the transmitted print will show transmission of scan lines, about 144 per inch. These scan lines are much like the scan lines that can be seen when looking closely at a television picture.

However, for the first time since wire photos were first sent via telephone lines in 1935, the transmission of wire photographs will take a major technological leap forward. Using a new electronic scanner called the "Leafax," photographers will no longer need to make a photographic print to send to

Figure 18.6   Photo print scanner

Figure 18.7   Leafax scanner

either an AP office or their home newspaper (Figure 18.7). Using only the negative—or a color transparency—the photographer or picture editor can send a digital image in less than one minute. Even a color negative can be sent as either a color image or a black-and-white. The Leafax will be installed in all of the AP's main offices and is the first step toward a completely electronic photo transmission system.

How Wire Photos Are Distributed

The AP's main distribution point is its New York City headquarters. Photographs from this point are sent out over two wire photo systems—LaserPhoto and LaserPhoto II. The LaserPhoto network is the main photo service for most newspapers; LaserPhoto II is a supplemental service that provides additional photos of major events and additional color photo projects.

The New York City headquarters receives photographs from bureaus and stringers worldwide and from national and local points. In addition to distributing photos to the U.S. networks, the AP picture editors in New York also serve as editors for wire photo networks in Europe, Asia and Latin America. More than 700 photos are received daily in New York for distribution on U.S. and foreign wire photo networks. Strong photographs of national or international

interest are offered to the entire AP network.

The AP can electronically *split* its national network into smaller networks serving several states, a single state or even a metropolitan area or city. The national network is split into regional networks that are based on several states with common readership interests. These regional centers can split off from the national network to move an important regional or local photo to a member newspaper. For example, one regional photo network serves Illinois, Indiana and Ohio and is handled by picture editors in Chicago. Another serves Southern California and is handled by editors in Los Angeles. Pictures that move on the Southern California split might involve the mayor of Los Angeles or Dodgers baseball.

One regional split photo was of California Governor George Deukmejian preparing to go on television to propose a refund of $700 million to state taxpayers (Figure 18.8). The photo probably did not have great interest to readers outside of California, so it was moved to the AP's California members from Sacramento during a "regional" split.

There are times when the AP has to cross-split lines and make sure that more than one region receives photos. For example, if the service wanted to transmit pictures showing pollution in the Ohio River, it would have to send them to Ohio and Pennsylvania because the river flows in both states. But regional photos for Ohio are handled in Chicago, and regionals for Pennsylvania are handled in New York. By crossing split lines electronically, the AP is able to send the pictures to both states.

UPI's photo network is set up similarly to the AP's and can distribute its photographs in a variety of ways, including splitting off various states or parts of states.

Wire Service Photo Editing

During the 1987 British political campaign, the AP editors in New York City received from their staffers, from the British press association and from local newspapers six or seven pictures daily on Prime Minister Margaret Thatcher and her opponents. The photographs were of great interest in Britain, but they were of limited interest to most U.S. newspaper readers. Part of an AP picture editor's job was to decide which photograph or two to transmit on each *daily cycle*.

Daily cycles include **AM** for morning newspapers and **PM** for evening newspapers. The wire services also can send visuals *BC*, which can be used in both cycles. The cycles are important for the wire photo services because most newspapers prefer to run photos different from the ones seen in their competitors' morning or evening publications.

An AP picture editor tries to find a different angle or a fresh approach when selecting a picture for the next cycle. If a major event occurs late in the afternoon, only morning publications on the AM cycle can use the wire photos. The afternoon papers on the PM

(SCI)SACRAMENTO, Calif., May 19--PROPOSES $700 MILLION REFUND FOR TAXPAYERS-- Governor George Deukmejian, with a California budget summary at hand, prepares to go on statewide television Tuesday where he proposed refunding at least $700 million to taxpayers this year.(AP LaserPhoto)C(WJ23l4l3stf/Walt Zeboski) --SLUGGED:BUDGET--1987

Figure 18.8   AP wire photo moved to California by regional split

cycle will want pictures that reflect the "second-day" nature of the event. That *second-day photo* may be a different angle from the same coverage or a "follow-up" photo assigned and photographed early in the morning.

When Thatcher won the British elections and a third term as prime minister, the first pictures received from the AP's London offices of her acknowledging the victory were sent quickly over the AP's national wire photo network from New York City at about 4 a.m., according to Rich Kareckas, day (picture) supervisor. They were moved on the wire photo network in time to meet the first deadlines of the East Coast's afternoon newspapers, but were too late to make the final deadlines of the West Coast's morning publications.

Later that day, photos were taken of Thatcher going to work at 10 Downing St. and waving to the crowds outside her office. These pictures, along with additional photos of Thatcher and her defeated opponents, were sent in the next cycle, giving morning newspapers something fresh.

The AP picture editors had more to worry about than just the British elections. When the first picture of Thatcher moved at 4 a.m., there was little else contending for wire transmission time (only one photo can move on each network at one time). Later in the day, however, there were other photos that newspapers wanted to see, especially those of President Reagan visiting the Berlin Wall. The AP picture editors had to juggle pictures and transmission times to make certain that Reagan and Thatcher were transmitted in timely fashion so that newspaper editors would have the choice of what to play where.

In the case of Thatcher, the first picture received in New York was sent quickly. The wire service's picture editors then waited to see all the other photographs from London before sending additional ones. By doing that, they avoided clogging the network with secondary photographs. Such editing and juggling enables the AP to service its members with both breaking news photos and feature, sports and business photos.

INSIDE LOOK

Pete Leabo

News Photo Editor   The Associated Press, San Francisco

A wire service photographer has to be a jack-of-all-trades, according to Pete Leabo, news photo editor of the Associated Press bureau in San Francisco. "There are no specialists in the wire services," he said. "We shoot news. We shoot sports. We shoot fashion.

"Wire service photographers have to have the technical knowledge of all the equipment, such as computers and circuits. They have to know how to build a darkroom in a bathroom full of windows. They need to know how to send a photograph from anywhere. They have to handle every aspect of an assignment, both in black-and-white and color. There is no edition deadline here. A wire service photographer is always on deadline."

Leabo said the wire services want to provide newspapers throughout the United States and world with immediate pictures that they otherwise would not have. "We go for the picture that best illustrates the story, bearing in mind that because of technological restraints we are limited to one or two pictures. Our job is to sum up an event. We might not be able to meet sidebar or offbeat demands."

The AP supplies its member newspapers with pictures from staff photographers, free-lancers and other member newspapers. Leabo and the three photographers in San Francisco shoot pictures throughout the country and world. "The photographer brings the film into the lab and it is processed and printed," Leabo said. "An editor or the photographer types the caption containing identifying elements of the photograph. It is affixed to the picture, which then is wrapped onto the drum of the transmitter.

"Next, the picture is scheduled on our system of leased telephone lines called the LaserPhoto Network. It is scheduled with the national monitor (the person who controls the routing of pictures on the network) in New York or the regional monitor in Los Angeles. The monitor will put the picture on a schedule and will tell us when to start the transmission. The transmission also can be triggered automatically from the control bureau. The picture then is scanned, and receivers throughout the system will receive the signal simultaneously. It takes eight or nine minutes per picture to transmit."

At more and more bureaus worldwide, computers are replacing this older method of transmitting wire photos. "The technology is there to transmit photos in under a minute," Leabo noted. "Computers are bringing higher quality and faster handling of wire photos."

Besides shooting assignments from the AP, the photographers in San Francisco respond to every request from member newspapers for pictures. For example, Leabo said, a staffer of an AP member newspaper in the Midwest may call the AP in San Francisco and request that a photo be taken of a news or sports event of interest to the newspaper. An assignment is made and the photograph is taken. The photo then is sent by a transmitter connected to a standard telephone. The member newspaper has a similar telephone connected to a receiver. This type of transmission is called an LD. By transmitting the photo on this one-to-one basis, the AP network does not have to be used.

SUGGESTED EXERCISES

1. Explain the similarities and differences between the Associated Press and United Press International wire photo services.

2. Clip five wire photos from a local newspaper. Which wire service supplied them? Are they used effectively? Does the paper use photos from more than one wire service?

3. Go through the inside pages of a local newspaper. Are wire photos used? Clip examples of pages where a wire photo could have been used but was not.

4. Can you find an example or two of "lazy photo editing," where an editor used a wire photo when a local assignment could have been made? Explain what the local picture could have shown.

5. Clip two examples of effective combo photo treatments.

6. Clip two examples of stand-alone wire photos. Were they used effectively?

7. Clip examples of a first-day photo and a second-day photo of the same event. How are they different? Do they do a good job of illustrating the stories?

CHAPTER NINETEEN

Photo Manipulation and Illustration

Reality. It is the most important part of a photograph's image. Newspaper photographs are supposed to portray reality for readers who could not be at an event. Yet, despite protests by many photographers, some visual journalists and editors continue to treat photographs as just another design device that can be manipulated and adapted to the needs of the page's appearance at the expense of reality.

WHITEOUTS AND CUTOUTS

One of the most common means of distorting reality is through the use of a **whiteout**, or **cutout**, a process in which a photograph's background is removed either by painting it white or by cutting it out, leaving only the image that an editor or artist decides is important. Supporters of whiteouts or cutouts argue that the process takes a weak photograph and focuses attention on what is really important. Critics claim such treatment creates an image that no longer represents the reality the photographer saw in the camera lens.

A major drawback to photos with whiteouts or cutouts is that readers look at them and sense non-reality. They realize immediately that a photograph

has been distorted. For example, the whiteout of a cowboy photo exaggerates the cowboy's arm, hand and gun to an almost comic extent (Figure 19.1). And the photograph of Walter Mondale makes his fingers look misshapen—readers cannot tell if the picture is a news photograph or an illustration created to mark an event (Figure 19.2). Finally, when displaying excerpts of a historic Supreme Court ruling, one newspaper decided to take out the justice who did not participate in the decision (Figure 19.3). By using paints, a new pillar was created and "placed" where the justice once stood (Figure 19.4).

Throughout the history of newspapers, artists have been called upon to "create" photographs for one reason or another. For example, in a 1931 photograph that appears to be a family scene, the children actually were cut from another photo and positioned next to the man (Figure 19.5). The original photograph also shows a young man with a hat on the left side of the man, not the right side as in the manipulated picture.

Many whiteouts or cutouts look crude and misshapen because of the process required to create them—physically cutting out the background image or painting it out and then using dyes and paints to blend or create a

Figure 19.1   Photo whited out to almost comic degree

Figure 19.2   Photo whited out to the extent that image seems unreal

Figure 19.3   Photo of Supreme Court justices

Figure 19.4   Photo of Supreme Court justices with one member whited out

new background. With today's sophisticated computers, however, it is possible to do in minutes what once took an artist hours to achieve. And because the computer deals with *pixels*, or electronic elements of the picture, it is impossible for readers to detect the photo manipulation.

INSETS AND MORTICES

Insets and **mortices**, in which a photo, map or other visual device is placed into a different image, are another form of manipulation (Figure 19.6). Insets and mortices are used to create a "relationship" between two images by combining them, but they often create visual confusion or clutter. For example, in the photographic treatment on signing up voters in the South, the

a   b

Figure 19.5   (a) "Photo" of family and (b) separate photos from which image was created

Figure 19.6   Example of inset and whiteout

Figure 19.7   Photo inset on another photo, weakening both images

images of Tampa residents are super-imposed on a photograph of a house in Mississippi (Figure 19.7). Such treatment creates two weak photographs. Or note the inset of the map into a photograph accompanying a story about drivers using an unopened part of a new freeway (Figure 19.8). The purpose of the photograph is to show the empty expanse of the unopen road; the inset of the map adds visual clutter. Finally,

a strong photograph showing children in a Haitian hospital is weakened when a map is cut into the image (Figure 19.9). The map, not the photograph, now attracts the reader's eye.

The use of a morticed or inset image often represents a move made to avoid a layout or design problem. The visual journalist must avoid such treatment to preserve the reality of the photograph and not distract from its communication.

Figure 19.8 Visual clutter created by inset of map into photo

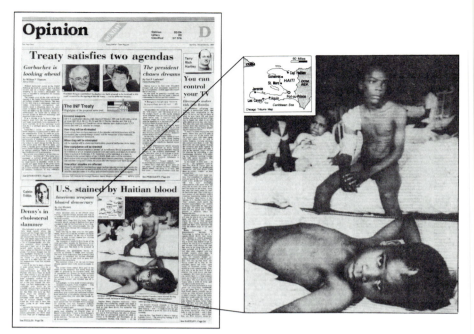

Figure 19.9 Photo weakened by inset map

ELECTRONIC MANIPULATION

What has been done by an artist's hands and knife now can be done by computer. An **electronic imaging device**, often called a Scitex machine after one of the pioneer manufacturers in the field, allows its users to electronically scan a print negative or transparency and manipulate the image. Photographic images can be manipulated subtly to remove blemishes or other imperfections, or their entire content can be altered.

With an electronic imaging device, a user breaks down the image of a photograph into pixels. Because the device's computer stores and displays the pixels as digital information, the picture elements can be changed, erased and otherwise manipulated. For example, a green apple could be turned to red (or blue) by telling the computer to identify all of the pixels in the apple that contain the color green and then change their color. It is possible to publish a "realistic"-looking purple apple.

Digital information from one or more pictures also can be combined, much as part of one story in a computer can be moved to another story. Once the editor or production worker is finished using the electronic imaging system, the photograph can be transformed into color separations that are ready for the printing process.

A major reason that more newspapers currently are not using electronic imaging devices is their cost. Their price tag of $1 million to $2 million makes them too expensive for most newspapers.

ETHICAL QUESTIONS

In the 1990s, as new equipment is introduced and prices fall, more newspapers may be manipulating pictures. Even personal computers such as the Macintosh will have the power to do complex photographic manipulation such as whiteouts and cutouts. The PC systems will cost less than $30,000. These advances are sure to raise new ethical questions.

For example, when editors of the 1986 "Day in the Life of America" book changed their cover photo from a horizontal to a vertical picture by electronically moving the cowboy and a tree closer, critics called "foul." Visually, there was no way for readers to tell that the picture was not "captured" by a photojournalist. The book's editors insisted that such manipulation was acceptable because it was done on the book's cover and not on any inside pages, that the cover represented a selling device for the book and was not "pure" photography. One of the crowning ironies in this case was that many of the country's best photographers worked on the project, some of whom were unaware of the manipulation being done by the book's editors.

The ethical questions raised by electronically altered photographs has many journalists concerned over the potential loss of credibility among readers. And because the general credibility of newspapers among readers has fallen in the past few decades, the potential for further damage from fake pictures must be taken very seriously. Some editors even argue that the use of electronic imaging could undermine faith in photography as a recorder of human events. As Robert Gilka, former director of photography at *National Geographic* magazine, said in a *New York Times Magazine* article, "It's like limited nuclear warfare. There ain't none."

Figure 19.10 Humorous and obviously staged photo illustration

Figure 19.11 Obviously staged photo illustration

Figure 19.12 Photo illustration that readers might interpret as documentary or real photo

PHOTO ILLUSTRATION

The use of illustration to make a photographic point is a more recent phenomenon in newspapers. Unlike the standard newspaper **documentary photo**, which is taken by a photographer, acting as a journalist who records events or faithfully shows the reality of people or places, a *photo illustration* is a posed photograph that has been conceived and executed for the purpose of illustrating a point in a story. It also is called a *conceptual photo* and often uses abstract ideas or symbols to illustrate feature stories. The roots of photo illustration can be found in advertising photography, where photos of people enjoying a product often are staged or taken to make a statement about why consumers should buy a product or service.

Photo illustrations often are used as attention-getting devices or visual illustrations of points being made in a story. Frequently, they are humorous. One such example of a photo illustration is in the Food section of the *Statesman-Journal* of Salem, Ore., in which the photographer used the idea of scores of zucchinis taking over a kitchen (Figure 19.10). Obviously, the photograph is not reality, but it attracts attention to the story. In another example, the *San Jose Mercury News'* photo illustration in its Garden section attracts readers to the page because it shows something that cannot be real (Figure 19.11). The reader knows that the photograph is a "trick."

But what about a more subtle example from *The Providence (R.I.) Sunday Journal* in which the photographer created the messy scene for the purpose of illustrating the story about

clutter in homes (Figure 19.12)? Although there is a credit line at the bottom of the photograph that says "photo illustration," how many readers would know that the picture of the messy dresser is "unreal"?

Photo illustrations present bigger problems when they accompany more serious subjects, such as a story concerning children who start fires (Figure 19.13). In these cases, the readers can be fooled into thinking that a picture is real. For example, in the picture shown in Figure 19.13, who is the child? Is he related to the story in the same way most news photographs are to news stories? Once again, there is a **credit line** that says "photo illustration," but the reader might miss it, thinking instead that the child is indeed connected to the story. Although it might be difficult to take a "real" photograph of children who start fires, the use of a photo illustration on such a story could bring the newspaper's credibility into question. As a visual device, the illustration could cause more problems than it solves.

Another example of misleading photo illustrations concerns a story about protest groups that is accompanied by a photo illustration of a child painting graffiti (Figure 19.14). However, the story is about joining protest groups, not about painting walls. Not only does

Figure 19.13 Deceptively realistic photo illustration

Figure 19.14 Photo illustration that misrepresents accompanying story

SUGGESTED EXERCISES

1. Find and clip an example of a white-out or cutout in a daily newspaper. Can you tell if it was done by hand or computer? Was it used effectively? Can you think of a better way to use the picture?

2. Find and clip an example of a mortice or inset in a daily newspaper. Was it used effectively? How can the page be designed to avoid the mortice or inset?

3. Find and clip an example of a photo illustration. Do you think it was used effectively? What type of picture could have been assigned for the story to avoid the illustration?

---

the picture give one impression and the story another but also the use of a socially unacceptable form of behavior to illustrate an acceptable form would probably upset those in the protest groups mentioned in the story. Those readers might ask whether the newspaper is implying that its members spray paint graffiti.

The photographer, picture editor and other visual journalists thus must establish a working relationship to develop the best ideas for illustrative photographs so that the image works best with the story and headline being planned. George Wedding, director of photography at *The Sacramento (Calif.) Bee*, offers the following tips for better illustrative photography:

✔ Provide visual clues to let the reader know the image is not real. Wedding suggests injecting whimsy or fantasy into illustrations so that readers do not think they are documentary pictures.
✔ Avoid trite visual puns.
✔ Use professional models when possible, and avoid "free models" from the newsroom because staffers seldom possess professional actors' ability to express emotions.
✔ When models are used, make it clear that they are actors posing as symbols of humanity in illustrations. When a recognizable face is used, readers will want to know more about that person by reading the accompanying story.
✔ Clearly label the work as an illustration.
✔ Keep illustrative photography out of the news sections. When an illustrative picture mimics a documentary photo, it confuses readers who expect to see factual reporting on the news pages.

"To create images that re-create real life in documentary style is not an appropriate style in photojournalism," Wedding said. "It might be appropriate in movies and annual reports, but not in journalism. Our challenge is to use illustrative photography in a way that it won't compromise documentary photography."

PART FOUR

Art and Illustration

CHAPTER TWENTY

History of Newspaper Illustrations

Before photographs, before informational graphics, before color, there were newspaper illustrations. Based on the standards of today's artists, those illustrations were crude, but they represented the first attempt by newspapers to show readers the faraway places, people and events that were shaping their lives. As with the color and informational graphics of the late 1900s, the illustrations of the late 1800s had a profound influence on the U.S. newspaper industry. These early visual elements opened new ways of presenting information (Figure 20.1).

THE FIRST ILLUSTRATIONS

The earliest illustrations in printed books, magazines and newspapers were reversed images of fancy letters, symbols or drawings carved by hand on small wooden blocks and then placed onto a page with the rest of the movable type. These *woodcuts* were used as a design device to break up gray columns of type. Because it took a great deal of time for an artist to carve the wooden block, woodcuts that illustrated actual news events were rare. The illustrations tended to be small and completely unrelated to the words on the page. Large illustrations also were unusual because they made it more difficult to run the newspaper's press.

By the mid-1840s, almost all U.S. metropolitan newspapers had abandoned woodcuts as they changed from flatbed to revolving-cylinder presses—woodcuts could not be used on such presses. Meanwhile, advances in engraving technology, just like today's advances in computer technology, changed the way newspapers were published. In the 1880s, a new soft-metal process allowed newspapers to create *engravings* of artists' drawings in hours rather than the days it took to create a woodcut.

When the *New York World*, under the direction of Joseph Pulitzer, began running sketches of important local citizens in 1884, the response was so overwhelming that New Yorkers were begging to get their "pictures" into the paper. As the demand for more illustrations grew and newspaper publishers across the country saw them as a way to increase circulation, artists and engravers were hired by the hundreds to re-create news events and draw portraits of famous people (Figure 20.2). They even drew comics and political cartoons.

The artistic boom in the late 1880s and 1890s was short-lived, however, as photographs were introduced into newspapers. Although some journalists

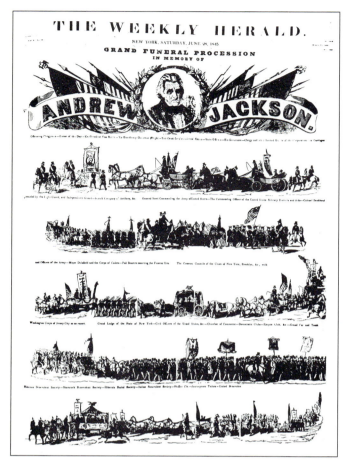

Figure 20.1   Sample woodcut use

Figure 20.2   Early newspaper portraits (1892)

Figure 20.3   Retouched photo

of the time complained that photographs were a waste of space, the reading public enjoyed reproductions of actual events and people.

THE EVOLVING FUNCTIONS OF THE NEWSPAPER ARTIST

Newspaper photography did not squeeze out artists completely, but it did help change the role of artists. From the early 1900s until the 1960s, artists were used mainly to prepare photographs for publication. A skilled artist equipped with paints and an **airbrush**, which sprays water-based paints in a fine mist, could create ornate photo layouts or designs out of discrete images. For example, a person in one photograph could be cut out and placed in a different location. Then, using an airbrush and paints, an artist could blend the two photographs so that most readers would think the

image was real. Newspaper artists also cut photographs into various shapes in an attempt to create different designs. Fortunately, most airbrush work was limited to the process of **retouching** a photograph, which generally meant using paint to cover the background in a photograph so that the image was cleaner and hence easier to reproduce (Figure 20.3). Occasionally, drawings depicting events were even placed on a photograph in an effort to have the illustration tell the complete story. These illustrations were early informational graphics.

Newsroom artists also traditionally have been used in courtrooms where cameras have not been permitted. Much like the artists who covered the Civil War with pencil and charcoal, a courtroom artist illustrates a major trial by sketching witnesses, defendants, plaintiffs, judge and jury. Often, the artist works under tight deadlines.

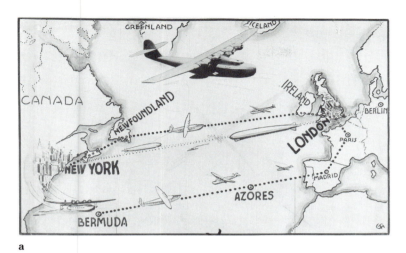

a

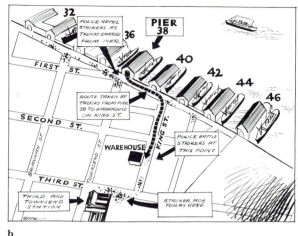

b

Figure 20.4 Early hand-drawn, hand-lettered maps showing (a) likely inaugural trans-Atlantic air passenger routes and (b) details of labor strife in San Francisco

Map Drawing

Newspaper artists always have been needed to draw maps, particularly during war. From the time of their introduction in newspapers in the 1850s, maps and their counterparts, charts and illustrations, were finely drawn creations, full of detail and information; even the words needed to be hand-lettered at first (Figure 20.4). It would be years before high-quality proofs of map information were available, and not until the 1970s did artists use type created by electronic typesetting equipment. By the late 1980s, artists were creating maps on computers.

THE ROLE OF THE MODERN NEWSPAPER ARTIST

Today, the need for an artist to merely retouch photographs has, for the most part, disappeared. Instead, the newspaper artist has evolved into a new and important player in the newsroom. From drawing maps and creating graphics with a computer mouse and keyboard to contributing to the overall look of the newspaper, the function of the newspaper artist has changed with the technology.

The newspaper artist now plays an important role in the creation of informational graphics and the design of the newspaper. Today's editors understand

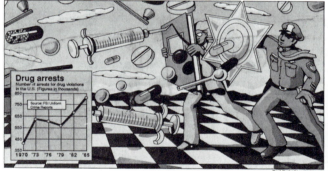

Figure 20.5 Page One artwork that creates cartoonlike appearance

the vital role design plays in attracting and keeping readers, and they are turning to the paper's artists to develop pleasing designs. At some newspapers, a member of the art department attends all news planning meetings, making certain there is a link between the visual and words in the newspaper.

Illustrations

Besides creating information graphics and designing pages and sections, today's newsroom artist is responsible for the illustrations or drawings in the newspaper. These drawings, or *artwork*

as they often are called, are used primarily in the feature sections and sometimes in the business and sports sections. Although some smaller newspapers have run drawings on Page One, this generally is not a good idea, because it can give the page a cartoonlike appearance. For example, when the *Reno* (Nev.) *Gazette-Journal* used a Page One illustration with a story on the fight against illegal drugs, the page took on a "feature-like" look and did not have the appearance of a traditional front page (Figure 20.5). Other papers have used illustrations instead of photographs on their front pages to capture

Figure 20.6 Illustration used instead of photo on front page

Figure 20.7 Illustration used instead of photo on front page

Figure 20.8 Editorial page cartoon

the spirit or essence of the newsmaker. Two examples, from two different periods in journalism, are shown here; in both cases, photographs of the person in the news were available (Figures 20.6 and 20.7).

Even on inside pages, illustrations can present problems. Because there is so much illustration used in advertisements, inside page news illustrations often are perceived as ads. Stories with illustrations thus should be placed on a page where the illustrations will not clash with other elements.

Editorial Page Cartoons

When an illustration is placed correctly, it can be more powerful than a photograph, as editorial page cartoons have proved. Editorial cartoons are powerful pieces of commentary, and some newspaper readers pay more attention to the opinion of an artist than to a written editorial (Figure 20.8). In the early part of this century, editors and publishers knew the value of editorial cartoons; they often placed them on Page One. The limitations of newspaper printing techniques made drawings easier to create and print than photographs, and hence this type of illustration was a device to attract readers (Figure 20.9). Although by the 1960s most newspapers had moved the editorial cartoon to the editorial page, in the 1980s *The Des Moines Register* still ran one in color, on Page One (Figure 20.10).

ILLUSTRATION AS COMMUNICATION

No matter what artistic style it takes, illustration is a powerful method of communicating ideas and images. Because illustration can communicate a message concerning an abstract or theoretical subject, it is especially helpful with stories dealing with issues that cannot be photographed easily.

However, illustration also requires more thought and work than most visuals. Unlike an informational graphic or a story containing hard facts, an illustration must convey the tone or feeling of the story. And it has to be in an appropriate style. For example, an illustration accompanying a story about the homeless or cancer must reflect the serious nature of the topic. A cartoonlike drawing would be inappropriate. The artist thus must be capable both of understanding and of expressing the underlying message in a given subject, because the subliminal feelings an illustration conveys are sometimes almost as powerful as the message being presented (Figure 20.11).

Understanding the power of illustration does not mean, however, that visual journalists cannot have fun with stories and illustrations. Humorous illustrations, found mostly in the feature pages, also attract readers and keep them interested in stories.

Figure 20.9   1930s editorial cartoon placed on front page to lure readers

Figure 20.10   1987 editorial cartoon on front page

Figure 20.11   Example of illustration that communicates the underlying message in a story

SUGGESTED EXERCISES

1. Go to a library and make a copy of an early map in a book or newspaper. Clip a map from a current newspaper. Discuss their differences and similarities. Which do you prefer and why?

2. Do the same for a newspaper illustration.

3. Clip two examples of newspaper illustrations, one serious and one humorous, that accompany stories. How good a job do they do of illustrating the stories they accompany?

4. Discuss the layout of two editorial pages that contain editorial cartoons or other illustrations. How do the illustrations help the design of the page?

CHAPTER TWENTY-ONE

How Art Directors Work

Most of the daily newspapers that have art departments—and many do not—have only a few artists assigned to the news pages. Far more newspaper artists work in the advertising department, helping the sales team prepare ads for clients.

Even though this chapter will focus on newsroom artists, whether a newspaper has two or 20 of them, artists are the same in any newspaper department. With communication, cooperation and creativity, they can produce quality work that is successful as art and that works as a visual product in a newspaper.

COMMUNICATION, COOPERATION, CREATIVITY

Communication and cooperation among the art director, artist, section editor and reporter help prevent art projects from going astray. *Communication* and *cooperation* also nurture an artist's *creativity*. These "three C's" of newspaper art begin with basic news questions:

- *What is the story about?* Without this information, the tone and direction of the illustration could be wrong. If the story is not com-pleted, the artist needs an accurate summary of it.
- *When will the story run?* The artist needs to know the deadline for finished artwork because different processes take different amounts of time. It is the responsibility of all parties involved—the artist as visual journalist, the section editor, the reporter—to be as honest and accurate as possible when dealing with issues of time. All parties need to know the minimum amount of time required to produce the artwork before the run date of the story.
- *Where in the newspaper will the illustration run?* The artist needs to know the potential audience for the illustration. Some sections, such as lifestyle or features, are "softer" than others, such as sports or business or opinion. Some sections provide more freedom than others. For example, whereas the business section may require illustrations that fit within the normal multicolumn format, features may allow the artist the freedom to create illustrations that totally dominate the page, with odd shapes that integrate type and artwork. The artist, as a visual journalist, thus should know the tone and direction of every section of the newspaper. Too often, staff

members (both visual and word journalists) know little about the parts of the paper on which they are not working.

- *Who is doing the illustration?* Who does an illustration is sometimes as important as the direction and execution of the work. The art director, as a visual journalist, must keep in mind all of the special skills of each artist and give assignments accordingly. Like a city editor who gives certain assignments to certain reporters, the art director must hand out assignments based on the strengths and weaknesses of artists. Not every staff artist can do everything equally well.

THE ROLE OF THE ART DIRECTOR

Not every newspaper has an art director, who performs a specialized function in the newsroom. Generally, only metropolitan newspapers have art directors. At some newspapers, the graphics editor or design editor also serves as art director.

The art director has management responsibility for the artists working for the editorial or news side of the paper. In addition to managing, scheduling and budgeting, the art director coordinates the projects in the art department. He or she also gives a sense of direction to the artists and maintains the illustration standards of the newspaper.

To be successful, an art director must develop a sense of unity of purpose between the art department and the rest of the newsroom. Too often, there is a lack of cooperation between the newsroom and art department because word journalists do not understand and

Figure 21.1 Art and type harmoniously combined on section front page

appreciate the function of the art directors and vice versa. Although this gap is being closed at many newspapers, the art director still must act as "mediator" between the words and the visuals so that readers can benefit from both. That means the art director must read stories being illustrated to make sure the artists are on the right track. He or she also must work closely with top editors of the newspaper, discussing concepts of illustration and the nature of a page's design.

A successful art director knows how the newspaper is produced, what stories are likely to be important and on what days color is available. That knowledge can prove beneficial even in subtle areas. For example, familiarity with the newspaper allows for the placement of art in a section's nameplate, an artistic touch that helps harmonize illustration and type on the page (Figure 21.1).

FROM IDEA TO ILLUSTRATION

Time and creativity are the keys to quality artwork in newspapers—it takes time for an artist to articulate creativity. An art director can help the creative

process by persuading editors to plan ahead. Artists need time to develop ideas, discuss them, refine them and then create the illustration. Adequate time helps ensure that artwork in the paper pleases the artist, the editor and, of course, the reader.

Usually, the art process begins with the artist reading a copy or summary of a story. If there is no story or summary, the artist and the art director, if possible, should meet with the section editor and the reporter and thoroughly discuss what the reporter is working on. The artist should take careful notes.

Next, the illustration's concept should be discussed. Some artists will do accurate and complete sketches of their ideas; others will sketch only a rough outline. In either case, the art director should make sure that the direction of the art matches the direction of the story. As the work progresses, the art director should check on it periodically. In most cases, there will be little need for changes, but the art director should be on the lookout for problems that can be spotted early and corrected.

Depending on the newspaper, the artist also may design the pages his or her artwork will fall on. If that is the case, the editor needs to inform the artist as to the number of stories planned for the page, the length of each story and the inclusion of other visuals, such as informational graphics or photographs, on the page. Again, the more cooperation between artist and editor, the higher the quality of the finished product.

TYPES OF ILLUSTRATION

There are various techniques used to produce newspaper illustrations:

- *Acrylic wash with pastels.* In this method, an artist lays down a background wash of acrylic to make a good surface for a layer of pastels, which can be applied by pencil, soft chalk, inks or oils. Acrylic is a water-based medium that is more like plastic than paint. It provides a permanent base for other mediums, such as pastels.
- *Gouache with pastel paint or colored pencil.* This commonly used newspaper art technique is similar to acrylic wash. The water-based gouache provides a good surface upon which to put other materials, such as pastel paints, colored pencils, soft chalk or ink. Oil paints cannot be used because of the water base of the gouache.
- *Dr. Martin dyes and colored pencil.* In this technique, transparent dyes, usually applied with an airbrush, serve as a base, and colored pencils are used for the top layer. This method is common at newspapers.
- *Coquille board and black pencil.* In this technique, an artist draws with a black pencil on a highly textured surface such as heavyweight paper. It is commonly used at newspapers when strong line work is required.
- *Pebble board and colored pencil.* A pebble board is another textured surface, and it comes in different colors. Colored pencils are used on the board.
- *Oil paints.* Oil painting is seldom done at newspapers because of its production time—it simply takes too long for the paints to dry.

- *Acrylic paints.* Acrylic is similar to oil, but it dries much quicker, making it more common than oil painting at newspapers.
- *Scratchboard.* In this process, a painted black surface is scratched away to reveal white. This commonly used method makes for a strong black and white image that is easy to reproduce.
- *Watercolors.* Watercolor is a water-based paint that is often used at newspapers. It requires special watercolor paper.
- *Woodcuts.* In this subtractive type of artwork, an artist carves away areas that will be white in the finished piece of art. Most artists use linoleum glued to a wood block. Once the carving is completed, ink and then paper are applied to the remaining surface. The carved image is a reverse of what the final image will be.
- *Cut paper.* Different colors and pieces of paper are used in this process to build a piece of art. When completed, a photograph is taken of the artwork.
- *3-D cut paper.* This cut-paper method allows the artist to create paper models of events or subjects. When completed, a photograph is taken of the artwork.
- *Sculpture.* Clay or other materials can be shaped into images and then photographed.
- *Xerox.* In this method, an artist copies a photo or sketch and then applies paint or pencil to enhance the image.
- *Pen and ink.* In this commonly used newspaper art method, the artist draws with water-based or lacquer-based ink and quill pens or

Figure 21.2 Illustration using cut paper

mechanical pens with points ranging from fine to heavy.
- *Collage.* Here, the artist takes various images from printed, painted or illustrated sources and pieces them together to make a finished product.
- *Charcoal.* An artist uses charcoal, usually charred, soft wood, to draw images on white paper. This method is common at newspapers.
- *Macintosh.* This artistic technique is one of the newest. By using a Macintosh computer and special software, an artist can create various types of artwork, in black-and-white or color. The finished piece usually is printed on a laser printer.

Possible results of some of these techniques, or combination of techniques, can be seen in the accompanying examples (Figures 21.2–21.11).

Figure 21.3   Collage using photos, paint, colored pencils and airbrush

Figure 21.4   Illustration using scratchboard

Figure 21.5   Illustration using oil-based washes

Figure 21.6   Illustration using airbrush

Figure 21.7   Collage with pen and ink

Figure 21.8   Illustration using airbrush

Figure 21.9 Illustration using gouache with pastel paint and color pencil

Figure 21.12 Illustration that draws reader's eye away from accompanying story

Figure 21.10 Illustration on coquille board using ink and crayon

ART'S RELATIONSHIP TO THE REST OF THE PAGE

Unlike artwork in a museum, a newspaper illustration does not hang alone. It is surrounded by other elements—words, headlines, captions, photographs—that must be considered when deciding on its placement. In fact, placement can be so crucial to successful communication of the artwork that the artist often designs the page on which it will appear. No matter who designs the page, however, the design must allow for easy reading of words and optimal viewing of the visuals.

Proper placement of an illustration on a page is like the proper placement of any other element. The location of an illustration on the page, its size in relationship to other elements and the use of color in the illustration and elsewhere on the page are important considerations. If the illustration is to be the dominant visual element on the page, the visual journalist must make certain that the other elements on the page do not distract readers.

Placement

An illustration should be placed on a page so that it draws readers to the story being illustrated. Illustrations,

Figure 21.11 Illustration in watercolor and pen and ink

like photographs and typography, have lines and shapes that move readers' eyes in certain directions. The art director should look for those lines and ensure that the movement of the artwork aids in the reading of the page.

For example, in an illustration concerning consumer debt, the upward shape of the money bag combined with the upward direction of the eyes and arms of the people holding the bag moves readers to the top of the page (Figure 21.12). The eye is "forced" upward before the brain realizes that the story the illustration accompanies is below the drawing. Subtle changes, such as altering the direction in which the people holding the bag are looking, could prevent the reader's eye from wandering too far from the start of the story.

By contrast, in the *Chicago Tribune* Business section drawing on banking, the artist successfully uses movement to bring the reader's eye around to the start of the story (Figure 21.13). No matter where readers start to look at the drawing, they end up with the figure in the foreground and the start of the

Figure 21.13   Illustration that draws reader's eye to start of accompanying story

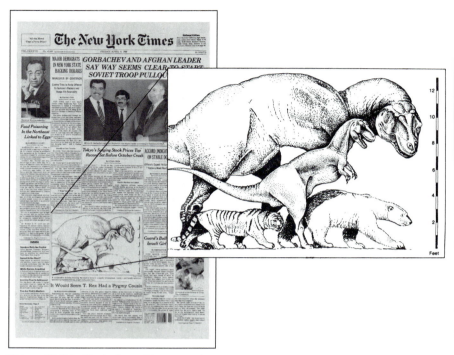

Reprinted by permission of the *Chicago Tribune.*

Figure 21.14   Illustration set in proper size

story. In this case, the artist understood that illustration and design go hand in hand.

Size

An illustration's size can enhance or harm its impact. If it is too big, it overpowers the page; if it is too small, readers might not see it. The art director must understand size and its impact on a newspaper page.

The New York Times illustration about a pygmy dinosaur is a good example of proper size (Figure 21.14). If the illustration had run smaller, the photographs and other elements on the page would have overwhelmed it. If it were larger, it would have been out of proportion to the rest of the page.

A newspaper's design and content goals also help determine the sizes of illustrations. A full-page Food section illustration might be acceptable in the *Minneapolis Tribune* (Figure 21.15), for example, while a half-page illustration is more than enough for the *Seattle Times* (Figure 21.16).

Figure 21.15   Full-page illustration appropriate for paper's design and content goals

Figure 21.16   Half-page illustration appropriate for paper's design and content goals

INSIDE LOOK

Lynn Staley

Editorial Design Director   *The Boston Globe*

"An editor may have a conception of how his or her page will feel, but it is the designer's job to make that conception explicit," said Lynn Staley, editorial design director of *The Boston Globe*. "The editor has a vague vision; the designer makes it complete. A designer doesn't see a story in the upper right corner. He [or she] sees a nice shape in there with grays and shades."

It is Staley's job to synthesize the editorial and artistic approaches at *The Globe*. She supervises 13 full-time and six part-time designers (they are not called artists at *The Globe*) who are responsible for specific pages or sections in the newspaper, such as food or science. She also supervises the designers who do informational graphics.

"There are several levels of intricacies that we get involved in," she said. "We have a standard chart style for the paper, so some of the things we do are quite utilitarian and just get banged out. Other things require decorative elements or color. Sometimes, we are presented with raw data and the designer has to come up with ways to display it. We also have designers who are responsible for total pages or sections that run on a weekly basis."

Staley said it sometimes is a challenge bringing artist and editor together. "There is a fair amount of tension. Many of the best pages are the result of collaboration. But some people find that difficult. Egos come into play, and it may just be that newspapers attract people with these egos. It is hard to incorporate an editor's vision into a designer's thought process. The best editors are those who can use the strengths of the designers to get their points across. The best designers are those who have a firm artistic sense of a page and can look at it the way a reader would."

Despite the tensions, Staley said *The Globe*'s design department has had some tremendous successes since 1980, when she started at the paper as a designer. She added: "When the department was young, there was tremendous resistance to what we did. News judgment is such a prized attribute for editors. To endorse a different way of prioritizing information was a real challenge for some of them.

"In 1980, design was uncharted territory. *The Globe* was a very traditional daily paper. The function of art director was not one that many people would identify as being part of a newspaper's process. First, we worked only on the feature pages. Little by little, however, we have made inroads in the way the daily paper uses art, design and packaging. At this point, design is much more integrated into the workings of the paper."

Today, *The Globe*'s infographic department does everything from elaborate science illustrations to location maps using Macintosh computers 95 percent of the time. "I don't think there are many places as reliant on the Mac as we are," Staley said. "We use it for everything. We very rarely get into doing informational graphics by hand. The people who do charts here are on the forefront of a technological revolution. Many of them do quite intricate and wonderful illustrations on the computer."

Staley noted that design is becoming more sophisticated at newspapers. "We have page designers who have never done anything for the daily paper. They take their design skills very seriously. They work with editors but are charged with creating very sophisticated pages. They have little to do with the day-in and day-out needs of the newspaper. They deal in weekly fantasy pages such as the travel pages. They want to make it easy for the reader to access the information, but there is a lyric quality in what they do. There is an increasing need for people on that end of the spectrum. I believe the word *journalism* is too narrow to define what goes on in a newspaper these days.

"At the other end of the spectrum are the people who work on the daily pages. Their work has to be done in two hours. It has to be energetic and engaging, day-in and day-out, but it can't be too intricate. These people must have excellent reflexes. They must be hardened to the realities of producing a page on deadline."

Staley said that in the 1990s there will be more computer-generated artwork in newspapers. She added: "The industry will become even more dependent upon the Macintosh. I sense that the use of illustration has peaked. We'll see more combinations of photographic images and illustration. There will be more photography used in a conceptual way.

"There will be more art direction. Newspapers will be more sensitive to images, whether they are photographic, illustrative or computer-generated. As newspaper readers become more sophisticated visually, newspapers will have to look at how they package things. They will have to think more about how a newspaper page is assembled."

Color

The proper use of color in an illustration can be just as important as the concept of the artwork itself. Color does attract readers, but the art director must be aware of how much color is enough and what mix of colors is best for a page containing an illustration. For instance, if the illustration contains bright, primary colors in large amounts, other visuals on the page with subtle, small touches of color will be overwhelmed. Conversely, an illustration with subtle colors would be overwhelmed by visuals with brilliant primary colors.

The art director must view a newspaper page as a whole, looking at all of its color elements together. By dividing a blank page into grids, he or she can visualize the color impact of the page before it is printed. Once the page is divided into grids, colored pencils can be used to sketch where color photographs, informational graphics and illustrations will be used on the page. The sketched colors should be as true as possible to the major colors in the page's elements. By viewing just colors and not the art, the art director can spot areas where colors might clash.

SUGGESTED EXERCISES

1. Examine the visual elements in the news section of a daily newspaper and compare them to other sections, such as features, business or sports. Discuss their differences and similarities.

2. Examine the visual elements in a Sunday newspaper. How do those in the news sections compare to those in the weekly sections, such as travel, real estate or entertainment?

3. Discuss how placement of and color in an illustration are related to other elements on a newspaper page. How important is size?

Appendix

In the following pages are listed books, journals and other materials dealing with newspaper typography, informational graphics, color and computers. This list is based on excerpts from a report prepared for the Society of Newspaper Design Annual Workshop, October 13–15, 1988, Louisville, Kentucky. (© 1988 by David B. Gray). The list is updated almost every month; please send corrections, updates and suggested additions to David Gray, Managing Editor–Graphics, *The Providence Journal*, 75 Fountain St., Providence, RI 02902, or call (401) 277-7323. Many of the books listed here are available at reduced prices; see the addresses for Print Book Store, Dover Publications, Dynamic Graphics Bookshelf and Graphic Artist's Book Club on pages 254–255. The asterisk (*) indicates items of interest to Macintosh users.

TYPOGRAPHY

Baseline, The International Typographical Magazine. Designed and published by Typographical Systems International, Limited, a member of the Letraset Company. Classy publication, slanted almost exclusively toward typography. Write TSI Limited, St. George's House, 195-203 Waterloo Rd., London, England SE1. Free.

Designing with Type: A Basic Course in Typography, 2d ed., by James Craig. A reprint of a book that's been around for a while and contains sections on terminology, design, copy fitting and phototypesetting. Watson-Guptill. 176 pp. 200 illus. 9 x 12. ISBN 0-8230-1321-9. Print Book Store, $22.95.

Dover Alphabets, selected and arranged by Dan X. Solo. Ten books containing more than 1,000 copyright-free complete alphabets. 1,000 pp. $8\frac{1}{2}$ x 11. Print Book Store, $43.85.

Glossary of Typesetting, Computer and Communications Terms, by NCA. This glossary is well-illustrated and tries to include all the terms we use daily. National Composition Association, 1730 N. Lynn St., Arlington, VA 22209. (703) 841-8165. 65 pp. $20 for nonmembers.

"History of Letterforms," 6-ft. x 3-ft. poster. Call (800) 424-TYPE. Free for Compugraphic customers. All others pay $20.

A Manual of Comparative Typography, The Panose System, by Benjamin Bauermeister. A nifty job of organizing typefaces according to similarities and effects by breaking down over 200 typeface characteristics into seven groups. Also lists suppliers. 257 pp. $8\frac{1}{2}$ x 11. Print Book Store, $29.95.

Phototypesetting: A Design Manual, by James Craig. The enormous range of phototypesetting capabilities is broken into four major categories: terminology, design, copyfitting and phototypesetting. Watson-Guptill. 224 pp. 700 illus. $8\frac{1}{2}$ x 11. Print Book Store, $24.95.

Tips on Type, by Bill Gray. Good hints with focus on practicality. Uses over 100 different faces in showing samples of various settings, measures, etc. Paper. Print Book Store, $7.50.

Type and Typography, the Designer's Type Book, revised by Ben Rosen. Displays more than 1,500 samples, based on design excellence, utility and general availability. 406 pp. Illustrated. $8\frac{1}{2}$ x 11. Print Book Store, $13.50.

Type Design, Color, Character and Use, by Michael Beaumont. New guide for picking typefaces, and guidelines for the use of appropriate faces. Has many examples on how the look of a piece will change by changing the font. 176 pp., 96 in color. $9\frac{3}{4}$ x $8\frac{3}{4}$. Print Book Store, $21.95.

*"Type Is to Read." A typography poster/calendar from Adobe. Call (800) 292-3623. Free.

Typographic Design: Form and Communication, by Carter, Day & Meggs. A really comprehensive book covering history and education of designers, and with a glossary of type and typography. Van Nostrand Reinhold Co. Inc., 135 W. 50th St., New York, NY 10020. 262 pp. $8\frac{1}{4}$ x $10\frac{3}{4}$. Paper. $35.

Typography. The annual "Best of Show" of the Type Directors Club, showing how type works in layouts, ads, logos, editorial design, etc. 384 pp. 350 color plates. 9 x 12. Print Book Store, $32.95.

Typography for Photocomposition, by A. S. Lawson & Archie Provan. Good, rational discussion on whether ragged right is good or bad, how to correctly do cap initials, with historical perspectives on both. Good typographic spacing examples and guidelines. National Composition Association, 1730 N. Lynn St., Arlington, VA 22209. 26 pp.

Typography: How to Make It Most Legible, by Rolf F. Rehe. Back to the basics, but surprisingly, very few newspaper people are aware of many of them. This compilation of research provides guidelines and recommendations for the most legible applications of typography. Design Research International, P. O. Box 50129, Indianapolis, IN 46250. (317) 842-0596. 80 pp. $8\frac{1}{4}$ x $8\frac{1}{4}$. $12, plus $3 postage.

U&lc. The title stands for upper- and lowercase and is a big favorite with type designers and art directors. Published quarterly. Some back copies are available. Write *U&lc* Subscription Dept., International Typeface Corp., 2 Hammarskjold Plaza, New York, NY 10017, or call (212) 371-0699.

What Every Editor Should Know About Layout and Typography, by Bill Chadbourne. Sections illustrated with movie stills to show principles, including "Grabbing & Holding the Reader's Attention" and "Sizing the Art." National Composition Association, 1730 N. Lynn St., Arlington VA 22209. (703) 841-8165. 38 pp. $5.95 non-members.

GRAPHICS: HOW TO DO

Chart and Graph Preparation Skills, by Tom Cardamone. Cardamone shows you how to adhere to all plotting principles and formulas as well as how to be creative in your production of graphs and charts. Easy-to-follow instructions are given for preparing column, bar, pie, line and layer charts. 128 pp. $8\frac{1}{4}$ x $9\frac{1}{4}$. Print Book Store, $18.95.

Clip Bits. A publication from Dynamic Graphics for subscribers to their Clipper Creative Art Service. The June '86 issue had an intelligent article about newspaper design, plus a good article, with appropriate illustrations, on using the Macintosh computer. You might look in your ad department, or try to get a copy by calling (309) 688-8800.

DeadlineMac. A stand-alone monthly publication, for members of The Society of Newspaper Design, specifically on how to make the Macintosh computer more useful for newspapers on deadline. The first dozen or so have been reprinted in one booklet. $8\frac{1}{2}$ x 11. Write to SND, The Newspaper Center, P.O. Box 17290, Dulles International Airport, Washington, DC 20041, or call (703) 620-1083. $20.

Designer's Guide to Creating Charts and Diagrams, by Nigel Holmes. Must reading for all who deal with visual information. Watson-Guptill, 1515 Broadway, New York, NY 10036. 192 pp. $8\frac{1}{4}$ x 11. ISBN 0-8230-1315-4. Print Book Store, $29.95

Designing Pictorial Symbols, by Nigel Holmes with Rose DeNeve. This second Nigel book explains how to create those little symbols and story-tracing devices that *Time* magazine uses. Watson-Guptill, 1515 Broadway, New York, NY 10036. ISBN 0-8230-1327-8. Print Book Store, $24.95.

Desktop Graphics for the IBM PC, by Corey Sandler. Unlike most other "how-to" computer books, this one digs into the nature of business graphics, and how they can lie. Gives good examples of how numbers should be presented and what the pitfalls of graphics are. Also has a very good bibliography. Creative Computing Press, 39 E. Hanover Ave., Morris Plains, NJ 07950. 190 pp. $14.95.

Graphis Diagrams, 4th ed., by Walter Herdeg. A stunning book that shows hundreds of ways statistics can be presented in new and meaningful (and interesting) ways. Samples of bar charts, pie charts, family tree diagrams, maps, organizational diagrams, scientific material, tables, etc. For the extremely visually sophisticated. Graphis Press Corp., 107 Dufourstrasse, 8008 Zurich, Switzerland. 208 pp. Print Book Store, $37.50.

*HardCopy, by the staff at Knight-Ridder Tribune News graphics network. Packed full of good examples and more useful tips on how to get the best from your Mac. Published quarterly. Contributions wanted: via Presslink to HARDCOPY, or mail to KRTN, 774 National Press Building, Washington, DC 20045. (202) 383-6065.

How . . . The Magazine of Ideas & Techniques in Graphic Design. Another magazine that shows in detail how things get done by the people who do it all the time. Published bimonthly by the publishers of *Print* magazine, 6400 Goldsboro Rd., Bethesda, MD 20817-9969. $33 a year.

How to Draw Charts and Diagrams, by Bruce Robertson. A new entry in the field, the 400-plus illustrations will help you expand your horizons on ways to do charts and graphs. Many techniques, however, have been overtaken by the Mac. 160 pp. $7\frac{3}{4}$ x $9\frac{3}{4}$. Graphics Artist's Book Club #30041, $19.95.

How to Lie with Statistics, by Darrell Huff. Great little pocket book on the basics of how to deal with numbers and their display. Now in its 37th printing. W. W. Norton & Co., 500 5th Ave., New York, NY 10110. 142 pp. with illustrations. ISBN 0-393-09426-X. $2.95.

*Macintosh Users' Group Newsletter deals with problems and suggests ways of overcoming them in working with the Macintosh. Designed for Gannett papers that are networking their graphics. Contact Gannett Macintosh Users' Group Newsletter, *USA Today* Graphics Department, P.O. Box 500, Washington, DC 20044.

Maps—A Visual Survey and Design Guide, by Michael and Susan Southworth. Over 200 beautiful and informative maps in color, with an extensive section on mapping techniques. Good references and index. A must for editors and mapmakers. New York Graphics Society: Little, Brown & Co., Dept. GF-81, 34 Beacon St., Boston, MA 02106. 224 pp. ISBN 0-8212-1503-5. $39.95.

Step-by-Step Graphics. A how-to-do-it, step-by-step idea bimonthly that covers lettering, making overlays for color, airbrushing techniques, etc. Has already profiled some newspaper designers. Write to P.O. Box 1901, 6000 N. Forest Park Dr., Peoria, IL 61656-1901, or call (800) 255-8800. $42 a year.

Using Charts and Graphs, by Jan V. White. Explains how charts can convey information and persuade readers. Generally a useful book, full of examples and ideas, with a section on mapping. R.R. Bowker Co., 245 W. 17th St., New York, NY 10011. 212 pp. Approx. 1,000 illus. $8\frac{1}{2}$ x 11. ISBN 0-8352-1894-5. Print Book Store, $22.95.

The Visual Display of Quantitative Information, by Edward R. Tufte. Beautifully printed, it traces the history of informational graphics and gives many practical suggestions on how to present data and on how data is perceived in charts, graphs and maps. Must reading for those who prepare charts and diagrams. Graphics Press, P.O. Box 430, Cheshire, CT 06410. 197 pp. 220 illus. $8\frac{1}{2}$ x $10\frac{1}{2}$. Print Book Store, $29.95.

GRAPHICS: SOURCES OF INFORMATION

The Anatomy Coloring Book, by Wynn Kapit and Lawrence M. Elson. Here, in one place, is the whole human anatomy: bones, muscles, nerves and all the other details. Harper & Row, New York, NY. 8 x 11. 142 plates. ISBN 0-06-453914-8. $9.95.

Atlas of Surgical Operations, by Robert Zollinger. Diagrams of a variety of common surgical procedures. Macmillan Publishing Co., New York, NY.

The Book of American Rankings, by Clark S. Judge. Same as *The New Book of World Rankings,* but with much more data on just the United States. ISBN 0-87196-395-7.

Coloring Books. Dover has dozens of coloring books on subjects ranging from flowers to animals, birds, cars and anatomy. Perfect as line illustrations, or as a sourcebook for artists. Various sizes and prices.

Comparisons, by the Diagram Group. This one is copyrighted, so you can't steal from it. Compares things in terms of size, speed, weight, volume, etc. and, with a little imagination, could make nifty source material for locally produced graphics. St. Martin's Press, 175 5th Ave., New York, NY 10010. ISBN 0-312-15484-4. $15.

The Complete Dover Clip Art Series can be had for only $179. 51 volumes, 1,632 plates printed on one side only. 10,000 images. Dover Publications.

Design on File, published by Facts on File. This loose-leaf binder is full of black-and-white designs and includes human forms, projections, diagrams, geometric shapes, etc. Good source material for some of the basics. Facts on File Publications, 460 Park Ave. South, New York, NY 10016. $145.

Dictionary of Sports, by Graeme Wright. Known in the UK as the *Illustrated Handbook of Sporting Terms,* from Hampton House Productions, this American version is good and should be on the sports department's shelf.

Rand McNally & Co. 189 pp. ISBN 528-81078-2.

Dover Clip Art Series. Two collections, 17 volumes each, of copyright-free books. 928 pages each with over 2,500 illustrations. Printed in black on glossy stock, one side only, the images are ready for stealing in three sizes. Collection includes frames and borders, illustrations for sports and food, alphabets, logos, banners. Dover is asking $59.50 for these. Print Book Store will sell them for $53.95. They can be had individually for $3.75 each or less.

Dover Full Color Design Library. A new collection of 38 of its color clip art books, heavy on Art Deco and Victorian stuff like borders, patterns, motifs and textiles. Dover Publications. $3.95 to $20.90.

Dover Pictorial Archive Series. A collection of six volumes of old cuts, engravings and photos on specific topics such as hands, transportation, women, men, music and animals. 639 pp. $47.25. Print Book Store, $42.50.

Encyclopedia of Associations, edited by Katherine Gruber. A four-volume basic guide to information on 20,000 trade, business and commercial organizations, all of which are sitting on a wealth of information. Published yearly. Volume I is really the only one you need. Gale Research Co., Book Tower, Detroit, MI 48226. Available also on-line through Dialog. About $225.

Encyclopedia of Source Illustrations (Vols. I and II). 1,100 illustrations. Morgan and Morgan, Inc., Publishers, Hastings on Hudson, NY 10706. $26.

The Encyclopedia of Sports, 6th ed., by Frank G. Menkie. This is a great source of statistics to use in graphics. Covers everything from angling to yachting. Paperback edition by Doubleday-Dolphin. 1,132 pp. ISBN 0-385-12262-4. $8.95.

Etcetera, Graphic Devices, by Typony. Copyright-free ornamental designs. Floral motifs, suns, stars, hearts, fleur-de-lis, butterflies, ships, anchors, snowflakes, animals, nymphs(!) and many other modern and antique designs. 176 pp. $8\frac{5}{8}$ x $11\frac{3}{8}$. Paper. $12.95.

Gray's Anatomy, by Henry Gray. This medical classic will help you understand some of the more complicated medical aspects of stories. Bounty Books, Crown Publishers, 1 Park Ave., New York, NY 10016.

Guide to Statistical Materials Produced by Governments and Associations in the United States, by Juri and Jean Stratford. This gem is a directory of statistical publications, what they include, what they cost and how to get them. Meticulously annotated. Write to American Demographics, P.O. Box 68, Ithaca, NY 14851, or call (800) 828-1133, ext. 506. $85.

Handbook of Pictorial Symbols, by Rudolph Modley. This little book could give you all the standing "logos" you'll ever need, from sports to finance to news to just about anything. Dover Publications. 3,250 illustrations. $8\frac{1}{2}$ x 11. $5.95.

Illustrated Encyclopedia of Commercial Aircraft, by Exeter Books. Diagrams and charts of domestic and foreign passenger airlines.

Illustrated Science & Invention Encyclopedia (or *How It Works* in the UK). Twenty-three volumes, organized alphabetically, explain not only graphically but also in great detail how almost everything, from an abacus to a weather satellite, works. Yearly updates. H. S. Stuttman Inc., Westport, CT 06889.

Jane's All the World's Aircraft and *Jane's All the World's Fighting Ships.* Two musts for any news library. Hundreds of details on ships and planes, with facts and figures.

Jane's Pocket Books. Unknown to many is the fact that, in addition to the expensive annuals, Jane's also publishes paperbacks, including the following: *Commercial Transport Aircraft, Research and Experimental Aircraft, Major Combat Aircraft, Helicopters, Missiles, Naval Armament, Towed Artillery, Modern Tanks and Armored Fighting Vehicles, Pistols and Sub-Machine Guns* and *Rifles & Light Machine Guns.* Available through Collier Books, Macmillan Publishing Co., New York, NY.

Logotypes of the World, by Yasaburo Kuwayama. Great source of ideas from more than 2,600 examples, showing how to pull, stretch and shape new logotypes from existing type. 312 pp. $8\frac{1}{2}$ x 12. Graphic Artist's Book Club, $55.95.

Lore of Sail, by an international team of maritime experts. This is a scaling-down of a gorgeous coffee-table book into a decent paperback. A handy reference to ships as well as the names of nautical things. Sections include The Hull, Spars and Rigging, The Sail and Navigation and Ship

Handling. Facts on File Publications, 460 Park Ave. South, New York, NY 10016. 256 pp. ISBN 0-87196-211-7. $5.95.

The Map Catalog, edited by Joel Makower. Lists almost every kind of map and the major sources of them, as well as descriptions and examples. Land, sky, water and map products are covered. Provides a list of state agencies that have maps. Tilden Press Inc., 1001 Connecticut Ave. NW, Suite 310, Washington, DC 20036. ISBN 0-394-74614-7. $14.95.

Maps on File, published by Facts on File. This loose-leaf binder is full of maps, ready for reproduction. And they are all for use; the fee you pay includes the right to use them. Facts on File Publications, 460 Park Ave. South, New York, NY 10016. $145. Annual updates are $35.

NASA has everything you'll ever need to know about the space shuttle and the rest of the space program. Latest is a 1,000-page, 3-ring publication chock full of drawings and information. Write Ed Medal or Jerry Berg, Marshall Space Flight Center, AL 35812, or call (205) 544-0034. Or write Bill Green, Public Relations/Technical Communications, Rockwell International Space Transportation Systems Division, 12214 Lakewood Blvd., Downey, CA 90241, or call (213) 922-2066. Or write Sarah G. Keegan/Barbara E. Selby, NASA HQ, Washington, DC 20546, or call (202) 453-8536.

Navy Fact File, 8th ed. Includes specs, photos and drawings of ships, planes and missiles, as well as listings of which ships are part of which fleets

and their home ports. Loose-leaf for easy scanning and copying. Issued by the Department of the Navy, Office of Information, Washington, DC 20350-1200. Ask for number 0515-LP-945-6010. Free.

The New Book of World Rankings, by George T. Kurian. From the folks at Facts on File, this one has statistics, social and economic indicators, and quality of life information for most of the developed countries of the world. Facts on File Publications, 460 Park Ave. South, New York, NY 10016. ISBN 0-87196-743-X.

Random House Encyclopedia. A seven-section visual extravaganza, with sections on the Universe, Earth, Life on Earth, Man, Man and Machine, Man and Science, and History and Culture. 884 pp. 13,500 illustrations, diagrams and photos (11,325 in color), with a full-color atlas. ISBN 0-394-52883-2. List is $110, but seen on discount counters in bookstores for $40–$50.

The Rule Book, by the Diagram Group. This one, like *Comparisons,* is a superb set of instructions about all sports and should be in the sports as well as the graphics library. St. Martin's Press, 175 5th Ave., New York, NY 10010. ISBN 0-312-69576-4. $9.95.

Statistical Abstract of the United States, from the U.S. Bureau of the Census. Also ask at one of the 12 regional offices for the *Summary* of the *Statistical Abstract of the United States.* U.S. Government Printing Office, Washington, DC 20402. Credit card orders, call order desk at (202) 783-3238. Number 6390 S/N 003-024-06707-2. $25.

Trademarks and Symbols. Vol. I—*Alphabetical Signs,* Vol. II—*Symbolic Signs,* by Ysaburo Kuwayama. Yet another collection, this time organized by type. More than 1,500 samples. Each volume is 228 pp. 7 x 10. Print Book Store, $19.95.

The Ultimate Clip Book. 10,000 illustrations in six $8\frac{1}{2}$ x 11, loose-leaf binders, printed on glossy stock, one side of the sheet. Fully indexed and all copyright-free. From Print Book Store at special discount price of $449.

United States Government Printing Offices, Superintendent of Documents, Washington, DC 20404. (202) 783-3238.

U.S. Air Power, by Anthony Robinson. Specifications and diagrams of U.S. military aircraft. Bison Books, 17 Sherwood Place, Greenwich, CT 06830.

U.S. Department of State has a publication called *Background Notes* in $8\frac{1}{2}$ x 11, three-hole format that is updated periodically. It contains some good base maps, flags and statistics of all the countries of the world. Contact U.S. Department of State, Bureau of Public Affairs, Washington, DC. About $30 a year.

The Way Things Work—An Illustrated Encyclopedia of Technology (2 vols.). A good book to look through to figure out how things work. The next time a bridge, a plane or even a sparrow falls, this book will tell you how and why it happened. Simon & Schuster, Rockefeller Center, 630 5th Ave., New York, NY 10020.

What's What—A Visual Glossary of the Physical World, by Bragonier and Fisher. A great sourcebook for informational graphics, either to steal the items or to use as an idea generator. Ballantine. ISBN 0-345-30302-4. Paper. About $13.

World Trademarks & Logotypes II, by T. Igarashi. A collection of symbols and their applications. More than 1,500 works in color from 26 countries. Background information on their development also provided. 400 pp. 9 x 11. Print Book Store, $63.75.

GRAPHICS: SERVICES AND ORGANIZATIONS

*Accu-Weather's weather maps are available through the Macintosh. More than 40 standard maps and charts, as well as custom maps. Based at Penn State. Call (814) 234-9601, or write 619 W. College St., State College, PA 16801.

American Demographics via The Register and Tribune Syndicate, owned by Dow Jones. The syndicate has a once-a-month package of stories and graphics dealing with census statistics and such; it includes some graphics. Check with Carolyn Arthur, Managing Editor in Ithaca, NY, at (607) 273-6343.

*The Associated Press. AP Access and GraphicsNet are now used by more than 500 members via Macintosh. Contact your nearest AP bureau chief.

The Business Wire is moving pictures and graphics through Independent Network Systems (INS) receivers at no cost. Write to Bob Sweet at 44 Montgomery, Suite 2150, San Francisco, CA 94104 or call (800) 227-0845.

The Chicago Tribune Graphics Service, 64 E. Concord St., Orlando, FL 32801. Call Walter Mahoney at (800) 322-3068.

Copley News Service has a set of infographics it calls Fillers & Graphics with health, travel, kitchen, money, entertainment and sports categories, and new science categories called Discover and Your Body. It also provides graphics for special sections such as auto, weddings, home and fashion. Call (800) 445-4555 for free samples, or write to Copley News Service, P.O. Box 190, San Diego, CA 92112-0190.

Cowles Syndicate has a Demo Memo five-day-a-week package done by Cheryl Russell of American Demographics. The graphics are designed to simulate the *USA Today* lower left corner "snapshots."

Design: The Journal of the Society of Newspaper Design. Back issues are available in two sets. Set #1 includes issues 1 to 10, 1980 to 1982. $44. Set #2 includes issues 11 to 20, 1983 to 1986. $49. Write or call SND.

Feature Photo Service offers *free* feature photos, without any restrictions or requirements. May be ideal for those papers without any wire services. Most seem to be of the business PR-type that have people peering at you through stainless steel tubing. Write to Meyer Goldberg, Feature Photo Service, 216 E. 45th St., New York, NY 10017, or call (212) 661-6120.

Gallup Graphics has a five-day-a-week package of graphics based on the Gallup Organization's statistics, and it also simulates the *USA Today* lower left corner stuff. The graphics are all two SAU columns wide and are available in color. Done by Gallup artists in their Princeton, NJ, headquarters, they are available from Los Angeles Times Syndicate. Call (213) 972-5000 or (800) 528-4637.

*Gannett is on-line with all its 96 papers through Gannett News Service to share Macintosh graphics. For Gannett newspapers only.

*Infographics. Marketed by North America Syndicate, 235 E. 45th St., New York, NY 10017. Call (800) 526-5464.

INS Photo/Graphics Network is a way to get not only the Business Wire but also the NYT News Service pictures and graphics, Agence France-Presse, Sygma Syndication International photo agency and Cox Business Wires faster if you are a client. Contact Linda Fishler, INS, at (212) 330-1620 or (212) 809-7921.

INX provides topical editorial or op-ed drawings from some well-known New York artists. The service is available through United Features Syndicate, 200 Park Ave., New York, NY 10066, or call Brad Bushell at (800) 221-4816.

*Knight-Ridder Tribune News graphics network. Currently supplies more than 100 papers, providing an on-line data base of base maps, file and spot news graphics done on the Macintosh. KRTN supplies the software and training for you to get the stuff to your paper. Call Walter Mahoney, Tribune Media Services, at (800) 322-3068.

*The Meyers Report does more than 100 business graphics a week. It also sells a custom service in which it will do graphics for you using local numbers (for example, create a local business index or compile local bank interest rates). Contact Brad Bushell at United Features Syndicate, (800) 221-4816, or write to Gary S. Meyers at 20 W. Hubbard, Suite 500, Chicago, IL 60610, or call (312) 670-2440.

NEA Graphics Package. A graphic service from the Newspaper Enterprise Association, 200 Park Ave., New York, NY 10166. Call Brad Bushell at (800) 221-4816. It also has a base map package for its "full service" clients.

*The New York Times Graphics Service. The NYT Picture Service has begun transmitting Macintosh graphics. No details are yet available.

The Society of Newspaper Design. Write SND, The Newspaper Center, P.O. Box 17290, Dulles International Airport, Washington, DC 20041, or call (703) 620-1083. Membership is $55 per year, students $35 (add $10/year for outside United States), and you get copies of *Design,* the journal of the Society. In addition, SND runs an annual design contest and a workshop/convention. Books with contest results include the following (second, third and sixth editions are no longer available from SND):

First edition: *The Best of Newspaper Design 79–80.* A limited number were recently discovered in the warehouse. $8\frac{1}{2}$ x 11. $5.

Fourth edition: *The Best of Newspaper Design 82–83.* 350 examples from more than 3,900 entries. 123 pp. $8\frac{1}{2}$ x 11. $5.

Fifth edition: *The Best of Newspaper Design 83–84.* 400-plus examples from more than 6,000 entries. 180 pp. 9 x 12. $5.

Seventh edition: *The Best of Newspaper Design 85–86.* 400-plus examples from almost 10,000 entries. 220 pp. 9 x 12. $25.

Eighth edition: *The Best of Newspaper Design 86–87.* Available in hardcover only. 256 pp. 547 illus. in color. 9 x 12. $53.95. SND members get one soft-cover book free at time of book release. Additional copies at $43.46. Print Book Store, $44.95.

Ninth edition: Available mid-1989. Contact SND at above address for price information.

U.S. Department of Energy. Free photos and captions (one supplement about energy had 82 photos). Write to U.S. Department of Energy, Office of Public Affairs, Photo Office, C-460 GTN, Washington, DC 20545, or call (301) 353-5476.

*Weather Central, a section of Color-Graphics Systems Inc., gives you twice-a-day, full-color separations of weather maps, historical weather graphics, summaries and custom graphics. Sent Mac-to-Mac, or retrievable through KRTN. Write to 5725 Tokay Blvd., Madison, WI 53719, or call Charles Sholdt, General Manager, at (608) 274-5789.

*WeatherData Inc. provides custom data and maps through a service it calls WeatherPage. Write to Pat Cooper or Mike Smith at 833 N. Main St., Wichita, KS 67203, or call (316) 265-9127.

*Weather Services Corp. *USA Today*'s map is now done by these folks. Write to Bill Saulnier, 131A Great Rd. Bedford, MA 01730, or call (617) 275-8860.

COLOR

Color and Communication, by Favre and November. Another reference book that explores how we react to color, how to communicate with color, and what works and what doesn't work. Basic data on color vision and psychology. 180 pp. 200 illustrations in color. $10\frac{1}{4}$ x $10\frac{1}{4}$. Print Book Store, $53.50

Color Harmony: A Guide to Creative Color Combinations, by Hideaki Chijiiwa. This is a great book to develop your color palate with; we've got seven of these scattered throughout the building. More than 1,600 color combinations grouped by hue, shade and purpose, as well as a section on how to choose color. 158 pp. $5\frac{3}{4}$ x $8\frac{1}{4}$. ISBN 0-935603-06-9 Graphics Artist's Book Club #07310, $12.75. More than two copies from Print Book Store, $11.95 ea.

Color in American Newspapers, by The Poynter Institute for Media Studies. Results of some basic research on how readers react to color, as well as articles on how newspapers use and abuse color. Also contains an excellent bibliography on color. Poynter Institute, 801 3rd St. South, St. Petersburg, FL 33701. 70 pp. $8\frac{1}{2}$ x 11. Paper. $7.95

Color Separation Techniques, by Miles Southworth. This is a hard-cover version of *Pocket Guide to Color Reproduction, Communication and*

Control with much more detail on scanners and the separation process. Now in its second edition, it's a good reference for color committees to have. Graphics Arts Publishing Co., 3100 Bronson Hill Rd., Livonia, NY 14487. 270 pp. ISBN 0-933600-00-3. $23.

Designers Guide to Color. A three-volume set, each volume containing over 1,000 color combinations that would be useful to newspapers using four-color tint blocks and tones. Each is made up of 50 basic colors in 10 or 20 tints that show more colors than we could possibly reproduce. 124 pp. 6 x 7 and 6 x $8\frac{3}{4}$. Paper. Print Book Store, $8.95 each.

The Elements of Color, by Johannes Itten. Based on "The Art of Color," an excellent treatise on what color is, how we see it, and why it's important to understand the "seven color contrasts" principles. Van Nostrand-Reinhold Co. 96 pp. ISBN 0-442-24038-4. $18.95.

Enjoyment and Use of Color, by Walter Sargent. First published in 1923, this book explains little-known and interesting facets of color. Explores color values, intensities, effects of illumination, harmonies and complimentaries. In other words, what works and what doesn't work! Dover Publications. 274 pp. $5\frac{5}{8}$ x 8. $4.95.

The Forms of Color, by Karl Gerstner. The Swiss artist continues his examination of color begun in *The Spirit of Color* by drawing on artistic, literary and scientific sources to explore the basics of color and form. MIT Press, Cambridge, MA. ISBN 0-262-07100-2. $29.95.

Interaction of Color, rev. ed., by Joseph Albers. *The* book on colors and how they behave with one another. It's a record of a way of studying and teaching color. It explains why color is never seen as it physically exists. Yale University Press, New Haven, CT. ISBN 0-300-01846-0. $6.95.

Mechanical Color Separation Skills, by Tom Cardamone. For those of you who are still cutting color and preparing art for stripping, this might be helpful for the tricks and hints it contains. 128 pp. $7\frac{3}{8}$ x $7\frac{3}{4}$. Print Book Store, $13.95.

Pantone puts out a color-matching system used throughout the graphic arts industry. It manufactures markers and tint sheets and sets ink standards as well as producing many guides for the accurate reproduction of color. Some of its books include:

Color Selector/Newsprint. Has samples of 33 Pantone colors and three process colors to produce more than 2,000 various tints and combinations with black. (A Euro-color edition is also available.) Print Book Store, $33.75.

Process Color Selector. Shows almost 9,000 colors made from the four process colors, in 10 percent steps. They are all labeled so you can reproduce the same (or almost the same) colors. Print Book Store, $180.

Two Color Selector. Handy to broaden your range of spot color use. Shows various combinations of two-color inks. Print Book Store, $89.50.

Pocket Guide to Color Reproduction, Communication and Control, by Miles Southworth of the School of Printing at RIT. Originally written in 1979 and now in its fourth printing, this handy book starts with the basics of color theory and moves through standards, choosing transparencies and prints, separation process, proofing, printing and, most importantly, identifying and correcting color problems. Graphics Arts Publishing Co., 3100 Bronson Hill Rd., Livonia, NY 14487. ISBN 0-933600-01-1. About $10.

Pocket Pal, by International Paper Company. Everybody in the business from publisher to copy kid should have a copy of this paperback classic. First published in 1934, it's now in its 12th edition and second printing. International Paper Company, 77 W. 45th St., New York, NY 10036. About $1.25.

Principles of Color Design, by Wucius Wong. A practical examination of the effects that can be achieved with color. Contains a section on the use of black, white and gray as well. 101 pp. 195 illus. in color. $6\frac{1}{2}$ x $7\frac{3}{4}$. Print Book Store, $12.95.

S. D. Scott Process Color Guide. 5,000 three-color tint screen combinations of process colors create almost every color. On glossy and uncoated paper. S. D. Scott Printing Co., 145 Hudson St., New York, NY 10013. $12\frac{1}{2}$ x 12.

The Spirit of Color, by Karl Gerstner. Gerstner spent 30 years exploring color and the relationships to form, and he presents his findings in a clear, formal style. MIT Press, Cambridge, MA. 224 pp. 70 color plates. ISBN 0-262-070484-7. $45.

Theory and Use of Color, by Luigina De Grandis. Chapters on analyzing color, the theory of color, physical and chemical factors, visual apparatus, psycho-physical parameters of color and perception and color equilibrium. Harry N. Abrams, Inc., 100 5th Ave., New York, NY 10011. 160 pp. $7\frac{5}{8}$ x $10\frac{1}{2}$. Bibliography and index. ISBN 0-8109-2317-3. Paper. $16.95.

COMPUTERS/ELECTRONICS

Computer Images, by Joseph Denken. 250 illustrations on all aspects of computer graphics, not especially for newspapers, but a mind-expanding collection nonetheless. 200 pp. $9\frac{3}{4}$ x $9\frac{3}{4}$. Paper. List price, $16.95. Print Book Store, $14.50.

The Jeffe Report on Computer Graphics for Design. A monthly devoted to brief rewrites and reviews of equipment and software of interest to graphic designers. Good to see how many fields (design, publishing and pagination) are coming together through hardware and software. Pratt Center, 45 Stephenson Terr., Dept. G, Briarcliff Manor, NY 10510. $89 a year.

Microcomputer Graphics and Programming Techniques, by Harry Katzan, Jr. Good basic book (pardon the pun) on how to do graphics on home computers in "basic" computer language. Gives 20 sample programs to get you up and running. In the process, you can begin to understand how graphics are done with computers. Van Nostrand Reinhold Co., 135 W. 50th St., New York, NY 10020. 229 pp. 6 x 9. Indexed. $22.50.

Overcoming Computer Illiteracy, by Susan Curran and Ray Curnow. A lot of controversy over this one: some reviewers have loved it, and some have hated it. It's a reprint from an English book and has many British phrases, but it's still pretty good if you know nothing and want to start from scratch. Penguin Books. ISBN 0-14-007159-8. $12.95.

The Pratt Center for Computer Graphics has conducted annual seminars in New York for a couple of years now, and much of the proceedings have been about publication and newspaper design. Transcripts may be obtained. Write to the Pratt Center at 45 Stephenson Terr., Dept. G, Briarcliff Manor, NY 10510, or call (914) 741-2850 to get details and prices.

The Seybold Report on Publishing Systems. By far the best source of up-to-date information. Copies of this 22-issues-a-year publication are probably already in your building and available from the "systems" people. Hellishly expensive, but worthwhile if you really want to know what's happening with pagination, digitized imaging and digital typesetting. Seybold Publications, Inc., P.O. Box 644, Media, PA 19063. (215) 565-2480. Many back issues are available; write or call for list. $192 a year for 22 issues; additional copies in the same envelope are $96 a year.

The Seybold Report on Office Systems. Same thing for "word processing." Of less value overall to newspapers. $105 a year.

The Seybold Report on Professional Computing. Same thing for "personal computers." $120 a year.

The World of Digital Typesetting, by John W. Seybold. An excellent book, though dry, on everything you'll need to know about typesetters, including a pretty good history of typography, and how and why we got the typographic compromises we have now. Good computer primer and lots of good illustrations. Seybold Publications. 426 pp. 7 x $9\frac{1}{2}$. $32.95.

Understanding Digital Type, by Edward Bunnell. A 32-page report for the National Composition Association that deals with the design problems of digital type for CRT typesetters. National Composition Association, 1730 N. Lynn St., Arlington, VA 22209. (703) 841-8165. $5 for non-members.

MISCELLANEOUS

The Book of Graphic Problem-Solving, by John Newcomb. Presents a way to "brainstorm" graphics problems. Some chapters deal with a word-oriented method for creating visual solutions to problems of communication. Lots of examples to stimulate you. R. R. Bowker Co., 245 W. 17th St., New York, NY 10011. ISBN 0-8352-1895-3. $34.95.

Communication Arts (*CA Magazine*). Catering to an audience similar to *Print*'s, it offers detailed reports about designers, illustrators, photographers, art directors and design firms. Published bimonthly, as well as an annual "Best of . . . " edition. $28 per year.

Illustrators Annual of American Illustration. Many editions of the award-winners from the Society of Illustrators' Annual Competition. Many pages in full color. Available through Print Book Store and other magazines of interest to Art Directors. $34.95.

Print Magazine (America's Graphic Design Magazine). Primarily magazine design, illustration and typography. Helpful to newspaper design people for keeping abreast of new styles, techniques, talent, products and ideas. Lately, the magazine has been doing some stories on newspaper art departments. Circulation Dept., *Print*, 6400 Goldsboro Rd., Bethesda, MD 20817-9969. Yearly rates for the bimonthly can go from $29 for special introductory offers to $60 for the newsstand price. A subscription includes the *Regional Design Annual*, which, by itself, is $25.

Print also offers some great annuals, such as:

ADLA (Art Directors Club of Los Angeles).

American Illustration. $44.

Art Directors Annual. $39.95.

Graphic Design USA. $49.50.

Graphis Design Annual (European). $54.50.

Print Casebooks. Six volumes of the best there is. $115.

Publication Design Annual for the Society of Publications Designers. $34.95.

Problems: Solutions, Visual Thinking for Graphic Communicators, by Richard Wilde. Fifty-three design problems presented with dozens of possible solutions offered for each.

Includes designing with type, symmetry and combining images. 244 pp. 400 illus. $9\frac{1}{4}$ x $9\frac{1}{4}$. Print Book Store, $39.95.

Visible Language. "The research journal concerned with all that is involved in our being literate." Published quarterly since 1967. A folder is available listing all past journals and their contents. Visible Language, P.O. Box 1972 CMA, Cleveland, OH 44106. (216) 421-7340. $20 per year; $30 for institutions. The best of the reprints for a good understanding of how readers read are Vol. 15 numbers 2 and 3, Vol. 18 number 2, and Vol. 19 numbers 1 and 2, $5 each plus 50 cents handling.

WHERE TO GET THE STUFF

Dover Publications. There are literally thousands of books, all copyright-free, and most are printed for easy copying. *Write* for its *Graphic Design & Art Instruction Book Catalog*, the *Dover Clip Art Sampler*, the *Dover Pictorial Archive Catalog* or a full list of catalogs to: Dover Publications Inc., 31 E. 2nd St., Mineola, NY 11501.

Dynamic Graphics Bookshelf is a telephone/mail order service that will take your order on the phone with a credit card. Many of the books listed in this Appendix are available from this service, which also conducts many workshops around the country on graphics, production techniques, and electronic publishing. Call or write Dynamic Graphics, Inc., P.O. Box 1901, 6000 N. Forest Park Dr., Peoria, IL 61656, or call (800) 255-8800.

Graphic Artist's Book Club has many of the books listed here at 20 percent less than list prices. But like most book clubs, you have to sign up to purchase a certain number in the course of a year. If you're going to buy a bunch at once, this might be the way to go. Write to P.O. Box 12526, Cincinnati, OH 45212-0526, or call (800) 543-8677.

Print magazine has a "Print Book Store" with a lot of the books on this list available at discount prices. Write to *Print*'s Graphic Design Book Store, 6400 Goldsboro Rd., Bethesda, MD 20817-9969, and ask for the latest catalogs.

Glossary

A.M. A newspaper that publishes for morning delivery.

Absolute defense A libel defense that has no conditions or qualifications.

Actual malice defense A constitutional libel defense first articulated by the U.S. Supreme Court in the 1964 *New York Times Co. v. Sullivan* case. The ruling nationalized the law of libel to provide a constitutional defense when public officials are the plaintiffs. Under the ruling, the public official must prove that the defendant acted with knowledge that the information was false or with reckless disregard of whether it was false or not.

Ad Abbreviation for advertisements.

Ad dummies Sheets showing the placement of advertisements on a page; supplied by advertising department and used by editorial department in placing news and feature material.

Additive primary colors Three colors—red, blue and green—that, when added together, produce white.

Agate Smallest type used in newspapers; traditionally 5.5 points, many newspapers now consider 6-point type as agate.

Air brush A tool used to spray paints or watercolors to create illustrations.

Analog Type of information that is continuous and cannot be broken into small pieces.

Anchoring Continually publishing the same column or feature in the same location within the paper.

Area composition Computer generation of part or all of a page that has "holes" or spaces open for the placement of photographs, ads or graphics.

Art play Plan as to which stories will have photographs or informational graphics accompanying them.

Background facts box A visual device that describes what is being discussed in the story or the key people in the story.

Banner headline Main head on Page One that stretches across the top of the page; also refers to a large headline that extends across a page. Sometimes called a *line* or a *flag*.

Bar chart A horizontal display of information, with the vertical axis on the left side of the chart serving as the baseline.

Basket Place where a computer files a story. Also called *queue* or *desk*.

Bastard width Type that does not conform to the newspaper's standard column set.

Body type Type used in text of stories, usually 8- to 10-point.

Boldface Type that has **thick, heavy** lines.

Brace Page layout in which the lead news story so dominates the page visually that it detracts from all other news elements on the page; usually used on Page One.

Breakfast standard A standard used by some visual journalists to determine if a photograph will be shocking to someone at the breakfast table.

Briefing column   Abbreviated rundown of the top news stories and features of the day that also tells where the stories are located inside the paper; used as a promotional device. Also called a *summary box.*

Broadsheet   The standard size of a newspaper page, generally about 13 inches by $21\frac{1}{2}$ inches.

Bumped heads   See **Tombstone heads.**

Bumped/bumping headlines   When headlines are placed side by side on a page.

Byline   The signature or identification that precedes a story.

Byte   The sequence of adjacent binary digits; generally, 8 bytes represents a character of information.

Caps   Abbreviation for capital letters.

Caption   Type under a photograph (or other visual device) that provides additional information, such as identification of the individuals in the picture.

Chart   A visual display of quantitative information, such as the charting of data over a period of time.

Cheesecake   Slang term for photographs that show women's legs or scantily dressed women.

City editor   Individual in charge of reporters who cover local news.

Classified ad   A "want ad" that generally is set in small type, usually does not contain visuals and appears in a separate section of a newspaper.

Clippings   Previously published stories, photos and graphics that are clipped out of the publication and kept on file.

Color   Design tool that adds anything from a full-color photograph to spot color to a newspaper page.

Color separation   Made up of three color negatives—magenta, cyan and yellow—used to create printing plates that, when used with their corresponding inks, produce a color reproduction; sometimes, a fourth color—black—is used.

Column chart   A chart format that displays statistics in vertical bars.

Column rule   A thin rule or line, usually $\frac{1}{2}$- to 1-point, used to separate columns of type on a news page.

Composograph   A staged news photograph in which the faces of real people are pasted over actors' faces.

Condensed typeface   Characters spaced closely together, or narrow-set type that looks squeezed.

Conditional defense   A libel defense that is viable if certain conditions or qualifications are met.

Consent   A conditional libel defense in which a source gives permission to use a libelous statement about himself or herself.

Copyright   A person's or publication's claim to ownership.

Country facts map   An informational graphic that includes specific information about a nation.

Credit line   The identification or byline for an illustration, photograph or informational graphic.

Cropping   Editing or removing the part of a photograph that is unnecessary or that impairs effective communication by the picture.

Cursor   A flashing line or square on a computer screen to indicate the point in the text of the story where the reporter is working.

Cutout   See **Whiteout.**

Data map   A map that presents statistical information in a geographical form.

Dateline   Type appearing under the nameplate on Page One; contains volume number and date of publication.

Deadline   The last moment to get copy in for an edition; also applies to the last moment to send art to the production department and the time that the last page should be completed.

Deck   A supplemental headline that runs under and amplifies a main headline.

Diagram   A device that shows how things work or how events occurred. Also called a *schematic.*

Digital   Type of information that is not continuous, that is divided into measurable pieces.

Digital imaging system   See **Electronic imaging device.**

Display ad   An advertisement that generally combines visuals and words and appears anywhere in a newspaper.

Distribution map   A map that shows the distribution of, for example, oil deposits or endangered species in a given area.

Documentary photo   A photograph that records an event as it happens or faithfully shows the reality of people or places.

Dogleg layout   The layout of stories in irregular shapes, such as inverted L's.

Double-truck layout   Two facing pages that are laid out as a single unit.

Dummy   A layout guide or instruction sheet that represents a miniversion of a newspaper page.

Dutch wrap   See **Raw wrap.**

Ears   Little boxes or other devices along the side of a newspaper's nameplate; generally they contain the weather, price and edition name.

Electronic camera   Filmless camera that records pictures on a video or computer (floppy) disk.

Electronic imaging device   Device that allows for the digital adjustment of a photographic image; generally used as part of the production process for color.

Electronic photo transmitter   A piece of equipment that requires only a negative or transparency to send photographic images from a remote site to a newsroom.

Electronic picture desk   A computerized system that allows for the "digital" reception of photographs sent via satellite or telephone lines at extremely high speeds and the editing of such images on the computer screen before the picture is printed or sent to a pagination system.

Event map   A map that traces an event as it progresses over time.

Extended typeface   Fat characters spaced widely.

Facts box A device used to highlight certain points of a story.

Fair comment and criticism A conditional libel defense that covers journalists who write or illustrate opinions about matters of public concern.

False light When a subject in a photograph is placed in an untrue setting or situation.

Feature photograph A non-news photograph, generally timeless in its subject matter. Also see **News photograph.**

Fever chart See **Line chart.**

Filming Typesetting a story electronically in the front-end system; the filmed story is the "type" used to make up the page.

Flexography A form of letterpress printing that uses a raised, flexible printing surface and water-based inks.

Flopped image When a photograph is printed backwards. Also called a *reversed image.*

Floppy disks Devices for storing data for use with personal computers and electronic cameras.

Font A complete set of type in one size and style; the assortment of type of a single style.

Front-end system Computerized equipment that typesets elements for the printed page.

Galley A copy of a news story that has been produced or typeset on a piece of photosensitive paper.

Geographic map A map that shows formation of mineral deposits and other geologic features situated under the surface of the Earth.

Graphic An umbrella term for a piece of newspaper artwork; can include photographs, charts, maps, diagrams and illustrations.

Graphics editor Person serving as liaison between reporters, editors, photographers, artists and designers to coordinate the production of visuals.

Gray wrap See **Raw wrap.**

Grid Newspaper design term referring to the standardized column widths or measurement units that serve as the framework for laying out a page.

Grouped-bar chart See **Grouped-column chart.**

Grouped-column chart A graphic that shows multiple items in a bar- or column-chart presentation.

Gutenberg, Johannes The inventor of movable type in the 1450s in Mainz, Germany.

Halftone The reproduction of a photograph as a continuous tone image through a series of dots of various sizes; the larger the dot, the darker the image.

Hammer A one- or two-word headline that runs above or alongside a main headline and is set in larger and often heavier type.

Hard copy A paper printout of a story or informational graphic written or created on a computer.

Hardware The physical components of a computer system.

Head Abbreviation for headline.

Head shot A photograph of the face of an individual. Also called a *mug shot* or *face photo.*

Header An information field at the top of a story in the computer; contains data on author, basket, file date, etc.

Headline Type over a story that indicates subject matter; headlines also are used to indicate subject matter of informational graphics.

Heavy news day A day when there are many news events or stories.

Highlights box A visual device accompanying a story that summarizes the story's key points.

Illustration A drawing of people or things.

Input Process of typing a story into a computer using a keyboard that has more functions than a typewriter has.

Inset When one visual element is placed inside another one, such as a map placed inside the image area of a photograph. Also called a *mortice.*

Interactive pagination system System that allows for both the copy editor and the person using the pagination computer terminal (an editor, designer or printer) to edit or change a story.

Italic Any *slanted* typeface.

Jump The continuation of a story from one page to another.

Jumpline A guideline at the termination point of a column of type that tells the reader the story continues on some other page.

Justified A typesetting function that adds white space between words or letters so that each line of the story is set flush right and flush left.

Key points box A graphics device that contains the major points in a story.

Kicker A two- or three-word supplemental headline that runs above, and usually is set half the size and width of, the main head.

Land use map A map that shows the location of residential and industrial areas within a community.

Layout The design of a newspaper page; the arrangement of headlines, stories, photographs and other visuals.

Letterpress A "relief" method of printing in which a printing plate with raised, reversed images is coated with a thin layer of ink and rolled against paper.

Libel Statements that are communicated to a third party, clearly identify a person and hold the person up to public hatred, ridicule or scorn.

Lightface A weight of type lighter than medium or bold.

Line chart A chart that shows an up or down trend with a continuous line. Also called a *fever chart* and a *rectilinear coordinate chart.*

Location map A map that geographically locates the subject of interest in a story.

Mainframe   A powerful, central computer that drives the VDTs of reporters and editors.

Map   A visual device that aids readers in locating where an event occurred.

Mechanical color   Newspaper color created by an artist who cuts individual acetate flaps for each color or color combination.

Medium face   A weight of type heavier than light but lighter than bold.

Megabyte   Electronic data storage term, equal to 1 million bytes.

Menu   A computerized list or directory of items or stories.

Misappropriation of a name or likeness   When a photographer uses an image for commercial purposes without permission.

Modem   A device that allows a computer to transfer information to and from another computer via telephone lines.

Modular layout   The layout of stories in short, squared-off columns or blocks.

Morgue   A newspaper's in-house library; now more commonly called a *reference center.*

Mortice   See **Inset.**

Mouse   A small computer device used to move the cursor on a VDT screen. See **cursor.**

Mug shot   See **Head shot.**

Nameplate   The name of the newspaper as displayed at top of Page One; not to be confused with *masthead,* an inside box listing the names of the paper's executives and subscription information.

News hole   The space left for editorial matter throughout the newspaper after advertisements have been placed.

News photograph   The image "captured" on film by a newspaper photographer either on the scene of a news event or during a prearranged meeting.

Newspaper design   The stylized overall appearance of everything in the paper, from headline typeface to design of stock table pages.

Offset   A method of printing in which an ink-covered plate is offset against a rubber cylinder that picks up the ink and then comes in contact with paper.

Optimum column width   The length of a line of type that can be scanned easily and repeatedly without quickly tiring the human eye; about 14 picas.

Organization   When related to design, how a newspaper is physically put together and presented day after day.

Output   The process of producing a physical copy of something stored electronically in a computer.

Overline   A promotional device that runs above the nameplate on Page One and refers to stories on inside pages.

Overprinting   When a black-and-white or color screen or pattern is printed over body type or a headline.

P.M.   A newspaper that publishes for afternoon delivery.

Packaging   The gathering of related material on a single subject for easy-to-follow presentation.

Page board   Grid sheet used to assemble or paste-up a full-sized facsimile of a news page.

Page designer   The newest breed of journalist; blends all the visual elements and stories into an attractive page.

Page One   The main news page, the first page of a newspaper.

Pagination   The computer-generated production of a complete newspaper page, including stories, headlines, visuals and ads.

Partial defense   A defense such as a retraction that may help mitigate libel damages.

Passive pagination system   Typesetting a newspaper through two separate computer systems.

Pattern   A consistent presentation of visuals.

Personal computer   The self-contained system of VDT screen, keyboard and memory storage.

Photo illustration   A photographic image created by a photographer to make an editorial point or comment; a posed photograph that has been conceived and executed for the purpose of illustrating a point in a story.

Photocomposition   An electronic form of typesetting.

Photograph   An image reproduced on surfaces through the interaction of light and light-sensitive chemicals.

Pica   A unit of typographic measurement, equal to 12 points or one-sixth of an inch; usually used to measure the width of elements on a news page. One inch equals six picas or 72 points.

Pictographic   A graphic that uses symbols instead of lines, figures or columns to present data.

Picture editor   The editor at a newspaper who is in charge of managing and editing the day's picture report.

Picture package   A special layout of pictures, usually run inside a newspaper.

Picture page   A page devoted exclusively to pictures; some picture pages have short text blocks or stories.

Pie chart   A chart that shows the relationship of various items to a total.

Pixel   Abbreviation for picture element, a basic rectangular unit that, in combinations, forms a digital photographic image.

Point   The smallest unit of typographic measurement, equal to approximately a seventy-second of an inch; usually used to measure the size or height of type.

Pool camera   When a single camera or a few cameras are allowed in a limited-access setting, as in a courtroom, and the pictures are shared with all of the media.

Printing plate   The metal or plastic plate containing a page's image that is put on a printing press.

Privilege of reporting   A conditional libel defense that flows from fair and accurate reporting of official proceedings and of information from official documents and court records.

Process camera   A special camera that uses a transparent screen to alter the light reflected from photographic images during exposure to a high-intensity light in order to create the halftone dot pattern necessary for printing photographs.

Promotional device   An index, or overline, that tells the readers what is inside a newspaper.

Proportion wheel   A device used to compute commensurate sizes of an original photograph and size planned for publication.

Pyramid ad layout   A style of advertising layout in which the largest ads are placed at the bottom of a page and smaller ads are stacked on top to imitate a stair step; usually arranged left to right on a page.

Quotes   Words or sentences that report precisely what a source said.

R.O.P.   A term meaning run of paper, signifying that an ad or piece of color is part of the normal newspaper.

Ragged   A typesetting term meaning lines of a story do not end at a set point and do not align vertically.

Raw wrap   Body type without a headline over it, or when type is wrapped around the right-hand side of a short headline. Also called a *gray wrap* or a *dutch wrap*.

Readout   See **Deck**.

Rectilinear coordinate chart   See **Line chart**.

Refer   A line or sentence placed noticeably within a story to tell the reader where a related news article can be found. Sometimes called a *refer line* or *refer box*.

Reference center   See **Morgue**.

Reflective color   Photographic prints, transparencies or color artwork that is reproduced in a newspaper.

Retouching   Process of removing blemishes and other marks on a photograph or removing background or elements of a photograph; often done with paints or an airbrush.

Retraction   A statement that admits erroneous reporting.

Reversed image   See **Flopped image**.

Reversed type   Printing process in which letters are set white on a background of color or black.

Rules   Straight lines used to visually segment a page, to underscore words and headlines or to box in related stories and visuals; may be thin (1 point) or thick (up to 12 points).

Runsheet   A daily list that contains the names of advertisers and the sizes of their ads but generally does not contain the content or design.

Sans serif   Type that lacks cross strokes at the tops and bottoms of its characters.

Schematic   See **Diagram**.

Screen   Gray tint used as a background to accent a headline or story or in a graphic.

Section front   The lead or first page of a section.

Sectionalization   Presentation of common or specialized stories in separate sections of the newspaper: main news, sports, business, food, etc.

Series highlights   A box that highlights other parts of the series, if the story is part of a series.

Serif   Type containing cross strokes that accent the tops or bottoms of its characters.

Sidebar   A secondary news story that offers additional information to or a different focus on the main story.

Single-copy sales   Newspapers sold to individual readers on an occasional basis rather than on a daily, subscription basis.

Sizing   The scaling of a photograph to fit it into an allotted space.

Sketch   See **Illustration**.

Software   A computer program that tells the computer what to do.

Source line   A credit line at the bottom of a graphic that tells the source of the information.

Spot color   A block of one or more colors that accents the placement of a story or visual. Also called a *tint block*.

Spot news   Unscheduled events that make the news, such as earthquakes and traffic accidents.

Stand-alone photo   A picture and caption that do not accompany a news story; the caption must fully explain the news event. Also called *wild art*.

Standing headline   A headline that introduces a column or page and appears in the newspaper every day.

Statistical map   See **Data map**.

Statute of limitations   A specified period of time set by state law in which a libel suit must be filed.

Story play   Plan for where stories will be positioned on the page and which will have larger headlines.

Structure   When related to design, refers to such items as the width of type and the kind of type used for body copy and headlines.

Subheads   Small one- or two-word headlines within a story that denote a shift in subject matter; used as visual aid to break up long columns or large blocks of type; in long stories can provide additional "mini-headlines" and provide a new point of entry.

Subtractive primary colors   The colors—cyan, magenta and yellow—that are used in color printing.

Summary box   See **Briefing column**.

Surface map   A map that shows the location of such features as roads, cities, airports—all features on a flat surface.

Table   A list of information displayed in tabular form; the most common display of tabular information is the daily stock market report or sports box scores and standings.

Tabloid   A newspaper that is about half the size of a typical broadsheet newspaper page.

Tint block   See **Spot color**.

Tombstone heads   Headlines of the same size and weight placed side by side.

Topographic map   A map that shows visible geographic surface features, such as mountains and elevations.

Traffic   Design term denoting the number of elements on a page, including all stories, visuals, promos, refers, etc.

Trip map   See **Event map.**

Typography   The appearance of type in text and headline; the process of printing material; the arrangement of material on a page.

Unreasonable intrusion   When a photographer intrudes upon a person's privacy and does not have the right to take pictures.

Velox   A halftone print that is pasted up on a page board along with stories, headlines and advertisements; made up of varying concentration of black dots that create the illusions of "gray" found in a photograph.

Vertical layout   Stories run in long, often single, columns.

Video display terminal   VDT; computer terminal that looks much like a television set, with a typewriter-style keyboard.

Visual journalist   A journalist who may work with graphics, photographs or design.

Visual pacing   The editing of images so they are from different vantage points.

Visuals   Photographs, illustrations, graphics, color and page design.

Weather map   A map that shows temperatures for featured areas.

Well ad layout   A style of advertising layout in which ads are stacked on each side of a page, creating a "well" for news material.

Whiteout   A process in which part of a photograph's background is removed by either painting it white or cutting it out.

Wild art   See **Stand-alone photo.**

Zero basing   Starting the scale on the vertical axis of a graphic at zero to avoid visual distortion of data.

Acknowledgments

Agence France-Presse: Fig. 8.14

Albuquerque Journal: Fig. 5.9

Amarillo Globe-Times: Fig. 5.11

Anchorage Daily News: Figures 3.7, 3.20

Anderson Independent-Mail: Fig. 4.17

Apple, Inc.: Fig. 2.10

Arizona Daily Star: Figures 6.2, 20.6, 21.5

Arizona Republic: Figures 3.8, 3.9, 3.10, 3.11, 3.12, 3.13, 11.6, 11.10, 15.6, 16.16, 17.5, 17.6

Edmund C. Arnold: excerpts, pp. 38–39

Asbury Park Press: Fig. 5.12

Associated Press: Figures 2.14, 8.1, 8.2, 10.7, 10.8, 16.12, 18.1b, 18.4, 18.8

Atlanta Constitution: Fig. 12.7

Bakersfield Californian: Figures 8.7, 8.9

Billings Gazette: Fig. 5.14

Binghamton Press: Fig. 8.12

Boston Globe: Figures 10.2, 17.7, 21.9

Boston Herald: Fig. 21.6

Bradenton Herald: Fig. 12.16

Butler Eagle: Fig. 5.15

Morning Call-Chronicle: Figures 5.10, 11.17, 12.13, 12.14

Candian Press: Fig. 8.10

Chicago Daily News: Figures 1.3, 1.4, 9.7, 15.7

Chicago Sun-Times: Figures 4.5, 4.22, 5.16

Chicago Tribune: Figures 1.5, 1.6, 1.7, 1.8, 5.2, 5.17, 6.12, 9.12, 9.13, 9.14, 9.18, 11.16, 12.11, 12.17, 13.5, 13.6, 13.8, 14.4, 14.8, 16.4, 16.5, 16.14, 16.19, 17.20, 19.4, 20.9, 21.13, Color Plate 2

Christian Science Monitor: Figures 5.18, 9.16

Cincinnati Enquirer: Figures 3.24, 21.1

Citizen Tribune: Fig. 6.19

Rich Clarkson: excerpts, p. 188

Columbia Daily Tribune: Fig. 20.7

Concord Monitor: Fig. 5.19

Contact Press Images, Inc.: Fig. 16.6

Contra Costa Times: Fig. 12.1

Courier-Journal: Fig. 19.8

Daily Breeze: Fig. 4.10

Daily Herald: Figures 3.18, 3.19, Color Plate 19

Daily Iberian: Fig. 18.5

Daily News: Fig. 8.3

Daily Oklahoman: Fig. 17.12

Daily Report: Fig. 5.5

Dallas Morning News: Figures 4.12, 5.20, 6.18, 6.25, 17.82, 19.13, Color Plate 15

Dallas Times Herald: Figures 4.4, 5.1, 6.20, 11.1, Color Plates 4,6

Dayton Daily News: Fig. 10.12

Des Moines Register: Fig. 20.10

Detroit Free Press: Figures 4.18, 21.4

Detroit News: Figures 11.7, 12.5, 12.6, 12.8, 12.9, 12.10

Dow Jones & Company, Inc.: Fig. 11.3

Bill Dunn (*The Orange County Register*): excerpts, p. 148

William Dunn (*The Orlando Sentinel*): excerpts, pp. 4–5

El Paso Times: Fig. 14.13

Erie Daily Times: Fig. 5.21

Evansville Press: Fig. 6.4

Evening Sun: Figures 3.25, 5.13, 9.19, 14.11, Color Plate 5

Howard Finberg: Figures 2.1, 2.2, 2.7, 2.8, 2.11, 2.12

Robert Finch: excerpts, p. 35

Gary Fong: Fig. 17.3

Fort Worth Star-Telegram: Fig. 3.23

The Fresno Bee: Figures 5.22, 13.11

Gazette Telegraph: Figures 3.16, 3.17, 4.14

Gloucester Times: Fig. 8.6
Graphics Press: Figures 9.4, 9.5
Houston Chronicle: Fig. 4.2
John Hutchinson: excerpts, p. 35
Journal-News: Fig. 10.4
Kansas City Star: Fig. 20.2
Knight-Ridder Graphics Network: Figures 10.9, 10.10, 11.5, 11.8
The Lawrence Eagle-Tribune: Fig. 5.24
Pete Leabo: excerpts, p. 222
The Ledger: Fig. 5.23
Carolyn Lee: excerpts, p. 202
Robert Lockwood: excerpts, pp. 52–53
Los Angeles Herald Examiner: Fig. 5.4
Los Angeles Times: Figures 4.19, 5.26, 6.13, 19.6
Tony Majeri: excerpts, p. 11
John Merrill: excerpts, p. 107
Miami Herald: Figures 5.27, 6.16, 9.11, 16.15, 21.2, 21.3, Color Plate 12
Miami News: Fig. 5.28
Milwaukee Journal: Fig. 4.21
Bryan Monroe: excerpts, p. 34
Pat Murphy: excerpts, p. 33
New York Daily News: Figures 4.25, 15.3
New York Times: Figures 5.30, 6.15, 10.1, 11.4, 16.2, 21.14
Newsday: Figures 4.24, 5.29
Nikon: Fig. 2.13
Oakland Tribune: Fig. 8.16
Orange County Register: Figures 4.6, 4.13, 4.23, 6.8, 6.28, Color Plate 16
Oregonian: Fig. 4.7
Orlando Sentinel: Figures 1.2, 14.3, 14.20, 16.18
Frank Peters: excerpts, p. 129
Philadelphia Inquirer: Figures 5.31, 8.5, 12.20
Phoenix Gazette: Figures 13.20, 19.1
The Plain Dealer: Fig. 21.10
Playboy: Fig. 8.13
Post-Star: Figures 10.3, 19.9
Post-Tribune: Fig. 17.23
Press Democrat: Figures 4.11, 6.5
Press-Telegram: Figures 5.25, 6.23, Color Plate 13
Providence Journal: Figures 3.22, 5.32, 10.11, 19.12
Quad-City Times: Fig. 13.12
Raleigh Times: Fig. 8.4
Register Guard: Fig. 5.8
Reno Gazette Journal: Figures 14.1, 20.5
Reuters: Figures 18.1a, 18.3a, 18.3b
Richmond Times-Dispatch: Fig. 3.21
Roanoke Times & World-News: Fig. 5.33
Rockford Register Star: Fig. 6.21
Sacramento Bee: Figures 6.17, 6.27
San Antonio Light: Figures 5.7, 10.13

San Francisco Chronicle: Figures 4.9, 8.11, 8.15, 11.13, 11.14, 12.4, 13.23, 14.15, 16.3, 16.7, 16.11, 17.4, 17.8, 20.4b
San Francisco Examiner: Figures 13.22, 16.8, 16.9
San Jose Mercury News: Figures 5.36, 6.7, 8.8, 12.2, 16.1, 16.10, 19.11, 20.11, Color Plate 18
San Luis Obispo County Telegram-Tribune: Fig. 6.3
Sarasota Herald Tribune: Fig. 17.19
Seattle Times: Figures 6.11, 12.3, 21.11, 21.16
Warren Skipper: excerpts, pp. 100–101
St. Paul Pioneer Press & Dispatch: Fig. 16.17
St. Petersburg Times: Figures 5.35, 12.12, 19.7, Color Plates 3, 7
Star Tribune: Figures 9.17, 13.10, 17.14, 17.22, 19.14, 21.15
Pegie Stark: excerpts, p. 159
The State: Figures 13.9, 20.8
Statesman Journal: Fig. 19.10
Sun News: Figures 3.14, 3.15, 5.3, 6.26
Sun-Sentinel: Figures 5.6, 10.5, 12.18, 12.21, 17.21, 21.8, Color Plate 20
Tempe Daily News: Fig. 17.16
Times Herald: Color Plate 17
Times-Union: Fig. 5.34
Topeka Daily Capital: Fig. 9.15
Tulsa World: Fig. 17.1
UPI: Figures 18.2a, 18.2b
USA Today: Figures 1.1, 5.37, 13.14, Color Plate 1
John Walston: excerpts, p. 22
Washington Post: Figures 5.38, 9.20, 12.22, 14.19, 17.18, 21.7
George Wedding: excerpts, p. 115
Cecil Whig: Fig. 11.5
Wichita Eagle & Beacon: Fig. 21.12

COVER CREDITS

Front

Back

Index